BRUNO SCHULZ AND GALICIAN JEWISH MODERNITY

JEWS IN EASTERN EUROPE

Jeffrey Veidlinger
Mikhail Krutikov
Geneviève Zubrzycki

Editors

BRUNO SCHULZ AND GALICIAN JEWISH MODERNITY

Karen Underhill

INDIANA UNIVERSITY PRESS

This book is a publication of

Indiana University Press
Office of Scholarly Publishing
Herman B Wells Library 350
1320 East 10th Street
Bloomington, Indiana 47405 USA

iupress.org

© 2024 by Karen Underhill

All rights reserved
No part of this book may be reproduced or utilized in any form or by any means, electronic or mechanical, including photocopying and recording, or by any information storage and retrieval system, without permission in writing from the publisher. The paper used in this publication meets the minimum requirements of the American National Standard for Information Sciences—Permanence of Paper for Printed Library Materials, ANSI Z39.48-1992.

Manufactured in the United States of America
First Printing 2024

Library of Congress Cataloging-in-Publication Data

Names: Underhill, Karen, author.
Title: Bruno Schulz and Galician Jewish modernity / Karen Underhill.
Description: Bloomington, Indiana : Indiana University Press, 2024. | Series: Jews in Eastern Europe | Includes bibliographical references and index.
Identifiers: LCCN 2023031835 (print) | LCCN 2023031836 (ebook) | ISBN 9780253057273 (hardback) | ISBN 9780253069931 (paperback) | ISBN 9780253057280 (ebook)
Subjects: LCSH: Schulz, Bruno, 1892-1942—Criticism and interpretation. | Modernism (Literature) | Jews—Intellectual life. | Polish literature—Jewish authors—History and criticism. | BISAC: HISTORY / Europe / Eastern | LITERARY CRITICISM / European / Eastern (see also Russian & Soviet) | LCGFT: Literary criticism.
Classification: LCC PG7158.S2942 U53 2024 (print) | LCC PG7158.S2942 (ebook) | DDC 891.8/5372—dc23/eng/20231122
LC record available at https://lccn.loc.gov/2023031835
LC ebook record available at https://lccn.loc.gov/2023031836

For Elijah

CONTENTS

List of Abbreviations ix

Preface xi

Acknowledgments xv

Introduction: Bruno Schulz and the Archaeology of Polish Jewish Modernism 1

1. Leading the Word Out of Its Golus: Rokhl Korn Reads *Cinnamon Shops* 28

2. "A Creation Born of the Longing of Golus": Schulz's "E. M. Lilien" and the Jewish Renaissance Movement 54

3. The Sunday Seminars of Bruno Schulz and Debora Vogel: Rachel Auerbach's "Un-Spun Threads" and Vogel's "Human Exotics" 90

4. Sanatorium under the Sign of the Hourglass: Reading Schulz with Kafka, Manger, and Ahad Ha'am 125

5. Acculturation without Assimilation: Polish Contexts for a Translational Poetics 154

6 "What Have You Done with the Book?":
Schulz's Exegetical Encounter from the *Book of Idolatry* to the "Mythologizing of Reality"   177

Notes   207

Bibliography   253

Index   269

ABBREVIATIONS

Works by Bruno Schulz

The following abbreviations are used within the text for frequently cited editions of works in Polish and in English-language translation by Bruno Schulz.

KL   *Księga listów* – Correspondence of Bruno Schulz
     Księga listów. Dzieła zebrane, Tom 5. Edited by Jerzy Ficowski and Stanisław Danecki (Słowo/obraz terytoria, 2002)

L   Madeline G. Levine English-language translation
     Collected Stories of Bruno Schulz (Northwestern University Press, 2018)

O   Ossolineum critical edition of Schulz's collected writings
     Bruno Schulz: Opowiadania, wybór esejów i listów. Edited by Jerzy Jarzębski (Zakład Narodowy im. Ossolińskich, 1989)

SF6 "E. M. Lilien" by Bruno Schulz, as compiled and republished in *Schulz/Forum 6* (2015)

W   Celina Wieniewska English-language translation
     Street of Crocodiles and Other Stories (Penguin, 2008)

WE   Celina Wieniewska English-language translation
     The Collected Works of Bruno Schulz. Edited by Jerzy Ficowski (Picador, 1998)

PREFACE

Through the prose of the Galician Jewish author and graphic artist Bruno Schulz in the 1930s, the Polish language became the linguistic raw material for a profound exploration of the modern Jewish experience. Rather than turning away from the language like many of his Galician Jewish colleagues, themselves native speakers of Polish, Schulz used the Polish language to explore his own and his generation's relationship to East European Jewish exegetical tradition, and to deepen his reflection on *golus* or exile as a condition not only of the individual, and of the Jewish community, but of language itself, and of matter.

In 1937, Schulz published a lengthy essay that he had prepared and delivered as a public talk on the artist Ephraim Moses Lilien—a native of Schulz's hometown, Drohobycz, now Drohobych in Ukraine, and a pioneering contributor to modern Jewish art and an emerging Zionist cultural imaginary. Published in the *Subcarpathian Review*, a local periodical with a small print run, Schulz's article on Lilien lay forgotten, unknown, for almost eighty years. It was discovered only in 2015 by researchers Piotr Sitkiewicz and Bohdan Lazorak, working separately but simultaneously in Poland and Ukraine with newly digitized periodicals from the Drohobycz-Borysław region where Schulz lived.

In his Lilien article, the author speaks directly about his understanding of the challenges and existential questions facing Jewish artists of his generation, and specifically his Galician milieu. Since Schulz's untimely death during WWII, generations of readers, artists, and authors have read and been influenced by his mystical, oneiric, and also modern landscapes, informed by east European Jewish life and tradition, meaningful for many as landscapes of Jewish memory and longing. Yet until the discovery of his article on Lilien, no surviving documents remained that could provide readers or scholars direct access to the author's stance or thoughts on his experience as a Jewish artist, on the challenges and existential choices that faced the Jewish artist in his Galician Jewish generation, or on the challenges of producing modern Jewish literature in the Polish language. In the present short study, Schulz's Lilien article presents an opportunity to revisit his innovative poetics and to read them more carefully against the realities of the Galician Jewish experience out of which Schulz's writing emerged. Specifically, the language Schulz uses in his essay makes it possible to reframe his Jewish modernism as a writing in Polish that harnesses the fact of its use of Polish, the author's native vernacular, to reflect on golus or exile not only as a condition of modern Jewish life in a post-WWI Europe of nation-states but also as an ontological principle: the exile of matter in the world of form and of language—understood as the pure potential of the word—in the languages of everyday communication.

My modest goal in the chapters that follow is to make room for this diasporic poetics and to understand some of its sources. I am interested in how it took shape, why it could and did happen precisely in Galicia and not in Warsaw, and how it can change the way that we think about Jewish modernism, Polish modernism, and literatures produced in both post-Imperial contexts and contexts of rising nationalism. To the extent that my reframing of Schulz's poetics contributes to these discussions, it owes its success to the indefatigable scholarship of historians in the field of Polish Jewish History, and specifically the cultural history of Galicia, who have over recent decades restored an increasingly complex picture of the social and cultural dynamics of Jewish communities in the late nineteenth and early twentieth centuries in Galicia. Schulz's ontological-poetic project emerged, in its mature form, in a very specific context: that of his contact with the Yiddish and Polish writer, essayist, and aesthetic theorist Debora Vogel, and with the Yiddishist literary milieu of Lwów (today L'viv, in Western Ukraine) with which, through her, he came into contact. It is my hope that by turning attention to the Lilien essay and to textual conversations between Schulz and members of his Galician milieu, my study may bring even a slight adjustment to the categories through which we think about prewar Polish Jewish culture and experience.

Schulz's work has never fit easily into categories used to frame Jewish modernism. At a historical turning point when the Polish language was being ever more tightly grafted to the project of integral nationalism, when many Polish Jewish writers, themselves native speakers of Polish—Schulz's closest colleagues were choosing to write in Yiddish or Hebrew, languages traditionally associated with diasporic Jewish modernism in literature— Schulz not only treated Polish as the Jewish vernacular that it already was; he occupied it and owned it with a spiritual and sensual intensity that would change the literary language forever. At a moment when history demanded sober realism, solutions, and commitments, Schulz was working on a poetic paradigm of escape from history. The route would move through history's transient forms—the everyday language of communication, the material storehouse of a Drohobycz childhood—into the exegetical "margins" where commentary enters the realm of the transhistorical.

ACKNOWLEDGMENTS

My gratitude goes first and foremost to Geneviève Zubrzycki, Mikhail Krutikov, and Jeffrey Veidlinger, editors of the series Jews in Eastern Europe, and to Dee Mortenson, Gary Dunham, and Anna Francis of Indiana University Press, for taking on the project and seeing it through to its completion.

I am indebted to many teachers and colleagues who generously read and provided insights and valuable criticisms on earlier versions of the material here, and whose mentorship, support, and interest lie behind its completion: Samuel Kassow, Bożena Shallcross, Paul Mendes-Flohr, Michael Fishbane, Adam Lipszyc, Agata Bielik-Robson, Emily Finer, Antony Polonsky, Eugenia Prokop-Janiec, Kenneth Moss, Benjamin Paloff, Michał Markowski, Julia Vaingurt, Harriet Murav, Shana Penn, Beth Holmgren, and David Goldfarb.

I have gratitude and deepest admiration for Wiera Meniok, who has worked tirelessly to connect care for the legacy of Bruno Schulz and restoration of the knowledge of the community from which he came with living faith in the power of cultural work that crosses national and linguistic borders. The study in its current form is possible thanks to the pioneering work of Ukrainian and Polish researchers Bohdan Lazorak, Piotr Sitkiewicz, and Lesya Chomych, whose archival discoveries of previously unknown work by Bruno Schulz have reinvigorated the field of Schulz studies and had a decisive influence on the shape several chapters in this study would take. The present study developed and changed in conversation with colleagues and predecessors in the field of Polish Jewish studies who, over the past three decades, have succeeded in restoring a vibrant and nuanced picture of a multilingual prewar Poland and its diverse Jewish communities. My interpretations of Schulz's place in that prewar context owe a particular debt to the work and inspiration of colleagues and friends Sam Kassow, Karolina Szymaniak, Antony Polonsky, Kamil Kijek, Marci Shore, Joshua Shanes, Natalia Aleksiun, Michael Steinlauf, Michael Alpert, Agi Legutko, Pasha Lion, and Daniel Kahn.

A generous research fellowship from the Institute for the Humanities at the University of Illinois Chicago enabled me to complete the book, for which I thank all involved, especially Linda Vavra and Susan Levine. I am grateful for the support and friendship of my departmental colleagues

Michał Markowski and Julia Vaingurt and for the broader community of colleagues at the University of Illinois Chicago, whose spirit of intellectual generosity and workplace solidarity are a continual source of inspiration.

For support, encouragement, and intellectual fellowship that made the project possible, I thank Karl Fogel, Janet Underhill, Renee Melton-Klein, Angela Jakary, Margarita Cygielska, Rick Perlstein, Monica Campbell, and my closest and most patient friend, my husband, Rick Meller.

BRUNO SCHULZ AND GALICIAN JEWISH MODERNITY

INTRODUCTION
Bruno Schulz and the Archaeology of Polish Jewish Modernism

THE SMALL BODY OF PROSE BY GALICIAN JEWISH writer and graphic artist Bruno Schulz that was published between 1934 and 1938 has entered into, transformed, and enriched Polish, Jewish, and Central European modernisms, stretching the boundaries of how each of these bodies of modern literature is understood. It has also earned a place, together with Schulz's graphic works, within the field of Holocaust studies. Born in 1892, in the Austro-Hungarian Empire, Bruno Schulz died in 1942, murdered by Gestapo officer Karl Günther during the wartime occupation of his hometown Drohobycz, today Drohobych in Western Ukraine, even as plans for his escape had been prepared.[1] His maturing artistic goals and projects, as his friend and supporter Rachel Auerbach would write after the war in "*Nisht-oysgeshpunene fedem*" ("Un-Spun Threads"), her memoir of both Schulz and Yiddish/Polish poet Debora Vogel, would remain unrealized.[2]

The final works of art that Schulz produced before his death were fairytale themed frescoes that he painted on the walls of a children's bedroom in the wartime Drohobycz home of SS Commander Felix Landau, who had taken Schulz under his temporary protection in order to exploit his artistic talents.[3] Discovered under layers of paint in 2001, the frescoes, which offer a striking metonymy for a buried and overwritten Jewish past that is in the process of returning to visibility, and to memory, in Poland and Ukraine, were partially removed to the Yad Vashem museum in Israel, where Schulz is memorialized as a Jewish artist and Holocaust victim.[4] The circumstances of Schulz's last years in the Drohobycz ghetto, and his death, speak lastingly to his fate as a Jewish artist and victim of the racist politics of the twentieth century. Yet they can tell us little about the early twentieth-century and interwar sources that inspired his art, or the intellectual and cultural contexts that surrounded its emergence. For this reason, numerous critics have bemoaned the backreading of Schulz's work from the perspective of his fate at the hands of the Nazis, asking that his work be read as the expression of a universally human, and not specifically Jewish, vision.⁵ It is also true that in the decades following World War II, knowledge of the modern Jewish experience in Poland was largely lost to a majority of readers of Polish literature. The destruction of prewar Jewish life in Poland produced a fabric of discursive absence that continues to inform the entire landscape of postwar and contemporary Polish literary and cultural studies. A full understanding of the complex sources and subjectivities that contributed to literary modernism in the Polish language, the product of a multilingual prewar context, was severely restricted for over half a century by a lack of access to and familiarity with the Jewish realities out of which so many of the seminal works of Polish modernism arose. This included familiarity with the Jewish cultural and political contexts and questions that informed the work of Jewish writers in all three major literary languages of Interwar Poland: Yiddish, Polish, and Hebrew. With the murder of a great portion of the Polish-speaking Jewish readership of modern Polish literature written by Jewish authors, the polyphonic and often intentionally translational nature of this literature had slipped, if not out of reach, at the very least out of the dominant discourses on Polish modernism. This includes this literature's complex resonances with Jewish public discourse of the interwar period, as well as with Jewish theological, hermeneutical, and exegetical tradition.⁶

These resonances and conversations were also actively pushed out and suppressed. For over half a century within both Polish studies and Jewish studies, separately and for complementary reasons, there existed varying degrees of reticence about emphasizing or exploring the Jewishness of canonical works of Polish-language literature—particularly those that do not openly and directly focus on Jewish themes, or that employ veiled or allusive textual strategies, that intentionally allow the Jewishness of their subject matter and sources to be overlooked.⁷ As a result, the discourses of archaeology and spectrality and the evocative trope of the palimpsest offer themselves as productive tools in the study of Polish-language Jewish writing in Poland, and in the field of Polish Jewish studies more broadly. The decades following Poland's transition to democracy in 1989 have brought a growing reintegration of knowledge about the Jewish past of Poland into scholarly, cultural, and public discourse in Poland; and thirty years on, Poland has become a world center for the study of East European Jewish history and multilingual modern Jewish culture and literature. As a result, and combined with the growing study of Yiddish language and literature worldwide, with the East European turn in Jewish studies scholarship, and with the renewed interest in diasporism and diasporic cultural formations, the Jewishness of the Polish physical and cultural landscape—and with it the Jewishness of Polish-language modernist writing—is becoming more legible.

This process, by no means specific to Poland, represents an interdisciplinary paradigm shift underway within scholarship on all aspects of multilingual pre- and post-WWII East European Jewish culture and history. For scholars of prewar Yiddish culture, it involves rediscovering and restoring a picture of the ways in which Yiddish literature and culture were in conversation with the other-language literatures and intellectual communities beside which, and against which, they developed. As Mikhail Krutikov had written in his study of Galician Jewish critic Meir Weiner, "Our picture of the past has become fragmented, with past relationships severed, and the separate pieces being reassembled into different, and often conflicting, narratives."[8] Indeed, the language of recovery and unearthing is widely used by scholars to frame the study of pre-war Jewish literatures. Yiddish literary scholar Karolina Szymaniak has pioneered multilingual and comparative methodologies in the study of prewar Polish and Yiddish literatures, in part by reconstructing and centering within scholarship of interwar Lwów the multilingual cultural production and pioneering Yiddish cultural activism of two women writers long marginalized or entirely ignored: Rachel Auerbach and Debora Vogel, a central figure in the present study.[9] Kamil Kijek's 2017 *Dzieci modernizmu* (*Children of Modernism: Awareness, Culture and Political Socialization of Jewish Youth in the Second Polish Republic*), an analysis of autobiographies submitted in three languages to the YIVO Institute for Jewish Research in the 1930s, is one of the first studies in Poland to give voice to a largely forgotten generation of Jewish youth. They were the first generation to grow up as citizens of an independent Poland, within what Chone Shmeruk has described as Poland's "trilingual polysystem," developing new and complex forms of Polish Jewish subjectivity.[10] In their work on the poetic language of Yiddish writer Itzik Manger, which is also informed by a multilingual approach to Jewish literary history, Hana Kronfeld and Robert Peckerar explain that their research "aims to unearth the ideologically silenced dialogue between Hebrew and Yiddish modernisms in the first half of the 20th century."[11] Harriet Murav, in her study of Russian and Yiddish-language Jewish literatures in post-revolution Russia, *Music from a Speeding Train*, turns attention to "hidden quotations that can reanimate silenced voices." Her study is presented as "a work of restoration": "an attempt to recover Jewish literature and culture from the Soviet

Union, in order to tell a story long overshadowed by the teleology of 'hope to ashes.'"¹² These are but a few examples of a generation of archival scholarship that is making visible a previously palimpsested, multilingual Central and East European Jewish cultural landscape.

Perhaps no better example of the archaeological metaphor exists than in the international field of Schulz studies, which as gained the name "Schulzologia." The field has been defined by the knowledge that a draft of Schulz's final novel, *Messiah* (*Mesjasz*), was lost during the war and has never resurfaced, and that the author's collected oeuvre and biography will forever remain fragmentary.¹³ Since 2012, the seventieth anniversary of Schulz's death, the journal *Schulz/Forum* under the direction of Stanisław Rosiek has become both an international platform of Schulz scholarship and a central forum for the publication of "unknown archival material, and documents shedding new light on Schulz's biography," as well as a reference library for Schulz scholars, readers, and amators.¹⁴ In 2017, the project launched the web resource *Schulz/Forum: A Calendar of the Life, Work and Reception of Bruno Schulz*, which has undertaken to reconstruct in the form of an online archive all available knowledge on Schulz's work and biography.¹⁵

The present study of Bruno Schulz's work in its Galician Jewish context also developed out of one striking example of the archaeological metaphor: the 2015 discovery by Polish and Ukrainian researchers Piotr Sitkiewicz and Bohdan Lazorak, working separately but simultaneously, of a previously unknown 1937 article by Bruno Schulz on Jewish artist and fellow Drohobyczan Ephraim Moses Lilien (1874–1925).¹⁶ The article, which discusses at length the work and career of an artist famous for his widely reproduced Zionist-themed graphics, is the first known document in which Bruno Schulz openly presents his views on the contemporary political, cultural, and spiritual concerns of his Jewish generation in 1930s Poland. In the essay, Schulz uses his analysis of Lilien's artwork before and after his emigration to Palestine to publicly situate himself in relation to debates on cultural and territorial Zionism, modern Jewish messianism, and the relation between diaspora existence and Jewish creativity. Schulz speaks in highly laudatory terms of Lilien's early illustrated collaborations *Juda* (1900) and *Lieder des Ghetto* (1903), and at the same time indirectly of his own Polish-language writing, as a "creation born of the longing of golus."¹⁷ The image, together with his assessment of Lilien's art and career, signals a commitment on Schulz's part to what I will call here an affirmatively diasporist ethos and a reluctance to capitulate artistically before the "realistic" pressures of rising ethnonationalism in a post-WWI, post-Imperial context. The language Schulz uses throughout the article draws substantially from the arguments and perspectives of both cultural Zionists and representatives of the fin de siècle Modern Jewish Renaissance movement: it points to Schulz's commitment to artistic proposals, achievable or not, forged in the particular and local context of Galician Jewish diaspora, drawing on East European Jewish thought and exegetical tradition. The disappearance of Schulz's Lilien article from readers' consciousness for over three quarters of a century and its reemergence in 2015 represent an exciting next episode in the quest, initially undertaken by Schulz's biographer Jerzy Ficowski, to recover Schulz's existing oeuvre. They also offer a fitting metaphor for the larger phenomenon taking place today within the fields of both Polish and Jewish studies.[18]

In the opening of the Lilien article, Schulz makes direct allusion to his semi-autobiographical, "mythologized" story *"Księga"* ("The Book"), published in the collection *Sanatorium under the Sign of the Hourglass* (1937). The *"mityzacja rzeczywistości,"* or "mythologizing of reality," is a much-explored premise of Schulz's poetic practice—one that he named and described in essays and interviews—but in his Lilien essay, through intertextual allusion to his own stories, Schulz also invites his readers to *demythologize* his literary texts, understanding them as a direct expression of his engagement with the Jewish questions of his day.[19] For Schulz, the relationship between the individual and the history in which they find themselves embedded was of central concern. He conceived of a poetic text as both a border region where multiple temporalities intersect, and as its own form of linguistic polysystem—a dynamic locus of exchange and of translation in which the languages of history, of transhistorical myth, and of individual experience are constantly being translated into one other: "That strange border, where the person becomes myth, and myth takes human form." In such a text, for Schulz, "History passes over into embodied characterology [the study of an individual personality] and the author speaks about that history and about that individual personality not with the language of retrospection, but rather in the dynamic language of a living story, that is in the act of creating itself."[20]

In the chapters that follow, I accept the invitation Schulz puts forward in his 1937 Lilien essay, and seek to intentionally re-historicize and re-contextualize selected passages from his mythologized and universalized literary landscapes, allowing them to shed light on, and give voice to, the experiences of Polish-speaking Jewish writers and intellectuals in Schulz's Galician region of Poland in the interwar period. How was Schulz's model for a diasporic Jewish/Polish/world writing shaped by his specific Galician experience? How did his contact with the Yiddishist milieu of Lwów, and with the Polish/Yiddish writer Debora Vogel in particular, contribute to the emergence of his aesthetic? How did the need for solutions to the Jewish Question in interwar Poland inform the aesthetic theories developed by Schulz and his Galician Jewish contemporaries? Using the Neo-Romantic language of myth, Schulz wrote that the dramatic changes taking place within European communities in the twentieth century must also play themselves out in the "mythic depths . . . where art operates" and where the contours of a present-day ethics are continually reimagined (SF6, 88).[21]

Since the 1990s, a growing constellation of Schulz scholars have contributed to identifying specifically Jewish cultural sources of Schulz's poetics, demonstrating the extent to which his mythologized literary landscapes—the "mythic depths" activated in his modern texts—draw on biblical, exegetical, kabbalistic, and Hasidic tropes and narrative techniques.[22] Schulz's adaptation of the Lurianic model of repair, or *tikkun*, in particular—a central paradigm of Lurianic Kabbalah—has been discussed by Henri Lewi, Władysław Panas, Bożena Shallcross, myself, and Agata Bielik-Robson.[23] In the present discussion I am interested in complementing these earlier studies by turning attention to contemporaneous conversations that were taking place within the Jewish communities of Interwar Poland, and Habsburg Galicia before it, with which Schulz's texts also engage, during a period characterized by rising ethnonational tensions, and by a sense of heightened existential concern for the future of Jewish life and cultural continuity in Central and Eastern Europe.

A comprehensive discussion of the multilingual and culturally diverse political, social, and cultural climate of interwar Jewish life in Poland and in Galicia is well beyond the scope of the present study. I point the reader in the chapters that follow to a wealth of new scholarship that has made Jewish cultural dynamics of the interwar period more accessible—chief among these historian Kenneth Moss's 2021 study *An Unchosen People: Jewish Political Reckoning in Interwar Poland.*[24] I limit myself here to a re-evaluation and re-reading of Schulz's aesthetic theory and practice that gives consideration to two distinct periods: fin-de-siècle Austrian Galicia under the Habsburg monarchy—the political and cultural context in which Schulz was born and educated, and in which he began his career as a graphic artist—and independent post-WWI Poland, a context that was both favorable to modernist artistic experimentation and increasingly fraught for Polish Jewish artists, particularly by the second half of the 1930s. The movement or transition between these two periods, between multiethnic Empire and Nation-state, was a defining experience for Bruno Schulz's Galician Jewish generation—and the arc of that movement becomes a subtext and a structural element within the stories and writings that I will explore here.

A Galician Inheritance: The Jewish Renaissance Movement

During Schulz's childhood the population of his hometown, Drohobycz, in the Austro-Hungarian Empire, was approximately one-quarter Polish Catholic, one-quarter Ukrainian, and almost half Jewish (44% in 1910). It was a turn-of-the century oil boomtown in the eastern reaches of the empire, in a region characterized for Jewish citizens by the early rise of Zionist thought and activism, by the continued vitality of Hasidism, and at the same time, by a strong degree of Polish patriotism among acculturating Jews.[25] Under the Habsburg Monarchy, Galician Jews had been granted legal emancipation in 1867, fully two generations before their contemporaries within the Russian partition, and joined eleven other ethnic groups as citizens able to participate fully in both economy and regional and local governments of the empire.[26] Also in this year, Galicia, consisting of the territories of the former Polish-Lithuanian Commonwealth that had been annexed by the Austrian Empire in the Polish Partitions of 1772–1775, was granted substantial political and cultural autonomy. In an historically Polish province where Polish gentry retained political power on a local and province-wide level, autonomy meant that Polish would become the language of regional government, courts, and education for all Austrian citizens of the province, including Poles, Jews, and Ukrainians.[27] For Jews, Polish joined German as a language of middle-class acculturation.[28]

Bruno Schulz's family belonged to the acculturating Polish Jewish middle class. His parents, Henrietta Schulz (née Kuchmarcher) and Jacob Schulz, owned a cloth shop on the main square of Drohobycz, and it is in the apartments above this shop, mythologized in his later stories, that Schulz was raised with both Polish and German in the home, and with a secular upbringing. He attended a Polish high school, The Franz-Joseph Royal-Imperial Gymnasium, like Martin Buber ten years earlier in precisely this region.[29]

Culturally and linguistically, the Drohobycz of his youth was a multilingual and ethnically pluralist environment in which translation was a part of everyday life. In daily discourse and on the street Hasidic tales mingled with discussion of the speeches of Zionist luminaries; poetry and prayer with the languages and imagery of advertising and commerce; Polish and Yiddish with German, Ukrainian, Hebrew. These linguistic and narrative components were part of life in Drohobycz's streets, homes, and schools, and also in the lanes and dining rooms of the sanatorium at Truskawiec, where he summered with his family.

Schulz, himself a member of Drohobycz's Jewish community, is known to have taken an interest in the prayers, services, and pageantry associated with Eastern Orthodox and Catholic holidays. At the cinema house in Drohobycz, one of many owned by his elder brother Izydor Schulz in and around Lwów, he would have taken in the images and plots of movies from Warsaw, Berlin, and Hollywood; and he read widely at the well-stocked antiquarian bookshop owned by the father of his friend Mundek Pilpul, who allowed him to borrow books at will, all before he left to study in Vienna. As an aspiring artist, Schulz spent significant portions of his young adult life in the cultural capital, Vienna, during World War I—both to escape the war together with other family members and also to pursue studies in art and architecture that he was not able to complete. It was an environment and a period steeped in the aesthetics of the Viennese Secession, including its decadence and eroticism, and fascination with myth, qualities that would define Schulz's graphic and written work from that point on.

When Schulz began to write fiction himself, after he returned to Drohobycz following World War I, it was in Polish, the language in which he had the greatest poetic facility. Unlike other members of the Galician Jewish artistic and literary milieu of Lwów, who were also native speakers of Polish, including the poets Debora Vogel and Rokhl Korn, Schulz did not choose to become a Yiddishist, and to learn Yiddish as a literary language. When he did decide to begin writing in a language other than Polish, he chose German. "I'd very much like to capture that prize," he wrote to his friend Romana Halpern in 1938, referring to the prestigious *Wiadomości Literackie* (Literary News) award out of Warsaw, "chiefly because it is the steppingstone by which to break *through* the boundaries of the Polish language."[30] One completed text in German, entitled "Homecoming" ("*Heimkehr*") and written in 1938, he sent to Thomas Mann in hopes of initiating a correspondence with the writer who'd had a formative influence on him. Had Schulz survived the second world war, he may well have gone on to join the canon of modern German-language as well as Polish-language literature. But it is in the Polish language that Schulz would carve out a Galician Jewish modernist poetics that set in motion an artistic genealogy of its own—and that continues to generate a growing international lineage of artistic responses in the visual arts, literature, theater, and cinema until the present.

I propose in chapter 2 of this study to the that the sources of Schulz's diasporic Polish Jewish modernism can be found in part in the fin de siècle Galician intellectual heritage of Cultural Zionism and the Jewish Renaissance Movement. In the pre-WWI period, Galician Jews a decade older than Schulz, including Markus Ehrenpreis, Martin Buber, Berthold Feiwel, Ephraim Moses Lilien, and August Thon—citizens of the Habsburg Empire from Schulz's Lwów region—were leading contributors to a current of cultural activity associated with the Berlin journal *Ost und West* (East and West) which Nathan Birnbaum and later Martin Buber would call the "Jewish Renaissance Movement."[31] Addressing themselves to a German-speaking, acculturated Jewish readership in Austria and Germany, these Galician-born cultural activists argued that East European Jewish culture—the rich religious and communal life that had developed over centuries on Polish and Russian territories—represented the authentic and indispensable spiritual and cultural source on which any successful project for the development of an affirmative, secular Jewish identity must draw. Schulz would later go on to bring the ethos of the fin de siècle Jewish Renaissance Movement into his literary work in the 1930s, in a Polish context. Indeed, his writing may represent a singular literary expression of the goals and values of the modern Jewish Renaissance Movement in the Polish language.[32]

The contexts of influence and exchange described in the chapters that follow turn particular attention toward a central challenge to which Schulz's work addressed itself: how to negotiate and to reimagine the forms of Jewish cultural continuity in a secularizing age. This was the project and challenge most urgently emphasized in Markus Ehrenpreis's and Nathan Birnbaum's statements on Jewish cultural renaissance, and in the programs of Cultural or spiritual Zionism and diaspora nationalism that influenced many Jewish writers of the interwar generation. Schulz's work, too, as he reveals in his essay on Ephraim Moses Lilien, developed as a response to a calling felt by many in his generation to consider the future of Jewish cultural heritage in an era of national state-formation. "I knew that the Book is a postulate, that it is a task [*zadaniem*]," says the character Joseph, the young protagonist of many of Schulz's short stories. "I felt on my shoulders the weight of a great mission [*posłannictwa*]" (L, 85).[33] For the author, too, the book was a mission that involved in particular the search for modernist forms of continuity for the Jewish textual and exegetical tradition, and for what Schulz called the tradition of Jewish "mystical messianic" tradition.

"Historians," writes Joshua Shanes, "have tended to overlook Galicia by focusing either on the numerically more significant Russian Jewry or on the other emancipated communities in Western and Central Europe. Most Zionist historiography has also under-emphasized the importance of this community, particularly in the pre-Herzlian period, by which time Galician Zionists could already boast a considerable degree of organizational infrastructure."[34] While a wealth of historiography has moved in to address this lacuna,[35] a similar dynamic within literary studies has led to an under-theorization of the development of Polish-language Jewish culture in Galicia, including conditions that could give rise to the mature and complex expression of Jewish modernist writing in the Polish language that Schulz's work represents.[36] Working within dominant paradigms for understanding Polish-language modernist writing, critics have traditionally situated Schulz's work in relation to what was the new, post-1918 cultural center of a reunited Poland: Warsaw. He is canonized as one of the three leading innovators within Polish modernist prose—Stanisław Ignacy Witkiewicz (Witkacy), Bruno Schulz, and Witold Gombrowicz—also recognized as leading experimenters in Form. In this context, his art has been understood as a writing from the Polish periphery or margins, a provincial writing, that gained recognition at the center.[37] At the same time, several critics have noted that the poetic landscapes of his fiction seem to register no reaction to Polish cultural and political developments unfolding at that center. Schulz is "deaf to the call of any and all politics—artistic as well as social. The words of Żeromski, Peiper, if not Peiper than Słonimski, must have made their way to Drohobycz . . . and yet they seem not to have struck any chord with Schulz."[38] In another evaluation, he is "not particularly burdened by the Polish past and the weight of its literary tradition."[39] Indeed, the landscape of Schulz's prose work is oriented both thematically and discursively less toward the Polish-language cultural center of the reconstituted Republic, or Polish literary tradition, than toward two alternate cultural poles or centers that were of seminal importance to Galician Jewish artists. The first was represented by German-language literature of fin-de-siècle Austria and Germany. "I am looking for a new author who would dazzle and enrapture me," Schulz wrote in a letter to his friend Rudolf Ottenbreit. "For quite some time, I haven't found anything except Rilke, Kafka, and Mann."[40] The second, a cultural capital of both local and trans-historical dimension, was the deterritorialized center represented by Jewish scriptural and exegetical tradition.

Through attention to these Galician contexts, pre- and post-WWI, I am interested in identifying a third position within modern Polish-language literature that Schulz's work occupied and also carved out for itself in response to the call felt by modern Jewish writers. That is a category of Jewish writing in the Polish language separate from both that of the assimilated or acculturated writers associated with the Warsaw-based *Wiadomości Literackie* and Skamander milieux[41]—who avoided Jewish thematics to a strong degree—and also from the emerging cohort of Zionist or "Palestinocentric" Polish-Jewish writers whose work was brought to light in the first major study of Polish-language Jewish writing, Eugenia Prokop-Janiec's *Polish-Jewish Literature in the Interwar Years*.[42] Differently from either of these trends, Schulz's translational and polyphonic form of diasporic modernism seeks a way to leverage the very fact of writing in Polish, by this time a Jewish vernacular for Schulz's Galician generation, to develop a Jewish writing that explored and embodied, through its linguistic form as well as through its thematic contents, the condition of diaspora in the newly formed Polish nation-state.

From Habsburg Galicia to the Second Republic

For ethnic Poles, the reconstitution of Poland as a nation-state following World War I marked the realization of national aspirations that had shaped Polish literary discourse since the final partitioning of Poland in 1795. For Poland's Jewish citizens, the Polish Second Republic was a newly constituted, majority Polish nation-state in which Jewish residents of the former Russian Pale of Settlement, Austrian Galicia, and Prussia—the former Polish Partitions—would now make up a sizable, diverse minority—and for many Poles, an unwanted minority.[43] Non-Jewish Polish political sentiment was deeply divided over the question of whether Jews represented an integral part of the new social and cultural body that must be tolerated, accepted, or embraced to a greater or lesser degree, or a fundamental threat to its purity. From the formation of the Second Republic, national, ethnic, and linguistic lines were increasingly tightly drawn. Cultural production in Polish by Jews, and a de-ethnicized cosmopolitanism more generally, were increasingly perceived by Polish nationalist critics as direct threats to the purity of Polish language and literature.[44] Yet it was precisely in this context that Jewish poets and prose writers, filmmakers, and songwriters in the Polish language played a central role in shaping Polish literary modernism, and the twentieth-century Polish cultural imaginary more broadly. In the 1920s, Polish culture and the arts celebrated the cultural freedom and individual freedom of expression that came with independence, and Polish Jewish writers were leading contributors to modernist literary experimentation and literary formations, including the Skamander poets, Polish avant-garde and Futurist movements, and the country's leading literary and intellectual newspaper, *Wiadomości Literackie* (Literary News). Simultaneously, trilingual Jewish culture flourished in post-WWI Poland, in the form of Jewish newspapers, schools, theaters, and literary publications in Yiddish, Polish, and Hebrew. Warsaw had become the center of the Yiddish literary world. The literary weekly *Literarishe bleter*, a Yiddish-language corollary to *Wiadomości Literackie*, was founded in 1924, supporting the continuation of a vital contemporary literary scene in Yiddish. Already since the turn of the twentieth century, Jewish writers and artists had found themselves at the center of what Chone Shmeruk and Benjamin Harshav have termed the "modern Jewish revolution" and the "Jewish language wars."[45] Each had to choose the language or languages in which they would create modern Jewish and modern European and world culture, as well as in which, if any, of the existing utopian or soberly realistic projects to place their hopes: diaspora nationalism, associated with Yiddishism; political Zionism, associated with Hebraism and modern Hebrew literature; acculturation and the embrace of Polish patriotism; Communism, Socialism (in all three languages), or emigration to the US and other countries, while immigration policies permitted.[46]

In a post-WWI period characterized by the rise of integral and extrusionary nationalism and vocally antisemitic politics, both in neighboring Germany and within Poland's nationalist right, Narodowa Demokracja (National Democracy), the "secular messianic" tenor of these Jewish political and cultural programs increased. Each held out the promise either of escape from the untenable or unsustainable present, or recommitted to the hope of full participation in a future Polish democracy that might fulfill its obligation to grant all of its citizens, including a full third that were not ethnically Polish, equal rights. "What elsewhere is a utopia, among the Jews is a necessity," the socialist-Zionist activist Nachman Syrkin (1868–1924) had written in his 1898 essay *Die Judenfrage*.[47] His assertion encapsulates as well a mood of urgency and uncertainty that many Jewish artists felt in interwar Poland, whether they wrote openly about it or not, whether they wrote in Polish or in one of what were recognized as the two national Jewish languages: Yiddish and Hebrew. In Poland's interwar climate, members of the Jewish intelligentsia—including assimilated or acculturated Jewish writers in the Polish language—faced qualitatively different dilemmas, a different set of cultural and linguistic choices, and a far more existentially threatening political reality than their fellow Polish citizens, members of the non-Jewish Polish intelligentsia.[48] What was the place of Jews in this new, post-Imperial order, and in the nation-states that emerged on the basis of national self-determination? In such a context, how should one react to the living of Jewish life and the debating of possible Jewish futures, to the expression of one's Jewish selfhood and strivings, in the Polish language? And to the extent that many treated literature as a metonym for the national body and a medium for the expression and solidification of national consciousness, what was, or should be, the place of Jewish writers in the literary and cultural landscape of the Polish Second Republic?

This tenor and political climate also had a defining influence on the work of Bruno Schulz, and on the forms that his aesthetic philosophy and his modernist textual experiments would take. Attention to it illuminates his model of storytelling as, in part, a negotiation between the impulses of escape and rootedness—and between parallel and coexisting temporalities. The poetics of a "mythologized reality" that Schulz developed offered on the one hand a way out—movement onto a second track of time; the construction of a sanctuary space; and an escape into the world of childhood memory.[49] Yet at the same time, the specific, translational Jewish Polish poetics Schulz developed in the Polish language represented precisely a strong commitment to place—to, in his words, "his epoque, and the community from which he came." They inscribe into European and world literature an affirmation of Galician "golus-existence" or diaspora existence as the source of spiritually, ethically, and aesthetically charged forms of Jewish artistic expression that could have come into being nowhere else. Within the "republic of dreams" that his texts sought to recover, one entered a "fortress," a "citadel," or a realm "beyond all borders"—an idealized "no-man's land, and God's land" associated with childhood memories but also with the enduring, transhistorical haven represented by Jewish textual tradition. The construction within his stories of models of literary sanctuary or alternate time-space represented a conscious resistance to the call of both Jewish and Polish political nationalisms, and the demands that these calls placed on the modern Polish Jewish writer. Schulz's poetics figured themselves as a movement onto a "second track" of time, illicit or dubious. This image brings to mind the emergence of what could be called a "second track" of Polish culture—modern Polish-Jewish culture—emerging in the interwar period. In the newly created state, the Polish language itself was in the process of becoming the new vernacular of Europe's largest Jewish population. Recent scholarship on this process has drawn attention to the interwar phenomenon of *acculturation without assimilation*. As historian Sam Kassow writes, "Although young Jews received a Polish education, they did not become young Poles."[50] Instead, interwar Poland, on territories that had been an ancestral homeland of Ashkenazi Jews for over seven centuries, was beginning to see the emergence of a distinct Polish Jewish cultural imaginary, shaped by life in changing political and geographical realities, including a new and deeper exposure to Polish literary and cultural traditions, and yet developing along a separate, parallel track or tracks.[51] As one part of this emerging second-track of Polish consciousness, Galician-born Jewish historians Mojżesz Schorr, Meir Bałaban, and Yizhak Schiper, writing in Polish, would lead the way in establishing the field of Polish Jewish historiography, bringing a secular, scholarly understanding to the deeply rooted history—even indigeneity—of Jews in historically Polish lands and the integral role they had played in building Poland, past and present.[52] In chapter 5 I consider a number of historical factors that helped to lay the groundwork for the emergence of such a two-track cultural imaginary. These include first, the fact that after Poland gained independence, a new generation of Jewish students, both secular and religious, began to attend Polish state schools. Second, the existence in many Polish cities and towns of what were effectively Jewish-majority cultural environments, determined by historic patterns of Jewish demographic concentration, and by the history of autonomous Jewish social and legal structures that had characterized Polish Jewish communal life over centuries; and finally, the fact that even in a context of rising antisemitism and ethnonational polarization, Polish was quickly becoming the language of the Jewish street. In this respect, reconstituted post-war Poland was catching up with Galicia. A culturo-linguistic dynamic was underway of which Schulz's work may be seen to represent a striking Galician precursor. On the one hand, Polish-speaking Jews were contributing to the creation of a new, parallel Polish

Jewish cultural imaginary. On the other, through their creation of a modern Polish literature that was pluralist, non-Catholic, and non-ethnically Polish in its ethos and its intended audiences, Polish Jewish writers were contributing to an overhaul of the Polish symbolic imaginary itself. The effects of this shift continue to define the Polish canon to the present day. This dynamic also contributed dramatically to the reactionary response of Polish nationalist critics in the interwar period.

Diasporic Modernism in the Polish Language

It is precisely in this fraught, conflicted, and quickly changing environment that the Galician graphic artist and short-story writer Bruno Schulz made the choice to enter and to boldly transform Polish modernist letters. Indeed, he succeeded in this endeavor. Amidst portrayals of Schulz by both critics and acquaintances as a painfully shy, even self-loathing individual who lacked the courage to leave his provincial hometown in Galicia, this simple, astonishing fact remains. His essays and letters suggest that Schulz's model for this undertaking was Franz Kafka, whom he referred to as "a little-known mystic," and who had changed the landscape of modern German literature with a new form of Jewish/universalist prose. In 1936, Schulz began to write a novel that he referred to in correspondence to friends as "Messiah" or "The Messiah" ("*Mesjasz*").[53] The novel belongs to the unspun threads of Schulz's developing oeuvre; yet the author's intention and desire to publish a modernist novel in Polish that openly engaged Jewish messianic discourse and traditions speaks to his sustained commitment to the project of developing a diasporic, Polish Jewish modernist literature in the Polish language.[54] Franz Kafka, whose work Schulz read unequivocally as a reworking of theological subject matter, had done precisely this—had brought a modernist engagement with elements of Jewish scriptural and textual tradition to the center of German letters.

A basic assumption underlying Schulz's experiments, one based on central tenets of the Haskalah or Jewish Enlightenment, and of the fin-de-siècle project of *Bildung*, was that Jewishness and a modern European culture could coexist—and Jewishness could be expressed within the forms and the languages of European art and literature. This premise had been promoted in Habsburg Galicia throughout Schulz's pre-WWI childhood by outspoken leaders in the secular and "progressive" or reform Jewish community, including Markus Ehrenpreis, the uncle of Debora Vogel, who would later play a formative role in Schulz's artistic life. By the second half of the 1930s, however, in Poland this vision was increasingly being recognized as untenable. In a period of growing disillusionment with the promises of acculturation or pluralism, and just as Schulz was emerging as one of the most original voices on the Polish literary scene, emphasis among the majority of Jewish intelligentsia had shifted decisively toward participation in the creation of modern Jewish literature in either Yiddish or Hebrew, recognized as the two national Jewish languages.[55] By the 1930s, for many Jewish writers and cultural activists, a Jewish writer who chose to write literature only in Polish and who aspired to recognition not only among Jewish readers but also at the center of the Polish literary establishment in Warsaw (albeit itself a hybrid Polish/Jewish cultural formation) could be seen to have turned their back on, and to have become irrelevant to, the urgent, existential cultural demands of their nation.[56] Alongside the criticism of Polish ethno-nationalists, this form of literary-linguistic censure from within Jewish literary and intellectual circles arose at a moment when, again, Polish was itself becoming a Jewish language. This was an emerging reality that activists advocating for Jewish cultural autonomy and equality were far from comfortable with or ready to accept. For his part, Schulz's work belied the binary assumptions of critics on both sides. Though written in Polish, his work did not represent a turning of the back to the call placed on his own generation of Jewish artists and writers by influential theorists from Ahad-Ha-Am to Martin Buber to Y. L. Peretz. Instead, his decision openly tested the potential of Polish as a Jewish diasporic language—one as capable of expressing the modern Jewish experience as German, and one particularly suited to capturing the complex subjectivity of a Galician Jewish generation that had lived through the shift from Austro-Hungarian Empire to Polish nation-state. Nevertheless, to use Polish as a language of cosmopolitan and world literature, as Kafka had used German, was far from an unproblematic gesture. The fraught nature of this experiment would itself become a central theme of Schulz's stories in his second volume, *Sanatorium under the Sign of the Hourglass*, published in 1937.

Schulz was by no means alone in his rejection of literary parochialism or in his search for a world literature platform. For many writers who felt unable to embrace political ethno-nationalism as the foundation of their cultural work, socialism was an obvious choice and point of reference. In his study of literary critic Meir Wiener, a fellow Galician writer of Schulz's generation, and one who shared Schulz's cultural Zionist sympathies, Mikhail Krutikov writes:

> As I interpret Wiener's intellectual evolution, it was his rejection of post-World War I nationalist politics that drove him from the orientalist utopia of the cultural Zionism of Ahad Ha'am and Martin Buber to the Marxist-Leninist internationalist utopia of communism—and from Austria to the Soviet Union. . . . His reading of the political situation in interwar Europe convinced him that the only way for Jews to avoid the danger of the total "nationalization" of Jewish culture—a process he believed was well under way in many Central European countries—was to come under the protective wing of the Soviet multinational affirmative action empire.[57]

Marci Shore's study of a "Warsaw generation" of Marxist intellectuals and writers contemporary with Schulz, including Julian Tuwim, Antoni Słonimski and Aleksander Wat, similarly details these Polish-language writers' movement "from the cafés to the corridors of power": from avant-garde modernist literary experimentation toward increasingly activist engagement with communism, in many cases commitment to the Soviet project and, for some who survived, to the political and cultural project of post-WWII communist Poland.[58] While Schulz was likely sympathetic with socialism, his texts address the challenges of his generation differently—through aesthetic and spiritual, rather than political, means.[59] His response to the challenges that faced Jewish writers of his generation was rather to increase his literary and artistic engagement with Jewish exegetical and scriptural tradition, as well as with imagery and paradigms drawn from Hasidic culture and Lurianic Kabbalah. This set him apart from many Polish Jewish writers of his period, in particular those working at the Warsaw center of Polish literary life.[60] For this reason, his work is particularly productive when re-read in the context of neo-Hasidism: that is, when placed in conversation with the thought of both Martin Buber and Hillel Zeitlin. These philosophers developed parallel formulations, in German and in Hebrew and Yiddish, respectively, of a modern Jewish spirituality informed by Hasidic philosophy and tradition. Their dual influence is reflected prominently in Schulz's modernist poetics, with its focus on exegesis, its direct allusion to and tradaptation of kabbalistic and Neoplatonic metaphoric tropes of emanation, shattering and recuperation of shards or fragments, and its recurring atmosphere of messianic anticipation. Finally, when juxtaposed with his nostalgic attachment to *Bildung* and the Jewish/universalist renaissance of Vienna and Berlin, Schulz's sympathy with neo-Hasidic thought further highlights his Galician positionality at the intersection of *ost und west*—of east and west European Jewish intellectual trends.[61]

Schulz used the word *golus*—the Yiddish term for both 'diaspora' and 'exile'—only once in his published work known to date, in his 1937 article on E. M. Lilien. Yet throughout his work as a graphic artist, writer and literary critic he continually explored what it meant to be an artist creating in 'golus'—in diaspora. He also plumbed the ontological potential of the figures of exile and diaspora, turning his texts toward reflection on the exilic state in which language and all matter itself are to be found. In this study I describe Schulz's modernist writing as a concerted attempt to explore the potential of diasporic discourse in the Polish language. At the same time, I specifically do not intend to suggest identification or affinity on Schulz's part with the political program of Diaspora Nationalism that was adopted by the socialist Bund (the General Jewish Labor Bund in Lithuania, Poland and Russia) in interwar Poland, and that was associated with support for Yiddishism in literature and culture. What I do suggest is that Schulz's modernist aesthetics developed in self-conscious dialogue with Yiddishism, and with Yiddish writers' reflections on '*golus-existenz*.' This dialogue took physical form in 1930 when Schulz met the aesthetic philosopher, critic, poet and Yiddishist Debora Vogel, with whom he engaged in a series of intense debates on aesthetic theory. These conversations took place during his visits to Vogel in Lwów in 1930 and '31, and in letters that would famously become his first volume of short stories, *Cinnamon Shops*. Both writers' work would address the themes of diaspora and exile from both the specific historical perspective of the Jewish minority experience in Poland, and within a broader ontological framework, that considered the nature of language, matter and form. In chapter 3 I focus on this formative relationship, drawing on a memoir written by a member of Schulz's and Vogel's immediate Galician Yiddishist milieu, the essay *Nisht-oysgeshpunene fedem*, written by Rachel Auerbach, engaged Yiddishist and later survivor of the Warsaw Ghetto, for the Yiddish journal *Di goldene keyt* in 1964. It was during the period of his close contact with Vogel, recorded in Auerbach's personal memoir, that Schulz began to develop and experiment with a distinct form of non-Yiddishist "diasporist poetics"—in the Polish language.

Until recently, it was taken as a matter of fact that Schulz had not published any fictional writing until his correspondence with Vogel—and his debut as a writer with *Cinnamon Shops*. In 2019, however, a second remarkable archival discovery, made by Ukrainian researcher Lesya Khomych, revealed that Schulz had in fact published a short story entitled "Undula" in 1922, twelve years before *Cinnamon Shops* appeared, under the pseudonym of Marceli Weron.[62] In the context of the present study, the story "Undula" further highlights—through the striking contrast between its thematics and those of the later stories in *Cinnamon Shops* and *Sanatorium*—the formative influence that Schulz's contact with Vogel and with both the Yiddishist and the Cultural Zionist milieux of Lwów had on his emerging aesthetics of diasporic Jewish modernism. This would be an affirmatively Jewish writing in the Polish language that drew specifically on East European Jewish textual and literary traditions, including the centrality of textual exegesis, kabbalistic paradigms of creation and interpretation, and the Hasidic storytelling traditions native to Galicia. It can be argued that Schulz's intentionally "mythicized" prose gestured toward participation in the deterritorialized canon of Jewish literature, through the author's attempt to create a Jewish/world literature both born of and detachable from its Polish context.[63]

In their studies that introduce the terms "peripheral" and "diasporic" Jewish modernisms respectively, Marc Caplan and Allison Schachter identify formal characteristics of Yiddish and Hebrew-language literature written in Eastern Europe that textualizes the diasporic experience. Starting from the premise that "bilingualism or multilingualism is ultimately a precondition for all peripheral writing," both discuss narrative strategies and structural components that reflect the exigencies and also opportunities of writing in multilingual and diasporic contexts.[64] These include "self-conscious, modernist metaliterary framing devices" such as fictional prologues, multiple narrators, and embedded stories that, for Schachter, "enabled Jewish authors to wrestle with and represent competing linguistic, territorial, and political affiliations."[65] Caplan's study explores the coexistence of territorial and deterritorialized—spectral or imaginary—landscapes within both Yiddish and African peripheral modernisms, and the relationship of modernist writing to both folk storytelling traditions and Jewish textual and scriptural tradition—two narrative traditions that are inseparable in the case of East European Jewish culture. Both of their studies emphasize as well the abrupt nature of the movement from traditional, religious forms of Jewish expression to modern, secular forms. This was a temporal proximity characteristic of the emergence of modernist Jewish writing, that enabled complex continuities and conversations with traditional Jewish theological and communal discourse. This latter characteristic is particularly helpful in thinking the relationship between biographical and 'mythical' elements, and corresponding temporalities, in Schulz's Polish-language modernist writing.

Finally, these studies of diasporic modernism treat specifically modern Jewish literatures written in the "deterritorialized" languages of Yiddish and Hebrew, understood in their pre-WWII context as "languages that do not fit within the borders of a nation-state."[66] Because Schulz's writing exactly *was* produced in the dominant language of a newly formed Polish nation-state, it interferes with and productively problematizes a paradigm that associates the characteristics of deterritorialized writing specifically with Yiddish and Hebrew, and frames non-Jewish European languages as "territorial" by default. Schulz's Polish-language texts' imperfect fit reminds that affirmatively diasporist cultural forms— such as Schulz's translational Jewish/world literature—may also and frequently do employ the languages of European nation-states, while being committed from their inception to circulation within a broader context enabled by future translation or emigration. Jewish writing in postrevolutionary Russia, including in Russian, also enriches the category of diasporic modernism, through affirmative engagement with Jewish tradition. "The Soviet century, for all its emphasis on construction and mobilization," writes Harriet Murav in her study *Music from a Speeding Train*, "also gave rise to the reinvention of a backward-glancing Jewish temporality. . . . Traditional Jews saw ongoing reality in light of biblical precedent, according to a paradigm that linked each successive event to 'the continuum of Jewish sacred history.'"[67] Supporting Schachter's claim regarding the ability of texts produced in diasporic, multilingual and postcolonial contexts "to effectively produce counterhistories to the prevailing nationalist myths of literary production," Schulz's Jewish/world literature in the Polish language also belongs to and further expands both the constellation of diasporic and peripheral Jewish modernisms, and the landscape of central and east European Jewish cultural forms created in the interwar period.[68]

Historian Tara Zahra's introduction of the term "national indifference" also helps to frame the literary uses of Polish language as separate from identification with ethnically Polish cultural and heritage. In her 2010 article "National Indifference as a Category of Analysis," Zahra argues that "[m]aking indifference visible enables historians to better understand the limits of nationalization and thereby *challenges* the nationalist narratives, categories, and frameworks that have traditionally dominated the historiography of Eastern Europe."[69] And: "far from being a premodern relic, national indifference was often a response to modern mass politics," that "flourished in the eye of the nationalist storm in Europe between 1880 and 1948."[70] Scholarship on "national indifference" attempts to recognize forms of identity and positionalities that, while not necessarily indifferent to ethnic or cultural heritage, are defined by their unwillingness to become invested in the political project of nation-state building—specifically, in the organization of culture, society and identity around what were new post-World War I nation-states.[71] As a late and stubborn adherent of the fin de siècle call for a Jewish cultural renaissance that did not have territorialist aims, Bruno Schulz may be aptly described by this category.[72]

'The Encounter': Galician Modernity in a Picture-Riddle

Markus Ehrenpreis and his Galician colleagues repeatedly structured their descriptions of a modern Jewish renaissance around the image of a productive encounter between particularism and European 'universalism'—engaging a dialectical and an irreconcilable antinomy that accompanied and energized Jewish movement into modernity. The image of the Encounter would also serve as a scaffolding and a foundational paradigm organizing Schulz's literary and graphic landscapes. This was the encounter between the profane and the sacred; modernity and tradition; historical time and messianic time; material reality and Schulz's "mythologized reality." Within his short stories, prints, and sketches, images of such an encounter emerge as successive iterations in a series, conferring upon the same basic paradigm different faces or masks; testing the potential and the vitality of the encounter as a structural and thematic framework against different contexts, settings and plots; observing its metamorphosis across a variety of artistic media and forms. These forms included *cliché-verre* print, painting, letter, short story, essay, Soviet propaganda, and finally, fresco. In these final wall paintings, made during WWII, fairy tale and fate join in a self-portrait, in which Schulz lends his own visage to an elderly woman in a scarf, who peers from the wall of the childrens' bedroom with a piercing gaze. The image represents a distillation of Schulz's concept of the "thought image" or "picture-riddle": *"obraz-zagadka."*

The term appears in Schulz's story "The Dead Season" (*Martwy sezon*), where the organizing paradigm of encounter takes the form of an *"obraz-talisman"* ("picture-talisman") hanging on the wall of the narrator's father's shop. It is a dynamic, dialectical image that poses an ethical challenge to, and places a demand upon, the viewer, and upon the narrator's father, Jacob: "It was a picture-talisman, an unfathomable image, a picture-riddle, interpreted endlessly, wandering from generation to generation. What did it represent? It was an unending dispute being carried on for centuries, a never-ending trial between two conflicting principles. They stood there facing each other, two merchants, to antitheses, two worlds." In both volumes of Schulz's short stories, *Cinnamon Shops* and *Sanatorium Under the Sign of the Hourglass*, the space of the Father's shop is made available allegorically as a site for the encounter between Jewish textual and messianic tradition on the one hand, and modern life in the commodified landscape of exchange, on the other. It is an emotional and volatile space, in which the protagonist's father, Jacob, summons angels and curses idolaters, moves into the deep realms of introspection and calculation, struggles with ledgers and stores of cloth that become biblical landscapes; and transforms alternately into a prophet and into an insect. "For my father our shop was the place of eternal anguish and torment [. . .] a task beyond his strength, at once immense and sublime. The immensity of its claims frightened him. Even his life could not satisfy their possible extent. [. . .] Horrified by the laxity spreading everywhere, he shut himself off in the lonely service of his high ideal" (W, 224).[73]

The construction of a protagonist-narrator son, Joseph, who witnesses the struggles of his father, Jacob, with tradition, with faith, and with duty, becomes an alibi for the author's own exploration of a possible relationship with Jewish tradition: not legal or halakhic tradition, but in Schulz's own words, exegetical, messianic, and mystical. The father's struggles, his philosophical and artistic strivings, his attempts to defend and at the same time rage against tradition, and his impending demise, comprise an extended parable. I will read it as a tale of Schulz's own grappling, and that of his Polish Jewish generation, with the modern Jewish condition, and the specific historical and cultural moment in which they found themselves.

Within Schulz's 1937 essay on the artist E.M. Lilien that I discuss in detail in chapter 2, written in the same period as the story *The Dead Season*, the picture riddle emerges again, but in unmythologized form. Here Schulz discusses openly the existential choices that Jews of Schulz's generation are forced to make, between placing primacy on the continuity of the "mystical, messianic" Jewish tradition, or on the physical and material needs of the community in a time of rising economic and political crisis. In Schulz's poetic manifesto "Mityzacja rzeczywistości" ("The Mythologizing of Reality"), discussed in chapter 1, the sacred-profane encounter manifests as language in its twofold nature: the primordial Word on the one hand, that exists outside of time, and what Schulz calls the "mosaic piece," on the other: the fallen, fragmented language of everyday usage, available to recuperation by the poet.[74] Within Schulz's graphic works, explored in chapter 6, the picture-riddle condenses, into the form of a Book, whose existence describes a landscape that is both sacred and secular at once. In place of Scripture, here in Schulz's artwork and modern prose it becomes the fragmentary, material modern world, and the world inside of historical time, that lies available to interpretation by the child reader and exegete—whose act of reading discovers and releases the sacred from within the profane, where it lies trapped or scattered. The particular ways in which Schulz formulated the antinomy posed by the picture-riddle, and the specific contexts in which he was able to do so, were determined by his Galician environment.

The present study also proceeds by means of encounter, gesturing at the complexity of Schulz's pre-war and interwar Galician context by staging and restoring a number of representative encounters between Schulz's texts and those of his Jewish contemporaries, with the goal of allowing conversations and voices that have lain dormant within Schulz's work to be released. In chapter 1, I begin by reading the Yiddish poet Rokhl Korn's review of Schulz's first volume of short stories, *Cinnamon Shops*, allowing her text to offer insight into the resonances Schulz's modernist writing could have had for readers within his Galician Jewish artistic and intellectual milieu. In chapter 2 I turn to Schulz's own encounter with his Drohobycz predecessor, graphic artist Ephraim Moses Lilien, reading the multi-part feuilleton that he published on Lilien in 1937. The work, an expression of the diasporist ethos that I argue is central to Schulz's work, serves as a point of reference throughout the study, contributing to the selection and organization of conversations and textual encounters included here. I turn next to an exploration of the intellectual and personal encounter between Schulz and the Yiddish and Polish-language poet and aesthetic theorist Debora Vogel, that was formative to both of their development as Galician Jewish modernist writers. Chapter 4 stages a reading of the story "Sanatorium Under the Sign of the Hourglass" as an encounter of the author with the work of Franz Kafka. It also reads Schulz's story against themes and imagery common to modern Jewish literature and debate, including in work by Y. L. Peretz, Ahad Ha'am, Itzik Manger, Sholem Aleichem, and Aaron Zeitlin. As historians of Jewish Poland have argued, the paradigm of assimilation or acculturation inherited from studies of the German Jewish movement into modernity must be problematized in the Polish Jewish context, and chapter 5 returns to a consideration of the encounter between secular Jewish writers and the Polish language that had a defining impact on modern Polish culture of the interwar period, beyond Galicia. In closing, I return to consider the organizing image of the exegetical encounter, as it develops and shifts from Schulz's graphic works in *Xięga Bałwochwalcza* (*The Book of Idolatry*, 1921) to its emergence in "*Księga*" ("The Book," 1936) and in Schulz's mature aesthetic philosophy, based on the twin paradigms of *golus* and *tikkun*.

It is a goal of my study to give voice to Schulz's immediate Galician intellectual milieu, and when possible to his actual interlocutors—individuals who we know directly influenced him, with whom he discussed his own work and aesthetic concerns, and with whom he chose to explore the shared challenges of creating modern art in an interwar Polish context. In order to evoke the types of discourse that would have been a part of his daily life in this milieu, as well as the language and the concerns of the intellectual communities associated with the Galician periodicals in which Schulz was published, in my discussions I draw when possible on Lwów-based periodicals in which Schulz was either published or which he would have read—including the Polish-language, Zionist-oriented newspaper *Chwila*, the progressive cultural journal *Sygnały*, and the Yiddish-language *Tsushtayer*. My choices are meant to be suggestive, but by no means exhaustive. They aim to encourage further exploration of a rich and still understudied Galician context; to encourage not only new readings of Schulz's well-known work, but also interest in the Jewish and pluralist landscape of multilingual Polish modernism more generally.

Spectrality, Multilinguality and the Polyphonic Text

In reading Bruno Schulz in the context of Jewish modernity, my aim has been not to replace or negate existing interpretations that emphasize the ways in which Schulz's works transcend their Jewish specificity, but rather to establish or highlight those texts' polyphony: their harnessing of cultural multilinguality as a textual strategy. In Schulz's case, that multilinguality lies not in the author's ability to choose or to alternate freely between two or more literary languages, like many of the Jewish writers with whom I compare him in the present study. Again, Schulz was only in the early stages of developing his craft as a German-language writer when his life was cut short. By contrast, Debora Vogel published in Polish and Yiddish and was able to write in Hebrew; Auerbach wrote in both Yiddish and Polish. Instead, I use it to refer to Schulz's construction of texts that could speak simultaneously and differently to Jewish and to non-Jewish readerships. I also use the term to evoke the multiplicity of cultural traditions and symbolic imaginaries with which Schulz's Polish-language texts were in active conversation, and to which they contributed, and continue to contribute; the multiple cultural vocabularies and discourses on which he drew, simultaneously, in the creation of his Galician modernist texts.

With the loss and emigration of the vast majority of Polish Jews, the valences and voices of that pre-war context largely ceased to be activated or stirred up by readers following World War II. For different and complementary reasons discussed here, these voices were also actively repressed within both Polish and Jewish cultural and scholarly discourses, during what David Suchoff in his work on Kafka has called the period of "cold-war criticism."[75] For this reason, Schulz's Jewish/Polish literary language also belongs to the critical realm of spectrality and haunting.[76] While the Polish language itself experienced an unbroken continuity within Poland, it can be said that the pre-WWII writing of Polish Jewish authors represents a spectral voice *within* the living Polish language.[77] As a result, the Polish of today is both a continuous and a discontinuous language. What has been spectralized within it is the language, and the discourse, of *golus*, in both its positive and negative connotations.[78] The metaphor of spectrality introduced by Derrida in *Spectres of Marx* was adapted by postcolonial critics, including Homi Bhaba and Gayatri Spivak, to describe the ethical function within literature of repressed and marginalized voices—including voices of women and colonial subjects that were both silenced within dominant discourses, and reemergent within postcolonial literature. In her 1995 article "Ghostwriting," Spivak had adopted from Derrida's concept of spectrality the implication that the discovery of the spectral demand present in literature is oriented more toward the future than it is toward the past.[79] It involves recuperating repressed voices within literary texts, such that their valences, and their ethical demand, may become available to the reader in actively shaping a discourse of the future: "because it coordinates the future in the past, the ghost is not only a *revenant* (one that returns, the French for "ghost"), but also an *arrivant*, one who arrives."[80] Thus, the critical discourse of spectrality carries an implication of both demand or responsibility, and urgency—the ethical demand placed on the reader of the spectral text, together with a reminder that the critic's engagement with the past is oriented toward the future. It is also in this sense that I find the palimpsested layer of modern Polish Jewish discourse both compelling and timely.

Finally, my decision to read Schulz's work as an artistic expression not only of a modernist, universalist and ethical individualist ethos, as it has long been understood by critics and readers, but also of an affirmatively diasporist, Jewish ethos, reflects here a conscious choice to contribute to the recovery of forms of Jewish cultural identification that fell out of dominant narratives following the Holocaust. "The voices of pre-war European Jews," writes Mikhail Krutikov, "especially those who wrote in languages other than English, German or Hebrew, have been moderated by, and adapted to, various ideological and intellectual agendas, and sometimes silenced altogether."[81] Writing and art that expresses the goals, ideals and aspirations of prewar, affirmatively diasporist Jewish artists was not treated as useful for the urgent ideological and political projects of recovery and state-building that followed World War II in Poland and Israel, or in Jewish communities worldwide—at a time in which communal and scholarly narratives were dominated by what Arnold Eisen termed "the two events which have dictated the terms of Jewish existence in our generation—Holocaust and Statehood."[82] It is my hope that these prewar voices may speak more directly and readily to the concerns and orientation of the present historical and scholarly moment. The translational, diasporic poetics that Schulz developed in the 1930s captured the experience of a generation that had lived through the transition from multicultural Empire to European nation-state. It also marked the Polish-language writer's attempt to negotiate a dynamic marriage of Jewish and "universal," or European modernist, formal and thematic elements. Through this marriage, his texts have inscribed themselves simultaneously into two distinct, parallel, and at times competing cultural imaginaries: those of Polish Polish and Polish Jewish modernism, respectively. Schulz's dense and layered poetic prose undoubtedly draws a part of its enduring fascination for readers from the productive dialectical interplay between these two. While an affirmatively diasporic cultural model of this kind was not easy to incorporate into the ethno-national narratives that have dominated in both Polish and Jewish literary studies since World

War II, it lends itself much more readily to the present context, with its renewed interest, a century after Schulz lived and wrote, in diasporic, hybrid, and translational models of culture and identity, as well as post-secularist attention to cultural projects that arise at the intersection of materialism and theology.

1

LEADING THE WORD OUT OF ITS GOLUS

Rokhl Korn Reads Cinnamon Shops

CHONE SHMERUK AND LATER SCHOLARS HAVE DESCRIBED THE Jewish cultural landscape of Poland as a trilingual polysystem[1] in which spheres of Jewish daily life and communal life, public and private, conducted in Yiddish, Polish, and Hebrew, overlapped and coexisted, creating a variegated but interconnected multilingual fabric of Jewish experience—one that was in a state of constant flux. In the case of Schulz's Galician region and his intellectual formation, the term must be expanded to at least a quadrilingual system, to include German and, for some, Ukrainian. What came to be called the Jewish language wars, that characterized and accompanied Jewish entry into modernity in Eastern Europe, emerged in the late nineteenth century together with the rise of secular forms of Jewish national identification—Diaspora Nationalism and Autonomism, Socialism, cultural and political Zionisms, and Territorialism—and alongside assimilation and Polish patriotism. They accompanied the emergence of a Jewish public sphere[2] in Eastern Europe that included political parties, theater, public readings and speeches, newspapers, and journals in several languages, as well as the rise of the Central European café culture.[3]

Whether Jewish writers in Poland's multilingual interwar context chose to write and publish in Yiddish, Polish, or Hebrew, or to emigrate to the United States, the Soviet Union, Palestine, or Germany where they might again shift their primary medium of expression to English, Russian, Hebrew, or German, the choices that each writer made in this period reflected investment in a possible future, both as an artist and as a member of the Jewish community. Some chose affirmatively diasporist options, including Yiddishism, with the most clearly articulated diasporist agenda often associated with the political program of Diaspora Nationalism; but also the embrace of German as a language of modern Jewish renaissance and, as I will argue here, the increasing use of Polish as a Jewish vernacular. In contrast, the choice of Hebrew as a literary language signaled an affirmation that Jewish national revival would have to involve rejection of the condition and cultures of golus-existence, and a commitment to Zionism, with the goal of contemplating a Jewish future in Palestine. In his seminal study *The Modern Language Revolution*, Benjamin Harshav had proposed an additional dichotomy between "extrinsic" and "intrinsic" paths of entry into modernity among Jewish writers and intellectuals:

> What occurred in this period was a multidirectional, centrifugal movement away from the old existence, symbolized by the religious culture of the Eastern European small town, the *shtetl*, as mythologized in Jewish fiction. . . . The movement went in two directions, extrinsic and intrinsic. . . .[4] In other words: either go to the center of culture (in both the physical and spiritual sense), master its language, literature, ideologies, behavior, and science, and become a member of that language community (German, Russian, English), or create a parallel culture in Jewish languages [Yiddish and Modern Hebrew] that would have similar genres, norms, ideas, institutions, and achievements. Through either of those, you join cosmopolitan European culture as a whole.[5]

One way the texts that resulted from these divergent trajectories, "intrinsic" and "extrinsic," can be seen to have differed is in the degree of their internal polyphony. The latter or extrinsic case, as scholars of German-Jewish literature have argued, produced works of literature characterized by a structure of internal polyphony: texts that speak simultaneously, and differently, to Jewish and non-Jewish audiences.[6] Such a polyphonic or "translational" structure also provides an illuminating paradigm through which to reread Schulz's work.[7] Yet, I would also emphasize that the basic dichotomy proposed by Harshav, which assumes "intrinsic" literature to be that written in Yiddish or Hebrew, elides the quickly changing landscape that was making of Polish a modern Jewish language. If the question of the multilinguality of Jewish writing has undergone at least three generations of study in the case of Kafka's German-language writing, today it is allowing us to reopen and reexamine the large body of modern and modernist literature in Poland written by Jewish authors. A growing body of critical analysis on multilingual Jewish writing, including the attention of Polish critics to the "Marrano" phenomenon in Jewish literature, testifies to this.[8]

The quickly evolving interwar dynamics of Jewish multilingualism described here are relevant to understanding Schulz's work as an affirmatively Jewish writing, as well as to a study of diasporic cultural forms in Central Europe. One of the defining dynamics of diasporic and émigré cultural forms is their ability to decouple languages from ethnicity. Within the aesthetic vocabulary that Schulz developed to describe his own poetic practice, form is that which can be occupied, donned like a mask by matter and by the spirit—only to be discarded or exchanged later, when another mask is taken up. "The life of the substance consists in the assuming and consuming of numberless masks," wrote Schulz. "This migration of forms is the essence of life."[9]

> A principle of sorts appears in the habits, the modes of existence of this reality: universal masquerade. Reality takes on certain shapes merely for the sake of appearance, as a joke or form of play. One person is a human, another is a cockroach, but shape does not penetrate essence, is only a role adopted for the moment, an outer skin soon to be shed. A certain extreme monism of the life substance is assumed here ... for which specific objects are nothing more than masks (WE, 369).[10]

The image of movement through historically bound forms, recast in the empowering language of play, the prerogative of the "demiurge," also speaks to a historical moment when Polish Jewish communities and individuals were in the process of changing the most basic of representational forms: the languages in which they spoke, wrote, and thought, from Yiddish to Polish and, simultaneously for others, from Polish to Yiddish; or, for those in the process of leaving Poland, from Polish and Yiddish to Hebrew, Russian, English, or Spanish.

In this charged environment of competing political and cultural programs, then, as Harshav has written, there was no neutral position.[11] For Jewish authors, to write publicly, to employ language publicly, was always already to take a stand and to insert oneself into a complex of competing cultural programs and proposals. "The hostilities between all the intrinsic trends and the assimilationists, between the Socialists and the Zionists ... between Yiddish and Hebrew, between Western Jews and Eastern Jews, were in the center of social consciousness and public debate. No Jew in this secularized period seemed able to live without active consciousness, and in Jewish behavior there was no consciousness without a position in a debate."[12] Multilinguality was a starting point for Galician writers, many of whom were active in two or three languages, and as such having a position meant making a choice—or engaging, as Vogel would, in the difficult process of sustaining participation in two or more literary communities with differing ideological foundations. The texts that emerged in such an environment were characterized in part by an intentional activation of the polyphonic valences available in the specific languages in which one was writing.

For modernist writers, each of the competing projects also consciously and differently sought to negotiate a relationship between universalism and Jewish particularism. Each gave rise to forms of hybrid modernism, and to texts that participated in European and worldwide modern and modernist developments in literature and art, and at the same time contributed to contemplating the meanings and forms of Jewishness, and of Jewish cultural continuity in a changing and, for many communities, a secularizing age. To write in Polish, Yiddish, Hebrew, German, Russian, or English was, at least in part, to participate in imagining one or another possible future for Polish Jewry—a potential solution, however realistic or utopian that may be, to the existential question of Jewish cultural continuity.

Cinnamon Shops as a Translational Text

Bruno Schulz made his debut on the literary scene of independent Poland under his given name in 1934, with a small volume of short stories entitled *Cinnamon Shops* (*Sklepy cynamonowe*), published by Warsaw's Rój publishing house. The stories in *Cinnamon Shops* featured a first-person narrator—the author's own alter ego—whose memories of childhood in a small town unfolded in a dense and sensuous prose rich with allegorical potential.[13] Strongly influenced by Schulz's training as a graphic artist, the stories in *Cinnamon Shops* pulsed with an organic vitality that suggested a bold experiment in late or neo-*Jugendstil* art in words, transferred to the page. They took shape around constellations of imagery: the "heavenly geography" (W, 61) of the sky, the riotous ebullience of backyards; the alluring interiors of the "cinnamon shops" filled with the "aroma of distant lands and rare materials" (L, 47)[14] and the tawdriness of the commercial world at the provincial margins of the Austrian Empire; the winking eyes of peacock feathers and wallpaper flourishes; sexually charged household scenes (involving the family's housekeeper, Adela, and the employees of a cloth shop above which the young protagonist, like the author, lived); and the explosive figure of the protagonist's father Jacob, fashioned as a "metaphysical prestidigitator," defending "the lost cause of poetry" (L, 20)—and a second alter ego for the author himself. Jacob appeared in many of the stories, adopting successive roles as a biblical prophet in whose shop bolts of cloth unfurled into a Canaanite landscape; as a poet, a gnostic "Heresiarch" and theorist of matter, form, and creation; as a man shaken by illness—suffering and mad; even transformed, in a nod to Franz Kafka, whom Schulz both admired and emulated, into a cockroach and a stuffed bird.

The prose moved downward and inward more often than forward, opening or unfolding its layers and giving expression to states of perception, plumbing everyday objects and events to discover the mystical and mythical resonances within them. Combining expressionist, fin-de-siècle Neo-Romantic, and Neo-Hasidic elements with aspects of the oral tale and of memoir, the stories explored the region in which individual biography merges, in the author's words, with myth. "All poetry is mythologizing," he wrote in 1936, "and strives to recreate myths about the world"[15]—saving in his own work a special place for Jewish myth and tradition, with which his own generation of secular and secularizing Jewish intellectuals was negotiating relationships both spiritual and artistic.

"The substance of this reality exists in a state of constant fermentation," he wrote of *Cinnamon Shops*. It "exhibits a certain principle – of pan-masquerade" (O, 444). Aside from the loose continuity provided by portrayals of the protagonist's father, the fluid dynamism of these stories was fueled less by plot development than by the author's drive to experiment with a new form of modernist prose writing that could express "deep transformations taking place in the depths of the collective consciousness,"[16] by adapting the spiritual heritage of Jewish theological and hermeneutic tradition to a modern, secular form of expression that could transcend national boundaries.

In 1934, Yiddish poet Rokhl Korn (1898–1982), a close friend of Debora Vogel and Rachel Auerbach, reviewed Schulz's *Cinnamon Shops* for the Yiddish literary journal *Literarishe bleter*. Among the many known reviews of his work across the political, ethnic, and linguistic spectrum of Interwar Poland, Korn's presents a rare opportunity to read Schulz's work, and to hear his poetic language, through the ears of another member of the Galician Jewish artistic milieu of Lwów with which he was associated in the early 1930s, and among whom he began his modernist prose experiments. In it we hear how Schulz's work resonated for a Polish Jewish contemporary who knew him personally.

For Allison Schachter, a diasporic approach to modernism "underlines how communities of writers and readers relate to each other and to their shared languages."¹⁷ Shachar Pinsker writes of Yiddish and Hebrew modernisms that they were characterized by an "intense self-consciousness about the linguistic texture of a literature in a state of radical flux" and that "it is impossible to trace and understand Yiddish and Hebrew modernism without examining them in relation to one another."¹⁸ This holds true as well of Polish-language literature written by Schulz and other members of his Galician generation: this writing opens itself richly when placed within a multilingual context of Jewish diasporic modernism. I would argue that although Schulz wrote only in Polish, and not in either of what were considered the national Jewish languages, the cultural polyphony and translationality of his Polish-language texts emerge when prewar conversations and encounters between his texts and those of his Galician Jewish interlocutors are restored. I begin with a sample of the language Korn uses in her review "Bruno Schulz's *Tzimring gevelber* [Cinnamon Shops]":

> While reading this short novella, in which the imaginary takes on the fixed forms of reality, one has the impression that Schulz wants to lead the enslaved word out of its ages-long golus. . . . Entering between the covers of the book of Genesis, Schulz has found a way, through the spirit of words, to the essence of things. Suddenly we glimpse a world, a life that we had passed by indifferently and labeled with the collective name: *"nature-morte"*; a world that lives according to its own laws, ancient laws—engraved in the nervous system of a page. But in the shape of a warning. And we become witness to a bloody struggle for hegemony and equal rights, waged between man and violated nature. This is not a grotesque stage-play of Anderson's fairy-tales for children. It is revelation.¹⁹

Though Korn's choice of imagery and vocabulary reflects her own artistic concerns and her ideological and cultural alignment as a Yiddishist, it is also true that almost every line of her review resonates with Schulz's characteristic metaphoric formulations, and in so doing offers us almost a glimpse of what his writing might sound like had it been written in, or translated into, Yiddish.²⁰ In a discussion of what he terms "translational literature," critic and translator Waïl Hassan offers a suggestive formulation for the cultural and textual practice Korn's poetic review seeks—with a good deal of success—to effect. "My task," he writes, "was to strive to disalienate the novel, to end the linguistic exile in which it was written, to bring it home, so to speak—or indeed, to translate it into the original."²¹ Hassan's comments concern his experience of translating into Arabic a Portuguese-language novel by Alberto Mussa, *The Riddle of Qaf,* whose plot revolves around the protagonist's—and the author's—longing to be reunited with those very Arabic origins. "Mussa's declared intention was to write an Arabic novel even though he had to do it in Portuguese,"[22] Hassan notes, and the novel becomes for the translator "a love letter to the Arabic language."[23]

Though Hassan's proposed model of the translational text does not map precisely onto Schulz's Galician context, because Jewish diasporic culture does not have a single original language toward which to gesture, his theory points invitingly to a formal, architectural element of Schulz's "golus-writing": what we might call the exile of the author's Jewish text within its own native tongue. In almost every text aside from the Lilien article, Schulz's linguistic strategy involves actively encrypting or palimpsesting the Jewish layer of meaning through a slight universalization of Jewishly marked terms and images[24]—thereby inviting the reader to "lead the text out of its exile" in the Polish language, as Korn does. Such a reading does not replace or diminish his works' universal or world-literature resonances but instead restores an essential component of their polyphony and reveals the translationality that is a basic strategy of their construction.[25]

Thus the discourse for which Korn reaches to describe Schulz's work draws liberally on Jewish textual and theological tradition, and on Jewish communal practice. Again: "While reading this short novella," she writes, "one has the impression that Schulz wants to lead the enslaved word out of its ages-long golus." He effects this "leading out" by allowing his text, grounded in biography and the banal realia of small town life, to merge with the Bible, "drawing into its pages an aura of the Book of Genesis" ("*Er firt arayn tzvishn di tovln fun bukh Bereshit-shtimung*").[26] His art is a "form of holy worship before the newly discovered forms of life" and a "new year's ritual," that transforms what would seem to be unremarkable events of childhood into "a world that lives according to its own laws, ancient laws [*urgezetzn*], engraved in the nervous system of the page."[27] For Korn, the individual words in Schulz's texts are invested with autonomous existence, as vessels or carriers of "soul": "Through the soul of words," he finds his way "to the essence of things [*durkh der neshome fun verter hot Schulz gefinen a veg tzum tamtseysem fun zakhn*]." The author's relationship with his raw material—language, the word, form, and childhood experiences—are described by Korn using the vocabulary of slavery, liberation, and a "bloody struggle for equal rights," and she hears his prose as a writing characterized by both warning and "revelation."[28]

Korn's text is written in a metaphor-laden, densely poetic language that mirrors and adopts the style and tone of Schulz's own stories, at the same time selecting specifically those passages that contain an undertone of suffering, connected with the themes of exile, slavery—and also redemption. A discussion of Schulz's treatment of form in *Cinnamon Shops* becomes again in Korn's text an opportunity to reveal the centrality of golus or exile as an organizing principle of Schulz's aesthetic philosophy. As her approach highlights, Schulz's aesthetics treat not only language but also matter and the material world itself as existing in a state of golus, trapped within its given or assigned forms, longing for release. "'Who knows how many suffering, crippled, fragmentary forms of life there are'"—she cites at length a passage from Schulz's "Tractate on Mannequins—Conclusion," in which the father figure and "poet heresiarch"[29] in *Cinnamon Shops* continues his lectures on matter and form—"'such as the artificially created lives of chests and tables violently nailed together, crucified timbers, silent martyrs to cruel human inventiveness? The terrible transplantation of incompatible and hostile races of wood, their merging into one unhappy unity! [*vi dos kinstlekh tzunoyfgeshtikevete, bgvalt-tzunoyfgeporte lebn fun shafes un tishn, gekveytzikt holtz, shtile martirer fun akhzoyresdiker, menschlekher hamtsoe. Groyzame transplantatstiyes fun fremde, zikh hasndike baymerrasn, tsunoyfgeshmidte in eyn eyntsiker umgliklekher eynheyt!*]'"[30]

Directed at both a Polish Jewish and an international Yiddish-language readership, Korn's review allows these citations by Schulz to resonate with the experiences of Polish Jews in the postwar context of newly formed nation-states. In the case of Korn and Schulz specifically, both residents of formerly Austrian Galicia, these lines evoke the experience of not only Jews but also Ukrainians, fellow former residents of the Austro-Hungarian Empire, and other ethnic groups of the Carpathian Mountains, now forced into new costumes, as it were, appearing on the stage of history as citizens of the Polish nation-state. The violence highlighted in this particular citation—a note that appears rarely and thus pointedly in Schulz's texts—recalls that the moment of transition, this trading of costumes from Austrian to Polish, was accompanied for Galician Jews of Schulz's region by a shocking and sobering outbreak of antisemitic violence: the Lwów pogrom of November 1918, carried out by Polish soldiers and local residents, in which over two hundred Jews lost their lives.[31]

Korn's Yiddish-language review "hears" and allows us to hear the conversation with Galician Jewish modernity present in Schulz's early stories—lending his reflections on the artist as "heresiarch" greater urgency. "Weep, ladies, over your own fate," pronounces the father figure in "Tractate on Mannequins," "when you see the misery of imprisoned matter, of tortured matter which does not know what it is and why it is, nor where the gesture may lead that has been imposed on it forever" (W, 35; O, 38). In this context, Schulz's modernist reflections on the nature of matter and form connect golus as an ontological principle—the permanent exilic state of matter and of language—to the painful fate of the individual trapped in historical time, not yet redeemed, however momentarily, by poetry or criticism—who is subjected to the roles, stereotypes, and political and social complexes that the dominant languages and power structures of her day would impose upon her. They betray a quality of empathy and a sensitivity to what he calls the "terrible sadness of all the clown-like golems" ("*straszny smutek wszystkich błazeńskich golemów*") (O, 39)). But "all attempts at organizing matter are transient and temporary, easy to reverse and to dissolve." . . . "'The Demiurge,' said my father, 'has had no monopoly of creation, for creation is the privilege of all spirits. Matter has been given infinite fertility, inexhaustible vitality, and, at the same time, a seductive power of temptation which invites us to create as well. . . . It is a territory outside any law, open to all kinds of charlatans and dilettanti. . . . Matter is the most passive and most defenseless essence in the cosmos'" (W, 35).

In Schulz's conception of the artist as sadist ("Here is the starting point for a new apologia for sadism" [(W, 31]), the pliability of matter and of the self becomes both exhilarating and darkly threatening, and this duality is highlighted and preserved in Korn's review. Although Schulz's father figure's gnostic claim to a power equal to that of the contemporary engineers of the nation-state, and of human souls,[32] offers a plea for the removal of the boundaries that bind matter, and also individuals, into the forms and shapes into which history would squeeze them—for Korn, "the role of people, who reveal themselves to us in Schulz's stories only as a supplement to the quiet tragedies of the cosmos, has ended."[33]

Korn's review of *Cinnamon Shops* is of value in foregrounding a political and social context that has been largely absent from discussions of Schulz's work. This context includes, alongside the highly ambivalent relationship that Galician Jews had to the formation of the Polish state in the wake of World War I, the complex challenges of language choice that faced Jewish writers in this period. With the incorporation of this formerly Habsburg-ruled province into the Second Polish Republic, and the growing allegiance to Yiddishist and Zionist/Hebraist programs, the relationship of Polish-speaking Jewish writers to their mother tongue, Polish, grew increasingly conflicted.[34]

Korn was not alone in figuring the process of the Jewish writer's entry into and participation in Polish-language culture as a form of exile or even slavery, voluntary or otherwise. This was a common trope within polemics on the language question, and in literary criticism of the period that touched on the prominent role Jewish writers were playing in the new literary landscape of independent Poland. Chaim Löw, one of the first to offer an in-depth discussion of contemporary Jewish authors writing in the Polish language, wrote, "Thus, in the battle to secure and to hold onto a place in Polish literature, there is a good handful of poets of Jewish origin who have preserved and matured in the face of all obstacles, and who have given themselves entirely into the slavery of Polish culture, Polish language, and soon the Polish nation—though it is true they are forced now and again to recognize that sweet slavery of theirs."[35] A critic for the Poznań paper *Przegląd Poranny* writes, "It is commonplace today to speak with regret and bitterness about the role of Jewish poets as editors of *Wiadomości Literackie* (*Literary News*).[36] . . . As far as I'm concerned, Tuwim and Słonimski stopped being Jews long ago (if it is absolutely necessary to speak of the subject). Through their wonderful work they have grown into Polishness, and entered into the slavery of the Polish language of their own will."[37]

In his 1932 article "The Rebirth of Language," translator Hersz Buchman, writing for Lwów's Zionist-oriented Jewish daily *Chwila* (*Moment*), frames Jewish writers' use of Polish as the most recent iteration of a tragedy that has characterized Jewish life in golus for millennia. After seventy years in the desert, writes Buchman, "Jews betrayed their own language in favor of the speech of the all-powerful ruler of the time, Ramses. Arameisms crept into the poetic language of the prophets, the simple people began to speak in the Aramaic language, writers began to take stock of the situation to and write in Aramaic." Buchman points out and bemoans the fact that Jews have gone on to create hybrid Jewish languages everywhere they have lived in the diaspora: "later Arabic, for Spanish and Portuguese Jews the language 'Spaniolski'; for today's German Jews Yiddish; and currently it would seem we are witnesses to the coming into existence of a 'Polish Yiddish' [*polskiego jidyszu*—also 'Polish Jewish']. The Hebrew language has retreated to the quiet corner of religious life, making way in everyday life for different 'Yiddishes.'"[38]

For Buchman, a committed Hebraist, "most painful" is the fact that "Jewish writers have ceased to create in their own tongue, and they use foreign languages."[39] In the zero-sum game of national/linguistic territories posited here, which reprises arguments put forward by Ahad Ha'am, Jewish writers and thinkers who use the languages of diaspora allow the Jewish genius and spirit to become the treasure of foreign cultures, to the lasting detriment of Hebrew language and culture: "The first act of the tragedy is the Talmud, a monumental work, and encyclopedia of Jewish life written—not in Hebrew. Later acts follow one another in quick succession. Maimonides writes some of his best works in Arabic; there appear Arabic works by Jewish mathematicians and philosophers. When Jews take a voice in Western culture, they express themselves once again—not in Hebrew. Beginning with Spinoza, through Heine, even down to Tuwim, we see a whole gamut of Jews creating in foreign languages, and as such, belonging to foreign cultures; lost to Hebrew culture. Reclaim them we cannot."[40]

The *Chwila* piece reflects well the contradictions and ironies that characterized this fraught moment in language politics. Buchman must argue in Polish, in Lwów's most widely read Jewish newspaper, the Polish-language *Chwila,* against the emergence of Polish as the new Jewish vernacular. "There are no Hebrew dailies anymore.... We must prepare the ground of Jewish hearts," he concludes, "so that it will not be necessary to talk about the need to promote Hebrew language in Polish."[41] While framing Jewish cultural production in the Polish language as a loss for Jewish national culture, his article also lays out substantial support for a directly opposing diasporist viewpoint. His accounting reminds his readers of an illustrious intellectual, philosophical, and poetic lineage of Jewish writing in the languages of the diaspora that has contributed to the formation of modern Jewish culture and identity, and, now, to a modern Polish Jewish cultural imaginary. His suggestive list reinforces the extent to which foundational works of Jewish culture and religion, works that testify to and preserve Jewish difference, have throughout Jewish history emerged in and through the languages of diaspora, and become themselves textual embodiments of the experience of diaspora existence.

For Schulz, such figures as Spinoza, Heine, Kafka, Martin Buber and Ahad Ha'am help to crystallize his own Polish-Jewish task. His young protagonist states, "I knew that the Book is a postulate, that it is a task [*zadaniem*]. I felt on my shoulders the weight of a great mission [*posłannictwa*]" (W, 85; O, 108). For Schulz's *porte-parole* in the opening stories of *Sanatorium,* this involves discovering the Book (as *Księga, Kodeks,* and *Autentyk*) concealed in the Galician landscape, and in the ephemeral realia of a Galician Jewish childhood. For the author himself, this task entailed turning his ear toward those realia straining to be recuperated into a modern Polish Jewish poetry—and with them to contribute one chapter, a small set of texts, that could either carry the corpus of the Jewish book into a new Polish era or remain to commemorate his own generation's brief "Age of Genius" ("Genialna epoka").⁴² In the context of the language question, the "argument" that Schulz's texts present had already been made by numerous Yiddishists with regard to German. As Josh Karlip writes in his *Tragedy of a Generation*, Yiddish linguist Zelig Kalmanovich, speaking at the Czernowitz Conference of 1908, saw the history of the Yiddish language as "the story of how the Jews appropriated German and completely rebuilt it, reformulating it in the national spirit."⁴³ To concerns like those expressed in Buchman's *Chwila* article, Schulz's texts seem to respond in the affirmative: yes, Polish may be a new Yiddish, a new Aramaic—and if it is, then let it also resonate like those languages before it with messianic and eschatological import and "work its way in to the Bible."⁴⁴

In a separate interview for *Chwila*, the Yiddish poet Uri Zvi Grinberg, associated with avant-garde poets of Łódź's *Yung Yidish*, triangulates these considerations differently still. While he adopted a strongly Zionist orientation and had himself, by the time of the interview, committed to writing in Hebrew rather than Yiddish, Grinberg credits and embraces Jewish poetic creation in the languages of diaspora by relying on a racialized understanding of the sources of Jewishness in literature. "I recognize only 'race poetry,'" he states—"poetry that has a clear national tendency. Hebrew poetry [here: Jewish poetry] must have its distinct song and its national rhythm. Otherwise it will be nothing but a translation from foreign languages." But: "Hebrew literature is not Hebrew because it is written in the Hebrew language. Else Lasker-Schüler is in her German language more Hebrew than many poets in Hebrew. It's the same with Heine, a greater Hebrew race-poet than many of our contemporary poets."⁴⁵

These debates and comments highlight again the circumstances under which writers of Korn's, Vogel's, and Schulz's generation entered the Jewish literary scene in Galicia and the highly charged context of the Jewish language wars⁴⁶ that, since the late nineteenth century, had accompanied the development of modern secular Jewish literatures and the creation of a Jewish public sphere in Eastern Europe. The choices that artists and intellectuals would make in this context represent one of the most characteristic features of Jewish entry into modernity—against which Schulz's writing in his native Polish must be understood not as a neutral position but as a choice. While Schulz, like others in his milieu, would have understood spoken Yiddish.[47] It is also likely that he would have learned to read Hebrew letters in his childhood and as such could likely pronounce Yiddish texts at a basic level, scholars have not learned and likely will not discover whether he could write in Yiddish. Neither does any record exist as to what he thought about Yiddish-language literature, other than the negative space that this topic occupies in his own extant writing. Clearly the question of language choice was central to his aesthetic debates with Debora Vogel, and a trace of their discussions remains in a letter she wrote to Schulz in 1938—one of only five letters that were recovered from the totality of their correspondence: "For whom does one write in Yiddish (*po żydowsku*)?" she asked. Vogel had been a committed Yiddishist for many years at this point and was describing to Schulz a recent literary reading she had taken part in in Lwów. "Those who came understood some of it, but were hampered by their poor knowledge of the language. From among the Jewish poets and so-called Yiddishists *no one* came.... Today I am once again a bit resigned, meaning calmer, but for a few nights I couldn't sleep, and kept turning the pages of that sad book that describes my fate and inexorably marks out its next turns."[48] Even as Vogel continued to write and publish in both Yiddish and Polish, Schulz made great efforts to have his works translated into languages other than Polish, following up on introductions and sending his work to Italy, Austria (to Joseph Roth), and Argentina. "I'd very much like to capture that prize [the prestigious *Wiadomości literackie* award]," he wrote to Romana Halpern in 1938, "chiefly because it is the stepping-stone by which to break through the boundaries of the Polish language."[49] Also in that year he completed his short story "*Heimkehr*," written only in German.

Rokhl Korn, like Schulz and their mutual acquaintance Debora Vogel, was a native of the Galician region of Lwów[50] and a native speaker of Polish. Also like Vogel, she made the choice in the 1920s to become a Yiddish-language writer. This ideological choice is reflected in the ways that Korn, in her review of *Cinnamon Shops*, glosses and responds to the challenge Schulz had posed to himself: writing modernist Jewish literature in the Polish language. That choice is again figured in her review as a form of artistic-linguistic exile. Though Schulz continued to write in what was both of their mother tongue, revisiting this context and understanding the tension that surrounded Jewish writing in the Polish language in this moment can allow us to discover previously unnoticeable ways in which Schulz's writing and publishing strategies play with and respond to these tensions: how they seek to occupy and embody rather than to ignore the charged territory of Jewish writing in the Polish language.

In his postwar compendium of Yiddish writers, *Mayn leksikon*, Melekh Ravitch wrote of Rokhl Korn that "she spoke and mixed three languages, like all members of the national-Jewish [*natzional-yiddishe*] Galitzianer intelligentsia: Yiddish, Polish, and German."[51] Writing was more problematic. Ravitch also recalled that in 1919 Korn wrote cards to the newly opened publishing house *Der Kval* in Vienna, in her "broken and inept Yiddish." Until that year, Korn herself had not read or written Yiddish well, and in this sense she is again representative of Schulz's Galician Jewish Lemberg/Lwów milieu—a generation of Galician Jewish intelligentsia who grew up speaking Polish as a mother tongue, attended Polish-language schools, and used German as a second or third rather than a first language.[52]

Korn's first poems were published in Polish in 1918, but the next year, "after her husband introduced her to what she called the 'terra incognita' of Yiddish literature," writes Hellerstein, she made the choice to study Yiddish with him and committed to becoming a Yiddish-language rather than a Polish-language writer. Her translator, Seymour Levitan, understood this switch "as a direct response to the antisemitic post-WWI pogroms."[53] Like Vogel and Schulz, Korn also sought in her writing to negotiate a path between the twin poles of Jewish particularism and modernist "universality." As Kathryn Hellerstein writes, "Kadya Molodowsky, Dvore Fogel, Rikuda Potash, and Rokhl Korn all wrote poetry that derived from and complicated the desire to burn bridges between a religious cultural tradition and a new, secular, modernist, and political literature in Yiddish."[54] The poems in Korn's first Yiddish-language collection, *Dorf*, "commemorate the people and landscape of the Polish farming village Podliski, in East Galicia" where the poet spent "a solitary childhood, in a Jewish family that had owned and managed farmland for several generations."[55]

Both of these characteristic aspects of modernist writing by Galician Jewish authors in the interwar period—the highly charged question of language choice and the ideological identifications suggested by it, and the balancing act or dialectical relationship between Jewish particularity and modernist universality—are pronounced in Korn's 1934 review of *Cinnamon Shops*. Indeed, perhaps no other discussion contemporary to Schulz's work captures with such empathy and eloquence the internal struggles that animate his Jewish/universalist or Jewish/European experiment. The somewhat dark tone of Korn's language suggests that although she was sympathetic toward Schulz's project, she experienced it, through the lens of her own experience as a Polish Jew in postwar Galicia, and a committed Yiddishist, as a potentially anguished poetic and linguistic project, an aspect rarely identified by other critics.

Schulz's "Mythologizing of Reality": A Return-Yearning for the Pre-Fatherland of the Word

Korn's is not the only review of *Cinnamon Shops* to appear in the Jewish press. Herman Sternbach, mentioned earlier, also a Galician native of Drohobycz and an acquaintance of Schulz's,[56] reviewed his book for the Warsaw-based Polish-language journal *Miesięcznik Żydowski* (*Jewish Monthly*). In his reading, "the author gives such artful form to the simple, ephemeral, practically banal content that before the reader's eyes there arises, within the narrow boundaries of a petty-bourgeois Jewish context, a world boundless in its vastness, and bottomlessly deep. *Cinnamon Shops* is a reminiscence, a vision backwards, that brings to life people and events that have past, well-trodden roads, Jewish Saturday afternoons and autumn evenings that lie buried beneath layers of time; resurrected through the visionary powers of the poet."[57]

Whereas Sternbach's review focuses on the mimetic and nostalgic aspects of Schulz's prose, and the mundanity of his raw material—the quiet stuff of Jewish daily life—Korn's highly literary review is striking precisely in its grasp of how Schulz turns that material of everyday Jewish experience, including traditional theological discourse, toward his modernist philosophical and aesthetic concerns—drawing on it to articulate a new, modern aesthetic philosophy. Most notably, Korn's key formulation that "one has the impression that the poet wants to lead the word out of its ages-long golus" both predicts and echoes the language that Schulz would use in the essay "Mityzacja rzeczywistości" ("The Mythologizing of Reality"), considered to be his poetic manifesto.

In this essay, published in 1936 in the Polish-language journal *Studio*, Schulz wrote that: "what we call poetry" is a "striving of the word towards its home, its return-yearning, the yearning for its linguistic pre-fatherland" ("tę dążność słowa do matecznika, jego powrotną tęsknotę, tęsknotę do praojczyzny słownej, nazywamy poezją.") (O, 366). Language, or the isolated, fragmentary word, exists in a form of exile, separated—through a primordial event of tearing and dispersion—from its home in the "primordial word" ("*pierwotne słowo*") which was a "universal whole."⁵⁸ The work of the poet, precisely as Korn had proposed in her earlier formulation, is to lead the word out of that exile—figured as its exile within everyday spoken languages—and to allow it to return to its home in the primordial word, in "universal meaning" ("*sens uniwersalny*"), in age-old, "all-embracing, integral mythology." Schulz envisioned this primordial linguistic home as a *majaczenie*, a word that evokes simultaneously delirium (in this case presense or non-sense); something as-yet-unseen that draws near; and also a linguistic *tohu va-vohu*, "disorder and darkness above the abyss" (Genesis 1:2) that precedes creation: a swirling mass of unformed and undifferentiated language in a primordial state of pure potentiality—the spirit of language itself, or of language as such, before it enters or "descends" into form. The essay bears citing at length:

> The old cosmogonies expressed this with the statement that in the beginning was the word.... The isolated, mosaic word is a late creation, is already a manipulation of technology. The original word was an inchoate babble (*majaczenie*) circling around the meaning of the light ; it was a great universal whole (*Pierwotne słowo było majaczeniem, krążącym dookoła sensu światła, było wielką uniwersalną całością*). The word in its common usage today is only a fragment, a remnant of some former all-embracing, integral mythology. That is why it possesses a tendency to grow back, to regenerate, to complete itself in full meaning. The life of the word lies in that it tenses and stretches itself towards a thousand connections, like the quartered body of the snake in the legend, whose pieces search for each other in the dark. This thousand-formed but integral organism of the word was torn apart into separate words, into sounds, into everyday speech and, in this new form, adapted to practical needs; it was handed down to us as a means of communication (*organ porozumienia*). The life of the word, its development, was shunted onto a new track, the track of everyday life (*na tory praktyki życiowej*), and subjected to new rules of order (O, 366).⁵⁹

Here Schulz turns toward the role of poetry as agent of repair or return—though interestingly, he posits the agency of this process of return within language itself, consistent with proposals in his fictional works, including "Tractate on Mannequins," that it is matter itself that "longs to be released" from the forms into which it is pressed.⁶⁰

> But if in some way the rules of pragmatic reality (*nakazy praktyki*) loosen their grip, if the word, freed from their restraint (*wyzwolone od tego przymusu*), is left to itself and restored to its own laws, then a regression, a reversal of current

occurs within it; then the word strives for its former connections, strives to complete itself in *meaning*. And this striving of the word towards its origin (*do matecznika*), its return-yearning (*powrotna tęsknota*), the yearning for its linguistic pre-fatherland, we call poetry.[61]

Schulz's manifesto performs a modernist adaptation of the Lurianic creation myth of *tikkun*, but secularizes and adapts that Lurianic model as a theory of language or philology. It also universalizes and encrypts it, rendering it in non-Jewishly marked language. His retelling includes a version of the shattering of the vessels (*shevirat ha-kelim*) and the scattering of the sparks of the divine within the fallen world, where they are trapped in shells (*kelippot*), here figured as the languages of everyday communication,[62] (also a linguistic corollary to Schulz's ubiquitous *tandeta*, or tawdry and transient material) before they are finally returned to their source through an act of repair (*tikkun*), in this case a poetic act, which substitutes for the prayer and ritual observance that effects repair in the traditional model, and within Hasidic theology.[63]

In order to hear a back-translation from Schulz's universalized/mythicized version into a more Jewishly marked discourse of the same period, we can turn to Hillel Zeitlin, whose writings were widely read by members of Schulz's generation in the 1920s and '30s, in both Yiddish and Hebrew. In his writings on Hasidic philosophy, Zeitlin presented tenets of Hasidic philosophy in an accessible form, bringing them together with the thought of modern European philosophers such as Nietzsche and Bergson, and affirming the relevance of Hasidic thought for an interwar generation of acculturated and also secular readers:

> How did the "all" split apart into all these tiny pieces? The Hasidic answer is "the breaking of the vessels." The vessels, not able to bear the intensity of the light, were broken. Some of them broke into pieces, others into tiny fragments. . . . These were all scattered in every direction. . . . These castaways, wherever they are, sigh in longing for the sublime beauty of their original home. Holy sparks are bound up in matter, in nature, in coarseness, in body . . . they call out to God with all their strength: Please save us from captivity, from our scattered state![64]

Schulz's self-consciously translational "Mythicization" essay uses the familiar communal and traditional Hasidic discourse of golus, or exile, as the basis for its modern, secular theory of poetic practice, and in doing so fashions itself as both an inheritor of and a secular/modern continuation of or revitalization of that tradition.

Korn's review, though recognizing and employing Schulz's traditional references, repeatedly returns in its allusions toward contemporary, real-world contexts—highlighting once again the specifically Jewish challenges of acculturation and assimilation, both linguistic and national, that Schulz's writing negotiates. Her review opens with a reference to that context: "When transplanting a tree, one must take care to keep a bit of the native soil about its roots," she begins; "otherwise, the tree will not be able to take root—to acclimatize itself to the conditions of its stepmotherland. People too carry their earliest memories with them throughout their entire lives; and the more delicate a man's spiritual constitution, the more thickly are his soul-roots entwined in the experiences of childhood."[65]

With this image, Korn figures the experiences of childhood—the "spiritual home of childhood"—as a native realm, and the realities of the adult world, and, notably, of the new Polish nation-state in which both writers began to live as adults—as a "stepmotherland," the "hard shoals of real life," to which one must finally, or at some point, acclimatize. "In some cases people manage to make their way out of the spiritual home of childhood and to anchor themselves on the shoals of real life." The image also evokes the process by which Schulz has worked in *Cinnamon Shops* to *translate* or *transplant* his specifically Galician Jewish childhood experience in the Austrian Empire into the universalized/Europeanized "stepmotherland" of modernist Polish prose, making it accessible to a wider Polish and, as he hoped, through translation from Polish, to a wider European and world readership.

On the one hand, Korn draws attention in her review to the same characteristics of his prose that most favorable reviews of his work identify, including an emphasis on the organic in his work. She highlights the "richness of detail and event," the "true orgy of scents and colors, and the accomplishments of all that thrives in the soil of the wildest virility." She also continues her "apologia" for Schulz's Jewish writing in the Polish language by describing his literary landscape as his "*eygntum*" or "property"—a territory belonging uniquely to him; in other words, as a specifically Schulzian, rather than Polish, cultural space: not Julian Tuwim's "*ojczyzna-polszczyzna*" or "Polish-language fatherland," not the multicultural Kakania of his youth, but a private space that evokes *judentum*, and that straddles all of these spatial and discursive paradigms. Her image of a tree transplanted to foreign soil as a figure for Jewish cultural production in "non-Jewish" languages was used by Ahad Ha'am (Asher Ginsburg, 1856—1927), founder of cultural or spiritual Zionism, in his influential 1902 essay (and speech) "The Spiritual Revival."

"The fruit produced by a tree in the place where it grows naturally and freely," he writes, "is unlike that which it bears when it is preserved by artificial means in a strange soil; and yet the tree is the same in its essential nature, and so long as it lives it produces fruit of its own specific kind."⁶⁶ "When we finish reading," writes Korn, "and instead of within the covers of the book we become absorbed into the covers of our own reality," we become aware of what 'peculiar talent' it required to allow the reader to "pass over into that deep, mystery-filled world that . . . has become Schulz's *eygntum* (property)." Thus, although Korn hears the sources of Schulz's poetics in both the present-day experience of golus and in the Jewish exegetical tradition, she also recognizes that it is a goal of Schulz's project to create a literary space that privileges the mystery and complexity of individual experience over nationalism.

Korn's description of this artistic process also contains a warning and leaves room for failure. "One must take care," she notes: the spiritual homeland of childhood, simultaneously painful and idealized, can be dashed to pieces against the hard shoals of "real life," and the tree, uprooted from its native context, may not be able to take root and thrive in the new soil of Polish-language modernism, figured here as golus. How does Schulz respond? In a 1936 essay on Franz Kafka,⁶⁷ to whom he once referred as a "little known mystic writer," Schulz introduces a similar but inverse formulation, which we may read as a response to Korn's warning. His treatment of Kafka here includes yet another argument in favor of diasporism and against the argument for an exclusively bilingual (Yiddish and Hebrew) Jewish culture. For Schulz, Kafka had undertaken a project much like his own, one that could serve as a model within German-language literature for the Jewish modernist experiment he had undertaken in Polish. Thus in Schulz's text, the writer is accorded greater agency than in Korn's: he has the power of a prestidigitator, who can transform even the most resistant of raw materials, turning them to his own needs and to an expression of his own spiritual experiences. "Kafka sees the realistic surface of existence with unusual precision . . . but these to him are but a loose epidermis without roots, which he lifts off like a delicate membrane and fits onto his transcendental world, transplants onto his own reality. His attitude to reality is radically ironic, treacherous, profoundly ill-intentioned—the relationship of a prestidigitator to his raw material" (WE, 349; O, 414). Schulz's description of Kafka's and by extension of his own poetics is characteristically free of the Jewish linguistic markers and allusions that dominate in Korn's "translation" of the same. Yet the idea of the artist who redeems the material of everyday experience, or of golus-existence, raising it into his own spiritual realm, remains. "Aside from its mystical allusions and religious intuitions," writes Schulz, again about Kafka, "this work lives its own poetic life—ambiguous (*wieloznaczne*), not exhausted by any one interpretation" (O, 414).

Schulz's words, written after Korn's review, contain multiple resonances: they continue his reflections on the ability of the poet to redeem the material and temporal by returning it to the metaphysical or "mythical," to release historical into transhistorical, profane into sacred. But they also treat the ability of Kafka, the Jewish writer, to turn the non-Jewish language of diaspora into a vehicle for the expression of his individual spiritual reality. The poet does not have to secure himself a place in the new historical reality; on the contrary, through the work of poetry, real-life historical experiences are transplanted onto the realm of the poet's spiritual reality, where they may resonate with metaphysical content and join a transhistorical time of exegesis—affording the poet or prestidigitator both a measure of control and a means of escape, the ability to redeem or liberate the "raw material" of real-world experience; to return to Korn's words, "to lead the enslaved word out of its ages-long *golus*." In Schulz's interpretation, the type of text that Kafka strives for and achieves through this treacherous transplantation is a kind of textual alibi for the experience of a drawing near to the divine: "Kafka is able to render the atmosphere—the climate and aura—of a human life coming into contact with the superhuman, with the highest truth. . . . The astonishing artistic feat of this novel [*The Castle*] lies in . . . the creation of a *doppelgänger* or substitute reality," a "substitute material" in which even the secular individual in the twentieth century, "even the uninitiated may feel the chill breath of its distant majesty and realize that they are being offered a poetic equivalent (*adekwat*) of the actual experience" (WE, 349; O, 414).

In 1935–36, Schulz would continually revisit and elaborate upon his own maturing aesthetic philosophy in "The Mythicization of Reality," in several short and penetrating essayistic studies of writers and artists whom he admired, including Franz Kafka, Witold Gombrowicz, Moses Ephraim Lilien, Zofia Nałkowska, and Debora Vogel, and most notably in a 1935 interview with Witkacy that appeared in *Tygodnik Illustrowany*, and a 1936 open exchange of letters with Witold Gombrowicz printed in the monthly *Studio*. As his biographer Jerzy Ficowski writes, Schulz's essays on other writers also represent a substantial body of commentary on his own work. In his review of Witold Gombrowicz's novel *Ferdydurke*, for example, Schulz emphasized elements that echoed his own developing diasporic/exilic aesthetics: "Each of these forms, gestures and masks, overgrown with humanness, contained within itself fragments of those suffering, and yet concretely and singularly true depths of the human being. Gombrowicz recuperates them, brings them back, collects them, calls them out from their long exile and dispersal" (*"odwołuje je z długiego wygnania i rozproszeniu"*) (O, 386). He finds in Gombrowicz's writing a "love for the human creature, laughable, clumsy and also moving in its helplessness" (O, 386) and, once again, a sensitivity to the masks that individuals must adopt in modern society—perceived as a kind of golus of form into which the individual has been exiled but from which he or she may be redeemed through the redemptive power of the modernist text. Schulz's review reads in parts like a translation—now *into* the non-Jewishly marked discourse of Polish modernism—of fragments of Korn's earlier Yiddish-language review of his own work. The more these masks demask themselves, he continues, "the more their mechanism is revealed to be shoddy, transparent and scandalous, the more fully the individual can free himself from the forms that have bound him" (O, 386).

As Korn's and Sternbach's reviews of *Cinnamon Shops* demonstrate, already at the time of its publication, Schulz's work was read differently by critics connected to his Galician Jewish context and interested in its Jewish thematics one the one hand, who read it as a modern writing deeply rooted in Jewish communal experience; and on the other those who received it as a strikingly innovative, idiosyncratic example of experimentation with literary form within modern Polish letters. For Sternbach, again a Galician acquaintance of the author, *Cinnamon Shops* was "characterized above all by a subtle and intimate lyricism, unpretentious in its humanity, and not opportunistic but rather deep, true and fascinating in its Jewishness."[68] He concluded, "With this, his debut, the author has secured himself a leading position within Polish letters, and virtually the first place among Polish Jewish writers whose themes are drawn from Jewish life."[69] While for Sternbach it had appeared both natural and positive that Schulz's texts should bring him acclaim as both a Polish *and* a Polish Jewish author, for other critics in this period of increasing polarization, this straddling of literary worlds was not a quality to emphasize or to celebrate. The Yiddish-language writer and editor Rachel Auerbach, who met Schulz together with Debora Vogel in 1929 and who claimed to have played an instrumental role in encouraging Schulz to publish his literary postscripts to Vogel, wrote in her postwar memoir that while French critics had hailed *Cinnamon Shops* as the emergence of "a Polish Kafka," he was "*Nisht keyn Poylisher!*—By no means Polish! Jewish! An original and great writer of Jewish background! Polish is his language, Jewish is the background, the material of his phantasmagorias. And Jewish, without doubt, is his fate."⁷⁰ "Within Polish letters," she continued, "Schulz is utterly unique: a singular revelation of Jewish genius. Strange and original, with a power bordering on the ecstatic."⁷¹ It is significant that all three of these reviewers highlight their feeling of familiarity with the Jewish sources of Schulz's art. For each of them, elements of that background are recognizable, and their reviews express identification with and even a sense of ownership of those sources.

By contrast, reviews by non-Jewish critics in the interwar period frequently emphasized—and some also celebrated, or found exhilarating—precisely not familiarity and Jewishness but rather difference and otherness, the creation from whole cloth of an alternate reality.⁷² Many positive reviews described the power of Schulz's writing to defamiliarize what it touched: to carry the reader into a place of dreams, of the unconscious, the perverted, or the "mad," or of the metaphysical. Leading Polish modernist writer, painter, and aesthetic theorist S. I. Witkiewicz (Witkacy), who knew Schulz personally and discussed aesthetics with him on many occasions, both publicly and privately, wrote a lengthy and penetrating discussion of *Cinnamon Shops* for the journal *Pion*. Like Rokhl Korn's intentionally poetic review, Witkacy's language echoes and adopts Schulz's contagious formulations and reproduces elements of his ebullient baroque style. In Witkacy's reading, itself a literary performance, the theme of movement, of transformation from everyday experience into the realm of the metaphysical, also remains central. Yet, in place of resonances drawn from Genesis, or connected with the paradigms of golus, exile, slavery, or uprootedness that stand out in Rokhl Korn's reading, Witkacy chooses to position *Cinnamon Shops* for a new readership as "that diabolical book" that causes the Polish artist to connect with the transgressive, the antinomian, and the "satanic" within himself: "I began to feel—to put it poetically—rising from the depths of my being the satanic fumes (*jakiś szatański opar*) coming from the evaporating cinnamon grounds that had accumulated there during the night."⁷³ His text accesses primarily language associated with the transgression of boundaries: with the erotic, the unconscious, and the animal; with otherness, mystery, and madness. Considering Schulz's works today from the perspective of their intentional polyphony and translationality, it is possible to read in Witkacy's essay an alternate translation, as it were, of Schulz's literary project into the aesthetic discourse that the two Polish-language artists shared—namely, the un-Jewishly marked philosophical and psychological language of Polish-language modernism, characterized by experimentation with form, perception, and representation. Fascinating in Witkacy's explanation or "translation" of Schulz's style is the recurrence of vocabulary that frames Schulz's prose as being written in an incomprehensible or indecipherable language—one that the reader cannot fully hear, access, or understand but that nevertheless enters him and gains a kind of subconscious power over him.[74]

> Within me there was heard the gibbering of some unknown beast [*nieznanego jakiegoś bydlęcia*] who began to describe to me, in a cinnamon voice (inarticulate extract of Schulzean venoms), the objective world of a typical summer afternoon which I could see clearly with my own eyes. This world grew deformed in the stream of gibberish [*deformował się w tym bełkocie*], yet at the same time gained power, became "alienated" (otherized itself) ["*obciął (stawał się obcy)*"], uncannied itself [*niesamowiciał*], shimmered with all the colors of a madman's nightmare. . . .
> Schulz with a kind of outright metaphysical lechery paws the tiniest nooks and corners of his beloved reality. . . . Like meteors, Schulz's sentences illumine new, unknown lands, which are usually submerged in a sea of banality and which we, deluged with mediocrity, are not able to perceive. . . . His words are condensed pills which expand inside us—like the cotton soaked in fat used to poison rats in that hideous fashion—with an excess of content crammed into them under enormous pressure, spreading far beyond the boundaries of the prose itself and creating for us a metaphysical vista on the world."[75]

In Witkacy's characteristically performative and provocative rendering, Schulz's genre of Polish-language writing evoked not the familiar but rather proximity to the extreme Other, even to "ultimate Mystery of everything in the universe." He speaks of him as a master of defamiliarization, a technique central to Witkacy's own aesthetic goals—and seems to appreciate his achievement in this realm beyond discernable speech or language as much as Auerbach does Schulz's "singular revelation of Jewish genius," Sternbach does his nostalgic evocation of a deeply familiar Jewish world that was fast undergoing transformation, or Korn's text's ability to conjure a private mythical world resonant with the language of warning and "revelation."[76]

These reviews, all the reactions of people who knew Schulz personally and were engaged with him in literary and artistic debates, offer a glimpse into the divergent readings of Schulz's work that were born not only of individual subjectivity and interest but also of distinct and coexisting cultural imaginaries. That Schulz's writing could inhabit both simultaneously and could speak meaningfully to both readerships—Polish Polish and Polish Jewish, at times indifferent to or unknowable to one another—represents a constitutive characteristic of his experiments in diasporic modernism. This could be described as a play with translationality or the multiplication of subjectivity as a strategy of diasporic writing. Schulz's Polish-language texts added themselves to the margins, as it were, of different literary and philosophical traditions, depending on whether the Jewish cultural allusions and political and cultural realities were or were not available to or relevant to a given reader, as one discursive layer within a polyphonic text. As Schulz would write of the artist Ephraim Moses Lilien's work, which I examine in the next chapter: the result was an art form that strove to be "adequate to" and reflective of the specific community and historical moment out of which it came. That initial Jewish/non-Jewishly marked or Jewish/universal distinction has continued within criticism of Schulz's work until the present, producing two loosely recognizable streams of scholarship within Schulzology today.

How do Schulz's texts enable this two-tracked, or indeed multi-tracked reception on a formal level? Stefan Chwin and Thomas Anessi have convincingly detailed the choice to soften, to gently mock, to remove or to universalize markedly Jewish content in the stories published in *Sklepy cynamonowe* (*Cinnamon Shops*) and in Schulz's second volume, *Sanatorium*, as the author strove for readership and recognition at the center of the Polish literary world.[77] A single illustration of this process is quite telling. Schulz originally published the story *Wiosna* (Spring), which would appear in *Sanatorium*, as a separate piece in the journal *Kamena* in Chełm, founded by Zenon Waśniewski and Kazimierz Andrzej Jaworski, the journal's editor. Waśniewski knew Schulz from their studies together and had solicited the work from him for the journal. The original fragment of the story that Schulz sent him for publication contained a detailed description of a Passover seder at the young protagonist's home. In this scene, in what is portrayed as a collective, familial theatrical performance, and a movement into an alternate time or "side-track" of time—mythical or exegetical time—the family apartment transforms, much as Schulz's texts themselves, into a landscape animated by collective memory and myth:

> All of a sudden, from out of the frame of the week there emerged the Easter Holidays (*Święta Wielkanocne*) and suddenly, within the emptiness of those days, time began to take shape within its own depths, to take on color and meaning, and the entire great theater of Pesach emerged onto the stage; that

entire many-storied mysterium of the ancient Egyptian Spring; that wonderful and bottomless feasting at long, white tables, by the light of silver candles, flickering under the breath of that too great and too empty Pesach night. Those Pesach nights became like dark backstage wings just beyond the open doors of the house, growing deep with matters unfathomable, incomprehensible, while over the glittering parade of the table there appeared for a moment, in the order of the Bible [*kolejność Biblji*], the figures of its zodiac: the Egyptian plagues—before they crumbled away into the starry dust of that night that is different from all nights of the year.

And so that foreign and severe spring night grew large within its own depths with plagues and disasters, and amid the laughter of its stars, frogs, snakes and insects multiplied across the vast expanses, and that great space teemed with secret goings on; and within its core there opened out a dark labyrinth of rooms, of red chambers and painted cabinets, in which the first born died violent deaths and beyond doors slammed shut could be heard the parents' laments.

And when the holiday week [*tydzień świąteczny*] had passed, the many-tiered theater of Pesach was folded away once again into the indifferent wall of the week, which smoothed itself over, and once again the streets ran empty, and we forgot about spring, which once again had not yet come [*której jeszcze wciąż nie było*].[78]

The language used by Schulz to describe everyday time, non-holiday time as indifferent, "smoothed over" and empty recalls a distinction that would define Walter Benjamin's own writing at the intersection of materialism and theology—between "homogeneous, empty time" and a conception of the present as the "now-time" (*jetztzeit*) which is "shot through with splinters of messianic time."[79] In this passage from the original 1935 *Kamena* version, Jewish life and communal traditions appear in a less veiled, less universalized or Polonized form than in perhaps any other part of Schulz's fictional work. Most often the author's language in "Spring" and other stories strives for ambiguous, hybrid terms like the phrase *"tydzień swiąteczny"* ("the holiday week"), as opposed to either Pesach or the Catholic "Wielki Tydzień" ("Holy Week"). Other ambiguous forms include "Noc Wielkiego Sezonu"—"Night of the Great Season" as opposed to the Jewish High Holidays; or "those long days, free from school," (*"długie dni, wolne od szkoły"*)—universalized terms that open to both traditions. Here, in the original *Kamena* publication, the time of Pesach is directly named, and emerges (*"wynurza się"*) out of everyday time—"from the frame of the week." Like a wooden support that will later be removed from beneath a finished stone arch, the Passover seder can be seen in this text to provide a template for the practice of "mythologizing of reality," through which Schulz allowed both everyday time, and the language of everyday communication, to reunite as it were with the realm of transhistorical collective myth; or to be rerouted—if for a night, a week, or a page—onto an alternate, mythical sidetrack. The passage also speaks to the textual strategies of both performance and concealment. Here the Passover seder, and by extension Jewishness itself, are presented as a form of theater or a set of masks. They can be donned, and brought out onto the stage, but they may also be kept concealed behind the "indifferent wall of the week." When the story was included in the volume *Sanatorium pod klepsydrą* (*Sanatorium under the Sign of the Hourglass*), published by Rój publishing house in Warsaw in 1937, the passage describing the seder was removed. Such decisions contributed to producing the polyphony, and also the characteristic ambiguity or dislocation of subjectivity, that Schulz's texts share with those of Kafka.

Sanatorium under the Sign of the Hourglass, which followed two years after *Cinnamon Shops*, featured illustrations by Schulz himself, and included a number of the author's unpublished earlier short stories, several of them character sketches of outcast or lonely figures—"Dodo," "Edzio," "The Old Age Pensioner," "Loneliness." But it opened dramatically with a new series of three thematically connected stories—"*Księga*" ("The Book"), "*Genialna epoka*" ("The Age of Genius"), and the full (and edited) text of "*Wiosna*" ("Spring")—that offer the fullest expression of Schulz's aesthetic philosophy. Featuring the narrator Joseph—already known to his readers from his first volume—as the child protagonist, these stories drew more liberally on kabbalistic and Hasidic themes. Imagery introducing a tone of messianic anticipation, and plot structures that evolve around processes of repair or *tikkun*—the collecting and recovery of fragments—or the search to liberate the *Shekhinah* or divine spirit in exile in the material world from the palace in which she is imprisoned, were grafted onto the aesthetic project and onto the contemporary reality of the secular, modern artist.

From *Sanatorium* forward, a shift also becomes discernable in Schulz's work toward more direct engagement with political realities and communal discourses that were defining for the Polish Jewish street in the second half of the 1930s. This includes experiments that begin to reverse the implied temporal and linguistic directionality of the poetic program of "mythicization." *Sanatorium* and the short stories "Republic of Dreams" ("*Republika Marzeń*"), "Fatherland" ("*Ojczyzna*"), and the German-language "Homecoming" ("*Heimkehr*") enter solidly into the discourse of homeland, exile, and return, and of Jewish homelessness. The 1937 Lilien essay is the most direct example of this new willingness to engage present-day concerns, albeit with the requisite gesture of distancing or displacement—in this case achieved through the textual alibi of the critic and art historian. It is to that essay that I turn next.

2

"A CREATION BORN OF THE LONGING OF GOLUS"

Schulz's "E. M. Lilien" and the Jewish Renaissance Movement

THE FIRST INSTALLMENT OF SCHULZ'S 1937 ARTICLE ON Ephraim Moses Lilien (1874–1925), published in *The Subcarpathian Review* in August of 1937, opens with the following lines:

> When I was not yet 14 years old, my elder brother brought to me one day *Lieder des Ghetto*, an illustrated book by Ephraim Moses Lilien, and gave it to me with the words: "Have a look at this, I borrowed it for you, but I must return it this evening."
>
> I took it indifferently into my hand, but when I opened its cover with the weeping willow and the harp, I was dazzled. From the solemn silence that I suddenly felt within myself I knew that I stood at the threshold of a great and decisive experience, and with a kind of fearful joy I turned the pages of that great book, intoxicated and happy, advancing from delight to delight. I spent that entire day over Lilien's book, enchanted, unable to tear myself away from it, its interiors filled with the pathos of shining black and white chords that stood forth from the bright quiet of these pages and ornaments.
>
> There took place in me at that time a kind of internal shift. Lilien effected a powerful fertilization of my internal world, that revealed itself in an early, youthful and clumsy creativity (SF6, 83).[1]

The book that Schulz's elder brother Izydor brought to him that day—if indeed this significantly autobiographical opening, which reads like a demythologized translation of the opening scene in in Schulz's short story "Księga," of the same period is true—was *Lieder des Ghetto/Songs of the Ghetto* (fig. 2.1), a German-language translation by Berthold Feiwel (1875–1937) of a volume of verse by American Yiddish poet Morris Rosenfeld, one of the most popular of the so-called sweatshop poets of New York City's

Figure 2.1. Cover, *Lieder des Ghetto* (1903), poems by Morris Rosenfeld with illustrations by E. M. Lilien.

Lower East Side. The volume's album-size pages were lavishly illustrated and framed in the black-and-white Secessionist-style graphics of Ephraim Moses Lilien. First published in Berlin in 1902, one year after Lilien's celebrated participation in the Fifth Zionist World Congress held in Vienna, *Lieder des Ghetto* expressed the spirit and the ethos of Cultural Zionism and of the fin de siècle Jewish Renaissance Movement, with which both Lilien and Berthold Feiwel were aligned. A fellow native of Drohobycz, and twenty years Schulz's senior, Lilien would become the most internationally recognized and popular Jewish artist of his fin de siècle generation, developing the iconic style of Jewish-themed *Jugendstil*, based on Zionist and biblical imagery, that critic Michael Stanislawski has playfully described as "Judenstil."[2]

"Lilien was the first spring of my sensitivity," writes Schulz; he "was my mystical marriage with art; and it seems that this is the effect that he had on many of my generation" (SF6, 83). In the opening of this lengthy article, literary in its careful narrative structure and rich in allusion, Schulz tells his readers that his own artistic awakening began not only "in the dawn of childhood," (O, 105) as described in fictionalized and mythologized form in "*Księga*," but in the encounter of a young man, in his thirteenth year, with a new form of modern, secular, and proudly Jewish art—and more specifically, Galician-born Jewish art. Further, that artistic awakening is shown by Schulz to have begun in his encounter with a new form of the Jewish book, which gave sensual, rhythmic, organic, and liberating expression—and above all *modern* expression[3]—to what he describes in his essay as the "mythic roots of his tribe."

Though the article is not Schulz's missing novel, *Messiah*, it nevertheless contains something that many readers who have wished they could read *Messiah* have longed for: a more direct, less veiled or encrypted discussion by Schulz about the Jewish questions of his interwar generation. In it, Schulz uses his reading of E. M. Lilien's life and work as a platform to undertake a lengthy reflection on the Jewish cultural revival of his time, on the sources of the Jewish Cultural Renaissance and of Cultural Zionism as a form of secular messianic expression, and on the specifically pressing question of what political Zionism and emigration to Palestine, the choice of growing numbers of Jews in the 1930s, might portend for the vital continuation of Jewish culture, myth, and tradition that was taking place within his own generation in Galicia.

Schulz writes in the Lilien essay: "Zionism, as it was understood by its very best representatives, was not only an attempt to resolve the economic and political situation of the Jews, not only a question of the concrete realization of mystical and religious Jewish nationalism, but also, at least in its intentions, an idealistic movement like every deep movement, whose goal was to build life anew, to ground it in the principles of goodness, truth and beauty." (SF6, 86). He continues: "the young ideology of Zionism, born of a Europeanized stratum of intellectuals, felt itself deprived of roots, torn from the soil, without the flow of juices. It desired to root itself in the ground of myth, to forge a path toward the collective soul. Lilien represents this longing for myth, for the eternal source of all collective movements, in the most exemplary, decisive and straightforward fashion" (SF6, 86). But for Schulz: "as we will see later, that very straightforwardness, the very programmatic nature of this attempt hides within itself a certain danger" (SF6, 86). The danger signaled here applies to both Lilien's art, and to the text of Schulz's essay itself—whose realistic, sober presentation of content previously mythologized allows the author to speak to his own lack of immunity to the forces of history and politics.

Like every genre of writing and modern art with which Schulz experimented—letters, short stories, critical essays, *cliché-verre* prints, sketches, and oil paintings—the Lilien essay must be treated as both a discussion of its subject (in this case of Lilien's artwork) and, simultaneously, as a form of autobiography and self-criticism.[4] Throughout Schulz's lengthy essay, the arc of E. M. Lilien's career serves as a metonym for a larger process that described the shape of Schulz's own artistic development—namely, the flourishing of an ideal of Jewish cultural renaissance in the diaspora: the *Bildung*-inspired, humanist, cultural-spiritual project out of which Lilien's early work in the illustrated volumes *Juda* and *Lieder des Ghetto* grew, followed by its gradual waning or twilight, as political Zionism, fueled by rising antisemitism and economic insecurity in Central and Eastern Europe, would push aside and engulf that early universalist/nationalist idyll.

E. M. Lilien: In Exile in the *Subcarpathian Review*

Why was Schulz's essay on E. M. Lilien, which reveals so much about his relationship with debates surrounding Jewish cultural continuity and with traditions of the Jewish book, not discovered earlier? One of the most startling aspects of the Lilien piece—aside from the very *emergence* for present-day readers of Schulz's unguarded, un-mythologized, and, we might say, un-culturally translated Jewish voice—is where the author chose to stage this textual coming out as a Jewish artist, as it were. He published "E. M. Lilien" not in a leading cultural journal or paper out of Warsaw or Lwów, where he was by this time (1937) recognized as one of the foremost experimental Polish-language prose writers—one of Polish modernism's triumvirate of "experimenters in Form" that included his Polish Polish colleagues S. I. Witkiewicz and Witold Gombrowicz; not in the Polish Jewish press, on the pages of Lwów's *Chwila* or Warsaw's *Nasz Przegląd*, which regularly featured debates on Zionism of the kind in which he engages in the Lilien article; and not in the scholarly, Zionist-oriented Polish-language journal *Miesięcznik Żydowski* (*Jewish Monthly*), whose contributors had taken an express interest in the renaissance of Jewish culture in the Polish context. Instead, the piece appeared in *Przegląd Podkarpacia* [The Subcarpathian Review]: *Drohobycz-Borysław-Truskawiec*. More specifically, his Lilien essay appeared as a collection of fragments—installments published in 1937 and '38 across eight separate issues of this local, four-page weekly newspaper associated with the oil and gas industry of Borysław and Drohobycz, and with the popular sanatorium at Truskawiec—in other words, in the disposable margins of the press and publishing world.[5] It bears mentioning that Schulz had certainly taken time to contemplate this particular paper's commercial identity, as he was commissioned to create a new and modern banner for it that celebrated local industry (fig. 2.2). As Schulz's narrator Joseph asks in an evocative line from the story "Spring," "Where else would the exiled one [*wyklęta*, also "cursed"] take shelter, where find asylum, if not where no one is looking for it—in those cheap calendars and journals, in those canticles of beggars and old men?" (L, 140).[6]

With this reflection from "Spring" Schulz reprises the Lurianic and Hasidic paradigm of scattering or exile and, return, which posited that sparks of divine light, fallen or exiled during the initial catastrophe associated with creation (*shevirat ha-kelim*, or "breaking of the vessels") are trapped even, and especially, in the most profane, mundane, and unholy places. Hillel Zeitlin, who published some of the most popular writing on kabbalistic and Hasidic thought directed at secular readers of Schulz's interwar Polish generation, paraphrases for example these formulations by the Ba'al Shem Tov: "Divinity continues to dwell even in the very lowest of rungs ... has hidden itself in the world.... Hints and signs are to be found within existing things and the revealed world ... the *Lieder* that the Gentiles sing ... everything has its roots above in the *sefirot*.... God's own attributes, as it were, reduced themselves into physical forms ... until they reached into very lowly matters."[7] While Schulz's Lilien text is one of his most worldly, it is only in this text that he directly discusses, in untranslated form, the question of the "mystical, messianic" Jewish tradition.

Schulz's choice to publish his 1937 Lilien piece in such a "low" venue, *The Subcarpathian Review*, had the result of contributing to the continued encryption or occultation of the Jewish layer within his polyphonic discourse—and it virtually guaranteed the article's disappearance from scholarly attention for the better part of a century. At the same time, it generated a material object or artifact—a fragmented form of modern Jewish writing—that resonates delightfully with the author's mythologized vision of the lost "*Autentyk*," or primordial Book, from his short story "The Book," published that same year in the collection *Sanatorium under the Sign of the Hourglass*. In that text, the *Księga* (The Book), is a living and rustling

Figure 2.2. *Przegląd Podkarpacie*, 1937.

"*kodeks*" Codex evoked by the author, with a nod to Zoharic imagery, as emanating "a dawn of divine colors" (*dziewiczy świt bożych kolorów*) and an "invasion of brightness" ("*inwazja blasku*"); that opens like a many-petalled rose, releasing "flocks of swallows and larks" from between its letters ("*wypuszczając spomiędzy liter klucze jaskółek i skowronków*") (O, 106).[8] It is an ur-text that the child protagonist, Joseph, remembers in a dream and resolves to recover. After pleading with his parents to tell him where it is, to no avail, he discovers the Book accidentally, while looking over the shoulder of his maid:

> I read that story over Adela's arm and was struck by a sudden overwhelming thought. This was the Book. Its last pages, the unofficial supplement, the tradesmen's entrance full of refuse and trash! Fragments of rainbow

Figure 2.3. *I, Anna Csillag*, advertisement for Elsa Balm.

suddenly danced on the wallpaper. I snatched the sheaf of paper out of Adela's hands, and in a faltering voice I breathed: "Where did you find this book?"

"You silly boy," she answered, shrugging her shoulders. "It has been lying here all the time. We tear a few pages from it every day, and take them to the butcher's for packing meat or your father's lunch" (W, 119).

One of the most productive images that Schulz's protagonist "reads" over Adela's shoulder is that of the ubiquitous Anna Csillag (fig. 2.3), who appeared in advertisements throughout the Austro-Hungarian Empire and Central Europe during this period, and who was also "collected" by Walter Benjamin in his Arcades Project. It is while Joseph looks at an ad for hair tonic featuring Anna Csillag that the mythicized story in The Book is "released" from the advertising pages of a commercial supplement, unfolding into a textual landscape that "lives and grows" (W, 125). In the text of Schulz's story, an ad for hair tonic transforms itself into a version of the story of Job, set in the Carpathian mountains; of faithful devotees of Anna

Csillag [*wierni*, in a universalization of "Hasidim"], following their female apostle [*apostołkę*] through the hills of Moravia. Using the structure of a two-track temporality, it is a tale filled with the timeless and the kitschy, the street-song and the epic; with desire, melancholy, and longed-for redemption. "And what about the bearded ones [*brodacze miasteczka*], worthy townsfolk immobilized by their enormous growth of hair? . . . Who knows, perhaps they will all purchase the genuine Black Forest barrel organs and follow their lady apostle into the world, to search for her throughout the country, playing 'Daisy, Daisy' everywhere the go? O Odyssey of bearded ones, wandering with barrel organs from town to town in pursuit of your spiritual mother! When will the bard be found who is worthy to sing this epic [*rapsod . . . godny tej epopei*]?" (O, 116). On the following page devoted to healing salves, the sick arrive from across the Habsburg Empire (from Siedmiogród, Slavonia, and Bukovina, from "towns forgotten in the depths of time"). Reaching the last word of this fragment of the Book, Joseph is left with a "mix of hunger and excitement in his soul" (O, 115).

In the newspaper medium that agreed to publish Schulz's Lilien essay, in the same year as the story "The Book" was published, the author's reflections on the "flickering" remnants of Jewish messianic and artistic instinct, that, as he writes, has been "pressed deep into the soul of the people, where it smolders with a faint flame," share the pages of the *Subcarpathian Review* with advertisements for men's hair tonic, articles on the election or appointment of mayors and industry directors, vacation packages at the sanatoria in Truskawiec and Solna, and the Borysław crime report. The reader learns that 963 US dollars were stolen from the smoking jacket of restaurant owner Judy Kreppa by Piotr Kos, who cut a hole in the roof of her restaurant; that "the new Browning automatic is the best defense against attacks, and theft: 2 for only 13 zloties 50; sent by mail; Christian-run firm"; that the title of Miss Truskawiec was awarded to Janina Fogel, wife of the rich industrialist from Lwów: "musical accompaniment by the Eddie Boys, at the garden bar Jozia"; and so on. Critics rarely speak of Schulz's sense of humor, but the author would undoubtedly have enjoyed the particular juxtapositions that emerged with the publication of each successive fragment of the Lilien essay.

Thus the choice to publish in the *Subcarpathian Review* allowed Schulz to create a version of his mythicized *Księga*, scattered into the really existing urban landscape of his Galician region. By extension, it allowed him to give material form, in historical time and place—Drohobycz, 1937—to an organizing principle of his aesthetic theory—namely, the concept of a dialectical and also redemptive encounter between the spheres of high and low, sacred and profane, *"Autentyk"* (the Authentic) and *"tandeta"* (kitsch / trashy goods or literature / *shund*)—an encounter that is mediated by the figure of the exegete, whose act of discovery, reading, and interpretation liberates the fragment and allows it to fly up. In the story "The Book," the child-exegete of the fragmented material world appears in the text itself, as the protagonist Joseph. In the case of the Lilien essay, this role would have fallen to members of Schulz's Galician Jewish artistic milieu, including Debora Vogel, who would have had access to the *Subcarpathian Review* and would have read Schulz's text with interest—again, as far as we know today, his first public piece treating contemporary Jewish concerns—while it was coming out. Viewed in the context of the two artists' aesthetic debates of 1930 and '31, further developed in the chapter to follow, Schulz's essay emerges as a new contribution to the two artists' ongoing debate about new formal possibilities for a Jewish modernist aesthetics. As Schulz offered suggestively in the opening of "The Book," "Besides, any true reader—and this story is only addressed to them—will understand me anyway when I look them straight in the eye and try to communicate my meaning" (W, 116).[9]

Martin Buber and Fin-de-Siècle Orientalism

As a Galician Jewish artist raised in the Habsburg Empire, Schulz sits at the Galician intersection of Eastern and West European Jewish cultural trends. For this reason, it can be productive to return for a moment to Schulz's formative westward-looking gaze, and to consider the path by which neo-Hasidism, including familiarity with elements of Hasidic philosophy and popular kabbalah which is in evidence throughout Schulz's graphic works and writings, entered into intellectual and artistic discourse within German-Jewish letters. While a modernist adaptation of aspects of popular kabbalah was not unusual within Jewish literature in Eastern Europe, particularly in Yiddish, a discussion of Schulz's Galician context invites a closer look at one source of this intensely revived interest in Jewish mysticism and traditional Hasidic culture among secular Jewish intellectuals in the German-speaking and Austrian context of Jewish Renaissance. That source is the influence of German-Jewish philosopher Martin Buber's writings and charismatic speeches on an entire generation of 'assimilating' Jews in Central Europe. Of particular influence were Buber's early lectures on Judaism, later published as *Drei Reden über das Judenthum* (*Three Lectures on Judaism*)—which he was invited by the Bar Kochba Students' Association of Prague to deliver to the sizable acculturated public of Prague between 1909 and 1914. These lectures had transformative impact on their audiences, and on generations who later read them.

German-Jewish philosopher Martin Buber was a fellow Galician, and the son, like Schulz, of acculturated Jewish parents in the Austro-Hungarian Empire. Born in Vienna, he was raised at the home of his grandparents from the age of three on, in the outskirts of Lwów, and, like Schulz, attended a Polish high school, the gimnazjum im. Franciszka Józef in Lwów. While he wrote that "it was not Hasidism alone from which I was alienated at that time, but Judaism as a whole,"[10] in the home of his grandfather, the renowned Midrash scholar Salomon Buber, he learned Hebrew alongside Classical and European languages, and received a Jewish education. As a scholar with a growing interest in mysticism in both European and non-European cultures and author of *Ecstatic Confessions*, he was able, at the strong encouragement of his then-fiancée Paula Winkler (1877–1958), to draw on that earlier education to undertake a renewed engagement with the Galician Jewish cultural heritage from which he had distanced himself as a younger man.

Buber's early lectures on Judaism and his and his wife Paula Buber's retellings in German of Hasidic tales appealed particularly to those who had moved away from traditional religious practice, had been educated in German, Polish, or Czech, and had joined, or hoped to join, a cosmopolitan, secular European culture as citizens of their respective countries. Estranged to varying degrees from their ethnic and religious traditions, and often no longer speaking a Jewish language, whether Hebrew or even Yiddish, many in this generation developed a more or less-articulated longing for a revived relationship with Jewish tradition (even as their European compatriots around them were discovering new romanticized conceptions of traditional European folk culture), and sought possibilities for an affirmative relationship with that tradition that did not require adherence to halakhic law, or the separation of the Jew from the larger society and culture in which he or she lived. Buber's lectures became a kind of bellwether and inspiration for a generation of Jewish intellectuals—transforming the attitudes toward their Jewish heritage of such thinkers as Franz Kafka, Max Brod, Georg Lukács, Ernst Bloch, and Gustav Landauer; individuals who, like Schulz, took an "extrinsic" path of participation in European letters, and aligned themselves neither with Zionism nor with Buber's modern religiosity. Left-wing anarchist Gustav Landauer writing on Buber's influence said: "If I now say that [. . .] it is precisely through the mediation of Martin Buber that I have found Judaism, I must caution all who do not know the world of Jewish spirit to which Buber brings us, not to conjure up a formal religion and ritual practices."[11] What Landauer responded to in Buber's collection of Hasidic tales, *The Legend of the Baal Shem* (1908),[12] was rather a way of understanding his Judaism as an 'inalienable spiritual sensibility' which he shared with his fellow Jews, and which was independent of formal belief and affiliation. Drawing on categories proposed by his teacher Georg Simmel, Buber introduced the division between *religion* and *religiosity*.[13] Religion—as practice, observance of halakhic law—was staunchly rejected as no longer valid for the modern Jew. But "religiosity" was brought forward as a primary value, a quality present in the individual who was open to the perception of authenticity and wholeness or unity, and who sought in affirming this perception to restore meaning to life in modern Europe. For Buber, this sensitivity or openness was characteristic of the Jewish spirit, was latent in the soul of even the most deracinated modern Jew. Of relevance to our study of Schulz, Landauer "also learned from Buber that often those Jews who were most faithful to this sensibility were aligned with an unofficial, indeed heretical tradition."[14] This idea was central to Buber's reevaluation of Jewish tradition, and his understanding of the revitalizing role Hasidism had played in that tradition.

What Martin Buber offered, then, was a discourse and a new way of thinking about Judaism that this assimilated generation was looking for—and it was based in a revaluing of precisely the culture of the so-called 'Ostuden'—a negative epithet which referred to unassimilated Polish Jewry, and in particular Hasidim. Writes Paul Mendes-Flohr: "[Buber] rendered Hasidism respectable, as it were, by integrating this most distinctive manifestation of East European Jewish spirituality into the general discourse and idiom of the New Romanticism (and later, of Expressionism). By virtue of Buber's inspired presentation, Hasidism—and the millennial Jewish tradition from whence it emerged—was deemed relevant to the concerns of the educated individual involved in the spiritual quest of the fin de siècle."[15]

As Mendes-Flohr points out, the call that Buber made to his contemporaries, in these lectures and in his early writings on Hasidic culture, represents a specifically Jewish manifestation of a wider trend, or movement at the fin de siècle, and on into the inter-war period, then dubbed the "New Romanticism." The name was coined by German publisher Eugen Diederichs, who published Buber's collection entitled *Ecstatic Confessions* in 1909, and whose publishing house sought to promote "a return to a higher transcendent reality."[16] For Jews and non-Jews, this was a period of vigorous interest in mysticism, and, under the strong influence of Schopenhauer, particularly in many forms of Eastern or "Oriental" spirituality, including Hinduism and Buddhism and, as a result of Buber's efforts, later Hasidism—hence the term "fin de siècle Orientalism." Adherents of the New Romanticism sought—and found in the teachings of the Orient—material and language for a revived spirituality, while at the same time vehemently rejecting organized religion, whether Christian or Jewish. They turned for inspiration, both spiritual and artistic, to mysticism, folklore, and the occult, and sought meaning and even potential salvation in art, poetry, theater, music—in forms of cultural expression that were based on a return to myth and reconnecting with mythic consciousness.

Almost paradoxically, within the Jewish world, this new interest in Oriental spirituality and culture offered an opportunity to radically transform the relationship of assimilated Jewish intellectuals to their own past—to Jewish tradition. For within European discourse Judaism itself had been considered an Oriental religion and culture with all the negative connotations that that had previously carried. By the turn of the century, and since the Jewish Enlightenment or Haskalah and the entry of Jews into wider European society in Western Europe, the relationship of assimilated Jews to their "unenlightened" neighbors to the East had become a strongly conflicted, and even pained one. Assimilating Jews, particularly in Germany and the West but also in Poland and Russia, had internalized Europe's negative image of the Jew as Oriental, and transformed their own discomfort with Jewishness into a fear and scorn for the Orthodox and Hasidic Jewry of Poland and Eastern Europe. Viennese writer Karl Emil Franzos, also born in Galicia, referred to this Polish region in his very popular novels as *Halb-Asien*, "an exotic world characterized by squalor, ignorance, and superstition, and ruled by a fanatic mystical sect known as Hasidim."[17]

In the climate of fin de siècle Orientalism, however, with the rise of interest in Eastern religions and the new respect for eastern spirituality and mysticism, it became possible for Buber to effect a complete turn-around of this attitude among many members of his generation and the generations to follow. He was able to appropriate the image of the Jew as Oriental, to make it a sign of how Jews had in themselves and in their tradition a source of deep spirituality that modern European intellectuals and artists were now seeking. Hasidic culture and tradition, reexamined and repackaged as Oriental spirituality in the positive sense, could be seen as a source of living spirituality, and still vital myth and legend, that should be an inspiration not only to modern Jews but to European culture. In his speech "The Spirit of the Orient and Judaism," Judaism—in particular Hasidism—becomes, in fact, the highest expression of the Oriental spirit, and modern, secular Jews as the inheritors of this tradition are invested with a world-historical mission; they are a promise of spiritual hope to all nations. For this world-historical mission, he concluded his lecture, "Europe has at its disposal a mediating people that has acquired all the wisdom and the skills of the Occident without losing its original Oriental character, a people called to link Orient and Occident in fruitful reciprocity, just as it is perhaps called to fuse the spirit of the East and the West in a new teaching."[18]

As part of this shift in perception, Hasidic legends, and mythology drawn from popular kabbalah and the Hasidic oral storytelling tradition, could also become a rich source of inspiration for modern and modernist literature, in its many language incarnations. The Bubers' German-language renditions of Hasidic legends, and Martin Buber's essays which introduced Hasidic philosophy and basic principles of the kabbalah, opened the tradition up to assimilated or acculturated Jewish writers and artists, who would not have had access to this tradition in any Jewish language. Buber's translations were certainly not the only work on Jewish mysticism available in German; there were numerous scholarly studies on aspects of kabbalah published in German, including work by Marcus Ehrenpreis, himself a student of Salomon Buber, who published his dissertation on the doctrine of emanation in thirteenth-century kabbalah in 1898.[19] But they reached an incomparably larger audience of secular, assimilated Jews who likely would not have expected to be drawn to this material—in a way, at the time, and with a message that many of them wanted to hear. Yet it is also true that for Polish-Jewish readers, and especially Galician Jewish readers, the Hasidic culture 'recovered' or rediscovered in Buber's writings was neither foreign nor exotic, but a part of everyday life in Galician cities, and for many of family life. Buber's revaluation, then, could rather have served to complement and complicate existing relationships to the Hasidic world, as well as to place a *West-jüdische* imprimatur on intellectual and artistic engagement with the heritage of that culture, leading to what may have been perceived as a de-ghettoization or universalization of such thematic engagement, tantamount to a granting of permission to draw Hasidic cultural heritage into the center of European modernism. It is neither possible nor necessary to our study to establish which titles by Martin Buber Schulz himself may have read, though it is likely that he would have read the *Tales of Nachman of Bratslav* (1906), and Buber's extensive introductions on Hasidic philosophy, as did so many of his generation. More importantly, by including frequent allusion to kabbalistic paradigms and to the form of the Hasidic tale, Schulz also reveals sympathy with the wider trend within the Jewish intellectual community that Buber pioneered in a German-language context. Schulz's prose works cast themselves, and the Lilien article confirms as much—as an irreverent Galician response to the call that Martin Buber made to his generation—in tandem with other Polish Jewish writers, including Y. L. Peretz, Hillel and Aaron Zeitlin, and Markus Ehrenpreis, all of whom had likewise connected their modern Jewish forms of expression to a renewed interest in the potential of Hasidic and kabbalistic paradigms and exegetical traditions to inform modern and secular Jewish culture (SF6).

"Jewish Renaissance," Galician *Golus*, and the Fifth Zionist Congress

"The Jewish people are on the doorstep of a resurrection from semi-life to life," wrote Martin Buber in his earlier 1901 article "*Jüdische Renaissance*," in the inaugural issue of the new Berlin-based journal *Ost und West*.[20] "That is why their participation in the modern national-international cultural movement is seen as a renaissance."[21] The article expressed the goals and ethos of the fin de siècle Jewish Renaissance Movement: a grouping of acculturated and German-speaking Jewish intellectuals and artists whose program combined Ahad Ha'am's call to secular Jewish intellectuals to reject assimilation and to proudly affirm a distinctly Jewish culture, on the one hand, with an unwillingness to surrender the promise of belonging in Europe, represented by the concept of *Bildung*, on the other.[22] "We live in a period of cultural gestation," wrote Buber. "Goethe's dream of a world literature takes on new forms—only when each people speaks from its innermost essence does the collective treasure increase. . . . In this way we see an amalgamation of universal and national culture in the deep unitary evolution."[23] In the fin de siècle context, promoters of such a Jewish cultural renaissance called for the development of a new, unashamed Jewish artistic idiom that would both thrive within and contribute to wider European culture. Its imagery and forms were to be modern, European and able to cross cultural and linguistic boundaries, and it would include literature and writing in the European languages of the diaspora. For Buber, the work of Ephraim Moses Lilien, a fellow native of his Lemberg region, was exemplary of this amalgamation of European and Jewish, universal and national culture.

Buber came to know Lilien and work closely with him in Berlin in the early years of his editorship of the journal *Ost und West* (1901–03). Lilien became the magazine's artistic editor, and his boldly sensual illustrations filled the paper's pages, defined its proudly Jewish look, and reached tens of thousands of Jewish readers in Germany, the Austrian Empire, and throughout Europe. "He penetrated deeply into the miracle of our people," Buber said of Lilien in his 1901 "Address on Jewish Art" to the Fifth Zionist Congress; "he has recognized the meaning and value of our old themes and appropriated them. . . . We put all of our hope in him."[24] Interestingly, in Buber's speech, as in Schulz's later essay, Lilien stands for hope and promise, and for the aspirations of his generation, rather than for fulfillment: "His technique is rich and mature," says Buber, yet "just as the striving of our new generation . . . his art is more promise than fulfillment."[25]

Like Buber, several of the leading proponents of the national-international Jewish renaissance—inheritors of the Haskalah generation's ethos of *Bildung*—hailed from the Lemberg/Lwów region, or were most politically active in this region.[26] Two in particular who had a strong influence on Schulz's acculturated Galician generation and on his Lwów milieu were the Vienna-born writer and political and cultural activist Nathan Birnbaum (1864–1937) and Lemberg Rabbi Markus Ehrenpreis (1869–1951). Birnbaum, the son of Galician immigrants to Vienna, is credited with being the first writer to use both the term *Zionism* and the phrase *Jewish Renaissance Movement*, and he was influential in shaping the discourse of both of these movements in the late nineteenth and early twentieth centuries.[27] An early Zionist from the Galician region and participant in the First Zionist Congress, Birnbaum's views evolved—initially toward Cultural Zionism, later to Diaspora Nationalism and Yiddishism (ca. 1900–14), of which he was a leading promoter, and in the final phase of his life toward religious observance and a leadership role in Agudath Israel (1914–37). During his bid for election to the Austrian Parliament in 1907, and as a staunch supporter of Jewish cultural autonomy in the diaspora, Birnbaum gained enormous popularity and renown while touring and speaking in towns and cities throughout Galicia.

Among the most widely respected representatives of the Jewish Renaissance Movement in the Lwów region was the writer, cultural activist, and rabbi Markus Ehrenpreis (1869–1951), the uncle of Debora Vogel, with whom Vogel was very close. Ehrenpreis was a prolific scholar and publicist, a progressive rabbi, and an early Zionist activist in Galicia. Together with fellow rabbinical students Markus Braude (1869–1949) and Ozjasz (Yehoshu'a) Thon (1870–1936), who became chief rabbi of Kraków in 1897 as well as a member of the first Polish Sejm in 1919, Ehrenpreis helped to establish the First Zionist Congress. An early and leading cultural Zionist and Hebrew writer, he was himself inspired by the teachings of Salomon Buber (grandfather of Martin Buber) and Ahad Ha'am considered the founder of Cultural or Spiritual Zionism. Ehrenpreis went on to become head rabbi of Bulgaria and later chief Rabbi of Stockholm, where he founded the Swedish-language literary and cultural journal *Judisk Tidskrift*[28] and promoted the cause of modern Jewish cultural renewal not only in Hebrew but also in the diverse national languages of Europe. Like other members of his Galician constellation, Ehrenpreis called for a Jewish renaissance that would combine engagement in European-wide intellectual and cultural trends with a commitment to preserve and value Jewish textual traditions—in particular, the ethical and moral heritage of Jewish messianism. Here is where we can hear his language aligning closely with Schulz's in the Lilien essay. Ehrenpreis was also deeply interested in Hasidic literature, and, as Martina Urban writes, Buber proposed co-editing with him an anthology that would include an essay "on the mystical content of Hasidism and its inner relationship to other teachings (Neoplatonism, Vedanta, Eckart, etc.)" as well as "a selection of significant sections from Hasidic literature in carefully [aesthetically] stylized translation."[29] "In advocating a renewal of myth," writes Urban, "Ehrenpreis parted from Ahad Ha'am's studied distance from the popularization of folkloristic and non-rational elements in Judaism."[30] Of the specific Jewish intellectual and cultural climate of the Lemberg/Lwów region Ehrenpreis remarked, "In our provincial borderland between Austria and Russia (which has unfairly been given the name *"Halb-Asien"*), we had found the synthesis between Jew and citizen earlier than other Jewish groups—and without suffering their disappointments."[31]

Ehrenpreis urged his generation and younger generations of acculturating Jews to seek new cultural forms that would guarantee the continued vitality of Jewish culture. "We have liberated ourselves from the rabbinic culture," he wrote. "We are free men in order to begin our culture anew, a culture that will be born from the synthesis of the Hebrew spirit and the European spirit."[32] Thirteen years Schulz's senior, Ehrenpreis continued to visit his home city of Lwów and remained an important intellectual figure for Jewish communities in the region. Schulz was likely familiar—if not earlier, then through his contact with Debora Vogel—with the range of Ehrenpreis's writings published in German and Polish—from his dissertation on the concept of emanation in kabbalah published in 1895, to interviews that he gave to *Chwila* during his 1930 visit to Lwów.[33] It is possible that Schulz met Ehrenpreis personally during this visit, as it overlaps with the period during which Schulz was paying regular visits to Debora Vogel in Lwów. Schulz also took an uncharacteristic trip abroad in 1936, to Stockholm—quite possibly with the aim of visiting Ehrenpreis—though archival research to date does not show evidence of his having managed to do so. His work, however, reveals strong elective affinities with Ehrenpreis's own views about the role of Jewish art and literature in a broader European context.

In their different capacities, Buber, Birnbaum, and Ehrenpreis can be considered Cultural Zionists (though Birnbaum would become a Diaspora Nationalist and Yiddishist), and their writings and speeches promoted the ideals of what Birnbaum referred to in a 1902 article for *Ost und West* as the "Jewish Renaissance Movement." It is the ideas, aspirations, and characteristic rhetorical tropes of this movement, and of this influential turn of the century constellation of Galician writers, that are echoed throughout Schulz's essay on E. M. Lilien.

Proponents of a Jewish Cultural Renaissance and of Cultural Zionism envisioned Jewish national renaissance primarily in cultural and spiritual rather than political terms—a fact that would bring them into direct conflict with Theodor Herzl and the "Western Zionist" leadership of the World Zionist Congress. Buber's language in the 1901 article "*Jüdische Renaissance*" already reflects this strong reticence concerning the politicization of the Jewish revival. It also expresses his desire that Jewish national revival be understood not as a defensive strategy or a rejection of Jewish life in the diaspora but rather as an affirmation and rediscovery of national pride or individuality, including pride in belonging to the European community:

> On the one hand, we see forerunners of a great general culture of beauty.... The artistic feeling that awakens everywhere, the development of modern arts and crafts, the infusion of everyday life with a sense of beauty, the diverse attempts at an aesthetic education for our youth.... On the other hand, we see

nationalistic groups assemble around new flags. They are no longer moved by a basic impulse of self-preservation or by the need to defend against hostile attacks from the outside. These nations do not wish to exercise their desire for territorial possession and expansion, but their individuality. They wish to make conscious the unconscious development of the national soul.[34]

With this essay of 1901, Buber framed a tension that was still vital at the time of Schulz's writing, thirty years later—namely, the dispute between political Zionism on the one hand and cultural or spiritual Zionism on the other. The former, characterized by étatist aims, was represented within the Zionist movement by the West European or "Western Zionists" Theodor Herzl and Max Nordau.[35] Their focus from the start was on the practical economic, political, and diplomatic strategies that would lead to the creation of a Jewish nation-state. The motivating force behind their arguments was antisemitism: the growing untenability, as it was seen, of a secure and lasting Jewish life in Europe. The creation of a state that would guarantee safety from antisemitism, as well as political and economic autonomy, was the first and primary goal.

For the cultural or spiritual Zionists, by contrast, the creation of a Jewish state in Palestine, if it should ever be realized, could follow only after a lengthy process of cultural renewal, education, and "awakening of the soul of the people," which had to take place in the diaspora—in Europe. Wrote Ahad Ha'am:

> We must recognize at the outset that this programme of a *spiritual* "back to the land," if one may so call it, of the re-centralization of our spiritual potentialities, is not one which can be carried out easily. . . . To lay the foundations of a spiritual "refuge" for our national culture demands perhaps preparations no less elaborate, and resources no less extensive, than to lay the foundations of a material refuge for persecuted Jews. And besides the work of preparation for the future, there is also a great deal of work to be done in the present.[36]

Ahad Ha'am, whose imprint together with Buber's is strong in Schulz's language and thematics in the late '30s, wrote primarily in Hebrew, which he considered central to the project of national renewal. Schulz would have had access to his influential essays in both the 1901 German edition of *Am Scheidewege* (At the Crossroads) published by Jüdische Verlag, and the Polish volume *O Sjonizmie duchowym* (On Spiritual Zionism), published in 1928 by the Zionist Academic Corporation "Zelotia—Kanaim." The editors of the volume stress the urgency of addressing in Poland the "unfortunate lack of deeper knowledge" about the foundations of Zionist thought, especially among a young Polish-Jewish generation "who for one reason or another cannot unfortunately avail themselves of Hebrew sources, or even Yiddish ones."[37]

Buber, for whom Ahad Ha'am was an important inspiration, in his address to the Fifth Congress argued: "What we have today are cultural buds, artistic seeds; and we have to nurture these here in the Diaspora with a tender, loving hand until we can plant them in the soil of our homeland."[38] For his part Nathaniel Birnbaum, as Jess Olson writes, "was far more interested in the construction of a Jewish national culture than in the practical concerns, many of them insurmountable in the short term, of settlement activity in Ottoman Palestine."[39] He introduced the term "Jewish Renaissance Movement" in part because it allowed him to decouple activism for Jewish national and cultural renewal from the strictly political aims of the party—and even from the term "Cultural Zionism," which was strongly connected with the revival specifically of Hebrew-language literature. "These words [Jewish Renaissance] have become linked . . . with [Zionism]. However, I would say that they are more like a simple exercise of the intellectual Zionist opposition, which posits that 'Zionism' is not to be understood as simply the party but rather the grand spiritual movement behind the party. To describe this movement, the word 'Zionism' is at the very least too weak and too narrow for me."[40]

What the Jewish Renaissance Movement and Cultural Zionism did share with political Zionism, as with socialism, Diaspora Nationalism, and assimilationism, was a rejection of traditional religious observance. For the cultural or spiritual Zionists, influenced by the writings of Ahad Ha'am, Jewish cultural and also spiritual renewal required emergence from the "ghetto" and recovery from a period of ossification and assimilation, described by Schulz in the opening paragraphs of his Lilien article. Essential here was freedom not from physical or territorial golus through immigration to a new land, but from traditional rabbinism that, as Markus Ehrenpreis expressed it, "had shut us up in a narrow cage of laws and walls and decrees; that has been a barrier separating us from all that is majestic and mighty and lofty in life and in the world."[41] Buber as well referred to the "ghetto" not as a physical space but as "the chained spirit and the pressure of senseless tradition."[42] "It will be more difficult for the Jewish people than any other to enter into this rebirth," wrote Buber; "Ghetto and *galut*—not the external but the internal enemies by those names—hold them back with iron chains."[43]

The rejection of traditional observance and of the traditional system of Jewish education sustained in the cheder and Yeshiva did not imply rejection of Jewish spiritual, textual, and—in Buber's and also Schulz's Neo-Romantic language—mythical sources. Schulz's discussion of Jewish renaissance, like those of his predecessors, hinges on this distinction. Jewish Renaissance required both rejection and recuperation: liberation and sublimation. In Ehrenpreis's words, "Forget that which no longer is viable, but remember that which is strong, vital and eternal, the indisposable foundations of existence, which bygone generations have bequeathed us."[44] As Paul Mendes-Flohr writes, "The Jewish Renaissance sought to reverse the tendency to assume that Judaism was an anachronism, or at best, a private sentiment irrelevant to the larger concerns of the educated European. . . . [The movement] did not entail a retreat from *Bildung*, rather it reflected the valorization of Judaism *within* the project of creating a cultural discourse informed by the diverse historical voices constituting humanity's shared inheritance."[45]

The polarization of allegiances between cultural and political Zionisms figured prominently in the leadup to the Fifth Zionist Congress in 1901, when Martin Buber's focus on cultural and artistic renewal was openly dismissed by Max Nordau as a distraction that could divert energy and funds from the singular goal of political work. In his address on Jewish art to the congress, Buber argued that art, music, and literature must occupy a central place in the work of the Zionist movement: only art held the means to awaken the national soul and to educate a new, secular Jewish generation. "Jewish art is for us a great educator. It is a teacher for a living perception of nature and people. . . . No language is as urgent, as suggestive as the language of art; . . . And our art will also become a strong herald of resurrected Judaism, it will grip all slumbering hearts with the power of forms and melodies."[46] The language of Buber's speech returns, as we will see, in Schulz's emphasis on the melodic and rhythmic quality of Lilien's graphics.

In protest against Max Nordau's strictly political orientation, which Buber described as "blind hostility and apathy in regard to the development of the national soul" and an "unending sin against the spirit,"[47] Buber also presented a specific appeal to the delegates present at the Congress, to provide financial support for a publishing initiative—"a purely idealistic undertaking:"[48] the new *Jüdische Verlag*, which would promote modern Jewish cultural and artistic renewal. The congress did not vote to support this cultural project of the Democratic Faction, but Buber and the faction, who had broken with the congress in formal protest, nevertheless managed to raise independent funding for the initiative. They founded the Jüdische Verlag, whose editorial board included Buber, Lilien, Feiwel, and Ehrenpreis, a year later. Its aim was to bring to the public the finest examples of their vision of a modern, secular Jewish renaissance—that was cultural, artistic, and spiritual, but neither traditionally religious nor primarily political. *Lieder des Ghetto*, which would soon have its formative impact on a young Schulz, was a product of this moment: an expression of the ethos of the Democratic Faction and a result of the close collaboration among its core members, Berthold Feiwel and E. M. Lilien.

Reigniting the Flame: Image and Text

Returning to the essay "E. M. Lilien": like his predecessors, Schulz sets the stage for his discussion of Lilien as a representative figure in the fin de siècle modern Jewish cultural renaissance by evoking in emotional tones the repressed, withered, and ossified state in which Jewish creativity found itself at the turn of the century in both Eastern and Western Europe. In his essay, assimilation and traditional Orthodoxy are presented as the twin and competing forces that have prevented the still vital artistic instincts of the Jewish folk from finding modern expression. "Those at the top of the Jewish community," writes Schulz, "were partly or entirely assimilated, and belonged to European culture. The mass of petty bourgeois and impoverished Jewish intelligentsia had nourished itself on the great old Hebrew poetry—distorted as its impact was by the deformed scholasticism of rabbinical pietism that had made of this wealth of living poetry a narrow subject, a formula for cult" (SF6, 83–4). "Whosoever managed to leave this contaminated fount," Schulz continues, "encountered only *shund* [*"tandetną literaturę"*]—cheap popular literature, the anonymous literature of romance novels and tales" (SF6, 84). Drawing here on a set of tropes familiar in secular critique since the Haskalah Schulz presents the traditional lifestyle and system of education of Orthodox Jewry as a *"skażona krynica"* (contaminated spring) that has also shielded the majority of East European Jews from exposure to artistic developments in the secular world: "Cut off and walled off from European culture, the Jewish masses did not know fine art" (SF6, 84).

For sociologist Jacob Lestschinsky (1876–1966), in his influential 1918 essay "Jewish Autonomy Yesterday and Today":

The negative processes—the processes of decay—really only trapped the uppermost strata of the bourgeoisie and intelligentsia. The middle classes remained in the Jewish social milieu, and cultural assimilation did not leave deep roots in its midst. At the bottom there remained a large dense mass with great historical national inertia, with a hardened, petrified, and obscured heritage.... This same dense mass was also rich in as yet undiscovered *primitive* forces and was nourished by deep roots found in the subterranean foundations of every national culture....[49]

Schulz takes time in his essay to own this account of the social processes that led to the Jewish artistic renaissance in which both he and Lilien would participate. Schulz delivered his Lilien essay as a public lecture, at least once in Lwów and once at his home in Drohobycz. Once he had received public recognition for *Cinnamon Shops*, Schulz became for residents of Drohobycz a highly respected "Professor," and in this sense his essay on a Drohobyczan artistic predecessor becomes an opportunity for him to re-present this history of the Jewish Renaissance Movement and secular Jewish artistic expression to the community. Assimilation, as he writes, had turned the Jewish intellectual elite away from its own cultural traditions, and led them to repress their connection with the sources of Jewish myth and art. Even traditional religious education, which would seem to offer access to those sources, had in Schulz's view also lost its connection precisely to the living poetry present in Jewish textual and folk art tradition. Differently deracinated, the Jewish exegetical tradition itself had become ossified, had grown dead and cold: it no longer had its roots sunk into the mythic and vital "sources" of the community. The imagery he employs here resembles not only that of the Galician proponents of Jewish cultural renaissance including Markus Ehrenpreis and Martin Buber but also that once again of Hillel Zeitlin: "Even Orthodoxy," writes Zeitlin, "Orthodoxy which it seems commits itself to Torah and consequently to spirituality . . . lacks that spirituality that once wrought wonders for the Jewish people. . . . It is out of touch with that 'river' which flows forth from Eden to water the 'garden.'"[50] Zeitlin's form of "philosophical neo-Hasidism" was a deeply religious sensibility, and he remained committed to Orthodox Judaism and to halakhic observance; yet the language Schulz adopts in his own works is in many cases closer to Zeitlin's than it is to that of any secular Jewish writer of the period.

For Lestschinsky again, to whose social analysis Schulz's text also hews closely, "One thing is clear, the hidden primitive powers need to be discovered and the hidden roots had to be raised to the level of a national multibranched cultural tree. In order to access its historical treasures and inherited wellsprings, the primitive Jewish people and folkways had to evolve into a modern nation and a modern national culture."[51] In Schulz's account, similarly, the forces of both assimilation and Orthodox pietism had combined by the fin de siècle not to destroy the Jewish artistic instinct but to press it deep into the Jewish collective unconsciousness, where it would await its spring. "The artistic instinct, the talent for the plastic arts, retreated deep into the soul of the folk, where it continued to smolder with a faint flame" (SF6, 84). This passage finds its universalized, fictionalized corollary in Schulz's short story "The Book" (again, published the same year): "I lay the fragment [of the *Księga*] in the deepest drawer, 'says the narrator, covering it with other books to conceal it.' It seemed to me that it was the dawn I was putting to sleep in my dresser, the dawn, who reignited again and continuously of her own accord; who had walked through all the flames . . . and had come back yet again, and who did not want to end" (O, 115). Particularly poignant in this mythologized passage is Schulz's metatextual reference to his own poetic practice, of "covering [the Original] with other books to conceal it" ("*nakrywając go dla niepoznaki innymi książkami*").

The image of a cultural remnant or artistic spirit which waits for its moment to reignite returns in many writers of Schulz's generation. In a 1926 essay entitled "*Der kult fun gornisht un kunst vi zi darf zayn*" ("The Cult of Nothing and Art as It Should Be"), playwright and poet Aharon Zeitlin (son of Hillel Zeitlin), whose experimental kabbalistic futurist poetics in Yiddish bear comparison with those of Schulz, writes: "We Jews are a dead people, and a forgetful people [. . .] Somewhere we gave birth to a *Zohar*—now lying in the attic of our forefathers, among thousands of yet-to-be-unpacked heritage-boxes!"[52] But the time has come to reopen the boxes, and to reactivate within Futurist poetry, in Yiddish, the dynamic, image-based language of the Zohar: "Kabbalah-image! Kabbalah plastic-arts!" Schulz himself had begun to experiment in "The Book" with an allegorical image-based language that nods to Zoharic imagery. In his non-mythologized Lilien essay, however, he speaks of the artistic spirit of the Jewish people, in the period before the fin de siecle Jewish Renaissance, as still flickering with a dim flame, "bursting forth here and there in objects of folk handicraft—in the lovely metalwork of Jewish candelabras, among the naïve illuminators of the Haggada, and in masterpieces of ornamental carving on gravestones." Schulz's historically accurate attention to the sources of Lilien's work within Jewish ornamental folk art also contains an autobiographical element. Schulz had studied Jewish gravestone art and devoted considerable time and attention to designing the gravestones of his parents, Henrietta Schulz (née Kuhmerker) and Jakub Schulz, which stood in Drohobycz's sizable Jewish cemetery. Jerzy Ficowski was able to locate and speak with one of the stonemasons who executed Schulz's project and who described the design of the stones to the best of his memory. The entirety of their vertical structure was carved in a notched pattern to create a menorah—possibly in a geometrical, art deco style—whose arms extended to support grapes, a symbol of Israel in traditional Jewish gravestone art.[53]

With this introductory passage, Schulz has set the stage in his lecture on Lilien for an exploration of the question of Jewish cultural revival in the early twentieth century, and specifically the possibility for continuity and revitalization of the Jewish book. Schulz is most interested in Lilien's work when it represents a re-igniting of the flame of Jewish artistic spirit in a modern European form. "For Lilien the matter of reactivating Jewish myth," he writes, "of reawakening it and bringing it closer to his contemporary, Europeanized generation appears as a question of giving expression to one's own content—to those reserves of ore slumbering in the depths of the collective consciousness—within the forms of national European art" (SF6, 86). While speaking of Lilien, Schulz describes the same project he had set for himself, and that had taken form in the short stories "The Book," "Spring," and "The Age of Genius": "He adopted its artistic equipment, form and contents, but he poured into them an altogether new and different spirit. This is a spirit of pure poetry and high idealism, a spirit of optimism and affirmation.... In this way his contribution has entered into Jewish culture as an eternal and indestructible asset" (SF6, 95–96). For Schulz, Lilien's early illuminated volumes *Juda* (1901) and *Lieder des Ghetto* (1902), which he refers to as Lilien's "monumental works," both achieve this goal.

Schulz was especially concerned with the "adequacy" of an art form to the specific historical moment that gave rise to it. One of the qualities that makes Lilien's *Juda* an ideal expression of the Jewish Renaissance, in his estimation, is that it emerged as an actual collaboration between Jewish and non-Jewish artists. In this sense it represented a material embodiment of the overcoming of the "ghetto walls" or "prison walls" that separated Jews from non-Jews, and that was a primary goal of the Jewish Renaissance. The *Juda* collaboration, then, is both a record of that movement's aspirations, and a monument to their passing: "This is a collection of biblical ballads written by a German poet, the *junker* Baron Börries von Münchhausen," he writes, "who was a very close friend of the Jewish artist"—and here he adds, parenthetically, "how long ago were the times when that was possible!" (SF6, 88), a cry of regret that runs more quietly throughout his entire essay.

Reading Lilien's work as an illustration of the national-international Jewish cultural renaissance, Schulz situates Lilien within two lines of inheritance simultaneously: European and distinctly Jewish. First, with regard to the European graphic arts, he traces a line of development of the black-and-white print from the German medieval and Renaissance woodcuts of Dürer and Holbein to the English Pre-Raphaelites (Ruskin, Morris, Crane) and their revival of a total aesthetic of the typeset book. "Lilien," he writes, "belongs to the great ranks of the graphic arts pioneers of the new movement."[54] He places him in a constellation of fin de siècle contemporaries—"Munch, Beardsley, Puvis de Chavannes, the Viennese Klimt . . . Wyspiański" (SF6, 92), with their penchant for the romantic, decadent, erotic, and irrational. At the same time, Schulz writes Lilien into the previously mentioned line of inheritance with respect to both the ornamental folk art tradition of Jewish gravestones and the work of the "naïve illuminators of the Haggada" (SF6, 84). Foregrounding the simultaneity and multiplicity of cultural imaginaries out of which modern Jewish art in the Austro-Hungarian empire arose, Schulz's discussion of Lilien intertwines these histories—Jewish, Habsburg and more broadly European—understanding Jewish artistic contributions as an integral part of the development of European culture. He uses the terms "authentic," "revitalized," and "adequate" to describe Jewish creativity that both draws on folk tradition and participates in the contemporary European art movements of its time.

It is *Juda*'s success as a union of image and text, however, that raises the book to the highest of Lilien's achievements in Schulz's estimation. The volume combined Börries' biblical ballads with Lilien's illustrations, to become an "integral whole" ("*integralna całość*") that, through the artist's use of line, pattern, contrast of black and white, and visual "rhythm," achieves a quality of motion, and of living poetry (fig. 2.4): "This is a strong and intoxicating poetry, hypnotizing in its celebratory gesture and in the solemn, enchanting dance of slender figures, formed as if from white silence above the roaring accompaniment of chords black as night. From the contrasts of blackness and whiteness—and out of their encounter at the sharp border of the melodious line—Lilien has extracted, as it were, the crystalline music of the spheres" (SF6, 87). Through the slight shift in Schulz's imagery from the

"A Creation Born of the Longing of Golus" | 79

Figure 2.4. E. M. Lilien, *The Creation of Man*, illustration for *Lieder des Ghetto* (1903).

linguistic and musical to the geographical, Lilien's discovery of a modern, visual form of Jewish poetry also becomes an example of Ahad Ha'am's program of a "spiritual back-to-the-land"—not territorial but textual and mythical: "Perhaps this is the first time a book so complete, so rawly, unswervingly and contrapuntally tuned into an integral wholeness, had ever been created.... At the same time, this book was a first attempt [of the artist] to immerse himself in the world of his own tribe's past, an attempt to recover his mythic fatherland" (SF6, 88). Again, he specifically links Lilien's collaborations to the tradition of illustrated *haggadot*.

To create works that combined text and image was a goal of Schulz's as well. He insisted that the volume *Sanatorium pod klepsydrą* be published together with his own accompanying illustrations. We know from the letters of Schulz's fiancée, Józefina Szelińska, that the volume containing Aubrey Beardsley's illustrations to Oscar Wilde's *Salome* was among Schulz's very favorites. He brought the book with him during his sabbatical stay in Warsaw in 1936, and was particularly pleased with its illustrations, writes Szelińska, "because they were integrated into the text. Woven into the text. He spent a great deal of time thinking about the best, most successful way to illustrate a text. The ideal for him was illustrations in the margin, or within the text itself, not on separate pages, but directly tied to the words of the text."[55]

Lilien's early Jewish-themed, book-length collaborations *Juda* and *Lieder des Ghetto*, then, produced in a German-language, European diaspora context, represented for Schulz examples of an authentic, revitalized expression of the "mythological powers of the folk" (SF6, 86). But here is where the plot of the essay takes a turn. For the author, Lilien's work will lose its vitality and authenticity when the artist moves to Palestine, and his artistic practice, accordingly, changes—moves forward—to match its historical conditions. His art adopts a form adequate to capture the experience of that emigration—one that now accurately records not the messianic longing of diaspora, but the physical and realized present of the new/old territorial homeland. Like Schulz's own poetry in Korn's review, which was "transplanted" from its soul-roots, here the artist moves away from the native context of Cultural Zionism and Galician Jewish Renaissance in which his artistry was rooted. "Once Lilien encounters Palestine," writes Schulz, "he ceases to be the visionary of a lost fatherland; he even gives up his black and white technique"—a marker of connection to ornamental, textual, and non-realist traditions—"as no longer relevant, and reaches for the brush of the watercolor painter, in order to describe in countless graphics the landscape, people and buildings of this country as seen through the sober eye of an artist reconciled with reality" (SF6, 88). Few words in Schulz's vocabulary carry as great a suggestion of resignation as "reality." The key words here, "*pojednany z rzeczywistością*" (reconciled with reality), signal an antinomy and encounter—myth with reality, sacred with profane, exegetical with historical that structures this and so many of Schulz's texts. The essay's subtext, as his readers and listeners would have received it, comes to the fore: the realization that political and economic solutions for Poland's Jewish communities had gained the utmost urgency; that the co-creation of hybrid modern European artforms was becoming a battleground; and that the idealism that underlay the promise of Jewish spiritual renewal in a Central European context was faltering as it became reconciled with reality. His essay performs the twilight of a "genialna epoka" ("wondrous era").

Schulz's words, like others throughout his essay, also echo concerns about political Zionism as a real-worldly resignation from, rather than a *continuation* of, precisely the messianic longing born of golus, that for Schulz had provided a continued source of vital sustenance within Jewish art and culture. According to Schulz, as an artist Ephraim Moses Lilien represented "a transition from religious, mythic, messianic Jewish nationalism to a nationalism that is modern and realistic."⁵⁶ Schulz's Lilien essay also speaks to, and becomes an apologia for, his own inability to follow in Lilien's footsteps, and his decision instead to seek a continuation of the mythic and messianic Jewish traditions of his region not in political programs but through the medium of the living book. "Political nationalism has not discarded the deep and mystical strengths," he writes, "the subterranean reserves that made it a popular movement.... It has tried to salvage them, and to transpose them ... onto its new, Europeanized ideology" (SF6, 84). But, echoing Ahad Ha'am, he continues, "Political programs are only the rationalized surface, the external expression of deep transformations taking place in the depths of the collective consciousness. These transformations cannot complete themselves within the categories of political thought alone, but must ferment in the mythical depths, out of which are born longings, rapture, ideals, and the forms of the collective imagination. It is in these same depths that art operates" (SF6, 84).⁵⁷ These lines recall Hillel Zeitlin again, for whom historically it was not the realistic heroism of freedom fighters that preserved Israel and Judaism for centuries, but the "fortresses of Israel's tomes." As he wrote, "The sages of Yavneh, however, spiritualized Judaea, built her up with cities, surrounding them with fortresses no enemy could ever hope to penetrate."⁵⁸ It is in the same period as the Lilien essay that the image of a fortress comes to the center of Schulz's literary landscape, in the short story "*Republika marzeń*" ("Republic of Dreams"). In this story the narrator describes a childhood dream of establishing a "Republic of the Young" and a fortress of poetry, in a "no-man's land, or God's land" where "boundary lines petered out": "It was to be part fortress, part theater, part laboratory of visions [*na wpół twierdza, na wpół teatr, na wpół laboratorium wizyjne*]" (O, 330). "We dreamed the region was being threatened by an unknown danger, was permeated by a mysterious menace [*przesiąną tajemniczą grozą*].... Our gates drew fugitives out from under the knives of brigands [*Bramy nasze wchłaniały zbiegów spod noży zbójeckich*].... We played host to mysterious distinguished guests, and in the evenings everyone gathered in the great hall, where, by flickering candlelight, we listened to one tale or confession after another...." (W, 320). According to a striking account related to Jerzy Ficowski by Emil Górski, a student of Schulz's who became a close friend, "even in his final years in the Drohobycz ghetto during German occupation: '[Bruno Schulz] liked to spin for us, whenever it was possible, long stories about a miraculous Citadel [...] a fantastic product of his imagination [...] mighty and safe, unconquerable to the enemy. [...]

We all were to shelter ourselves there.'"[59] His account evokes the enduring element of escape from the political realities of his environment that had played a role in shaping the author's nostalgic and also utopian poetics.

Republic of Dreams

Where Schulz's essay uses imagery that is less than laudatory of the spiritual trajectory of political Zionism, it can also be seen as a response or reply to a *West-jüdische* discourse, common within the language of political Zionism, that was less than flattering toward Galician Jewish culture. An additional characteristic shared by many Galician Cultural Zionists was a refusal to accept political Zionism's pessimistic evaluation of the European diaspora experience, or "golus-existence," and a rejection of the negative portrayal of *Ostjuden* (East European Jews). In this aspect they followed Ahad Ha'am in seeing East European Jewish life as reserve of Jewish cultural authenticity that drew—in contrast to West European Jewish culture—on "a real link with a millennial culture."[60] This perspective rejected Western stereotypes that perceived the eastern and in particular the Galician Jew as suffering in exile, as downtrodden, unenlightened, backward, or uncultured; and in some language, as physically and psychically deformed, overly effeminate or parasitic, without productive or healthy livelihood. Such paradigms had become, alongside the very real specter of rising antisemitism, building blocks of Zionist discourse. In Schulz's essay Lilien's art figures as a kind of shifter between East and West in this sense. Emerging in and representing the Galician context of Cultural Zionism, he will later contribute substantially, through his mass-produced postcards, commissioned by the Fifth Zionist Congress, to the popularization and solidification of iconic images of East European Jewish suffering in the minds of Jews worldwide. "If there is a graphic representation of Zionism's message," writes Michael Brenner, "it can hardly be more clearly communicated than in this drawing by Ephraim Moses Lilien (1874–1925) published in 1900 and titled 'Passover' [fig. 2.5]. On the left side of the picture we see the Jew in exile, his eyes sad and his body entangled in thorns; on the right side, we see the rising sun with the Hebrew word 'Zion' (Tzion); and in the background the pyramids of Egyptian slavery."[61]

Schulz's participation in such push-back against stereotypes of Galician Jewish life can be interestingly highlighted by placing two of his texts—the essay "E. M. Lilien" and the short story "Republic of Dreams" ("*Republika Marzeń*"), published in *Tygodnik Illustrowany* in summer of 1936—in direct

"A Creation Born of the Longing of Golus" | 83

Figure 2.5. E. M. Lilien, *Passover* (1900).

conversation with another text about Lilien written by Schulz's Austrian Jewish contemporary, the author Stefan Zweig (1881–1942). Zweig's biographical sketch of Lilien appeared as the introduction to *E. M. Lilien: Sein Werk*, the first album of Lilien's collected works, published in Berlin in 1903. Schulz, working on his own Lilien essay for *Przegląd Podkarpacia* would likely have made use of this album and of Zweig's introduction—and he would have found plenty in it with which to take issue.[62]

In his short biography of Lilien, a young Zweig, then twenty-four and writing in Vienna, tried to evoke for himself and for his German-speaking, assimilated readers what Lilien's life and surroundings must have been like in the Drohobycz of his youth. He imagined them thus: "The land is poor and desolate. The *gray*, cold cliffs of the Carpathians sink there slowly down into the barren, monochromatic expanse, which stretches out far into the Russian steppes. And life is without beauty and captivating force in these harsh, inhospitable regions. An artist there could never be given the wondrous gift of seeing the world as a fan of jubilant and seductive colors, that unfold themselves into intoxicating forms. Life could never teach him to allow the thousand-hued spectrum of colorful nuances to echo in his artistic visions."[63]

As if written in direct response to Zweig's highly tendentious discussion of his hometown, Drohobycz, and indeed of his own *landsman*, Lilien, Schulz's story *Republika marzeń* (*Republic of Dreams*) opens with a description of this very same "*heimatsschölle*," or patch of homeland: "I am transported in my thoughts to the distant city of my dreams," he writes. "I soar with my gaze above this low land, expansive and undulating like God's own coat thrown down as a colorful canvas at the threshold of heaven. For this entire land underpins the sky, holds it upon itself, the colorfully vaulted, manifold sky, full of cloisters, triforia, rosacias, and windows onto eternity" (L, 245).[64] *Kolorowość* (colorfulness), which signifies here and in Schulz's stories the artistic vision and vital energy that inflames and animates empty form, had been central to Schulz's aesthetic vision and literary output since at least the time of his discussions on aesthetics with Debora Vogel. Here he draws on that premise in a repartee directed at German-speaking Vienna (though also at the knowing Galician reader—perhaps Vogel herself). Reveling in the lush, imagined Galician landscape as a source of poetic and artistic inspiration, the passage also suggests that the Western Jewish image of Drohobycz as desolate, both physically and culturally, could not be further from the truth—or further from an understanding of this region as the true source of Lilien's inspiration. Indeed, Schulz's text suggests, the intelligentsia of Vienna and Berlin may wish from a distance for the direct proximity that the Drohobycz artist had had—to the continued spiritual and linguistic vitality of the Galician Jewish world, that transforms the landscape into a boundless fount of narrative. In Schulz's prose this landscape "stretches like a cat in the sun" and takes on distinctly biblical qualities, becoming "that chosen land, that peculiar province, that town unique in all the world" that has "boldly installed itself at the brink of eternity" (WE, 266; O, 325). "Republic of Dreams" even comes, under Schulz's pen, to resemble the promised land suggested in Lilien's most renowned graphic from the Fifth Zionist Congress, over which Zweig and Schulz seem in their passages to vie for ownership (fig. 2.6): "The garden plots at the outskirts of town are planted as if at the world's edge and look across their fences into the infinity of the anonymous plain. Just beyond the toll gates the region turns nameless and cosmic like Canaan," writes Schulz. "How shall I express it? Whereas other cities developed economically, and in numbers—our city entered deeper into essence. Here events are not ephemeral surface

"A Creation Born of the Longing of Golus" | 85

Figure 2.6. E. M. Lilien, *The Jewish May*, illustration for *Lieder des Ghetto* (1903).

phantoms; they have roots sunk into the depth of things, and penetrate their essence" (O, 325).

Further, whereas in "Republic of Dreams" colorfulness becomes a dominant characteristic of the Galician landscape, in the Lilien essay itself Schulz takes the formal contrast of "black and white" in Lilien's graphic works, that Zweig had used to evoke the bleak golus existence of East European Jews and reverses its significance. Now the interplay of black and white stands for the living Book and living transmission—as Schulz's descriptions of Lilien's imagery as "figures of white silence on a background of riotous black chords" evoke language used within kabbalistic writing to describe the Torah or holy scripture as black fire written on white fire.

Schulz's essay's relationship with Berthold Feiwel's introduction to the volume *Lieder des Ghetto* is also interesting. Notably, in his discussion of that book so formative for him as an artist, he does not mention either Feiwel's introduction or Morris Rosenfeld's poems themselves (here translated into German), for which Lilien had provided the illustrations.[65] Schulz does mention that attention to themes of Jewish poverty in *Lieder des Ghetto* represents the volume's "greatest strength," but he does not refer to the actual content of Morris Rosenfeld's poems, which treat the condition of the

Jewish proletariat in the sweatshops of New York. He makes no mention as well of the fact that these poems were written in Yiddish; of the cooperation between Lilien and Berthold Feiwel, who translated the poems; or of the cultural program of the Democratic Faction, of which the volume is an expression. This displacement or removal of Lilien's art and his project from its full historical context represents a formal choice by Schulz, that is directly in line with his use of the Lilien essay as a platform to discuss and reflect on his own artistic development. Here the strategy of irony that Schulz had attributed to Kafka—the transplantation of the surface reality onto his own spiritual reality—applies equally to the Lilien essay. Those aspects of Lilien's work that Schulz does discuss at length include precisely those biographical elements that overlap with Schulz's own artistic experience and that allow the full pathos of the author's fragmentary confession to emerge. These include: the development of a distinctive black-and-white print technique; the fin de siècle context that shaped his aesthetic; the amount of attention given in his early career to the *ex libris* or bookplate, which he now describes as "a regrettable fad"; and the inability to create works as raw, authentic, and inspired as those that went into his first volume. In this regard, Schulz's mention of Lilien's Żupna Street origins reminds his readers that this art, like his own, is born of golus, and specifically of the Galician, Drohobyczan diaspora experience. His assessment of this existence as a source of vital creativity differs markedly from the arguments made by either Feiwel in his original introduction or by Zweig—both of whom offer decidedly negative assessments of diaspora existence. For Feiwel, the sweatshop workers of New York described and honored in Rosenfeld's poems become a metonym for the suffering Eastern European and Galician masses, who at the time of his writing were emigrating in growing numbers to Germany and to Vienna. The poems' content lends support to the volume's Zionist message and aims.[66] Feiwel attempts to describe to his German-language readership the miserable existence of the East European Jewish masses: "The Ghetto is full of almost superhuman, unutterable hardships, in which millions of people are imprisoned. People? The poorest slaves, and at the same time the greatest heroes they are, who carry the burden of 'Golus,' the most terrible burden that ever weighed down upon human necks. It is not people, but tortured human life instincts that reside in the Ghetto."[67] By contrast, but responding to the same political exigencies, Schulz uses *Lieder des Ghetto* as a platform to express regret at the seemingly inevitable twilight of an era of vital Jewish creativity in the diaspora. As neither the content of Rosenfeld's poetry nor the context and intent of Feiwel's introduction would have lent support to this positive assessment of Galician diaspora existence as the source of Lilien's artistic vision, they are left out of his essay. At the same time, Feiwel's text does turn toward that aspect of the messianic, and specifically the image of sanctuary, around which Schulz would construct so many of his narratives: "Here lives abstinence . . . an asceticism that for the sake of that heavenly pay bears the monstrosity of existence like destiny, almost like a debt, and [with it] the inextinguishable hope for the Messianic kingdom, for redemption through Zion, which can come at any moment. . . . Here lives a last anticipation, that somewhere on Earth there is peace, a last sigh for a place to rest, for a piece of homeland."[68]

As readers of Schulz's rediscovered Lilien article, we cannot know the extent to which Schulz fictionalized a true scene of encounter with Lilien's work at the age of thirteen. What we can say is that in staging his "coming out" as a Jewish artist and intellectual in the Polish-language press a quarter century later, Schulz chose *Lieder des Ghetto* with Lilien's illustrations as the prototype of a Jewish book that embodied the artistic and spiritual goals he had placed at the center of his own aesthetic project. Lilien's art and trajectory could encapsulate the encounter and the dialectical tension that defined his own relationship to tradition and to his historical moment—suspended between sacred and profane, exegesis and history. Schulz's article resounds with a sense of regret and wistful resignation. The arc that it traces is the aspirational arc of Lilien and Buber's generation: the rise and also the fall of a particular fin de siècle dream: that of Jewish Cultural Renaissance in central Europe. "But alas, such is the curse of history that has already weighed down upon this creation. The early Spring of that myth," writes Schulz, "outlived itself, and expired."[69]

"This Creation Born of the Longing of Golus"

In the same year that Schulz was writing and publishing successive fragments of the Lilien essay, he received a letter from his friend and colleague from the *Tsushtayer* days in Lemberg/Lwów, Yiddish writer and editor Rachel Auerbach, in which she wrote, "I am strongly convinced that your work can become a revelation on a worldwide scale; and since you don't write in Yiddish, and do not belong to the milieu/community out of which you grew, then may you at least belong to the world. . . . For my part I would like to try to translate something of yours into Yiddish."[70]

Some of the most emotionally tinged lines of the Lilien essay, written at most a few months later, read as a direct response by Schulz to Auerbach's—again, tendentious—statements, informed by her strong Yiddishist convictions. We may read these lines as a commentary by Schulz not only on Lilien but also on his own attempt to create a modern Jewish writing—a new and authentic form of the Jewish book that would represent, in Martin Buber's words, a vital continuation of Jewish myth and in Hillel Zeitlin's, a form of "Torah-worldview"—specific to his time and place and to his Polish-speaking, Galician positionality. "His soul was not cut off from the sources of his tribe, from inspirations drawn from the depths of his race," writes Schulz. And, in a phrase that echoes Auerbach's words, he concludes, "just the opposite—he was a representative of the community from which he came. . . . He gave bodily form to the myth that his époque, and the community out of which he came, could afford" (SF6, 96). Schulz had placed similar lines in the mouth of his narrator in the story "Spring," written shortly before the Lilien essay, who justifies his stubborn attachment to a utopian project of liberation by explaining, "I wanted to remain in the world destiny had allotted to me."

Abandoning his pretense of scholarly or historical objectivity, Schulz continues near the end of his Lilien essay: "with a naive and open heart, he listened to the dictates of his genius" (SF6, 96). We may read in these passages a reflection on the ethos and dream of Jewish cultural revival embodied not only in Lilien's early drawings but also in Schulz's own much more recent experiment in the art of the modern Jewish book, *Sanatorium under the Sign of the Hourglass* (*Sanatorium pod klepsydrą*). It was an aesthetic project that contained in its very structure, and in its title (whose *klepsydra* (hourglass)—points to a time that has run its course and is a symbol of death) the recognition that it was the expression of an earlier age and of the dreams of an earlier generation. Writes Schulz:

> It is here that the true longing of the artist for his spiritual fatherland found expression; here he found an expression adequate to the myth that spun itself in the depths of his soul. One can disagree as to the value of this incarnation perhaps—whether it embodied it only for a group of people accustomed to matters somewhat aestheticized and "*po inteligencku*," [for the intelligentsia] perhaps this was a myth for a group that could not afford a myth of a more creative, more active kind. . . . Perhaps, in its encounter with the reality of living Zionism in Palestine, that creature born of the longing of *golus* could not stand its ground (SF6, 88).

What Schulz's Lilien article describes, and also formally embodies, in its disposable, *tandetny*, or low-culture form, published at the margins of the literary world, is the impossibility, for Schulz, of a non-diasporic writing. The book that his texts continually imagine—and that they argue must constantly be sought—cannot be territorialized. His literary and critical texts from this period, including the newly discovered essay, perform this argument for a diasporic literature in myriad forms and across the full range of his artistic genres.

Schulz's article gives renewed expression to the deep reticence that members of this earlier constellation had about what Ahad Ha-am would label "political Zionism." As Schulz explains in his own version of the argument, political Zionism makes sense and is indeed necessary for members of the younger generation growing up in interwar Poland, for whom it represents an active response to untenable economic and political conditions. Schulz, however, aligns himself with a different constellation of thinkers, both religious and secular, for whom this solution does not address the most pressing spiritual and intellectual questions about the future continuation of East European Jewish culture in the modern world. These include, perhaps most centrally for Schulz's writing, the question of whether or how a modern and secular Jewish art could give expression to the mythic, messianic tradition in Jewish culture.

3

THE SUNDAY SEMINARS OF BRUNO SCHULZ AND DEBORA VOGEL

Rachel Auerbach's "Un-Spun Threads" and Vogel's "Human Exotics"

IN HER 1964 MEMOIR FOR THE YIDDISH JOURNAL *Di goldene keyt*, entitled *"Nisht-oysgeshpunene fedem"* ("Un-Spun Threads"), Rachel Auerbach wrote of Bruno Schulz and of her close friend, poet, essayist, and aesthetic philosopher Debora Vogel, as "two original, deep minds, two creators—the fine threads of whose concepts and visions remain unspun—like the un-lived days of their lives." A Polish and Yiddish writer and engaged Yiddishist before the war. Auerbach (in Yiddish, Rokhl Oyerbakh) would survive World War II in the Warsaw ghetto, and later in hiding on the Aryan side. She went on to devote her life to memory and testimony—both recounting her own memories of the Polish Jewish world that had been lost, as she knew it both before and during the war, and collecting the testimony of others.[1] In "Un-Spun Threads," she returns in her memory to an earlier period in her life, and to Galicia where she was born and raised, to prepare, for the Tel-Aviv based Yiddish journal *Di goldene keyt,* a memoir of two friends from her earlier years in Lwów, neither of whom had survived the war. In a final tragic echo that links the two, both were shot by Nazis in their home towns: Bruno Schulz in Drohobycz, and Debora Vogel in her home in Lwów, together with her husband Antschel and her son, Szulim, in 1942.

Auerbach's memoir is deeply personal in tone. She recreates in detail and in a dynamic, at times emotional mode of narration, details of her close friend Dvoyre Fogel's biography, including her memories of Dvoyre's meeting and relationship with the artist and writer Bruno Schulz from Drohobycz. Her love and respect for Vogel are palpable in the text, as is her respect and admiration for Schulz, and a tension and even sadness that surrounds her references to his choice to remain a Polish writer. In the context of the present study Auerbach's voice, like Rokhl Korn's in her review of *Cinnamon Shops*, allows readers access to the perspectives and experiences of the Jewish intellectual and artistic community in which Schulz's Galician Jewish writing emerged. I allow Auerbach to narrate the initial encounter between Vogel and Schulz, and to introduce their Sunday Seminars of 1930–31. These aesthetic discussions offer the single most striking iteration of the organizing theme of "Encounter" ("*Spotkanie*") that runs throughout Schulz's graphic and written work. After considering the strongly divergent artistic programs that Schulz and Vogel articulated in conversation with each other, I turn to two essays by Vogel herself—who was, in addition to being a poet in both Yiddish and Polish, a prolific and engaged essayist, writing on social issues from a left progressive position. Her essays "Human Exotics" ("*Ludzkie egzotyki*") and "A Few Observations on Today's Intelligentsia" provide additional insight into her perspectives on the nature and meaning of golus-existence; on the Jewish and universally human experience of otherization; and on the responsibility of the artist to her historical moment—all questions which would have figured prominently in her discussions with Schulz. In comparison to Vogel, whose radically experimental texts in the Yiddish language combined avant-garde, formalist poetic exercises with an increasing degree of Marxist social engagement, Schulz, so often read as a linguistic innovator and experimenter in form, also emerges as an aesthetic reactionary—as the critic Artur Sandauer described him, a decidedly Secessionist poet—with a greater attachment than Vogel to the mystical and spiritual elements in Jewish tradition. Through Auerbach's memoir it becomes clear that in their aesthetic debates, the two Jewish artists honed the sharp divergence in their poetic goals and strategies, held together as they were by the shared raw material of a life lived in the turbulent post-WWI period.

Schulz first met Debora Vogel likely in 1929, at the Zakopane home of the Polish painter, playwright, and theorist Stanisław Ignacy Witkiewicz, a leading figure in the experimental art scene of interwar Poland.[2] This meeting, and the relationship and later engagement that developed from it, played a defining and formative role in the artistic, intellectual, and emotional lives of both Schulz and Vogel. It would continue to influence the forms their work would take until the war broke out. The specific forms these artists' creative output took reflect contrasting solutions to the shared challenges that faced Polish Jewish writers of the interwar period and Galician Jewish writers in a post-Imperial, post-WWI reality: how to combine the Jewish and the universal, still-valued elements of tradition with radical forms of artistic innovation that responded to the modernist call precisely to break with tradition and to "make it new." Was the concern with such modernist formal experimentation itself a diversion of the intelligentsia, or a response to the ethical demands of the age—whether historical or spiritual, collective or individual? The writers' distinct aesthetic projects can be read as expressions of two competing, generationally opposed orientations: Neo-Romantic and avant-garde/Marxist, respectively. The debate that runs throughout their artistic projects in the 1930s also opens up reflection on the dialectical tension between theology and materialism—two halves of a dialectical picture-riddle that defined Jewish modernity.

Together Schulz and Vogel would develop a shared artistic and poetic vocabulary: a dictionary and a poetic imaginarium of recurring terms, images, and themes that appear in both writers' works and that provide the material for their reflections on the nature of matter and form; on the effects of commodification and commercialization on both the human condition and the nature of artistic representation; and on the relationship of the artist to the raw material of the Galician cityscape and of personal biography. That shared album of image-words included wardrobes and credenzas of oak and ebony; soldiers in formation in a town square; ubiquitous sales clerks and shop windows; and the terms *shund* and *tandeta*, which evoke, in Yiddish and Polish respectively, the cheapness of disposable commercial materials, advertising circulars, and second-rate literature. Even such specific elements as cockroaches and dishwater appear in both artists' work, in passages that often echo one another quite closely. Both writers' works treat of a recurring or ever-present sense of anticipation, longing and waiting, for someone's uncertain but long-announced arrival; of the onset of autumn or spring, the changing light of the sky and the changing colors of leaves; and, as Korn's review had highlighted, of the secret suffering of matter trapped in form.[3] Most memorably, central to both of their work in the 1930s is the figure of the mannequin. And finally, as if to complete the modern picture-riddle, both Vogel's first published story and Schulz's unfinished last work bore the title *Messiah*.[4]

These and other images and themes represent an accumulation of linguistic and conceptual "raw material" that each artist would submit to his or her specific artistic vision, rendering—to use the language that both artists employ—a different "extract" or "distillation." Each would be modern,

Jewish, "universal"/European, Galician, and also highly idiosyncratic: unlike other literature being written in its language, whether Polish or Yiddish, at the time of its publication. Near the time of their acquaintance, Vogel published her first volume of poetry in Yiddish, entitled *Tog figurn* (*Day Figures*, 1930) and wrote many of the poems for her second volume, *Manekinen* (*Mannequins*, 1934). Schulz began a four-part series of stories linked by the title *Treatise on Mannequins*, also translated as *Tailors' Dummies*, during his visits to Vogel. But the themes taken up in this period define both of their work for the next decade, or for as long as both would write. It is also the case that their respective treatments of these themes, and their essayistic reflections on the artistic process, underwent a marked shift in the mid- to late 1930s. This shift reflected a changing political environment and a renegotiation of the role and responsibility of the artist toward that evolving climate.

The details of Vogel and Schulz's relationship, and their shared exegetical encounter with the Galician landscape, provide an excellent example of the archaeology of Polish Jewish modernism that is shaping Polish and Jewish studies in the early twenty-first century. With her 2006 monograph *To Be the Agent of an Eternal Idea: The Changing Aesthetic Views of Debora Vogel*, Karolina Szymaniak brought to light and to scholarly attention the aesthetic theories, biography, and writings in both Yiddish and Polish of an influential Galician thinker and cultural activist of the interwar period-who, as both a woman writer and a Yiddishist, had been largely forgotten within both Polish and Jewish studies. Exploring Vogel's commitments not only to avant-garde aesthetic theory but also to Yiddishism, socially engaged writing, feminist thought and women's experience in interwar Poland, Szymaniak's work, and the later work of Vogel scholars Annette Werberger, Kathryn Hellerstein, Anna Torres, Anastasiya Lyubas, Allison Schachter, Sylwia Werner, and Anna Maja Misiak has continued to reveal the complexity and intellectual breadth of an individual whom Schulz's biographer Ficowski had described primarily as a muse to the male writer who was the focus of his own research.[5] With the publication by Anastasiya Lyubas of Vogel's collected work in English, together these scholars have opened the way for Vogel to join the ranks of both Jewish and European modernist writers and aesthetic theorists.

The story of Schulz and Vogel offers an apt metaphor for the layers of marginalization, forgetting, and illegibility that surround interwar Polish Jewish culture. In his short story "Cinnamon Shops," Schulz had used the image of a region of the map that fades away into white invisibility. The metaphor resonates with the invisibility that surrounded large swaths of the intellectual landscape of interwar Polish modernism for decades following the Second World War. For Ficowski to recover Schulz's work and undertake initial research into his biography with the materials and the individuals he could access within and from Poland in the 1980s, required a herculean effort in itself. A generation later, renewed research into the Polish- and Yiddish-language writings and the thought of Debora Vogel, enabled by and premised upon a multilingual Polish/Yiddish approach to interwar literary research, has contributed to redrawing the intellectual landscape of Polish and Galician modernism in the interwar period.[6]

Beginning with Chone Shmeruk in the 1980s, a growing number of Yiddish literary scholars have argued for the value of comparative work that restores the conversations, often uneasy, that existed between Yiddish and Polish literatures. As Adamczyk-Garbowska argues in her essay "I Know Who You Are, but Who I Am—You Do Not Know ...," such conversations or dialogues were largely uni-directional, with Polish-language modernist writers and the intellectual milieu at the Warsaw center much less interested in developments within modern Yiddish literature, if they deigned to acknowledge its existence at all, than Yiddishists were in Polish literature.[7] Comparative work continues to reveal the formative influence, however, of Polish literary models on modern Yiddish writers, many of whom were raised with an education in Polish literature and culture and were personally and profoundly shaped by that literature. Cammy and Figlerowicz, in their study of the formative influence of late Polish Romantic poet Cyprian Kamil Norwid on the work of Yiddish poet Avrom Sutzkever, write that as Polish literature developed, "it was marked by the paradox of its intimate—but also highly tense—relationship with Polish literary history." They continue, "On the one hand, Yiddish writers of the period expressed a strong awareness of their cultural distinctiveness and social alienation as they confronted the rise of Polish nationalism and its antisemitic offshoots. On the other hand, their contact with Polish literature was more pronounced—and more conscious—than it had been for their predecessors; many of them actively mined Polish history and literature for motifs through which they could communicate the ambivalences of their cultural and national attachments."[8]

In Schulz's case, there appears a rare example of influence in the opposite linguistic direction. Through his relationship with Debora Vogel, Schulz was exposed to the concerns, discourses, aesthetic theory, and debates that characterized the Yiddishist and more broadly Jewish literary and cultural milieu of Lemberg/Lwów.[9] It was during and out of this formative encounter and attendant lively debates that Schulz revisited his prose experiments, turning his efforts toward crafting an affirmatively Jewish writing in the Polish language, expressive of his own historical moment and experience: of a swiftly receding, fin-de-siècle Habsburg, Galician Jewish diasporic imaginary. Lesya Khomych's remarkable discovery in 2019 of the short story "Undula," which Schulz published in 1922 under the pen name Marceli Weron, further allows us to situate Schulz's encounter with Vogel as a turning point in his artistic and philosophical development as a modern artist and Jewish writer, and as the starting point for his experiment in a poetics that could adequately express the experience of golus, or diaspora existence.

Separated in age by a little under a decade, both Vogel and Schulz were raised as citizens of the multicultural Austro-Hungarian Empire and members of the urban bourgeoisie or petty-bourgeoisie in the Lwów/Lemberg region of Galicia: Vogel in Bursztyn and later Lwów, Schulz in Drohobycz. They spoke Polish as their mother tongue in the home and at Polish gymnasia, and German as a second language. In both of their homes, the use of Yiddish—which both artists undoubtedly understood but did not speak or write fluently—was discouraged. For Vogel, unlike Schulz, Hebrew was also a second and close to fluent language. Her immediate and extended family members—including her uncles Markus Ehrenpreis and Dovid Malz, and her parents, Anzelm Vogel and Lea *née* Ehrenpreis—were actively involved with the Zionist movement and institutions in Lwów. Their ties to maskilic and Zionist traditions in the region reached back several generations. As such, Vogel's family made it a priority that she learn to speak and read in Hebrew. Vogel herself was very close to her father, who was a teacher and the director of the Baron de Hirsch school in Bursztyn and, following World War I, director of a Jewish orphanage at Zborowska 8 in Lwów, at which Vogel also worked in young adulthood.[10]

In the case of Schulz's family, by contrast, little is known about either their political affiliation or the nature and extent of their involvement with Jewish community affairs. In the context of Drohobycz's infamously rough local city politics, Schulz's parents' generation may have aligned themselves, in terms of their voting and reading preferences, with the anti-Zionist "assimilationists" who controlled local politics in Drohobycz; but this is speculation.¹¹ Biographical information about Schulz's elder brother Izydor Schulz points to the priority the family placed on continuing social advancement and movement toward participation in the secular economic and civic life of Galicia—in a Polish language context. Izydor became a highly successful civil engineer, employed by the Polmin Gas company, moved to Lwów with his family in about 1930, and also opened a number of movie houses in Lwów and other Galician cities.¹² His wealth and his great admiration for his younger brother's artistic abilities were instrumental in allowing Schulz to pursue his career as an artist and later as a writer.¹³

Together with thousands of middle-class Jews whose families had the means to flee to the relative safety of the capitol during World War I, both Schulz and Vogel spent a substantial part of the war years studying in Vienna—Schulz in and out of technical arts academy, and Vogel, then of high-school age, at first a German-language and then a Polish-language gymnasium. For both, the cultural and artistic milieu of Vienna would have a formative influence.¹⁴ As students of modernism, of new forms in the graphic and plastic arts, both Vogel and Schulz would model their later literary experiments on the respective—and stylistically opposed—plastic and graphic art forms that had inspired each of them most. For Schulz, these were *Jugendstil* and the Secession, whose formative influence on him even before his Vienna years he described later in his 1937 Lilien article. Vogel, eight years younger, turned her attention to developing avant-garde artistic movements, with a focus on Cubism and Constructivism.

"We Need Pluralism": Zakopane and Galician Polish/Jewish Encounter

We learn from Auerbach that the paths of Vogel and Schulz initially intersected not in the context of national-Jewish artistic revival but at the Galician provincial center of Polish high culture: the home of S. I. Witkiewicz in Zakopane.¹⁵ Auerbach dates their meeting to 1930: "Dvoyre and I had spent ten days together in Zakopane, taking hikes in the Tatras and meeting in the evening with interesting people from all over Poland. In Zakopane there lived one of the best-known thinkers and artists, a painter and son of a painter, Stanislaw Ignacy Witkiewicz, whom those in the artistic world called 'Witkacy,'" and who "had launched his philosophical conception of 'metaphysical terror' and 'the end of art.'"¹⁶ Vogel, whose dissertation examined theories of art in Hegel and Polish art historian Józef Kremer (1806–75), had established contact with Witkacy likely a year earlier, in 1929, when she sent him her thesis, inviting him to engage with her in an aesthetic debate.[17]

Vogel's desire to engage with and be recognized at the Polish Polish cultural center, while simultaneously committing herself to the promotion of Yiddish culture in Galicia, is indicative of still understudied contexts and combinations possible within the multilingual cultural climate of the 1920s in newly independent Poland. Strongly influenced by her friendship with Auerbach, she made the choice to become a committed Yiddishist shortly before she met Schulz, and in 1930, during the period of their meetings and close contact, she joined Auerbach and Melekh Ravitch in founding the Yiddish cultural journal *Tsushtayer* (*Contribution*) which she co-edited together with Auerbach. Their goal was to identify and cultivate a distinctive Jewish Galician culture and to promote modernist Jewish art of Galicia and literature and criticism in the Yiddish language.[18] "May this second issue of *Tsushtayer* be a demonstration of our will and perseverance," wrote the editors in an opening note from the June 1930 issue: "one of the signs of the cultural vitality and engagement of Yiddish [Jewish] Galicia."[19]

At the same time, Vogel found it relevant and important to continue her engagement in cultural and philosophical debates at the center of Polish Polish modern culture.[20] Vogel had defended her doctorate, entitled "The Epistemological Meaning of Art in Hegel's Philosophy and Modifications Thereof in the Work of Józef Kremer," at the University of Lwów in 1926, and in the decade that followed she began to lecture on philosophy, psychology, and Polish literature, gaining renown and a following as an aesthetic philosopher and theorist of the avant-garde within Lwów artistic circles, particularly among artists associated with the *Légeristes* circle. Before their Zakopane meeting, as Auerbach writes, Vogel "responded to Witkacy's theories with a treatise that she had sent him in manuscript form.[21] They entered into a correspondence, and being in Zakopane, we went together to look for Witkiewicz in his atelier. He made one of his 'narcotic' portraits of Dvoyre, and it was in his atelier that, one evening, she met Bruno Schulz."[22] From the time of their Zakopane meeting, Schulz began making the hour-long trip from Drohobycz to spend Sundays walking with Vogel in the city streets and parks of Lwów. The two began a series of what Vogel referred to later, in a 1938 letter to Schulz, as "our conversations of long ago."[23] "Our interactions then," she continued, "were one of the rare wonderful things that happen only once in a lifetime, perhaps only once in several hopeless, colorless lives." As Auerbach recounts in her memoir,

"Back then they would talk, walk, meet—a deep unanimity, mutual inspiration. Sometimes I would take part in these autumn walks of theirs 'to the castle' or in the 'Jesuits' Garden.'²⁴ These were poetic-philosophic symposia of a high degree, that would nevertheless sometimes pass over into a mischievous mood."²⁵

The Sunday seminars were highly productive for both artists, initiating a decade-long conversation that took place in person, in epistolary form, and on the pages of both writers' published works—including in essays written over several years following Vogel's marriage to Barenblüth. As has become legendary within Schulz studies, it was in extended postscripts to letters that he wrote to Debora Vogel in 1930 and '31 that Schulz composed the first drafts of the stories that would become *Cinnamon Shops* and that would change the landscape of Polish modernism. When Vogel met Schulz in Zakopane, he was already a recognized artist, known for his *Book of Idolatry*, who had begun exhibiting his graphic work in 1922, almost a decade earlier. She would have approached him as both a viewer and a critic of his artwork, which would have provided rich material for their debates on objectification and the "sadism" of the artist. It is possible, and given her feminist orientation likely, that Vogel would have criticized and challenged Schulz's instrumentalization of the female form in his erotic graphic works as an allegory for profane or worldly form, the object of the artist's worship. I explore this line of thought in the final chapter of this study, in connection with the discovery of the short story "Undula" by Lesya Khomych.

In June of 1930, Vogel featured Schulz's artwork in *Tsushtayer*. Reproductions of three cliché-verre prints by "B. Schulz" appeared in the issue: "*Karlikes*" ("Dwarves"); "*Undula afn shpatsir*" ("Undula Taking a Walk"); and "*A bagegenish*" ("An Encounter")—a sketch that features two figures who can be read as young Jewish men or boys in traditional dress, with hats and long caftans, "encountering" two provocatively dressed women in the streets of a town (fig. 3.1).²⁶ These graphics share the pages of the *Tsushtayer* issue with artwork by Max Fayering and drawings by Fritz Kleinmann for the Vilner Trup's production of "*Bay nakht afn altn markt*" ("A Night in the Old Marketplace") by Y. L. Peretz. Other selections include an article by Vogel on "Themes and Form in Chagall's Art," a prose piece by Rachel Auerbach, a collection of "Galician Literature-Miscellany," or notes on Galician literature, by Naftali Veynig; a review of "The First Jewish Art Exhibition in Kraków"; and a poem by Mendel Naygroshel entitled "*Bagegenish*" ("Encounter"; "the first chapter of *Ballads from the Frosty Night*").²⁷

Figure 3.1. *A bagegenish* ("An Encounter"), in *Tsushtayer* I, no. 2 (June 1930). Original charcoal drawing, 1920 (lost).

In the same issue's section "From the Art World," a few paragraphs on Schulz's art, written by Vogel but printed without her attribution, place him within the family of comic-grotesque artists that includes Goya and Bosch, and among contemporary artists Otto Dix and George Grosz. In her brief and notably reserved description of his graphics, Vogel describes Schulz's primary subject matter as treating "the demonic aspects of the erotic sphere."[28] Her comments focus on the contrast between the beautiful female form and the comically humble male figure who prostrates himself before it. Noteworthy here is Vogel's reference to messianic themes in Schulz's graphic work. "Even his works on the theme of messianic times (*Meshiakh-tsaytn*)," writes Vogel, "are given an erotic coloring."[29]

According to Auerbach, due to either family and work obligations, illness, or his hypochondriac nature, it became increasingly difficult for Schulz to continue his regular trips to Lwów, and it was at this point that his and Vogel's discussions took on a primarily epistolary form. In her account, Auerbach credits herself with motivating both Schulz and Vogel to bring the texts of those letters to literary recognition:

The second winter of their acquaintance he began to weave into the letters, in installments, "Stories about My Father." These "post-scripts" in his letters were so strangely interesting and original that she gave them to me to read. I read them over and sent up an "alarm": These are not simply letters, this is poetry, this is gorgeous literature. And this is the genesis of Schulz's first book: we transcribed the "installments" in the post-scripts on a machine and sent a copy to Zofia Nałkowska.³⁰ That subtle, smart Polish writer did not hesitate for a moment—reading them and responding with a loud and determined "Yes."³¹ She recommended the book to the publishing house *Rój*, where it was quickly published, under the title *"Sklepy cynamonowe"* (*"Cinnamon Shops"*).³²

The story of this epistolary genesis is also recorded in a 1936 letter from Schulz to his close friend Romana Halpern, in which he regretted his inability to spontaneously produce stories similar to the ones that grew out of his encounter with Vogel: "I was still able to write beautiful letters then. It was out of my letters that *Cinnamon Shops* gradually grew. Most of these letters were to Debora Vogel, the author of *The Acacias Are Blooming*. These letters are mostly lost" (WE, 399).³³

Read alone, Schulz's statement might be taken—and was, by other critics of Schulz after Ficowski—to suggest an image of Debora Vogel as addressee, lover, and muse—as the recipient of a creative gesture born in the solitude of the artist's Drohobycz home, and of his "strange and original" imagination.³⁴ In fact, the reality and process that gave rise to Schulz's stories, as we learn from Auerbach's memoir and from Vogel's own letters, was not unidirectional or even primarily epistolary but deeply dialogic—the product of a rich real-time intellectual encounter. Joining Vogel in these walks in her home city and on her native streets, engaging the suggestive visual landscape of the Galician capital, its commercial shop windows and parks, its advertisements and passersby, the changing light and color of its atmospheres and its trees, Schulz was in fact the latecomer, or newcomer, to Vogel's ongoing reflections on the poetic "processing" of the modern urban landscape.

In a number of the stylistically and thematically defining stories of *Cinnamon Shops*, including "Street of Crocodiles" and the four-part "Tractate on Mannequins," Schulz proceeds by echoing and reworking themes already present in Vogel's first published volume, *Tog figurn* (*Day Figures*, 1930), including what are considered the characteristically Schulzian themes of the mannequin or tailor's dummy, of salesgirls and shop windows, and of tawdry, reproducible commercial goods—*tandeta*. He did so, however, by submitting these same themes and shared images to a dramatically different treatment. Indeed, in the prose experiments that they undertook in tandem during this period, Schulz and Vogel can be seen to perform a kind of literary duet in which each writer subjects a set of shared raw materials to artistic transformation through the lens of the period, and the aesthetic, that had had the greatest impact on their individual artistic formation: two periods, two seemingly diametrically opposed solutions to the challenge of creating a modern Jewish and also universal or "world" poetics. For Vogel, that ethos and influence were the cubo-constructivist aesthetic of the post-WWI avant-garde, coupled with a realistic and rigidly secular, increasingly historical-materialist worldview. In the case of Schulz, this ethos and this era were Jugendstil and the fin de siècle Neo-Romanticism of the last decades of the Habsburg monarchy: the idyllic childhood period that Schulz evoked later in *Sanatorium* as the *"Genialna epoka,"* or "Age of Genius." This secessionist aesthetic is clearly reflected in his baroque, metaphor-rich prose, filled with winking wallpaper and arabesques taken almost directly from the paintings of Gustav Klimt; with references to classical mythology, the Bible, Kabbalistic thought and Gnostic philosophy; and with the Neo-Romantic language of myth, roots, and primordial sources. Schulz's unrestrainedly metaphorical and allusive prose, characterized by an abundance of organic imagery and a vital dynamism, differed in almost every formal aspect from Vogel's avant-garde experiments and what she described as her poetics of "cool stasis."

Where Schulz claimed as his beloved and admired influences E. M. Lilien, Thomas Mann, Franz Kafka—whom he referred to in one letter as a "little known mystical writer"—and *"boski Rilke"* ("divine Rilke"), Vogel's models and inspirations in the plastic arts, by contrast, included the surrealist de Chirico and the cubist Fernand Léger. Her poems in *Day Figures* and *Mannequins* represent attempts to approximate in linguistic form the achievements of the cubist and constructivist movements in the plastic arts. As she wrote in the foreword to *Day Figures*, "In poetry it is the word that takes on the role of contour and color."[35] The material world itself is distilled down in Vogel's verse to its most basic physical and visual components: line, shape, color, and pattern, or "schema." The materialist story these tell, that corresponds to what Vogel calls in some texts the *"legenda czasu,"* or "legend of the age," is understood not as the story of a specifically Jewish experience of modernity but as one of global or international capitalism, production, and commercialization. In theoretical essays written to accompany and render more accessible each of her volumes of poetry and prose, *Day Figures* (*Tog figurn*, 1930), *Mannequins* (*Manekinen*, 1931), and *Acacias Are Blooming* (*Akatsyes blien*, 1935), Vogel explained that, taken together, her successive volumes represented a series of investigations intended to follow the trajectory of Hegel's "wonderful law" of dialectical development: from cubism, to constructivism, to montage.

For Vogel, the choice to write in Yiddish made it possible for her to create literary texts whose very Jewishness, as well, was given expression almost exclusively through formalist means. Both the linguistic raw material and the form of her Yiddish-language poems and prose montages in *Tog figurn*, *Manekinen*, and *Akatsyes blien* were Jewish: the sounds, words, and syntax of the Yiddish language and the lines, shapes and contours of the Hebrew letters in which they were printed. Their intellectual content and imagery, by contrast, are—in all but a few cases—intentionally emptied of markedly Jewish referent[36,37] Almost in a mirror image of Vogel's negotiation of language/form and content, in Schulz's textual experiments the written and spoken forms of the Slavic, "non-Jewish" language become a vessel-conduit, mask, or garment in which to clothe or animate a modernist continuation of the Jewish hermeneutic and exegetical tradition.

Schulz's Galician diasporic poetics placed him in a doubly marginalized position: that of a Jewish writer in the Polish language, decentered within both Polish and Jewish literary worlds. For Szymaniak, Debora Vogel can also be seen to have consciously chosen a form of "self-marginalization." Vogel's linguistic formation and also her earliest attempts at writing reflected the Zionist commitments of her acculturated Polish Jewish family—which included two of Galicia's most prominent and influential Zionist thinkers and activists: Dr. Markus Ehrenpreis and Dr. Dovid Maltz.[38] Explains Auerbach, at the time of their meeting in 1929, "Dvoyre had little if any relationship with Yiddish language or art. Her father, with whom she had an intimate, close spiritual bond, displayed at every opportunity a kind of aristocratic-maskilic contempt for the *folksprach*.[39] He had taught his daughter Hebrew. In the home they spoke Polish, mixed with German, and took care that the young generation should study Hebrew."[40]

Vogel had written a number of Zionist-themed stories in Polish in the early '20s, as a member of the Socialist Zionist youth group *Hashomer Hazair*, and her first experiments in avant-garde, "cubist" poetics were undertaken in German in the 1920s.[41] Given her upbringing, it might seem a natural choice for her to undertake her experiments in the context of modern Hebrew literature—particularly in the climate that followed the Lwów pogrom of 1918. Linguistically, it may also have been the easier path. Yet Vogel instead took two alternate and affirmatively diasporist routes simultaneously: she chose to enter into both Yiddish and Polish letters.

In the case of Yiddish, Rokhl Auerbach, by her own account, played a decisive role in Vogel's choice. Vogel and Auerbach had met one another while riding the tram to and from the University of Lwów, where both were attending the philosophy lectures of Professor Kazimierz Twardowski. "With time," writes Auerbach, "our collegial relationship grew into a close friendship that would have an influence on both of us, and especially on Dosia—and on the direction of her further development."[42] At Auerbach's urging, Vogel undertook the difficult project of turning herself into a Yiddish-language writer, though she had not grown up speaking or writing in Yiddish. Vogel herself wrote later in a letter to the Inzikhist poet A. Leyeles in New York, "I came to Yiddish literature from the outside, I did not grow up in it (earlier I wrote in German, later in Polish, but I published nothing or almost nothing of it, these were completely crazy experiments, and I felt that that form was ephemeral, temporary)."[43]

Auerbach recounts that even she was surprised by Vogel's tenacity and commitment to the Yiddishist project. "Up to today I find it almost impossible to understand exactly how and by what means I succeeded in recruiting this refined aesthetician to the idea that she should begin to read Yiddish literature, and switch to writing in Yiddish herself." Besides highlighting her personal influence on Vogel, Auerbach attributes Vogel's choice to "the strength of the formidable life-milieu, and of the open forums that we had at our disposal,—above all of the poor but dynamic younger literary community that had by that time crystallized in Lemberg."[44]

> Dvoyre Fogel had behind her years of belonging to the youth group "*Hashomer-Hazair*"—a portion of whose members left for *eretz yisroel* and another portion of whom became followers of Professor Juliusz Kleiner—studying the Polish language and literature. What writing she did was in Polish. Nevertheless, she began to become friends with the "Yiddishists," to write articles and reviews for literary columns that I edited for the weekly paper *Folk und Land*, published under the editorship of Dr. Nosen Meltzer. . . . She published her first verses in Yiddish in the literary column edited by Zalbe Tzwait and Ber Shnaper in "*New Morning*" ["*Naye Morgn*"]. She would write her things in Polish, and I would translate them into Yiddish.[45]

For Szymaniak, the poet's decision to write in Yiddish "signified the initiation of a new path as a writer"—the rejection of her earlier attempts at writing in a Zionist vein and the beginning of a "conscious construction of her own theory."[46] By the second half of the 1930s, Vogel's desire to find a way to incorporate a political component in her highly aestheticized project comes through in an interesting comment in one of her letters, again to Schulz. Describing to him a Yiddish literary event that she organized in Lwów, and at which she read her own work, she writes, "And yet that evening had a positive moment: if I was unsure at times whether I would manage to formulate a current political and social element (that was one of the difficult experiments)—I convinced myself during my strong, somewhat declamatory and emotional reading, that the thing worked. So perhaps that moment makes sense out of the whole event."[47]

Indeed, both Vogel's and Schulz's images reiterate a shared concern with the question of the individual refigured within early twentieth century industrialized society as moveable, moldable, and disposable component within a political, economic, and ideological system: as product, commodity, raw material, machine, and disposable trash. In a montage piece entitled "Military Parade" from the late 1930s, Vogel writes, "Out of the light and delicate blue, from the very heart of the first spring blueness—a row of soldiers and tanks. . . . And from across the grey asphalt and the dusty square-strips one can feel how the delicate and gentle grasses and the shining pink beetles are crushed and mixed with the dirty dust. . . . Men exist to die beneath tanks. . . . Women exist to give new life."[48]

"Can you imagine the pain, the dull imprisoned suffering, hewn into the matter of that dummy which does not know why it must be what it is, why it must remain in that forcibly imposed form which is no more than a parody?" Schulz's Jacob had asked in his "Tractate on Mannequins": "Do you understand the power of form, of expression, of pretense, the arbitrary tyranny imposed on a helpless block, and ruling it like its own, tyrannical soul?" (W, 35). But: "Figures in a waxworks panopticon," he began, "even Passion-play parodies of mannequins, must not be treated lightly. Matter never makes jokes: it is always full of the tragically serious" (W, 35).

The mannequin, or tailor's dummy, as it is alternately translated, occupies a central place in both artists' writing. During and after the period of the Sunday seminars, Vogel wrote the poems that would be published in her second volume of Yiddish poetry, *Manekinen* (1934). The verses in this volume, like cubist-linguistic still lifes, are peopled by individuals rendered in geometrical shapes and colored forms—"bendable blue ladies" and "stiff black glued-together gentlemen"—that move mechanically in the streets of a paper and canvas city. Display window dolls and mannequins, interchangeable with the pedestrians on the other side of the glass, wear "blue-colored eyes and precisely-drawn carmine lips."

Lalkes	DOLLS
A lange tzayt geshtanen iz zi Vi a halbacht in portzelay unter a milkikher shoyb FRIZUR-GESHEFT – BREYTE GAS – NUMER FUFTZN [...]	She's been standing for a long time like a half-nude in porcelain beneath a milky windowpane: COIFFURE BUSINESS— BROAD STREET— NUMBER FIFTEEN....
Mit halb-geefnt oygn hot geshmeykhlt dos portzelay glat un vaserdik vi farhidusht fun altzding vos pasirt af der velt fun der tzveyter, fun yener tzayt gloz.	The porcelain one smiled with half-opened eyes smooth and watery with astonishment at everything that passes through the world on the other side of that glass.
Un fun yener tzayt funem fentster shpatsirt hobn mit elastishkayt lalkes mit oygn zise mandlen lange un bavenleche hent un fis.	And on the other side of the window dolls walked lithely with eyes like sweet elongated almonds and moveable hands and feet.
Lalkes mit a hartz a baveglechs trogn oygn-aplen glezerne in tush-bremen un a shmeykhl in karmin marke kameleon un penimer fun portzelay vos shmeykhlt.	Dolls with moveable hearts wear glass pupils beneath inky eyebrows and a carmine-red smile Chameleon brand and faces of porcelain that smile.

This reverse gaze that effects an equivalence between mannequin and human, mannequin and woman—and discovers their shared status as embodiments of matter, trapped within those forms afforded them in a modern commercialized landscape, would continue to be reworked in Vogel's later montage experiments in *Acacias Are Blooming.*

"The girls sat motionless, with glazed eyes," writes Schulz in the story "Tractate on Mannequins:" "Their faces were long and stultified by listening, their cheeks flushed, and it would have been difficult to decide at that moment whether they belonged to the first or to the second Genesis of Creation" (W, 33). The "Tractate" is one of a mannequin series, that resulted from Schulz's letters to Vogel: "Mannequins," "Tractate on Mannequins, or the Second Book of Genesis," "Tractate on Mannequins—Continued," and "Tractate on Mannequins—Finale." Perhaps Schulz accepted a challenge—posed by Vogel or that he himself suggested—to posit himself as a fellow Demiurge, with the power to animate the mannequin and harness it to his own modernist experiments. The cycle takes shape around such a premise: "'The Demiurge,' said my father, 'has had no monopoly of creation, for creation is the privilege of all spirits. Matter has been given infinite fertility, inexhaustible vitality, and, at the same time, a seductive power of temptation which invites us to create as well. . . . In one word,' Father concluded, 'we wish to create man a second time—in the shape and semblance of a tailors' dummy'" (W, 31). Here a human-mannequin interchangeability is attached both to the tailor's assistants, Polda and Polina, who listen to Jacob's lectures on a Gnostic-inflected concept of a "second Demiurgy," and to the father himself—who is by turns an artist of prophetic ambitions and a victim himself, easily deprived of his humanity and agency: "My father took a step forward like an automaton, and fell to his knees" (W, 34). "He, the inspired Heresiarch, just emerging from the clouds of exaltation—suddenly collapsed and folded up. Or perhaps he had been exchanged for another man?" (W, 34).

In works that return again and again to the themes of matter and raw material, trapped and suffering, awaiting release, the quiet but strangely familiar life of objects and furniture, of mannequins, dolls, wax figures, *pałuby,* and tailor's dummies, both Schulz and Vogel weave their experiments in linguistic and aesthetic form and representation together with reflections on the trappedness of both matter and the individual in the modern world—as woman, as political pawn, or as Jew.

While it is true that Vogel largely avoids directly treating Jewish themes in her poems, in an interesting echo of the division within Schulz's work between the stories in *Sanatorium* and the Lilien article of the same period, she also used the essay form to address more directly her concerns about the specific experience of Jews in contemporary Poland and of golus-existence. In a 1936 article for *Przegląd Społeczny* (The Social Review) entitled "Human Exotics" ("Ludzkie egzotyki"), Vogel brought the theme of dehumanization and objectification to bear on the condition of Jews as a diasporic minority community, otherized and exoticized by members of the dominant culture, including those who have assimilated into that culture. Responding to a request that she write a review of Jerzy Giżycki's 1934 book on colonial Africa, *Whites and Blacks*, Vogel turned her essay instead into an impassioned plea for an ethics of pluralism within her own country: "After all, one doesn't have to seek out the dark continent of Africa: in the very heart of Europe researchers are discovering 'their'—'black continent.'" For Vogel, Giżycki's book warrants attention for its relevance to "current social realities. And here we must state that as a form of judgment and a protest it is . . . too gentle. It fails to adequately outline the sharp contours of the injustice that is taking place today in all the lands of Africa and Europe." But it is not entirely without effect, as "It stirs in us certain resonances, that require us to *speak about it*, to speak yet again of matters that political forces are trying so hard to silence—not only the politics of imperialism and acquisitiveness, but that other—who knows if not even more threatening kind: *the politics of our organism*, the mechanism of our very body and our soul. We must speak of the irrational sense of otherness that exists between human species."[49]

Vogel turns next to a critique of a series of reportage pieces written for the Warsaw-based *Wiadomości Literackie* by Wanda Meltzer, which for Vogel epitomize both the irrational human instinct to otherize, and the very rational urge of the publicist to capitalize on such instincts. In this series, entitled "*Czarny ląd*," or "The Black Continent," Meltzer describes in shocked and salacious language the life and conditions of Orthodox Jewish residents, of some of Warsaw's poorest and most desperate quarters. She attends a bris, and visits a kosher slaughterhouse and a cheder. Vogel, expressing outrage at what she perceives as the disingenuous and patronizing tone of "pity" the author uses in these reportage pieces, argues that the primary function of Meltzer's series of articles was to turn those she described into an exotic species: "It has come time for the latest new sensation: the time has come for the Jewish exotic! . . . There is no need to search the terrain of Africa in order to turn people into the exotic; into specimens incomprehensible in their mentality, in relation to which there arises a mixture of pity and scorn—*à propos* of which, is not pity a gentler form of scorn? . . . For this it is not necessary to search for Blacks. There are Jews."[50]

Vogel's discussion alternates between a critique of the otherization and racism to which unassimilated Polish Jews are subjected on the one hand and a reflection on the loneliness and sadness associated with assimilation on the other. Both of these experiences—being treated as the exotic Other and seeking acceptance through assimilation—are portrayed in her essay as involving forms of objectification, either externally or internally imposed on the body of the Jew. In the latter case, echoing the images presented in poems from *Mannequins* and *Acacias Are Blooming*, Vogel envisions assimilation as the individual's occupation of or entry into the reproducible social equivalent of the mannequin. Seeking in her article an allegory to convey this experience of assimilation as mannequinization, Vogel imagines a man at a series of social gatherings who gradually transforms himself into a reproduction of the "happy people" whom he feels he must try to be like and look like. Finally, after going through the motions long enough, he forgets that he had been any other way. The scene imagined here recalls a characteristic mood of melancholy in Vogel's verse that Schulz, in his review of *Acacias Are Blooming*, had described as the "tragic monotony of a world fundamentally finished and immovable."[51] Indeed, Vogel's essay on "Human Exotics," whether viewing the Jewish condition as determined from without or cultivated within, leaves little room for escape from the condition of the mannequin—a condition in which by turns respect, individuality, and authenticity remain perpetually elusive.

In the second half of her article, Vogel turns from a critique of Meltzer's portrayal of the conditions in Warsaw's Jewish quarter toward her own reflections on the experience of "golus-existence." With a degree of pathos that moves the article into the semi-literary realm, she attempts to consider the historical, psychological, and social factors that have created and preserved a very real sense of otherness and difference within the Jewish community, including among assimilated or acculturated Polish Jews. In her reflections on the diaspora experience—which she describes as "life in an eternally provisional state"—the themes of "external fate," determinism, alienation, and profound melancholy, which also run throughout her verse, come to characterize precisely the experience of Jewish otherness. She writes:

> On the plane of history and of the most recent reality, this phenomenon of Otherness can be explained in the following way: identical life conditions, in which the lives of entire generations have played themselves out, shape . . . certain ways of experiencing life—all the more so when they find fertile ground,

in the form of a disposition, acquired over many generations already, toward certain ways of experiencing and reacting. If we speak of identical "living conditions"—clearly this has to do not simply with the ghetto, but with thousands of social difficulties and anomalies of psychic life, all the snags and the inelegances of everyday life, into which a deterritorialized nation is forced, being always a tolerated (in the best case) minority. These anomalies at times take on a negative character, and at other times a positive one, from the perspective of refinement, and of a richly layered psychic life—they are anomalies tied to *life in an eternally provisional state*.[52]

Noticeable here are Vogel's defense of and positive evocation of unassimilated Jewish life, and in particular her multiple references to the enduring spirituality of Jewish communities and individuals in a context of "provisional" and diasporic existence. In another essay entitled *"Lwowska juderia"* from 1935 she had written: "In this world of bastardized streets and their attempts at emancipation, at assimilation, we long for the ghetto. It pulls us back." The tone of both respect and regret in the article is similar to that used by Schulz in his Lilien essay, and indicates an additional zone of overlap in the two writers' developing diasporic ethos. Vogel continues:

> It is precisely this external fate that binds a certain group of people into a closely-knit whole, despite far-reaching differences in type, character and beliefs. . . . The psychic structure grows to the scale of a factor decisive of external fate, to a kind of life *fatum*.
>
> This does not mean that such a collective of people does not also produce views and worldviews entirely similar and of equal magnitude to those the "others" create; but it means that they will forever be marked by the stamp of that *fatum;* that undefined quality that tells this group to differentiate itself from all others. . . . And if that stamp is perhaps the weight of sadness—then it colors even the most monumental and heroic, optimistic and constructive of worldviews. And this will be precisely "that melody, defiant and sad, that rises up and lingers above their heads, like a string of curses"—about which they—those others—had spoken.[53]

Vogel had written *"Lwowska juderia"* ("Lwów's Jewish Ghetto") as an entry in the *Almanac and Lexicon of Polish Jews*. Her entry included a description of her great-grandfather Nosn (Nysała) Suss, which is characterized by a similar nostalgic tone:

> He was called the *Silken Jew*. It was said that this secularly educated kabbalist, author of tractates, and publisher . . . was forever surrounded by an atmosphere of quiet celebration. Even on weekdays he wore a velvet caftan and a round sable hat—perhaps an expression of that celebratory light that shone within him? And behind him there stood an entire generation and a way of

life, in which the fullness-of-life and the sweetness contained in the individual would permeate the narrow everydayness of streets and experiences. This was life spent, as it were, wrapped within a velvet cloak, utterly undisturbed by the fact that the boundaries of the ghetto, where that Jewish world ended, were so nearby.[54]

As different as were their poetic and essayistic strategies formally, both artists' modernist experiments sought to disengage the discourse and imagery of Galicia from the nexus of negative associations that surrounded the terms *Ost-juden*, *ghetto*, and *golus*, and to reattach them to a distinctly modern Galician Jewish imaginary, based on their own lived experiences in a Galician context where traditional and secular Jewish life shared the same urban spaces—and where an unbroken chain connected their work as modern artists to the lives of their parents and grandparents, and to members of the Jewish community who were subject, with them, to the vicissitudes of history. Many of Schulz's graphic works portray Hasidim or religious Jews in the streets of a town—his Drohobycz, yet projected into an undefined time of the Bible. Reflecting again the contrast between the two artists' approaches, these images are a direct translation of the strategy of mythologization into the medium of the graphic arts. In one series, that may have been prepared as illustrations to accompany the unfinished novel *Messiah*, Jewish men dressed in robes are seated at a long table set out in a street or square, awaiting the arrival of the Messiah. Interestingly, while Schulz was willing to openly criticize traditional religious education and cultural self-ghettoization in his nonfiction essay on Lilien, he did not introduce such critique or imagery into his artistic works, as if intentionally taking care to ensure, like Vogel, that his literature did not contribute to narratives disparaging of Jewish life in Eastern Europe. One element of Vogel and Schulz's mutual and affirmative diasporist projects entailed a polemic with negative and incomplete portrayals of Galician Jewish life common within Western Jewish narratives. They sought instead to challenge Western stereotypes with new representations of the Galician cityscape and landscape that belied familiar and stereotypical portrayals of Jewish *golus-existenz*, both positive and negative.

Un-Spun Threads

As Auerbach writes, "the 'match' between Bruno Schulz and Debora Vogel was not to take place."[55] Vogel's mother strongly disapproved of her union with Schulz, whom she believed was, in Auerbach's words, "not a fitting candidate as a husband and the father of a family," in part, no doubt, due to his family's financial situation. Vogel, whom her friends describe as having been acutely resigned and accepting of her fate, and prone to depression, capitulated to her mother's wishes. In 1932, following her father's death and only two years after she had met Schulz, she entered into an arranged marriage with the wealthy Lemberg architect and engineer Szulim Barenblüth, and in 1933 she gave birth to a son, Antshel. She continued to live in Lwów and to write poems and critical essays for Yiddish journals in Poland and New York, and for Polish-language newspapers and periodicals, but complained to her friends of the difficulty of finding any possibility to devote herself to her work as she would like.

Following the failure of their marriage plans, Schulz too entered an increasingly difficult period of his life. In 1935, he became engaged to Józefina Szelińska, and would remain engaged until 1937.[56] This marriage also did not take place: Szelińska's family had converted to Protestantism, and according to the state and regional laws in force in interwar Poland, the two were not legally able to marry unless Schulz should agree to convert as well. He was not willing to do so, even on a purely bureaucratic or symbolic basis, to make their marriage possible. As is often discussed in scholarship on Schulz's relationship to Jewish subject matter, he did go so far as to publicly withdraw his official registration in the Drohobycz Jewish community, but he expressed in a letter to Romana Halpern that he was not willing to do more than that, even if it meant the failure of their plans for marriage.[57] This somewhat complex attempt to negotiate the harried legal terrain of Interwar Poland speaks to Schulz's affirmatively Jewish self-identification.

In the late 1930s, after several years of less regular communication, Schulz and Vogel reestablished close contact that evolved into an intimate correspondence once again. The details of this reunion are preserved in a remarkable set of letters, from Vogel to Schulz, that was recovered from the attic of Schulz's former home at 10 Floriańska Street by M. Schreyer, a former student of Schulz's at the Drohobycz gymnasium.[58] These are the only five letters that remain out of dozens or possibly hundreds that were lost before, during, and after the war, and that undoubtedly contained much reflection on the specific questions, challenges, and choices that faced the two artists as Jews in independent Poland. As it is, the five letters from 1938 that survived are fascinating for their focus on the artists' private relationship; for the vocabulary that appears in them, echoing tropes and imagery familiar from Schulz's narratives; and for the regrets and frustrations that they reveal, on both sides, at the failure of their plans for marriage. In one letter from 1938, Vogel responds to Schulz, who appears to have written to her to reopen the question of their marriage, and the reasons for its failure. She reflects on whether she may have treated Schulz's original proposal of marriage "as poetry rather than as a literal proposal" because "I didn't believe that you truly know how to desire life and happiness." Instead, she argues, "you continually transpose that longing into a purified, sublime experience, and with this you somehow placate yourself, with that poetry of life, with that extract of the sublime, not wanting and not knowing how to taste of its rough and grey raw material, full of boredom and difficulty. Probably this is how I felt."[59] For his part, Schulz saw Vogel as the one wrapped in a theoretical and philosophical armor that separated her from the fullness of "reality." In his at times emotionally inflected, pointed review of Vogel's Polish-language volume *Acacias Are Blooming*, he wrote, "The author does not have a talent for realism; acquiring material for the exemplification of her theses represents an insurmountable challenge for her, but precisely this difficulty, this resistance, this noble abstinence and inability to assimilate content from the outside—guarantees the purity of her vision."[60]

It is possible in Vogel's late letters to discern strong echoes of the Sunday seminars—the shared experiment, conversation, and duet that had been so formative for both artists eight years earlier. Writes Vogel, in connection with Schulz's planned trip to Paris, on which she is interested to try to join him, "I am enormously curious for the artistic results of this journey, for conversations about certain streets and pictures, that perhaps will even allow both of us to crystallize our attitudes, differing or alike."[61] The letters reveal that Vogel hoped the two might revive their mutually productive discussions and inspire each other to literary exegesis of the urban landscape once again. In a letter of November 1938, she writes about "yesterday, which I was so happy about, wanting through it to revive and initiate a new series of our Sundays of long ago." "After all," she continues, "our conversations of long ago, and our contact, were one of those few miraculous things that happen once in one's life, and maybe even once in a few or a few tens of hopeless, colorless lives."[62]

Vogel's letters also directly address the question of the writers' shared vocabulary of tropes, the thematic similarities between their works that resulted from their productive encounter, and the reaction this similarity elicited among critics and friends. "Maybe it is that all those voices about our similarity have done their work and we don't want to bare ourselves too completely before one another?" she writes, reflecting on her disappointment about the awkwardness of their first meeting (the first of their renewed contact), which took place at a friend's house: "How sad is this stinginess, and how unproductive. How much evil is caused by human stupidity, and how sad, that precisely it has so much power even over the most basic need and the deepest longing in man."[63]

Schulz himself had referred to the issue of critics' reception two years earlier, in his review of Vogel's *Acacias Are Blooming*. Here he emphasized precisely the distinctness of the sources and of the respective worldviews that informed and gave rise to his and to Vogel's work, respectively: "A number readers and even reviewers have discovered in this book a certain analogy to *Cinnamon Shops*. This observation does not reveal a penetrating insight. In essence this book (*Acacias*) is the result of an entirely other and original worldview."[64] For Vogel scholar Annette Werberger, this particular comment by Schulz serves as evidence that Schulz "categorically rules out intertextuality with the texts of Debora Vogel."[65] His comment, as she argues, while posing as a defense of Vogel's originality, in fact reveals Schulz's desire to publicly preserve an impression of his own autonomy and originality, and to downplay the possible view that his own work represents an intellectual response to Vogel's. She cites, effectively, the gendered and sexist structure of Schulz's own story "Tractate on Mannequins," in which "the narrator's father delivers lectures *to* three women (to the seamstresses: Polda and Paulina, and the house maid Adela) about (masculine) creation and formation of matter."[66] In support of Werberger's perspective, I would note that while the graphics in Schulz's "Encounter" series (see chap. 6) often portray two men in traditional Jewish dress, in conversation in the streets of the city, his most formative experience of two scholars "reading" and discussing as they walk through the city streets was the one he shared with Vogel. Yet the image of a man and woman mutually absorbed in discussion does not appear in his surviving graphic work, even after their meeting. While female figures are central to Schulz's graphic reflections on the "Encounter," they are portrayed as objects of the male gaze, and even as material, or form, available to male interpretation. Similarly in the story "Spring," while the protagonist Joseph approaches Bianca as a supplicant and reads his work to her, submitting himself to her judgment, Schulz's landscapes do not contain the image of a man and woman engaged as mutual partners and equals in the exegetical process. Werberger's line of argument opens Schulz's work to interpretation as a striking failure to overcome the gendered and sexist semiotics of his time, even as Vogel's work in this area was groundbreaking.

Metaphoric Style vs. Concrete Style

Though the Sunday seminars remained unrepresented in Schulz's literary and graphic landscapes, their content is present throughout both writers' work up until the Second World War. Schulz's 1936 review of *Acacias Are Blooming* is but one example of a series of essays published between 1934 and '38 that offer reprisals of, and reformulations of, the contrasting positions taken by Vogel and Schulz in their initial debates of 1930–31. In these essays, both writers associate qualities characteristic of Schulz's poetics with traditional or outdated approaches to representation, as contrasted with the new, experimental forms that Vogel introduces in her works.

In her 1931 essay "White Words in Poetry,"[67] Vogel presents a contrast between the outdated "metaphoric style" and a new "concrete style" that she will introduce. She also refers to this as a distinction between "dynamic lyricism" and "static lyricism" or a "poetics of cool stasis." Her approach presumes a Hegelian conception of artistic development, in which one artistic form and one ethos reacts against and supersedes those before it, allowing art to give expression and form to changing social and economic relations. Situating artistic periods and movements along a historical line of development, she argues that over time, all forms of representation cease to be effective artistic tools and must be abandoned: "used up and outdated categories" become comic clichés that must be discarded and superseded. "There are two ways to overcome the used-upness of words," argues Vogel. "The first—is metaphor:" the writer in the "metaphoric style" may strive to expand the palette of metaphor and allusion they employ: "In particular those types of representation that belong to seemingly foreign, distant material . . . can intensify the contents of things."[68] But "this kind of baroque, naturalistic-ornamental style is a misguided, impatient attempt to conquer the boredom of one epithet with an ever greater number of epithets." Such a piling of new associations on top of earlier ones "is like adding additional decoration to an old dress."[69]

The second way to overcome the banality of "used-up and abstract expressions"—each of which represents "a condensation of many distinct individual qualities of things, experiences and gestures"—drives in the opposite direction: "rather than through concepts, or their association in metaphor, such a poetry will function through the use of a few concrete things and gestures."⁷⁰ If "concepts are an accompaniment to things, an accompaniment attached to the facticity of life," the concrete style strives for a reverse movement from concepts to things, constructing a poetic space that foregrounds that facticity. Its textual landscapes translate into words common materials, shapes and also mundane experiences—both of the urban landscape, and often of women's daily lives and labors within that landscape. "These seemingly accessory, marginal moments are the only real (factual) expression of the unformed mass of life." That unformed mass "takes concrete form only in them, and not in the abstract bodies of concepts."⁷¹

In this formulation, Schulz's poetics would be seen to double down on the metaphorical style that has for Vogel run its course. His poetic prose employs precisely a baroque agglomeration of metaphor and mythical allusion, marking itself as a linguistic equivalent of the uncontrollable fertility of an untended garden. "August," the first story in *Cinnamon Shops*, by illustration, opens with the character of Adela returning from the market "like Pomona emerging from the flames of day, spilling from her basket the colourful beauty of the sun—the shiny pink cherries full of juice under their transparent skins, the mysterious black morellos that smelled so much better than they tasted; apricots in whose golden pulp lay the core of long afternoons" (W, 3; O, 7). In the characteristic reflex of his metaphoric style, rich with allusion to the poetry of Rainer Maria Rilke, the text moves through this sensuous and tactile image into increasingly mythical and "conceptual" realms of association:

> And next to that pure poetry of fruit, she unloaded sides of meat with their keyboard of ribs swollen with energy and strength, and seaweeds of vegetables like dead octopuses and squids—the raw material of meals with a yet undefined taste, the vegetative and terrestrial ingredients (*telluryczne ingrediencje*) of dinner, exuding a wild and rustic smell. (W, 3; O, 7)
>
> The dark first floor apartment of the house in Market Square was shot through each day by the naked heat of summer: the silence of the shimmering streaks of air, the squares of brightness dreaming their intense dreams on the floor; the sound of a barrel-organ rising from the deepest golden vein of day; two or three bars of a chorus, played on a distant piano over and over again, melting in the sun on the white pavement, lost in the fire of high noon. (W, 3; O, 6) . . .
>
> A bunch of ragamuffins [*kupka obdartusów*], sheltering in a corner of the square from the flaming broom of the heat, beleaguered a piece of wall, throwing buttons and coins at it over and over again, as if wishing to read in

the horoscope of those metal discs the real secret written in the hieroglyphics of cracks and scratched lines. Apart from them, the square was deserted. One expected that, any minute, the Samaritan's donkey, led by the bridle, would ride up in the shade of the quivering acacias and stop in front of the wine-merchant's vaulted doorway and that two servants would carefully ease a sick man from the red-hot saddle and carry him slowly up the cool stairs to the floor above, already redolent of the Sabbath. (W, 3–4; O, 5)

The decadent, "frenetic dynamism" to which Vogel opposes her poetics of "cool stasis" is heightened by Schulz's attention to the onomotopaeic potential of his word choice:

> A tangled thicket of grasses, weeds and thistles crackled in the fire of the afternoon. The sleeping garden was resonant with flies. The golden field of stubble shouted in the sun like a tawny cloud of locusts; in the thick rain of fire the crickets screamed [*w rzęsistym deszczu ognia wrzeszczą świerszcze*]; seed pods exploded softly like grasshoppers.... The air over that midden, wild with the heat, cut through by the lightning of shiny horseflies, driven mad by the sun, crackled, as if filled with invisible rattles, exciting one to frenzy (W, 6) [*Powietrze nad tym rumowiskiem, zdziciałe od żaru, cięte błyskawicami lśniących much końskich, rozświecionych słońcem, trzeszczało jak od nie widzianych grzechotek, podniecając do szału*]. (O, 7)

Vogel associates such baroque, frenetic, or anxiously productive metaphorical activity within painting and literature as a sign of the death throes of a given aesthetic. "Such a style appears in moments of transformation, and is an expression of an uneasy dynamism." In relation to Schulz, her critique would suggest the view that his style represents a holdover, the late excrescence of an earlier period. Perhaps with a bit of wink, Schulz stated as much himself, in his later Lilien essay.[72]

For his part, Schulz, in his 1936 review of the Polish-language version of *Akatsyes blien, Akacje kwitną (Acacias Are Blooming)*, offers a repartee: his own elaboration of the conscious contrast between his and Vogel's aesthetic worldviews. "Within the traditional novel," he writes, "a distinction is always preserved between two parts of a double logic: the autonomous logic of realistic material, and the logic of deeper meaning—the superstructure of the author's creation."

> The peculiar mental game that produces the charm of this genre of writing depends on the subtle movement from one to the other, on their consonance, and on the process of their becoming intertwined, and being teased apart. The particular originality of Debora Vogel's book, and what disorients the reader, pulling the ground out, as it were, from beneath his legs—is its total break with this agreed-upon form, with this basic principle of the traditional novel.[73]

The basic principle that Schulz attributes here to the "traditional novel" is its ability to distill the totality of a human life into a select number of "thought-figures"—a strategy central to his own writing. "It is often said of the novel that the author is able to capture within it 'an entire life,' he writes, " a 'sliver of life,' an entire 'human fate from birth to death.' In fact, it contains but a few or a few tens of exemplary episodes; a certain number of realistic shortcuts tied to one another by lines of so-called meaning, idea, or a point; or simply selected and grouped in such a way as to enclose within themselves a certain 'thought figure.'"[74]

For Schulz, differently than for Vogel, what is most real lies in the individual human experience, and the thought-figure is an attempt to extract and preserve that concreteness. Vogel's materialist and also democratizing proposal instead uses poetic language to record experiences that are common, representative of the historical moment and social condition. In Schulz's tendentious language, which rings as in invitation to continue the debate: "The author has neither feeling nor respect for individual experiences, for individual fates and characters. . . . She does not experience these states in the direct form of individual experiences in the entirety of their individual concreteness, but gives voice to them only when they pass through a thousand hearts, when they lose their color, become impersonal and exemplary, when they become a kind of circulating streetlamp, an anonymous formula, hackneyed and banal."[75] As Vogel would argue however, these "formulaic" (*szablonowy*) images and pieces contribute to the construction of a new "legend of the age," which is a legend of mass production and consumption. Further, and here Vogel would also agree with Schulz's assessment, this legend contains a democratizing gesture: its meanings and its story are not reserved, as are Schulz's, for a special category of "true reader," but should, at least in theory, tell a story common to the masses.[76] As Schulz frames this difference: "The author recognizes them and accepts them only on the level on which they become the property of everyone, the passerby in the street, shop girls and the barboy. Their reality is in a sense tested when they allow themselves to become a text set to the music of the street song."[77]

In another 1936 article for *The Social Review* (*Przegląd Społeczny*), Vogel explained her own commitment to trying to find a form of representation that would speak to and be relevant to the experience of the proletariat and the common man and woman, whose historical moment, as she saw it, was now. Interestingly, like Schulz's later article on Lilien, her essay reads as an apologia for the chasm that separates the artist from the masses. "In this brief essay," she writes, "my concern is to justify a certain type of feeling, characteristic of the intelligentsia.... This rehabilitation seems all the more urgent, to the extent that the intelligentsia today is losing faith in itself and increasingly attempting to merge with the proletariat."[78] Her essay, she explains, is a call for "equal rights" for the activities of the intelligentsia and poet in a time of historical materialism, an age that belongs to the proletariat. As the present age is the age of production, the artist must also be understood as a part of history—in this case, a contributor to the process of production—by helping to formulate its "legend," and in this way the artist is similar to a worker. "That raw material with which the intelligentsia deals: namely, the raw material of thought and feeling" is in fact "analogical to the literal raw material with which the proletariat deals."

> The symbol of such an experience could be the affirmation that this "longing for the full roundness and sweetness of rectangular things," for the elasticity of metal, for the coolness and quiet of glass—can become a stimulant of revolution—even as the experience of unemployment can for the proletariat. Both groups meet on the platform of the legend of production and of the processing of raw materials (literal and "psychic raw materials") into things contained within hard, geometrical, definable contours, and things contained within systems of form and concept.... Precisely this need for constructiveness in life ... and concreteness is the hidden spring that compels the intelligentsia to resist and to join forces with that class that, through its life, is bringing to fruition the legend of the age. The intelligentsia for its part is the one that describes, prepares and defends that legend.[79]

For this reason, the work of the intellectual and poet should be assigned "equal and parallel value" to the work of production that the proletariat does. Specifically, it should be treated as a form of "otherness" that is fully and equally legitimate, *to the extent that* it recognizes and speaks to the needs of the present: "The real legitimation for the belonging of the writer is the degree to which he has managed to grasp the needs of contemporary times and to understand the new social and individual reality."[80]

> This should in no way suggest a lessening of the historical valor of the proletarian class. Quite the contrary: the very recognition of the creative valor of the intelligentsia, to the extent that it moves along a line analogical to that of the proletariat—serves to underline the significance of the latter, and to underline clearly the position of the intellectual (*inteligent*) who advances such an argument.
> ... This is not a question of "injustice," of a concept that is abstract and incomprehensible from the point of view of history; it has to do with something

far more important and brutal: the inevitability and the rationality of the historical dialectic, that decides without . . . the emotional element. From this point of view the proletariat is today the class with a historical future.[81]

Interesting in Vogel's mix of avant-garde aestheticism and Marxist determinism is that her essay on the task of the intelligentsia, like her essay on racism against Jews or "Human Exotics," becomes a next argument against assimilation. The intellectual should not seek to "assimilate" into the proletariat, but should maintain their "otherness" within a context of "multiplicity" (*wielość*) and "simultaneity."[82] Intellectual diversity—within limits—is presented as her correction to doctrinal Marxism, in which the bourgeois, experimental, or avant-garde poet could quickly be put in the place of the exotic other, rather than—or as—the Jew.

In one of her final letters to Schulz of 1938, Vogel restated the central argument of both essays: "*Potrzebujemy wielość*"—we need multiplicity. Generationally, we may situate Vogel's concerted attempt to develop a discourse of otherness and multiplicity in these essays between the political thought of Polish linguist and public intellectual Jan Baudouin de Courtenay (1845–1929), a vocal advocate of the rights of national and ethnic minorities in Poland in the early twentieth century, sharp critic of the nation-state paradigm, and a nominee of the minorities bloc in Poland's first Presidential elections, and Hannah Arendt's post-war reflections on pluralism—"the paradoxical plurality of unique beings"—as the defining characteristic of the human condition.[83] In an essay on "The Jewish Question and the Polish State," Baudouin had mounted a spirited and elegant argument, not on behalf of acceptance of Jews on the basis of their future assimilation or acculturation into Polish society, but on behalf of a radically anti-nationalist program of pluralism ("*wielość*"), that called for coexistence and tolerance of a diversity of ethnicities *and languages* within a civic political structure.[84] In the same spirit, together and in tandem, both Vogel and Schulz developed affirmatively diasporist discourses of otherness and multiplicity born of their experience in Habsburg Kakania. Schulz reiterates this commitment consistently in his descriptions of art as originating in or drawing on a shared mythological fund, an originary matrix or humus containing in composted form the myths and stories of all cultures and religions. In Vogel's work, the conviction that cultural and ethnic multiplicity and diversity represent a core societal value is stated quite directly. In the conclusion to her "Human Exotics" paper for *Przegląd Społeczny*, she wrote that the goal for Jews and for other racial and cultural minorities should not be assimilation. It should be, instead, to continue to advocate for a public culture in which diversity and difference are recognized and nurtured. She used her essay to argue that the irrational element of human psychology that predisposes individuals and communities to recoil from "difference and otherness," "that impersonal figure of antipathy, directed at collectives, whether of family, nation, political party, class, or literary or artistic grouping," must be recognized and discussed rationally, so that those operating "within the world of rationalized convictions and views" can "create a common front." Reiterating Baudouin de Courtenay's image of the civic ethos that must underlay a reborn democratic Poland, and attaching to it the language of aesthetics, Vogel proposes that through this rational approach, "life in its entirety can be recognized and affirmed as the aesthetic principle of the diversity and multiplicity of the forms of life."[85]

For all four thinkers, Baudouin, Vogel, Schulz, and Arendt, this search for a vocabulary and discourse of pluralism was influenced by the lived experience of or scholarly attention to the multilingual, multiethnic fabric of the former Habsburg Empire, and by outrage at the disastrous experiment, as Arendt would call it in *The Origins of Totalitarianism*, that sought to divide that fabric along ethno-national lines following World War I.[86]

"Is Modernism an Immobile and Petrified Movement?"

Together with the increasing virulence of nationalist rhetoric and antisemitic policy to which citizens both Jewish and non-Jewish were witness in the new Polish state, many modernist writers displayed progressively greater political engagement in their writing over time. Vogel wrote in a letter to A. Leyeles of 1937, "Is 'modernism' an immobile and petrified movement? Do we not notice how it is transforming before our very eyes, in our work; how it is achieving social elements and relevance? We are all consciously and unconsciously agents of the Hegelian dialectic." Though an increasing politicization and shift in tone is present in the work of both Vogel and Schulz, in the latter's work it was universalized and concealed through the author's own strategies of linguistic "multiplicity," and thus less visible to his readers. If the author took accusations of depravity and perversion from some on the Polish right, he was not immune to charges of irresponsible bourgeois nonengagement from the left. In 1936, Kruczkowski, a member of the editorial team of Lwów's left-intellectual cultural journal *Sygnały*, to which both

Schulz and Vogel were contributors, mounted a lengthy and spirited defense of Schulz's writing. He cites an article by Anatol Mikulka that took aim at poets whose writing is "fascistically lyrical": "filled with 'melancholia, exoticism, star-gazing or humanitarianism.'" For Mikulka and other representatives of the leftist literary "police," such "exoticism . . . turns the attention of the reader away from the problems of the moment and carries his emotion on the paths of authorial fantasy—these elements of the verse are enemies of socialism. They are only a hindrance on the path of struggle for a future social order."[87] Kruczkowski summarizes the problem: "If an author is passionate about the secret inside lining of the forest (Leśmian), this has been considered a conscious turning away from essential problems of society. If he is a religious mystic—he has been met with even harsher critique." But "the work of Bruno Schulz, Rogowski or Leśmian contributes more to the victory of the idea of social progress than does the 'revolutionary' verse of Lec. . . . the works of these poets are superb manifestations of talent, revolutionary salvoes—that the proletariat cannot read."[88] For Kruczkowski, this is an opportunity to defend Schulz in particular. The author's mythicized poetics, Kruczkowski argues, should be understood as a spiritual complement to, and not an impediment to, the socialist project. "These are honest people. They are capable of being stirred poetically, for whole pages of a book, by the sweltering July day of a small-town afternoon. . . . Poets inhabit a plane of different problems and issues than critics and sociologists do. . . . I will never believe," he writes, "that the prose of Bruno Schulz or the verse of Rogowski were written with the intention to slow down the victory of that idea whose fulfillment will guarantee the fullest and most universal flowering of culture." Moreover, argues Kruczkowski, leftist critics who brandish the phrase "'the most important problems of our age' . . . have caused as much sympathy for the enemies of socialism as the agitation of National Democrats has caused Jews to turn to Zionism."[89]

Interestingly, it is also in the same period as this defense that Schulz's newer work does begin more directly to engage the political realities and concerns of his community. The stories *Republic of Dreams* (*Republika Marzeń*), *Fatherland* (*Ojczyzna*), and the German-language *Homecoming* (*Heimkehr*), and Schulz's 1937 essay on Lilien all enter solidly into the discourses of homeland, exile, return, and the relationship between art and diaspora-existence. The 1937 Lilien essay is the most direct example of this new willingness to engage present-day concerns, albeit with the author's requisite gesture of distancing or displacement—in this case achieved through the textual alibi of the critic and art historian. In chapter four to follow, I explore more closely the emergence of these themes in the stories from Schulz's second collection, *Sanatorium Under the Sign of the Hourglass*, and in his final text (known to date), *Ojczyzna* (*Fatherland*). It bears mentioning that such shifts in the degree and specific orientation of political engagement represented a key characteristic of the environment in which Jewish modernism took shape in Poland: its dynamism and fluidity. If Schulz's alignments, attitudes, and relationship with Jewish questions in interwar Poland were in flux, so were those of a majority of Jewish writers and artists in this period. Nathan Birnbaum, one of the most influential representatives of the modern Jewish Renaissance Movement in Galicia, was by turns a founding Galician Zionist, a proponent of Jewish cultural renaissance in the German language, a Yiddishist and founder of the Czernowitz conference, and a leading activist for Diaspora Nationalism. It is unnecessary to read Schulz's work as containing portents of the specific events that would befall his community, in order to recognize within it a dramatic shift, that is recorded and explored repeatedly on the pages of the work that Schulz published in the second half of the 1930s. The themes of idealistic and irretrievably lost childhood dreams, of literary spaces of refuge, escape, and fraternity, and also of resignation from overly utopian aspirations are present in Schulz's work, as they were in work by so many Jewish writers in this period. Few primary sources exist that tell us how Schulz himself experienced this shifting climate. In a 1938 letter to his close friend Romana Halpern, Schulz expressed his fears directly, writing that "as the currents flowing in our country become law," he wondered if he could be fired from his teaching position.[90] Edmund Löwenthal, a close friend of Schulz's nephew Zygmunt Hoffman, who lived for a time with Schulz, commented at length in memoirs written for Schulz's biographer Jerzy Ficowski on the limitations that the atmosphere of the '30s placed on Schulz's professional options in Drohobycz, and on the tremendous stress that such an environment put on Schulz personally. How accurately Löwenthal's perception reflects Schulz's own feelings, we cannot know; but his memoirs are one of the few accounts available that attempt to directly address Schulz's experience as an acculturated Jew in Drohobycz, offered by an individual who both lived in Drohobycz and knew Schulz intimately. Löwenthal chose to portray and to contextualize Schulz's experience and attitudes in the following way:

[He] made a decision to ignore antisemitism; to not notice it, to treat it as a kind of social unpleasantness. But that attitude was a pose—a poorly functioning defensive layer. Difficulties in keeping his position, resistance on the matter from the side of the local "defenders of Polishness," . . . these were painful and could not go unnoticed. And besides that—the encounters with other faculty members! There were a few downright pathological types, some hardline clerics. . . . They constantly threatened not to renew his contract; to set new conditions. The attitude he had adopted in fact only worked for him in his relations with a few representatives of the cultural elite."[91]

The sense of urgency surrounding antisemitism is very much in evidence on the pages of *Sygnały*, the organ of the liberal cultural elite to which both Schulz and Vogel contributed—as is the mood of resignation to an inescapable if unknown fate. In an issue from March 1936, Debora Vogel was invited to contribute an essay introducing trends in Yiddish poetry, and to curate a column of Yiddish poems in translation to Polish. Her selection, which included poems by H. Leivick and Aaron Zeitlin, is telling, and illustrative of the climate in which both she and Schulz were writing in the mid-1930s. "Whom should we blame, that we are perishing?" asks the lyric persona in Zeitlin's 1933 poem "Four Strophes," "that we can make nothing of our lives?" The speaker jumps forward: "Hundreds of years from now, there will again be an eye, that / drinks in the sun, and children will laugh . . . / And once again there will be hands; hands that give, instead of / Hands that raise bayonets / And there will come / Bucolic poets—unlike today's—great / in their no-longer-remembering. . . ."; but the present generation will not know this world. "Gases will choke us. We will lie beneath the ashes / . . . A young rain will wash the old earth / And objects will speak with new languages / And God will lean down toward the earth, and children will laugh. . . ."[92]

The same issue of *Sygnały* carried an essay entitled "The Jewish Question in Poland," by Stanisława Blumenfeldowa, a member of the journal's editorial staff, that is useful in conveying a sense of the discursive turn that was taking place among acculturated Jewish intellectuals in the 1930s. In her conclusion Blumenfeldowa offered a formulation that today's reader may find difficult to parse, but that was already a part of the discourse of the time: "Can one be surprised that . . . Polish society, realizing how fantastically complicated the whole matter is, has chosen the easiest and the simplest road: antisemitism and extermination, softened by a certain goodheartedness, disorder and lack of system?"[93] Qualifying her statement a moment later, the author adds "I don't know if my reflections needed to reach such drastic eschatological conclusions, as they are just coming to their most important purpose and main question . . . that of the creation of well-thought legal norms that, taking into consideration the Polish majority, would allow Jewish life to continue for some decades to come." Blumenfeldowa's reflections in *Sygnały* were written in 1936—and by this time such eschatological language was already common in Poland. The extent of the rising sense of crisis and helplessness within Polish Jewish communities in the 1930s has been compellingly documented in Kenneth Moss's 2021 *An Unchosen People: Jewish Political Reckoning in Interwar Poland*. This study, which allows for reevaluation of the environment in which Polish modernist literature was being created, excavates new material from the exact period of Schulz and Vogel's literary productivity—to reveal "thinking framed by a sense of danger and emergency, the painful limits of Jewish agency, a sharpening sense of the risks of Diaspora minorityhood, vernacular renegotiations of Zionism, and a creeping sense that the only practical politics available might be a politics of helping oneself."[94]

In Schulz's stories, elements reflective of this developing discourse include his young narrator's reflections on the possibility of re-creating or regaining the "Wondrous Era" now lost—the imaginative state of childhood with its "messianic promise;" a growing mood of resignation from plans for a Republic of Letters that transcends borders, present in his expression of defeat and surrender at the closing of the novella *Spring*; skepticism surrounding the meaning that emigration holds for Jewish artistic and spiritual continuity ("Fatherland"); and a nod to his inspiration Franz Kafka, in his reaffirmation of golus both as a permanent condition, and also as the treasured source of his particular artistic vision.

4

SANATORIUM UNDER THE SIGN OF THE HOURGLASS

Reading Schulz with Kafka, Manger, and Ahad Ha'am

How may a familiarity with Schulz's perspectives on Jewish renaissance in the Lilien essay, and a sense of how he positioned himself within cultural and political debates surrounding the Jewish Question, reopen his stories to new readings? How might attention to these contexts help one to read Schulz's stories as a conscious engagement with the challenges that faced Jewish artists in interwar Poland? Or as an attempt to develop a poetics that could give adequate expression to his specific Galician context of Jewish cultural renaissance in the diaspora?

Schulz's second volume of short stories, *Sanatorium under the Sign of the Hourglass*, was being prepared for publication in 1936. It would be a year of incredible productivity for Schulz. In 1936, he received a long-awaited six-month sabbatical from his teaching responsibilities in Drohobycz, much of which he spent in Warsaw, where he could turn his attention to writing and also join his fiancée, Józefina Szelińska, who had moved there to live and work.[1] Together with her, he also made efforts during this period to deepen ties with the Warsaw literary world. Between January and June of 1936, Schulz wrote numerous book reviews and nonfiction essays for *Wiadomości Literackie, Tygodnik Illustrowany, Pion, Studio* ("The Mythologizing of Reality" and an exchange of letters with Witold Gombrowicz) and *Nasza Opinia* (Lwów—a review of Debora Vogel's work). He also advised Szelińska on the translation of Kafka's *The Trial*, which the two agreed would be published by the Rój publishing house under Schulz's name and with an afterword written by him.[2] He prepared his collection *Sanatorium under the Sign of the Hourglass* for publication, in an edition that this time he ensured would include his own illustrations. His work was in demand, and before this second volume came out in 1937, he published six of the individual stories from the collection across a wide range of periodicals and began regularly to contribute book reiews to *Wiadomości Literackie*. Two of these—"Tragic Freedom," on Kazimierz Wierzyński's volume of verse by the same title, and a review of *At the Belvedere* (*Pod Belwederem*) by Julian Kaden-Bandrowski, became an opportunity for Schulz to continue his reflections, begun in the 1935 essay "Legends Arise" ("*Powstają legendy*"), on the death of Józef Piłsudski. That death had a profoundly sobering effect on Poland's Jewish communities, as it marked an end to a politics that had at least purported to be inclusive of minorities within the new Polish state. In these three essays Schulz further developed his reflections on poetry as a node of intersection between the individual and history; and on the constitutive antinomy that exists between an individual and the historical moment of which their own life is an expression.[3] In this productive period Schulz also worked on new stories: "*Jesień*" ("Autumn"), published by *Sygnały*, and "*Republika marzeń*" ("Republic of Dreams") that appeared in *Tygodnik Illustrowany*.[4] But what Schulz made repeated reference to during this period in surviving letters to friends was the new project on which he struggled to make progress: a novel entitled *Mesjasz—The Messiah*.

While a number of the stories that Schulz chose to publish in *Sanatorium* had been written earlier, in the 1920s, and never published, the striking texts that open, structure, and define the volume—entitled "*Księga*" ("The Book"), "*Genialna epoka*" ("The Age of Genius"), and "*Wiosna*" ("Spring"), written between 1934 and '36—likely represent early drafts on the thematic material of his *Messiah*, which Schulz described in one letter as "a continuation of my *Cinnamon Shops*."[5] "*Genialna epoka*," published in *Wiadomości Literackie* in 1934, carried the subtitle "A fragment from the novel *Messiah*."[6] "The Book," the opening story of the collection, was published in the Warsaw journal *Skamander* in 1935; "*Wiosna*" ("Spring") in 1935 in *Kamena*; and "Sanatorium under the Sign of the Hourglass," from which the collection drew its title, that same year in *Wiadomości Literackie*.[7] The stories feature the same narrator, Joseph, this time tracing his development as a young artist and his search for fragments and clues of a true "book of radiance" that has been scattered into the modern landscape. While the potential likelihood of overlap between these new stories and the text of the novel *Messiah* remains speculation, what they do demonstrate is a conscious attention at

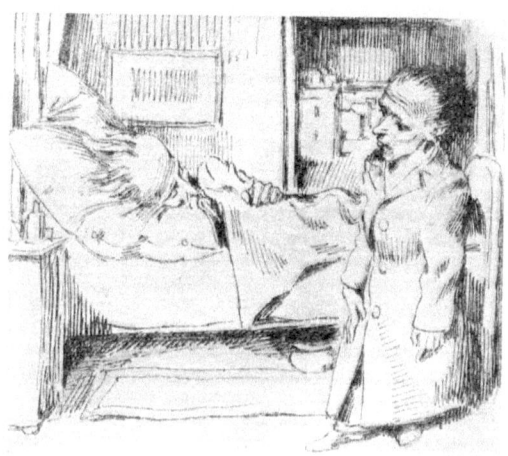

Figure 4.1. Bruno Schulz, Father, c. 1933, courtesy of Muzeum Literatury, Warsaw.

this stage of Schulz's work to articulating and experimenting with a poetics of golus and redemptive exegesis, connected to his own writing in the Polish language. About the remaining stories included in the collection, some written over a decade earlier, but never published, the author had remarked in a letter to his friend Tadeusz Breza that he had used them "as a kind of paralipomenon" to "fill out" the volume.

Several of Schulz's stories from *Sanatorium* forward invite interpretation as reflections on the condition of Jewish culture in the early 20th century; on diaspora existence and the specific fate of the Jewish writer in interwar Poland; and on the prospects for Jewish cultural continuity both in Poland and in Palestine. Schulz seemed to announce this turn with the title he gave to his second volume, also the title of the story which he placed eighth in the collection, "Sanatorium pod klepsydrą" ("Sanatorium under the Sign of the Hourglass"). This tale, dominated by an uncharacteristic mood of anxiety and dark foreboding, turns on a central conceit: the protagonist Joseph's father, Jacob, has already passed away in his "own country" (fig. 4.1). But his family has given him into the care of the management at the sanatorium "under the sign of the hourglass," where experts have devised a method of keeping him alive, suspended in a pseudo-life after death—a "pitiful substitute for life" and an eerily empty simulacrum of the life he had lived in his "fatherland."

Figure 4.2. *Józef with Doctor Gotard I*, c. 1933, courtesy of Muzeum Literatury, Warsaw.

"Is Father alive?" asks the protagonist. "He's alive, naturally," answers Doctor Gotard; "Of course within the boundaries imposed by the situation [*w granicach uwarunkowanych sytuacją*]. . . . You know as well as I that from the point of view of your home, from the perspective of your fatherland [*z perspektywy pańskiej ojczyzny*], your father has died. This cannot be entirely undone. That death throws a certain shadow on his existence here [*na jego tutejszą egzystencję*]" (L, 187; O, 253).⁸ The whole secret of the operation, explains the doctor, is that "we have turned back time;" "here we reactivate time past, with all its possibilities, therefore also including the possibility of a recovery. He looked at me with a smile," says Joseph, "holding his beard" (L, 188; O, 254).

Schulz's story, like many in his oeuvre, echoes and engages with imagery present in popular discourse of his time, which represented the Jewish communities of Eastern Europe as terminally ill, doomed to an unknown fate, not able to survive much longer in the current political and economic climate; or which described traditional Jewish culture itself as already dead or dying. The physician and early Zionist activist Leon Pinsker (1821–91), himself a native of Galicia, had spoken of Jews in his influential 1882 essay "Autoemancipation!" as a "dead but still living nation"—associating that state of suspension, of living death, with the very condition of diaspora.

"Among the living nations of the earth," writes Pinsker, "the Jews are as a nation long since dead. . . . After the Jewish people had ceased to exist as an actual state, as a political entity, they could nevertheless not submit to total annihilation—they lived on spiritually as a nation. The world saw in this people the uncanny form of . . . a living corpse . . . no longer alive, and yet walking among the living."[9] As elsewhere, Schulz subjects this real-world raw material to "mythicization"—what he describes in the case of Kafka's writing as the "treacherously ironic" transplanting of everyday political realities onto his own mythic and oneiric landscape. Further, Schulz also uses the image of the physical keeping alive of Jewish culture and communal forms, including here the life of a small-town shopkeeper, to reflect on the question of Jewish literature itself as a possible sanctuary, or sanatorium, for that dying culture. In one reading, Schulz's alter ego's conversations with Dr. Gotard bring to mind the projects of acculturating Jewish writers in the Polish language; but they also map allegorically onto both Hebraist and Yiddishist cultural programs, which sought to create protective "sanatoria"—linguistic and ideological strongholds that could keep Jewish culture alive in an era of emergent nation-states, assimilation, and emigration to the US. When read as a metatextual reflection by the author, on the place of his own literature in that process, the story also asks: to what extent can separate, national-language literatures, so many national-language cultural sanatoria, promise survival and longevity for Jewish culture? And if they do, then what kind? "Sanatorium" is one of Schulz's most skeptical stories, and a precursor to the disturbing *"Ojczyzna"* ("Fatherland") that followed. Thus, the director of the titular sanatorium invites Joseph's father, Jacob, in under the sign of the hourglass, *klepsydra*—a symbol of death and also itself an obituary notice, signaling that the sanatorium is a mausoleum, and the Jewish exegetical, prophetic, and messianic tradition that enters there is already a ghost or shadow of its former self.[10] The image of the hourglass, however, in its reversibility, contains within it a suggestion of the possibility of resurrection. Schulz's parable, presented under the sign of this reversibility, conceals the question of whether and how Jewish literature or exegetical tradition may be not simply put on hold but revived to live again.

Again, Schulz's premise was by the time of his writing a common trope: Israel as a patient who is either seriously ill, dying, or already dead. Sholem Aleichem's humorous 1903 *feuilleton* "*A konsilium fun doktoyrim*" ("A Consultation of Doctors"), for example, also employed the image of a dying father, Israel, to parody debates taking place among Cultural Zionists, political Zionists, and traditional Orthodox leaders. These are the same debates that Schulz references in his discussion of E. M. Lilien.[11] In "*Konsilium*," the patient, Yisrolik, is deathly ill, and a number of "doctors" and consultants have been called together to assess the best course of action to save him. The assembled include political Zionists Theodor Herzl, Max Nordau, and Max Emmanuel Mandelshtam; Cultural Zionist Ahad Ha'am and Autonomist Simon Dubnow; and a Rabbi Akiva, representing traditional Orthodox reaction to Zionist proposals.[12] As the consulting doctors argue about whether to prescribe "Zionistica," Herzl and Nordau take the upper hand, insisting that this medicine is definitely the only cure for the patient's illness, while Ahad Ha'am objects: "Professor Herzl, in my opinion, has accomplished nothing . . . because the patient is very forlorn and on top of that, the body of the sick Yisrolik is not prepared. In order for the prescription of Zionistica to have a good effect, one must first prepare the patient, give him a good dose of 'nationalism' and a proper course of 'culture.'"[13] The central conceit of Sholem Aleichem's *feuilleton*, as it emerges, is the introduction of the Uganda Plan as an alternate prescription, which is introduced when the British—the "producers" who control the distribution of the desired medicine, Zionistica—turn out not to be willing to sell it.

Y. L. Peretz would offer a similar formulation of this debate a decade later in his influential essay "*Vegn vos firn op fun yidishkayt*" ("Escaping Jewishness," or: "Paths which Divert from Yidishkayt"). Here, "one diagnostician felt for its pulse and could not find it, or else was slightly deaf and did not hear it, and so he concluded: 'Jewishness is dying!'. . . 'Let us sew for it a nice shroud; let us select for it a prominent spot in the mythological cemetery.' . . . A second diagnostician approached Jewishness with more piety. He advised: 'Don't just bury it. Embalm it! Keep it petrified in its present form unto all eternity!'"[14] In Peretz's essay, the perception that Jewishness is dead serves as a reproach of the diagnosticians themselves—Jews who in their acculturation and modernization are losing touch with the national instinct that, his essay argues, still lives on in the folk. In his "Konsilium," Sholem Aleichem's humorous treatment of the subject highlights a chasm dividing the motivations of the politicians whom his piece parodies, doctors inventing solutions or prescriptions, from those of the patient's family. Eager for any treatment that will save Israel, the family members in Sholem Aleichem's sketch are more than willing to administer Zionism if the doctors prescribe it. The hopes they place in the secular cure offered by Herzl and Nordau are interspersed with their recurrent prayers to God to save Yisrolik. "*Ana Hashem hoshea na—Got zol im helfn!*" ("We beseech thee, O Lord, save us! May God help him!")[15] Sholem Aleichem's Rabbi Akiva, speaking for the anti-Zionist Orthodox position, bemoans the proposed plan: "Woe to our patient! Woe to our Yisrolik! A beautiful marriage they've brought about with their remedy! A destruction of the Temple! The Third Destruction! First Zionism, and today—Uganda! A profanation of the Name!"[16]

In Schulz's 1935 parable "Sanatorium," the premise is also a form of spiritual tradeoff associated with accepting the proposal to move one's father to a new land offered by the director of the sanatorium.[17] Doctor Gotard's reanimation project is possible only through an effort of willful self-delusion on the part of the community. "It is clear that only by the solidarity of forbearance, by a communal averting of eyes from the obvious and shocking shortcomings of his condition, could this pitiful semblance of life maintain itself.... The slightest doubt could undermine it, the faintest breeze of skepticism destroy it. Could Dr. Gotard's Sanatorium provide for Father this hothouse atmosphere of friendly indulgence and guard him from the cold winds of sober analysis? It was astonishing that in this insecure and questionable state of affairs, Father was capable of behaving so admirably" (W, 249).

The story's protagonist, Joseph, visits his father out of concern for his welfare, and to determine whether they have sent him into good hands; and he increasingly doubts the wisdom of his family's decision. The sanatorium is eerily empty and the doctor seemingly absent and untrustworthy: "I sometimes feel a strong desire to open each door wide and leave it ajar, so that the miserable intrigue in which we have got ourselves involved can be exposed" (W, 258). His tirade on "the matter of the highly improper manipulation of time [the shameful tricks]" makes further reference to arguments being voiced within the Orthodox Hasidic community of Galicia—such as those of Chaim Elazar Shapiro (1868–1937), the Munkatcher rebbe, and a Galician contemporary of Schulz's—against prematurely "forcing the Messiah" through active creation of a Jewish state and mass return of Jews to Palestine. "Sometimes one feels like banging the table and exclaiming, 'Enough of this!'" says the narrator, Joseph, in "Sanatorium." "'Keep away from time, time is untouchable, one must not provoke it! Isn't it enough for you to have space? Space is for human beings [W, 259] . . . but for the love of God don't touch time!'" (L, 198; O, 268).[18] The choice of words also echoes the closing lines of Ahad Ha'am's influential 1898 article "This Is Not the Way": "I see him, but not now; I behold him, but not nigh" (Numbers 24:17).

In this essay, the author expressed reservations about what he feared was the premature and strongly commercial nature of early settlements in Palestine.[19] In Schulz's framing of the contrast between Jewish time, or messianic time, and historical time, the influence of Cultural Zionism, in this case not contradictory to but overlapping with the spiritual concerns of many Hasidic leaders, remains prominent.

The progressive, inclusive politics of "*wielość*," or "multiplicity," which were characteristic for Schulz's liberal intellectual milieu were combined with a skepticism about political Zionism, Poland's right-wing National Democracy Party, by contrast, in fact fully supported Territorialist and Zionist Revisionist proposals, sharing the belief that the only solution to the "Jewish problem" was mass emigration of a sizable portion of Poland's Jews to a new territory.[20] In interwar Poland, Madagascar was under consideration in addition to Palestine; the Soviet Union had created the Birobidzhan Autonomous Region, which attracted the interest of a small number of Polish Jews, and earlier Zionist proposals had considered, as in Sholem Aleichem's "Consultation," Uganda.[21] The language of Schulz's story resonates with the existence of projects like these, as it does with the inklings of danger, and the shifting winds of politics.

In Schulz's story, the sanatorium and its grounds are located in a dreamlike region to which the protagonist must travel by train, displaced in time, region, and climate from the father's home country, which seems to resemble his small-town Jewish world. In this "peculiar climate" with a "heavy, damp, sweet air," Joseph's father struggles to establish a shadow of his former life—though other characters in the story know that technically he is already dead and being lied to. Here Jacob, present in Schulz's stories since *Cinnamon Shops*, is given a noticeably different aspect. Not portrayed as the prophet or heresiarch of those stories, the character emphasizes instead his concerns with the most worldly, material aspects of his relocation.

> "I must tell you a piece of news," he continued. "Don't laugh. I have rented premises for a shop here. Yes, I have. And I congratulate myself for having had that bright idea.... Don't imagine anything grand. Nothing of the kind. A much more modest place than our store. Back home I would be ashamed of such a stall," says the Father, "but here, where we have had to give up so many of our pretensions—don't you agree, Joseph?" He laughed bitterly. "And so one manages somehow to live." The wrong word—I was embarrassed by Father's confusion when he realized that he had used it (W, 246).

Food figures prominently in the landscape of the sanatorium. Hunger and material satiation replace the poetic and moral heights to which both father and son climb in other stories. "I feel so lonely here. But I suppose one should not complain in my situation. I have been through worse things, and if one were to itemize them all—but never mind. Imagine, on my very first day here they served an excellent filet of beef with mushrooms. It was a hell of a piece of meat, Joseph" (W, 246).

The sanatorium's director, Dr. Gotard, identified physically only by his dark black beard, has sold the narrator's family a bill of goods, convincing them to send their father to his sanatorium for safekeeping. The doctor promises to keep Father alive, or at least not to let him think about the fact that he is already dead. In a nod to the tales of Nachman of Bratslav, Joseph, the narrator son, continuously searches the shadowland of the sanatorium for his father, who is elusive and often unlocatable, much as Nachman's Viceroy figure searches for the Shekhinah, in exile in a land of materialistic indulgence.[22] Joseph sees Jacob by turns plunged into deep sleep and ostentatiously ordering plates of food in the local restaurant, embarrassing his son. He cannot discern whether his father is real and does not know whether to trust the doctor.[23] "I am beginning to regret this whole undertaking. Perhaps we were misled by skillful advertising when we decided to send Father here." Meanwhile, the Sanatorium under the Sign of the Hourglass is guarded by a threatening and unpredictable man/dog—inviting allegorical readings as a figure for nationalism and also communist activism, both masters that the hybrid man/dog serves, or embodies as a guard dog. "Why does the management of the Sanatorium keep an enormous Alsatian on a chain—a terror of a beast, a werewolf of truly demoniacal ferocity? I shiver with fear whenever I pass his kennel. . . . He does not bark, but at the sight of a human being his wild face becomes even more terrifying. Its lines stiffen with an expression of bottomless fury and slowly raising his horrible muzzle, he breaks into a low, fervent, convulsive howl that comes from the very depths of his hatred—a howl in which there resounds the lament and despair of powerlessness" (W, 261; O, 270).[24] The story turns its attention toward the encounter between Joseph—established in the opening stories of the volume as the modern Jewish artist—and this beast. Despite his fear Joseph remains civilized and calm throughout the encounter, and he discovers that the dog is actually a man, angry, poor, and desperate, of an unclear party affiliation: "He could have been the elder, unsuccessful brother of Doctor Gotard" (L, 202; O, 273). "He was, rather, a bookbinder, a

Figure 4.3. *Joseph and the Man-Dog VII*, circa 1936, as printed in *Sanatorium pod Klepsydrą* (1937); original ink drawing lost. Courtesy of Muzeum Literatury, Warsaw.

tub-thumper, a speaker at rallies, a party activist—a violent man with dark, explosive passions" (L, 202; O, 273; fig. 4.3).

> Staggering on my feet, close to fainting, I raised my eyes. I had never seen him so close up and only now do the scales fall from my eyes. How great is the power of prejudice! How mighty the suggestion of terror! What blindness! For it was a man, a man on a chain, whom in reductive, metaphoric, undifferentiated abbreviation by some inconceivable means I had taken for a dog. Please don't misunderstand me. It was a dog, most assuredly, but in human form. (L, 202) The quality of a dog is an inner quality and can be manifested equally well in human form as in animal. (O, 273)

In Schulz's story, Joseph's decision to speak to the man/dog in a civilized manner precipitates a mounting wave of ominous signs: "the elements of some great and obscure intrigue, which was hemming [Father] in." There is a glare of fire over the town, his father is "somewhere in the thick of a revolution or in a burning shop." The man/dog latches onto Joseph and he can neither rid himself of his companion nor tolerate any longer his "spasms of growling." Seized with the desire to escape "at any cost. Anywhere," Joseph leads the man into his father's room, only to leave him there and sneak away. "I [. . .] began to run, breathlessly, my heart thumping, my temples throbbing, along the dark avenue leading to the railway station"

(W, 268; O, 275). While Father is left behind in the sanatorium where his fate remains ominously open-ended, the son—or, in the present gloss, the modern Jewish artist—barely escapes, fleeing the politically charged simulacrum of a homeland to take up an itinerant existence—curiously, in this case safer—on the thankless moving train of golus-existence. In a jarring shift of tone, the narration seems to move forward into the present of the telling, and into an undefined, continuous time: "*Od tego czasu jadę, jadę wciąż*" ("Since that time I have been riding, I am still riding"). The narrator is in motion on a moving train.

> Farewell, Father. Farewell, city that I shall never see again. [. . .] I have made my home as it were on the railroad and they tolerate me here, wandering from car to car (L, 204). The compartments, enormous as rooms, are full of rubbish and straw, and cold drafts pierce them on gray, colorless days.
> My clothes have become torn and ragged. I have been given the shabby uniform of a railway man. I sit on the straw, dozing, and when hungry, I stand in the corridor outside a second-class compartment and sing. People throw small coins into my hat: a black railwayman's hat, its visor half-torn away (W, 268; O, 276).

Abrupt and open-ended, of a different tone from the story that precedes it, this final scene, in its evocation of the trope of the Wandering Jew, also recalls the narrator's question from the story "The Book," in the same collection: "Where else would the cast-out one [*wyklęta*: the cursed or exiled one] take shelter, where find asylum, if not . . . in those canticles of beggars and old men?" (L, 140).[25] In its image of the artist-protagonist as an itinerant singer and a passenger aboard a moving train—the historical progression of this-worldly existence—Schulz's ending also echoes the language of Franz Kafka's parable "The Hunter Gracchus." In that tale the central figure Gracchus, long dead and yet also still alive, travels through history and from country to country aboard a ship, dressed in the ragged remains of a death shroud, reliant on the charity of others. As Gracchus tells the burgomaster his story, his present-tense narration evokes a similar mood of uncanny suspension:

> I am always moving. But when I go through the greatest upward motion and the door is shining right above me, I wake up on my old ship. . . . Julia, the wife of the helmsman, knocks and brings to me on the bier the morning drink of the country whose coast we are sailing by at the time. . . . My hair and beard, black and gray, are inextricably intertangled, my legs covered by a large silk women's scarf, with a floral pattern and long fringes. . . . Through a hole in the side wall the warm air of the southern nights comes in, and I hear the water lapping against the old boat.[26]

Schulz published "Sanatorium pod klepsydrą" as a separate story in *Wiadomości Literackie* in April of 1935.[27] During his sabbatical stay in Warsaw several months later, as Józefina Szelińska later recounted in her letters to Jerzy Ficowski, "he had [in his library] Kafka's *The Castle* and *The Collected Stories*, of which I translated 'The Hunter Gracchus' and 'The Bucket Rider.'"[28] In Kafka's story, the titular character, Gracchus—a play on Kafka's own name, "Crow"—shares aspects of both father and son from Schulz's "Sanatorium." He exists in a state of limbo, both alive and not alive, both inside of and beyond history. His condition, like Joseph's, evokes the trope of the Wandering Jew, who moves through history and is its viewer, coming ashore in different lands at different times but having recourse also to transhistorical memory. "Are you dead?" the burgomaster asks of Gracchus, who has arrived at a port. "Yes," answers the hunter, "as you see."

> "But you're also alive," said the burgomaster. "To a certain extent," said the hunter, "to a certain extent I am also alive. My death ship lost its way, a wrong turn of the helm, a moment when the helmsman was not paying attention, a distraction from my wonderful homeland—I don't know what it was.... I have no intentions," said the hunter with a smile and, to make up for his mocking tone, laid a hand on the burgomaster's knee. "I am here. I don't know any more than that. There's nothing more I can do. My boat is without a helm—it journeys with the wind which blows in the deepest regions of death."[29]

Kafka's parable seems to have served as an inspiration for Schulz's own reflections on the relationship between modern Jewish art and diaspora existence—and between his own creative work, his subjectivity as an artist, and his rootedness in the Galician, Polish Jewish diaspora. In drawing close to Kafka's language in the closing lines of his story, he foregrounds the literary and linguistic exploration of diaspora existence as a thematic link that connects the two authors. This story in particular owes much to Schulz's fascination with Kafka's parabolic tales, which multiply and also impede interpretation. It experiments with the tone of foreboding and anxiety that dominates in Kafka's novels, different from so much of Schulz's work. In place of the lush or riotous, baroque prose of stories such as "*Sierpień*" ("August") and "*Sklepy cynamonowe*" ("Cinnamon Shops"), or the erudite philosophical reflections and heretico-mythical landscapes of "The Book" or "Spring," in the story "Sanatorium" Schulz's primary idiom is an almost matter-of-fact realism, displaced, like Kafka's prose, into an uncanny realm outside of normal time. The protagonist approaches his circumstances rationally, while institutional forces at work, inscrutable, inaccessible, contribute to a sense of foreboding and growing powerlessness. Fate and survival are at stake in the story, and both the protagonist and the author seem to accept this fate—or that of the artistic or scriptural tradition with which their works are associated.

A Jewish citizen, like Schulz, of the Habsburg Empire, Kafka wrote in the language of that state—German, using that language differently than other non-Jewish German writers had, and developing literary landscapes at the intersection of Jewish exegetical tradition and German-language literary modernism. His texts provided Schulz a model of a golus-writing in the European vernacular, born in the Jewish diaspora. In paying homage to him in "Sanatorium under the Sign of the Hourglass," Schulz situates that story as a question about the future of Kafka's and his own forms of hybrid Jewish/universal imaginary.

Like many of Kafka's parabolic texts, Sanatorium's central conceit is also to place its own categories in flux—setting up an allegorical or parabolic structure that simultaneously invites and evades a one-to-one assignation of roles. Specifically, the story unfixes definitions of both fatherland (*ojczyzna*) and exile—asking its readers whether golus lies in Poland or in Palestine. Is it indeed a geographical category? Or is it again a characteristic of the human condition and of the primordial word, which aspires to escape the bounds of history and return to the *"praojczyzna słowna"* (linguistic pre-fatherland)? In this story, the titular sanatorium can certainly be read as a newly reconstituted Polish state in which Galician Jewish culture continues to live a simulacrum of its former autonomous existence—a state whose citizen guard dogs, impoverished and suspicious, are susceptible to increasingly violent nationalist postures. But Schulz's "Sanatorium" broadens its reflection on golus, allowing the concept of exile to apply to all political nationalisms and to ethno-nationalism itself as a fall—parallel to the scattering of the primordial word in *"Mityzacja"* ("Mythologizing")—into the world of realized nation-states, and also of boundaried and competing national-language literatures.

Through these associations, "Sanatorium" contributes to Schulz's argument that survival of those elements he considered most authentic and vital to modern Jewish culture and Jewish identity, or at least to the Galician Jewish identity that is his inheritance, was not only threatened in an environment of rising and extrusionary Polish ethnonationalism, but also that this survival may not necessarily be achieved or guaranteed by separatist, nationalist Jewish projects in politics, literature, and the arts, by territorialism or its linguistic equivalents: Yiddishist and Hebraist activism. According to this argument, the fostering of separate Jewish literatures in the national Jewish languages is not enough to fulfill the project of Jewish spiritual renewal and continuity. Rather, for Schulz this latter form of survival depends on the active and continual reinscription into a modern topos—be it a multilingual topos—of two key elements of Jewish culture: first, what he called "spiritual Jewish messianism," and second, the ethos of "The Book"—the centrality of the Jewish hermeneutic tradition of textual exegesis. Schulz's oeuvre, accordingly, reflects his continuing search for a literary form that might succeed in attaching itself to that exegetical tradition, and in so doing attempt to keep it alive. His protagonist muses in "Spring," "Ah, when writing down these tales, revising the stories about my father on the used margins of its text, don't I, too, surrender to the secret hope that they will merge imperceptibly with the yellowing pages of that most splendid, crumbling book, that they will sink into the gentle rustle of its pages and become absorbed there?" (W, 84; O, 92).

Toward a Modernist Midrash: Itzik Manger's "*Khumesh-lider*" and Schulz's "Mythologized Reality"

Concerns about territorialism and political Zionism as solutions to the challenge of Jewish renaissance and survival were voiced not only by cultural Zionists and Hasidic leaders but also by Yiddishists, Diaspora Nationalists, and neo-Hasidic philosophers of Schulz's later, interwar generation.[30] In widely read essays of the 1910s, Y. L. Peretz had provided Polish Jewish readers a diasporist discourse and set of images on which to draw for decades to come. In his 1912 essay "*Natsionalizm un Tsionizm*," he wrote, "Other nations have the following life questions: abundance, expanding the borders, strong armies, colonies; with us, if we desire to remain true to ourselves, the life question surrounds freedom of conscience, human culture and ethics; these are the only conditions of freely living life and being victorious. Fleeing from the battlefield to rescue the national physiognomy in a separate place is higher than submission and relinquishment of the flag."[31] Peretz's affirmations of a Jewish cultural-spiritual and above all ethical life in the diaspora influenced and were familiar to an entire interwar generation of Jewish intelligentsia in Poland.

An additional reference point for Schulz's generation remained the works of Baruch Spinoza, who both rejected the principle of chosenness and abandoned halakhic practice, and at the same time placed a critical engagement with the Hebrew Bible at the center of his metaphysics. He had distilled the teachings of Scripture down to a simple message. "I go so far as to say that such doctrines are very few and very simple," he wrote in the *Theological-Political Tractate*: "Obedience to God consists solely in love to our neighbor" (*TTP*, chap. XIII).[32] The two-hundred-fiftieth anniversary of Spinoza's death in 1927 and the three-hundredth anniversary of the philosopher's birth in 1932 became opportunities for a broad Polish Jewish readership to revisit the legacy of Spinoza's metaphysical philosophy for modern, secular Jewish culture and identity.[33]

To embrace central tenets of the ethical posture and structure bequeathed by Jewish tradition embodied in the Bible, but at the same time to use modern literature as a space in which to insistently universalize that inheritance, was characteristic of diasporist writing in Schulz's interwar Poland. This gesture is singularly well exemplified in the 1929 project of Yiddish-language poet Itzik Manger, entitled *Khumesh Lider* (*Bible Songs*), later republished as *Medresh Itzik* (*Itzik's Midrash*). Born in the city of Czernowitz in Habsburg Bukovina in 1901, and having helped to develop the Yiddish literary milieu in Romania after World War I, Manger moved to Warsaw in 1929, where he lived and worked until 1938, and became a transformative presence on the Yiddish literary scene. Considered by contemporary scholars to be the "preeminent modernist folk bard in the annals of Yiddish culture,"[34] he published prose, articles, and several volumes of his own verse, wrote lyrics for the Yiddish cabaret, and became popular among the wider public for his well-known song lyrics. He was also the husband by common law of Yiddish writer and publisher Rachel Auerbach, who had moved from Lwów to Warsaw in 1933 and who played a seminal role in his literary career.

Like Schulz, Manger also spoke of the great debt that he owed to German-language literature, and in particular the work of the poet Rainer Maria Rilke. The confluences in the influence that the German-language, fin de siècle literature would have on the two writers run deep. Kant, Kleist, Mann, and Hesse were among the other German writers Manger had read and listed in his notebooks of 1918–19. For David Roskies, "Manger might also have mentioned that German was the source of all his worldly knowledge.... [He] enlisted the compressed and conventional format of the ballad to combine the lyric sensibility of a German poet, the ethical sensibility of a modern secular Jew, and the dramatic sensibility of a born storyteller."[35] But beyond an ethical sensibility, writes his biographer Efrat Gal-Ed, "as a secular artist, he found a major source for his poetic strength in the themes, topoi, and literary techniques of Jewish traditions which he then rewrote in a modernist manner."[36] Also like Schulz, Manger's path to attaching his emerging modern, secular poetics to traditional Jewish sources and texts was not direct. "It took Manger several years to find his way from a strong identification with the world of German poetry back to Jewish motifs which he then recognized as universal," explains Gal-Ed. "Only toward the end of 1926 did he discover the wealth of Yiddish folk poetry and folktales as an important source for his own poetry." Interestingly, she suggests that "this artistic breakthrough in 1927 was not influenced by Peretz, but rather by Manger's intense engagement with Rilke's *Book of Hours, Book of Images,* and the *New Poems.*"[37]

Manger's *Khumesh-lider,* or *Bible Songs,* published in 1935 in Warsaw, represented a new genre that Manger described as a form of "*Literatoyre.*"[38] The term, which combines the European/latinate '*Literatura*' with the Yiddish/Hebrew 'Toyre/Torah,' had according to the poet, had been coined by his father. The volume recasts stories from Genesis, setting them, as he explained in his preface, in a Galician landscape: "The poems gathered in this book are a sort of mischievous toying with the gray beards of the Patriarchs and the head-shawl corners of the Matriarchs."[39] "The alert reader," he continued, "will recognize that the landscape in which these biblical figures move is not Canaanitish but Slavic. I was thinking of eastern Galicia."[40] In these gorgeous poems, to offer but one example, the maidservant Hagar (in a midrash on Genesis 21) sweeps the kitchen of a house in the Carpathian mountains for the last time, remembering the amber beads that Abraham bought her at the local market, and singing the blues: "How like the smoke of a chimney, / How like the smoke of a train / Is the love of a man, dear mother, / The love of any man"[41]; and while Isaac rides with his father, Abraham, to the market on a wooden cart, the roads of rural Ukraine become the roads of Scripture and of Jewish life: "'Sad and lovely,' the poet says, / 'Are the roads of the Holy Book'" ("*Troyerik un sheyn, zogt der poet, zaynen di vegn fun Tanakh*").[42]

Manger's *Medresh Itzik* was not original in transforming the Galician or Polish landscape into a site of Jewish group identity and belonging; rather, the poems attach themselves to a longstanding practice that had occurred throughout centuries of Jewish literature and folklore, beginning with legends of origin and place-name-*midrashim*.⁴³ Of Manger's new treatment of that tradition, heretical and unwelcome to some Polish Jewish readers, Roskies writes, "*Pour épater les orthodoxes*, Yiddish writers had merely to take a place already hallowed by tradition and turn it to secular ends. [They] had a surfeit of local legends from which to choose. This is how the Carpathian Mountains, birthplace of Hasidism, reappeared on the literary map."⁴⁴ Not surprisingly, he continues, "Manger's latter-day midrash met with opposition on two fronts: from the Orthodox camp, who viewed his mock-epic treatment of the patriarchs and matriarchs as sacrilege, and from the Zionist-Hebraists, who correctly understood his scripturalization of the shtetl to be a species of *doikeyt*, a valorization of the Diaspora."⁴⁵ This literature that embedded Jewish identity and tradition so deeply in the fabric of the Galician landscape was written in the spirit of Diaspora Nationalism, and evokes the Bundist concept of *doikeyt*, or "hereness." *Doikeyt*, corresponding to the socialist and Yiddishist political and cultural posture that affirmed Jewish belonging in Poland and Eastern Europe, signaled that Jewish culture was inextricably rooted in and identified with these territories—historically, the lands of the former Polish Lithuanian Commonwealth. According to proponents of Jewish "Autonomism," articulated by historian Simon Dubnow, and the later "Diaspora Nationalism" or "Golus-Nationalism" of Y. L. Peretz and others, Jewish culture, and in particular Yiddish-language culture, belongs "here"/"*do*"—that is, in Poland and on former Polish lands where it developed and flourished as a native European culture.⁴⁶ In the interwar period, the affirmation of rootedness in Polish territory and place was reiterated in the discourse and activism of the *Landkentenish* movement, which promoted the study of national customs through hiking and tourism.⁴⁷

Diaspora nationalism represented a clear rejection of the model of assimilation put forward during the Haskalah that had held promise for Polish Jewish maskilim in the nineteenth century. Proponents of the concepts of doikeyt and autonomism were not arguing for Jewish inclusion into Polish culture, but for the right to exist and to flourish where they lived. At the same time, insistence within Yiddishist narratives on working for the development of a distinct Jewish national identity did not make Jewish life and culture less native to Poland, to Russia, and to Europe. On the contrary, autonomism called for a societal model that transcends the nation-state. It envisioned a morally superior synthesis, as Simon Dubnow elaborated in his letters on autonomism, which was to follow after the immature extremes of isolationism (first) and assimilation (second): a "progressive nationalism, which balanced a Jew's national rights with secular universalism."[48] Jews, it was argued, should remain in their European home and work to build a just and democratic society that protected the rights of all its minorities.

As Schulz's Lilien essay makes more recognizable, his prose works participate in a diasporist gesture that overlaps with Manger's, by weaving together contemporary Galician landscapes and the landscapes of Jewish textual tradition. In her 1934 review of Schulz's *Cinnamon Shops*, Yiddish poet Rokhl Korn had described Schulz's writing as "drawing into itself the aura of the Book of Genesis."[49] Thus in a number of his stories Schulz restages or "reactivates" elements and characters from the Bible, setting them in his Galician hometown and specifically in his father's cloth shop. If Manger's Galicia contains the gardens, boulevards, and Yiddish-speaking homes of Abraham and Sarah, Adam and Eve, Schulz's Galicia emerges in a shop where the ties to or the burden of tradition confront the ineluctable onslaught of a burgeoning commercial age. If in Manger's *khumesh lider* the roads of the Carpathian countryside merge with the "roads of the Holy Book" ("*di vegn fun Tanakh*"), Schulz repeatedly conflates the streets of his childhood Drohobycz and the modern Galician landscape with the pages of that "great rustling Codex," the "*Oryginał*" and "*Autentyk*," allowing them to become interchangeable with the printed text, whether map, album, palimpsest, or tome of yellowed pages: "those elderly mornings, yellow like parchment, sweet with wisdom like late evenings! Those forenoons smiling slyly like wise palimpsests, the many-layered texts of yellowed books [*wielowarstwowe jak stare pożółkłe księgi*]! . . ." (W, 222; O, 230).[50]

Both of these authors' examples of diasporic modernism reinscribe the tradition and inheritance of "the book" into the Polish or Galician landscape, and they engage in universalizing and also challenging its ethics, testing their receptivity to a modern, secular Jewish experience. In his retelling of the story of Abraham, Sarah, and Hagar (Genesis 21:8–20), for example, Manger assigns to Hagar, Abraham's triply disenfranchised Egyptian maidservant and the mother of Ishmael, the status of protagonist and also lyric persona.[51] In places he allows her to sing what becomes a poem of exile, victimhood, and subjection to the winds of history. In "Hagar's Last Night in Abraham's House," Hagar sits in the kitchen, where "A smoking oil lamp spills / The shapes of shadowy cats and dogs / To flicker on the walls. / She weeps because her master / Fired her today. / "Beat it, you bitch," he told her. / "Can't you let me be?" A "toying with the long beards and prayer shawls of the Patriarchs and Matriarchs," Manger's ballads based on the tradition of the purim play, open to reflection on the injustices of class difference, of patriarchy, of ethnic and racial prejudice, and of fate. "It was Sarah who egged him on, / That proper deaconess, / Saying, 'You get rid of the girl / Or give me a divorce.'" "God knows where we will run to," reflects Hagar, "Myself and his bastard child, / Unless in some alien kitchen / We are allowed to hide."[52] Cast in the role of outcast and refugee, Manger's Hagar speaks to the experiences not only of Jews but of myriad ethnic groups during and after World War I—refugees, victims, forced to flee their homes or waiting with children in railway stations. In "Hagar on Her Journey," Manger allows his readers to linger with Hagar one ballad longer, extending his verses' reflection on the relationship of Jewish tradition to the non-Jewish Other.

Hagar oyf der mit fun veg

*Hagar zitst a farveynte
in mitn veg oyf a shteyn
un fregt bay ale vintn
vu zi zol vayter geyn.*

*Zogt eyner: gey keyn mizrakh
der tsveyter—keyn meriv gor,
un der driter, a voshne shtifer
shtift in ire hor. [. . .]*

*Veynt Hagar: "tate in himel,
kh'hob yorn getray gedint,
un itst tuen fun mir shpetn
der foygl un der vint."*

*Un hagar heybt oyf di oygn
un derzet a karavan,
faroys in a grinem mantl
geyt der terkisher sultan.*

*Er kumt tsu ir nenter, nenter
un zogt mit a fester shtim:
Zog, tsi du bist Hagar
di shipkhe fun Ibrahim!*

*Un der kleyner pempik
iz Yishmael min hastam,
der naviye hot getun undz meldn,
az mir shtamen fun zayn shtam."*

Hagar on Her Journey

Hagar, worn with weeping,
Sits on a highway stone.
She asks of every passing wind
The way that she must go.

One says, "Hagar, take the east."
Another, "West, that's where."
A third wind is a prankster
And plays among her hair. [. . .]

She weeps, "For years, O God,
I served him faithfully.
See now how any bird or wind
Can make a fool of me?"

Hagar lifts her head
And sees a caravan,
Led by the Turkish sultan
With a mantle all of green.

Nearer, he comes, and nearer,
Then speaks. His voice is firm:
"Tell me, are you Hagar,
Servant to Ibrahim?

And your little baby boy,
Is Ishmael his name?
We have heard our prophet say
That we descend from him."

Un er falt far ir anider	The sultan falls before her,
un knit far ir shtoyb:	He kneels down in the dust.
mir hobn dem yikhes gefunen,	"Our lineage finds its honor.
Allah, Allah a loyb!"	Allah, O Allah be praised."
Un Hagar zitst a farvirte	Not knowing what the truth is,
un veyst nisht tsi s'iz vor.	She can only stare
un a zilberne halb levone	While the moon is a silver crescent
finkelt in ire hor.	Glistening in her hair.[53]

Characteristic of Manger's *khumesh lider* is a playful anachronism, adopted from the traditions of purim shpil and midrash, that holds open two temporalities: historical and exegetical, or historical and mythical. Schulz's landscapes rely on a similar tension, but often with the Jewish source texts actively palimpsested, or concealed through the use of universalized language. At other times, as in "Night of the Great Season," the conversation with Biblical sources—and the "toying with the grey beards of the Patriarchs"—stays in. When it does, Schulz's imagery may take the form of an *"obraz-talisman," "obraz-zagadka"* or picture-riddle, that weaves together high and low, commerce and prophecy, *tandeta* and myth—presenting the modern experience as a recurring, unresolvable dialectical confrontation of these incommensurate temporalities. In the story *"Martwy sezon"* ("The Dead Season"), Schulz stages Jacob's struggle with the angel (Genesis 32:22–31) in his father's cloth shop. Here Jacob (the character's name, and also Schulz's father's real name) struggles with an angel throughout the night ("We never learned who this distinguished visitor really was" [W, 234]) and emerges blessed at the story's close:

> The black-bearded man lay on top of my father like the angel on top of Jacob. My father pressed against him with all the strength of his knees and, stiffly floating away into numbness, stole another short spell of fortifying sleep between one round of wrestling and another. So they fought: what for? For their good name? For God? For a contract? They grappled in mortal sweat, to their last ounce of strength, while the waves of sleep carried them away into ever more distant and stranger areas of the night. . . .
>
> The next day my father walked with a slight limp. His face was radiant. At dawn a splendid phrase for his letter had come to him, a formulation he had been trying in vain to find for many days and nights. We never saw the black-bearded gentleman again. He left before daybreak with his trunk and bundles, without taking leave of us. . . . From that summer night onward seven long years of prosperity began for the shop (W, 237).

The content of the story reflects its form: a modern prose parody, a product of its twentieth-century moment, that wrestles with visitors from a Biblical landscape and itself struggles to identify its relationship to Jewish myth and textual tradition. At the opening of the story Joseph describes a picture that hangs in his father's shop: "It was a picture-talisman, an unfathomable image, a picture-riddle, interpreted endlessly, wandering from generation to generation. What did it represent? It was an unending dispute being carried on for centuries, a never-ending trial between two conflicting principles. They stood there facing each other, two merchants, to antitheses, two worlds."

The structure of Schulz's narrative in "The Dead Season," both parodic and serious, suggests that it is through the very fact of Jacob's struggle with tradition—through his intense contemplation of the "*obraz-zagadka*" (picture-riddle) and the questions it asks of him—that he is successfully reinscribed in the pages of the great book. "He was the last of his race, the Atlas on whose shoulders rested the weight of an immense testament. Day and night Father pondered the thesis of that testament, struggled to understand its *meritum* in a flash. . . . Father wandered like a shepherd among that blind, woolen flock, those crowded obstacles, the undulating, bleating, headless trunks beside a watering hole. He was still waiting, delaying the moment when he would lift up all his people and move out into the noisy night like that oppressed, teeming, hundredfold Israel" (L, 181).

In the same story, the role of a scorned and victimized individual—in Manger's midrash, given to Hagar—is filled by a barefoot peasant (*chłopek*) from the countryside, who peers into the protagonist's father's shop, where the idle shopkeepers are passing a long and uneventful summer day: "Then it happened that a village yokel, barefoot and dressed in coarse cloth, [*kmiotek ze wsi, bosy i zgrzebny*] was standing hesitantly inside the shop door, timidly peeking into the interior. For the bored salesclerks that was quite a treat. Lightning fast, they descended from the ladders like spiders at the sight of a fly" (L, 177; O, 239). The shopkeepers descend on the man, asking him questions designed to reveal his ignorance, drawing him into the shop where they can continue to mock him, entertaining themselves at his expense. "Leon went behind the counter and pretended to pull out a nonexistent drawer. Oh, how he worked at it, how he bit his lip with effort! It was stuck and would not move. One had to thump the top of the counter with one's fists, with all one's might. The peasant, encouraged by the young men, did it with concentration, with proper attention. At last, when there was no result, he climbed, hunched and gray haired, on top of the counter and stamped it with his bare feet. He had us all in fits of laughter" (W, 229; O, 239).[54] The arrival of the protagonist's father, and the pain that the scene causes him, turns this moment of youthful cruelty into that "regrettable incident" "that filled us all with sadness and shame." "We noticed [Father] only when the sudden understanding of our little game distorted his face in a grimace of wild horror" (W, 229; O, 240). In its choice of encounter, Schulz's story empathizes not only with real or fictional customers from the countryside, standing at the doorstep of a new cosmopolitan and commercial world, but also with the experience of thousands of East European refugees or immigrants from the East Jewish and non-Jewish, in their encounter with the cosmopolitan West: experiences in which Schulz himself, during the war years in Vienna, figured as both witness and provincial newcomer.[55] The experience of being scorned and otherized is here universalized, as Schulz's peasant and the shopkeepers are not given ethnic markers. Like Manger's midrashim, the story negotiates a dialectical relationship with Jewish tradition: the re-inscription of the Bible as source, as literary landscape, the continued reference point and transhistorical locus of Jewish literature, and at the same time the secular universalization of its ethical demands. Here the premise of ethical treatment of the other and the stranger is summarized again in Spinoza's distillation of Scripture in *Ethics*—"that the worship of God consists only in justice and charity, or love towards one's neighbor;"[56] the philosopher's own modern midrash that can be seen to have provided Schulz's generation a kind of originary model for a writing at the intersection of theology and materialism.

In the story "The Dead Season," the mistreatment of the peasant puts Jacob in a state of shame and rage so great that, to the embarrassment of his employees, he transforms into an insect—a buzzing fly, the very intensity of his moral feeling rendering him more "other" than the peasant himself, who fits easily into their thoughtless economy of power. This scene of transgression and righteous anger unfolds at its core (a metaphor Schulz employed to describe his own texts) into the story's broader narrative: that of the anguished struggle of a community to negotiate relationships to and duty to Jewish tradition, to balance ethical demands against material needs or drives, and finally to reinscribe itself into that tradition—which is portrayed here again as a dying tradition, threatened by modern capitalism and by an innocently if boorishly frivolous, deracinated younger generation.

Fatherland, 1938

The last known story that Schulz published, "Fatherland" ("*Ojczyzna*"), which appeared in 1938 in the Journal *Sygnały*, has been received somewhat cautiously by critics and scholars, at times with confusion.[57] A short work seemingly of realist, psychological narrative, it differs noticeably in style and tone from the short stories that secured Schulz's place as a leading experimental modernist in Polish prose—enough so that some critics have questioned whether Schulz wrote the piece.[58] Yet, read within the context of the Polish Jewish experience, its thematics represent a direct line of continuation along the sobering trajectory that the author lays out in his Lilien article, and repeats through the arrangement of stories in the collection *Sanatorium*. "Fatherland," like "Sanatorium," is also in conversation with works in Yiddish, German, and Hebrew that explore the emerging realities of settlement in Palestine. These included, as the language of Schulz's text suggests, an early essay by Cultural Zionist Ahad Ha'am (Asher Ginsburg) entitled "The Truth from Eretz Israel." The subject matter and concerns expressed in Ahad Ha'am's essay, in which the author expressed reservations about what he saw as the predominance of materialistic underpinnings behind early settlement in Palestine, had gained new relevance for Jews in interwar Poland. It was a moment when emigration to Palestine was seeing a sharp increase motivated, as Kenneth Moss has recently argued, by a growing sense of "felt futurelessness" in Poland, and increasingly independent of specific commitment to earlier Zionist ideals of Jewish cultural and spiritual renaissance. Through his engagement with this topic, Schulz's work displays a marked shift in tone and an increased politicization that is characteristic of Jewish discourse in 1930s Poland.[59]

His story "Fatherland," revisits or directly translates the arc of Schulz's E. M. Lilien essay: an artist-protagonist moves from diaspora to homeland, becoming "reconciled with reality." In the Lilien essay, written in the same period, such a move is associated for Schulz with a turn toward realism both ideologically—in a shift from mystical to political "messianic" solutions to the Jewish Problem—and aesthetically, in the formal strategies of representation the artist employs. Accordingly, "Fatherland" represents an intentionally idiosyncratic, for Schulz, experiment in literary and spiritual *realism*: an imagination of what such a turn or return would imply for the author and poet were he to have undertaken a parallel artistic transition to that made by his early artistic inspiration, Lilien. For Schulz's protagonist in *"Ojczyzna"* ("Fatherland"), the movement home/abroad is equated with safety and rest; bourgeois comfort; superficial, materialistic pleasures; and death.

Here cast as a successful artist-narrator, Schulz's protagonist and alter ego in "Fatherland" moves into the role that the father figure had played in

"Sanatorium under the Sign of the Hourglass." "At last, after many vicissitudes and turns of fate that I do not intend to describe here, I found myself abroad, in a country fervently yearned for in the reveries of my youth" (L, 265; O, 354). In this story, which reprises elements of the plot of "Sanatorium," the artist knows that he has finally arrived at the fatherland overseas that he had dreamt of since his childhood—and, above all, that he is finally safe. The story's opening lines echo those of Ahad Ha'am in "Truth from Eretz Israel": "After many years spent contemplating and imagining the land of our fathers and the rebirth of our people in it, I have now finally been privileged to see with my own eyes the subject of my dreams, this land of wonders which captivates the hearts and multitudes."[60] The narrator of "Fatherland" continues, "The fulfillment of lengthy dreams came too late, and in circumstances entirely different from the ones I had imagined. I entered there not as a victor but as a castaway from life" (L, 265; O, 355). Rather than as a pioneer to a site of Jewish cultural and spiritual renaissance, such as that envisioned in Lilien's art and Buber's lectures, the author has come to this new homeland oversees like so many refugees from economic and political turmoil in Eastern Europe, exhausted, harried, seeking rest. "That country, imagined as the stage of my triumphs, was now the terrain of miserable, inglorious, little defeats in which I was losing, one after the next, my high, proud aspirations. Now I was struggling only for bare life itself and, knocked about, rescuing my wretched little bark as best I could from shipwreck, driven here and there by fate's changing inclinations, I finally stumbled upon the provincial city of medium size where in my youthful daydreams the villa, the *refugium* of an old and famous master from the turmoil of the world, was supposed to stand" (L, 265; O, 355).

The story opens with an image of respite: "I know: from now on no harm may come to me, I have found a peaceful haven. A long succession of years heavy with happiness and fulfillment now lies ahead, an unending mathematical progression of joyful good times" (W, 334). Here the familiar language of "mathematical progression" emphasizes that the narrator and narrative landscape have entered historical time—what Walter Benjamin would refer to in the thirteenth thesis of his *On the Concept of History* (1940) as "homogenous, empty time."[61] In Schulz's formulation, "one-track" as opposed to the "two-track time" characterized by a continual dialectical movement between reality and myth, mosaic fragment and primordial word, history and Scripture, that Schulz also identifies with diaspora existence. In "Fatherland" the mathematical progression of good times to come is also associated—in a reprisal of thematic motifs explored in "Sanatorium"—with the artist's death. While his wife plays cards with friends in the next room Schulz's protagonist muses, looking out the window on a dark garden: "The last few sighs, shallow and sweet, fill my breast utterly with happiness. I stop breathing. I know one day death will take me into her open arms [. . .] I will lie, entirely sated, among the green undergrowth of the beautifully manicured local cemetery. My wife—how beautiful she'll look in her widow's veil—will bring me flowers on those bright, calm midmornings we enjoy here" (W, 334).

The narrator, a musician, had previously believed his artistic life to be over—yet here in the fatherland he has unexpectedly achieved the recognition that had not been granted him in golus. He holds a good position as director of an orchestra. "My whole past of homeless wandering, the submerged misery of my former existence, separated itself from me and floated back like a stretch of country positioned crosswise against the rays of the setting sun"—here a reference to Lilien's golus imagery from the "Zion" postcard but in reverse—"rising one more time over distant horizons, while the train that bore me away rounded the last curve and headed straight into the night" (W, 330). The night and the community into which the protagonist artist is welcomed are characterized by shallow entertainment devoid of spirituality. It is a comfortable bourgeois existence of socializing, gambling, and relatively empty conversation between man and wife, which revolves around plans to furnish and decorate a modest home. With this premise, Schulz brings into play an image of the "Fatherland" as a material and also cultural refuge that is at the same time a resignation from spiritual searching.

"Fatherland," in transplanting the content of the Lilien essay into fictional form, displays Schulz's characteristic linguistic universalization, as directly Jewish markers have been removed; yet the subject matter of the Lilien essay, and the centrality that emigration to Palestine had gained within Polish Jewish discourse by the late 1930s, remain in palimpsested form. This time, however, the transplantation is less a (vertical) mythologization than a straightforward allegorization. In line with the thematics of a "realistic" Jewish messianism explored in "E. M. Lilien," the story "Fatherland" stubbornly resists being read mythically, as if performing its own inability to activate the second, or exegetical track of time. The setting resembles a modest drawing room in a realist novel. It is neither oneiric nor surreal, and is absent mythic allusions. The Jewishly marked language that signals to his reader that this homeland may be read, should the reader choose, as set in Palestine includes references—whose curious specificity makes them stand out—to "wooded groves of mulberry and walnut trees" (L, 267). The mulberry serves as a metonym for practical, present-day economic solutions: it was introduced into Palestine with the support of Baron Rothschild in the 1880s and '90s as part of a new industry, silk production, that could help to develop the economy of the early settlements in Palestine.[62] Again, as in the story "Sanatorium," Schulz allows his text to draw close to his generation's concerns about the fate of dreams, born in diaspora, of lasting Jewish spiritual and cultural renewal and continuity.[63]

"The Book" — "The Age of Genius" — "Spring"

Finally, the arc that Schulz revisits in a realist vein in both "E. M. Lilien" and "Ojczyzna" had already taken shape in the collection *Sanatorium*. In that volume, before and in contrast to the experimental realism of resignation in "Fatherland," Schulz had rallied the fullest spectrum of mythologizing that his "metaphoric style" could afford, to describe an arc from youthful commitment to artistic renaissance, to mature resignation. *Sanatorium* opens with a scene of reading, that is also an origin story: at the center, a young protagonist who opens a great "Book" that will unfold before him and initiate his artistic and spiritual journey. In the latter, mythicized version of this tale, the book is encountered by the young protagonist, Joseph, in a landscape outside of and before historical time—"mother had not appeared yet"—in a room "which at that time was as large as the world": "Somewhere in the dawn of childhood . . . the horizon had brightened with its gentle glow. The Book lay in all is glory on my father's desk" (W, 115; O, 105). In the Lilien essay—which could be identified in Schulz's translational poetics as the "vernacular" corollary to that story—Schulz figured himself as a youth of thirteen in his Drohobycz home: a child open to the influences of his artistic predecessors, Jewish artists living in the Habsburg Empire, involved in attaching modern European art forms to the project of secular Jewish cultural Renaissance. "When I opened its cover," he writes, "I was dazzled. . . . I knew that I stood at the threshold of a great and decisive experience, and with a kind of fearful joy I turned the pages of that great book, intoxicated and happy" (SF6, 83).

Following these openings, both the Lilien essay and the collection *Sanatorium* progress from artistic awakening and the experience of transformed vision toward a sober evaluation of the possibilities for that vision dream to flourish in the light of more recent history: a growing mood of resignation, foreboding, and also nostalgia for a time now decisively in the past.[64] Thus the story "The Book" opens with a creation scene whose poetic imagery nods to and translates elements of the neo-Platonic creation myth as portrayed in the *Zohar*.[65] "The blank pages grew opaque and ghostly with a delightful foreboding and . . . one's eyes turned toward a virgin dawn of divine colors. . . . O, that invasion of brightness, that blissful spring," (W, 115). From here it traces, through the two linked stories that follow it, "*Genialna epoka*" ("The Age of Genius") and the opening of "Spring," the young artist's artistic development, and his growing commitment to recover fragments of the original Book, to "gather up the wondrous things that God is throwing at [him]," and to stage a revolutionary liberation of the poetic word.

Lilien had illustrated and published *Die Bücher der Bibel* (*The Books of the Bible*) beginning in 1908 with the *Das Fünfbuch Mose* (*The Five Books of Moses*), which rendered the stories of Genesis in Secessionist-style images and decorated frames that for Schulz expressed the height of his poetic power as a graphic artist. Here, in the second story of *Sanatorium*, the "Age of Genius" ("*Genialna epoka*"), the landscapes of a new Bible flow spontaneously through the pencils and paints of the young artist, coming to life on the pages in front of him as the story recruits the reader in its celebration of the child's impulse to overwrite the "old Bibles" with "enigmas of bright revelation:"[66] "As in Noah's day, colorful processions would flow, rivers of hair and manes, of wavy backs and tails (W, 133):

> Then I understood what I had to do; and full of enthusiasm I began to pull from the cupboards old folios, Father's disintegrating business ledgers that were covered with his writing, and I threw them onto the floor under that pillar of fire that was lying upon the air, and burning. . . . And I sat among those papers, blinded by the radiance. . . . I drew hastily, in a panic, crosswise, across printed and handwritten pages. Inspired, my colored pencils flew across columns of illegible texts, raced in brilliant scrawls, in neck-breaking zigzags, suddenly knotting into anagrams of visions, into rebuses of luminous revelations (L, 96; O, 123).

"*Wiosna*" ("Spring"), the third story in the collection, is cast as a picaresque novella. Here the protagonist, now a young man, acts on the intuition that he must liberate the beautiful and inaccessible Bianca—whom he learns has a revolutionary and mixed-race ancestry—from her suffocating prison, a gated European villa. Combining parable with the structure of a tale by Nachman of Bratslav, in which the viceroy must liberate the princess, or Shekhinah, from a well-guarded palace, the story nods to the author's own Quixotic mission: to liberate language, and specifically the poetry of the Polish word; to discover the "mosaic" pieces within the prosaic or bourgeois vernacular forms in which they are hidden. The Joseph of "Spring" is also figured as an apostle of multiplicity, the reader of a new gospel—the Stamp Album—in which, to his amazement, God's voice speaks equally beautifully in the languages and colors of every country.

> I opened it, and the glamour of colorful worlds . . . spread before me. God walked through it, page after page, pulling behind Him a train woven from all the zones and climates (W, 152). You said whatever came into Your mind. You might equally well have said Panphibrass or Halleleevah, and the air among palms would flutter with motley parrot wings, and the sky, like an enormous sapphire cabbage rose, blown open to its core, would show in its dazzling center. Your frightening peacock eye, would shine with the glare of Your wisdom. . . . You wanted to dazzle me, O God, to seduce me, perhaps to boast, for even you have moments of vanity when You succumb to self-congratulation (W, 152; O, 145).

But as it does in the Lilien article, this celebratory mood shifts at the end of "Spring," as the author turns his parable toward metatextual reflection on the unrealistic idealism of his own literary endeavors. Central among them, as one reading allows, is his attempt to pursue the idealistic goals of the modern Jewish renaissance movement—and of his young adulthood in the Habsburg Empire—at the center of Polish letters. The protagonist, Joseph, arrested at the story's end, confesses, "I wanted to remain in the role destiny had allotted to me, I wanted to fulfill my task and remain loyal to the position I had usurped. . . . The spring has carried me away for a time. I wanted to harness it, to direct it according to my own plans. . . . I took its lack of [sensitivity] for tolerance, even for solidarity, for complicity. I thought that I could decipher, even better than Spring itself, its deepest intentions" (W, 199). But, he pronounces stoically, "In reality I have known my fate from the outset . . . my fate was that of Abel. There was a moment when my sacrifice seemed sweet and pleasing to God, when your chances seemed nil, Rudolph. But Cain always wins.[67] The dice were loaded against me [*ta gra była z góry ukartkowana*]" (W, 200; O, 206–207). For Schulz, in these stories, "the early young spring of that myth" had "outlived itself, and expired."[68]

After this third story, the stories that Schulz had included in *Sanatorium* "as a kind of paralipomenon" effectively play the role of a buffer before the volume advances toward its eponymous piece "Sanatorium under the Sign of the Hourglass." As a result of this arrangement, the arc of the volume bends toward skepticism and resignation at the increasing, and indeed inevitable, turning of history toward political nationalisms. This skepticism concerns not only the dream of a successfully hijacked Polish Jewish literary language but also, again, of Zionist/Hebraist and even Yiddishist projects that, willingly or not, were also establishing borders and walls within the multilingual territory of national/universalist Jewish writing.

Schulz had written of Lilien that in that artist's work the spirit of living, modern Jewish poetry, which expressed itself in the Neo-Romantic symbolism and decorative illuminations of his early Jewish-themed albums *Juda* and *Lieder des Ghetto*, could not survive the profound transformations taking place within the East European Jewish world as a generation prepared to make the transition to real-world safety, statehood and economic security in a new homeland. The reemergence of that essay has made it possible to highlight Schulz's own concerted engagement with the challenges of Jewish cultural continuity, and with the question of what statehood and growing ethno-linguistic division within the Jewish literary world could mean for a modern Jewish culture that was born in the hybrid, multilingual contexts of diaspora. It has also helped to foreground the dialectical tension between spiritual and material, sacred and profane that in Schulz's work is epitomized in the picture-riddle, or "*obraz-talisman*" from Schulz's "Dead Season," and that figures as a defining trope both in Schulz's oeuvre and in the modern Jewish experience.

The picture-riddle in which sacred and profane, spiritual and worldly motivations and aspects of the self face each other in endless debate had been a central theme in Schulz's graphic works before he met Vogel. In the shift from his pre-1930 work to the stories of *Cinnamon Shops* and *Sanatorium*, we see a process of development and maturation, through which Schulz embraces his commitment to the project of Jewish modernism. In the final chapter of this study, I turn to a closer consideration of that transition, examining the evolution of Schulz's poetics of redemptive exegesis, from the erotic-messianic iconography of the *Book of Idolatry* to a linguistic-ontological theory of poetic mythologizing modeled on the Lurianic paradigm of *tikkun-olam*, or repair of the world, that would characterize Schulz's lasting contribution to modern Jewish literature.

5

ACCULTURATION WITHOUT ASSIMILATION

Polish Contexts for a Translational Poetics

SCHULZ'S TEXTS FREQUENTLY PORTRAY THE LITERARY PROJECT IN which they are engaged as an illicit, questionable or subversive activity—an undertaking foreclosed by history, requiring the artist and his readers to enter a "second track of time." "What is to be done with events that have no place of their own in time," asks the narrator at the opening of "The Age of Genius," the second story in Schulz's collection *Sanatorium under the Sign of the Hourglass*: "events that have been left out in the cold, unregistered, hanging in the air, homeless, and errant?" (W, 129; O, 120).

> Have you ever heard of parallel tracks of time within a two-track time? Yes, there are such branch lines of time, somewhat illegal and suspect [*trochę nielegalne co prawda, i problematyczne*], but when, like us, one is burdened with contraband of supernumerary events that cannot be registered [*gdy się wiezie taką kontrabandę jak my*], one cannot be too fussy. Let us try to find at some point of history such a branch line, a blind track onto which to shunt these illegal events. . . . There is nothing to fear. . . . Don't let's panic; we'll take care of this quietly within our own sphere of operations [*we własnym zakresie działanie*].[1] . . . It will all happen imperceptibly: the reader won't feel any shock."[2]

Rachel Auerbach had described Schulz's poetic prose as "utterly unique: a singular revelation of Jewish genius. Strange and original, with a power bordering on the ecstatic."[3] But that writing also offers a glimpse of a cultural landscape that was in the process of emerging. Schulz's idiosyncratic creation can be viewed as an early herald of a second, Polish Jewish track of Polish letters that had only begun to be laid, and whose future trajectory would be lost to history. In this chapter, I examine more closely a number of demographic, linguistic, and social factors characteristic not only of Galicia but of Jewish life in historically Polish lands—the lands that made up the Polish-Lithuanian Commonwealth prior to partition—that helped to create the conditions for the emergence in the twentieth century of new forms of Jewish modernist writing in the Polish language. These factors include, first, the historically high concentration of Jewish populations in Polish towns and cities, which enabled what were effectively majority-Jewish cultural environments, and second, the fact that the Polish language was on its way to becoming a Jewish vernacular in the interwar period. In part, Schulz's early settling of this Polish Jewish linguistic territory owes its existence to a Galician head-start that saw Jews adopting Polish as a vernacular or a "new Yiddish" almost two generations earlier than Jews in Warsaw and the Russian partition and—what is of defining importance—adapting it in the context of a multiethnic, multilingual empire in which both Poles and Jews were minorities, while German was the language of the state.[4] A third factor that contributed to emerging Polish Jewish cultural imaginaries of the interwar period was a discourse of pluralism or multiplicity (*wielość*) that had distinct historical roots in both the Habsburg Empire and the Polish Lithuanian Commonwealth—two multiethnic, multilingual polities that preceded the emergence of Central European nation-states. Celebration of this multicultural landscape became a building block of the Romantic cultural imaginary of partitioned Poland through the literature of Adam Mickiewicz, and it figured prominently in pre-WWI Polish political debates. Though overshadowed in the 1920s and 30s by narratives of integral and extrusionary nationalism, a politics of multiplicity or pluralism still had substantial political support in the early twentieth century and in reconstituted post-WWI Poland. This minority narrative contributed to an environment in which Jewish writers could choose to imagine Polish-language literature as a territory open to non-ethnically Polish artists; a multiethnic or cosmopolitan, de-ethnicized territory—and could begin to transform it into one. The guiding value of "multiplicity" ("*wielość*") toward which Debora Vogel had turned at the end of her essay "Human Exotics," and to which she referred in letters to Schulz, also undergirds the Polish Jewish writing of many in their interwar generation.

Rethinking Minorityhood and Assimilation

Spheres of Jewish cultural "majorityhood" and the adoption of Polish as a Jewish language are Polish Jewish realities of the interwar period that present a challenge to still-dominant scholarly paradigms of minorityhood and assimilation that have been associated with Jewish writing in non-Jewish European languages. The long-held assumption that integration, acquisition of the non-Jewish national language, and cosmopolitanism forged a quick and sure path to assimilation and even conversion is connected to a German Jewish model associated with the Haskalah or Jewish Enlightenment in Germany that, until recently, dominated within studies of Jewish entry into modernity. The predominance of this West European model, in which Jews "exchanged their values for those of the dominant culture in the hope of acceptance, politically and socially," and that "involved varying degrees of self-rejection," as Gershon Hundert writes, has continued to obscure the vastly different demographic and cultural conditions that existed in the Habsburg and Russian Empires on the lands of the former Polish-Lithuanian Commonwealth, where Ashkenazi Jews were concentrated, and that distinguished Jewish movement into modernity in formerly Polish lands from that in Western Europe.[5] In recent years, however, scholars of East European Jewish history have placed renewed emphasis on discourses of Jewish autonomy and majorityhood that were first introduced into Jewish historiography at the turn of the twentieth century by historian Simon Dubnow in his *Letters on New and Old Judaism* and given further sociological grounding by the pioneering demographer and Jewish sociologist Jacob Lestschinsky.[6] In his analysis of the rise of competing modern Jewish cultural movements in the late nineteenth and early twentieth centuries, and of the actors he terms "culturalists," historian Kenneth Moss addresses the distinctiveness of the East European Jewish experience of entry into modernity. If in Western and Central Europe Jews "were offered an emancipatory contract that they essentially fulfilled: societal and cultural integration as individuals in exchange for the dissolution of all Jewish corporate identity other than the conventional," in Eastern Europe "mutually reinforcing factors such as the ethnic discriminations of the Tsarist state, the ethnopolitics of coterritorial Polish and Ukrainian nationalism, and the persistence of separate Jewish language and associational patterns on a mass scale ensured that Jewishness remained a powerful axis of group mobilization and individual self-identity for millions ... even as its meaning became ever more contentious." [7]Lestschinsky, in his 1918 essay "Jewish Autonomy Yesterday and Today," offered an early scientific discussion of this phenomenon, examining "the processes in Jewish life that led to new ideas of autonomy, which in turn ... established the conditions for an independent national life and unique cultural creativity."⁸ But the East European context to which these discussions refer, so distinct from the German Jewish model that strongly influenced the uses and meanings of the very terms *assimilated* and *acculturated* within scholarly discourse on modern Jewish culture, had its earlier roots in the political, economic, and demographic structures of the Polish-Lithuanian Commonwealth (1569–1791), whose territories were partitioned among Prussia, the Russian Pale of Settlement, and Galician Austria at the end of the eighteenth century. In *Jews in Poland-Lithuania*, Gershon Hundert argued as well that the forms of social organization and communal life that developed on the lands of the Commonwealth, and later under Russian and Austrian rule, challenge received notions of both minorityhood and assimilation. "The term minority," argues Hundert, "has a set of connotations that are misleading when applied to Jews in the Polish Commonwealth. . . . The experience of Western European Jews has been the template for the story of modernization told by virtually every Jewish historian of the period," but "that narrative concerns only small Jewish communities comprising tiny portions of the total populations of the countries in which they lived."⁹ In the Commonwealth, by contrast, "most Jews lived in communities that were quite large enough to support the living of the dailiness of life in a Jewish universe. For these reasons, the term 'minority group' . . . used to describe groups outside of the imagined homogeneous citizenry in modern nation-states . . . is entirely misleading."¹⁰

Present in the territories from the tenth century, Jews began moving to the Polish-Lithuanian Commonwealth in large numbers from the fourteenth to the eighteenth centuries, making the historical lands of the commonwealth the home of the majority of world Jewry by the seventeenth century. It was here that Jews built the institutions and patterns of autonomous communal life that characterized Ashkenazi Jewish civilization for centuries: the educational structures of the cheder and Yeshiva system; communal patterns of local organization, regional representation and courts of law, including local *kehillot* and the *Va'ad Arbat Aratzot* (Council of the Four Lands); and the social organization that from the eighteenth century on developed in connection with Hasidic courts. In the eighteenth century, approximately one-half of the entire population of cities and towns in the commonwealth was Jewish. The majority of Christian residents of any given municipality were involved in agriculture, and their homes were located outside of the town's center or in the surrounding villages.¹¹ In such a context, Jews' experience of living in towns was again one of living in a Jewish-majority space. This early social framework that established the patterns of Jewish autonomy on Polish lands has relevance for the forms of modern literature, art, film, and theater that would emerge much later in post–World War I Poland, including in the Polish language, with the strong participation of Jewish artists.

While the demographics of urban and small-town Polish landscapes shifted dramatically with modernization, industrialization, *embourgeoisement*, and the movement of both peasants (from villages) and Jews (from smaller towns) into cities, the paradigm of Jewish separateness remained a constant within the now Russian- and Austrian-controlled lands of the partitions, which began to see the emergence of a modern Jewish public sphere in the late nineteenth and early twentieth centuries.[12] As Moss writes, in this East European context "it was logical that some East European Jews rejected—or simply never considered—the notion that the price of modernity was the erasure of their Jewishness" and that they "sought instead a majority of their own making. As historians have long recognized the concept of Jewish culture stood at the center of the search."[13]

The reality of the living of daily life in majority-Jewish cultural environments in the towns and cities of Poland, then, and in particular Galicia, renders the concepts and discourses of assimilation and acculturation problematic and of limited use in the Polish context. Here modernization, movement to larger cities, and even secularization, where it applied, were marked not by the gradual assimilation of Jews into Polish or Polish Catholic culture and language, with attendant loss of Jewish identity, but instead by the gradual adaptation of the Polish language as a Jewish vernacular and a language in which to articulate and debate diverse and developing forms of modern Jewish identity.[14] In their discussion of Jewries in Galicia and Bukovina, Lichtblau and John cite a telling passage from the novel *Prophet Johannes* by German Jewish poet Alfred Nossig, published in 1892, and set in Lemberg Lemberg/Lwów in 1880: "the protagonist depicts a group strolling along the Lemberg Promenade: the adults walk at the head of the group, among them the narrator who 'hears only chitchat in German all around him.' The young people follow slightly behind, 'conversing among themselves in splendid Polish.'"[15]

Within independent Poland following World War I, the paradigm of relative autonomy, separateness, and even cultural majorityhood was transformed by Jewish citizens' legally guaranteed ability to participate in all aspects of political, economic, and cultural life. Yet at the same time, it would also be newly sustained and reinforced by the steady and later sharp rise in antisemitism throughout the 1920s and '30s. Paradoxically, it is in this interwar environment of growing polarization that a new generation of Jews—now citizens of the reconstituted Polish state and students in the Polish-language public schools—made the shift in much greater numbers to speaking Polish as a native language. It is the shift that members of Schulz's Galician Jewish milieu had begun to make a full two generations earlier, in 1867, as a result of the granting of political autonomy to the Galician region of Austria.[16]

Toward a Polish Jewish Cultural Imaginary

Like other newly formed states in Central Europe, Poland adopted a minorities treaty following World War I, which included a provision that state funding should support schooling in the minority languages of Poland—including Yiddish.[17] In reality, such support did not materialize. While privately funded secular schooling in Yiddish and Hebrew was the focus of a great deal of activism across the political spectrum, in practice it became a reality for a fairly small percentage of students of the school-age generation in the 1930s. Families that did not have the money to pay for private schools—a demographic that included the majority of all Jews in the interwar period, including a majority of religious Jews, both Hasidic and non-Hasidic—sent their children to Polish-language public schools, where they quickly acquired Polish as a native language. Additionally, even as Yiddishism and Hebraism gained adherents, many Jews wanted a secular, Polish-language education for their children who were now citizens of a Polish state. Thus, in 1936, records indicate that 69 percent of Jewish students were attending Polish public school.[18] Such attendance was not equivalent, however, to going to school in a Polish Catholic–majority environment. A growing percentage of secular Polish-language schools had a virtually all-Jewish student body—creating environments all the more attractive as students could be more or less protected from the daily experience of antisemitism at school.[19] These details help to confirm again that while the dynamic of majority-Jewish cultural environments continued to change with time, it endured and took on new forms.

The existence of majority- and all-Jewish Polish-language public schools was one more contributing factor to a dynamic that historian Sam Kassow has described as "acculturation without assimilation". The phrase can help to draw attention to the emergence of a distinct Polish Jewish cultural imaginary shaped by Polish literary and cultural traditions to which Jewish students were exposed, in Polish-speaking environments, but running along a separate, parallel track or tracks. Again, as Kassow writes, "although young Jews received a Polish education, they did not become young Poles."[20]

Students of this generation were, however, becoming some of the country's most attentive readers of the Polish literary canon—including foundational works of Polish Romantic nationalism, and building blocks of the Polish national identity, by the poets Adam Mickiewicz, Juliusz Słowacki, and Zygmunt Krasiński. They also read and memorized, both as children and as adults, the exuberant modern verse being written by Polish Jewish writers Bolesław Leśmian, Julian Tuwim, Jan Brzechwa, Antoni Słonimski, and Aleksander Wat, among others. Even those students and adult readers who were neither privy to nor engaged in Jewish cultural activism were reading these works as Jewish citizens of Poland, and not as Catholic Poles, allowing this literature's themes and imagery to resonate with their own Polish Jewish experiences, and incorporating them into a new Polish Jewish cultural imaginary. The process of reading and reverse-acculturating works of Polish culture was translingual, taking place in Yiddish and Hebrew as well as in Polish. Thus Polish Romantic national literature and culture informed the emergence of a Polish Jewish national imaginary within modern Yiddish and Hebrew poetry. Works by non-Jewish Polish authors were also becoming, in translation to Yiddish, the most popular titles available for Yiddish-language reading, to the concern of some Yiddishist activists. The novels of the immensely popular Polish writer Henryk Sienkiewicz, for example, were by far the most borrowed books in every Jewish library and reading room, including the Strashun Library in Vilna/Wilno. For Polish Jewish readers, who could read Sienkiewicz's classic *Quo Vadis* either in Polish or in its 1928 translation into Yiddish by Itzhak Daytsher, the central trope of martyrdom at the hands of the Roman rulers could and would have become available for interpretation by the Jewish reader not only as a story about Poland's martyrdom in the Polish Uprisings against the Russian Empire—the original allegory understood by readers of Sienkiewicz during the Partitions—but also as a story about Jewish suffering at the hands of rightwing Polish nationalists. James Loeffler has fascinatingly argued that this was precisely the case for the Polish Jewish Raphael Lemkin, who would go on to theorize the concept of genocide.

Kamil Kijek in *Dzieci modernizmu* (*Children of Modernism*) draws attention to forms of symbolic violence that also characterized the experience of this interwar Jewish generation—students who received a Polish literary and cultural education at a time when the dominant national narratives and discourses did not consider Jews an integral part of the Polish nation.[21] He writes that "both the elite and the Jewish masses held strong convictions regarding the difference between the idealized '*Polska Mickiewicza*' ['Mickiewicz's Poland'], the Poland that had struggled for freedom, that was open and tolerant toward Jewish difference; and the present-day [interwar] Poland"—here he refers to the 1930s—"that was oppressive toward minorities, and was often referred to as '*Polska Narodowej Demokracji*' [the Poland of the right-wing National Democratic (*Endek*) Party]." For both the elite and the Jewish masses, "that first Poland—that of Mickiewicz—represented a usable history." It contributed to "a historical narrative that the majority of the Jewish intelligentsia—including its most nationalist elements—were directly involved in constructing."[22] The idea of two Polands, one of which was open and tolerant, argues Kijek, helped to keep alive Polish Jewish patriotism and also faith in pluralism as a cornerstone of what was perceived by some as the more authentic Polish national historical narrative—and thus, theoretically, of a possible Polish future.

A number of studies of Polish language acquisition among Jewish youth were conducted in the interwar period by Yiddishists whose goal was to sustain Yiddish-language use in the next generation. As Nathan Cohen writes, the picture that emerges from these studies is that by the 1930s, Polish was becoming the Jewish vernacular of the great majority of Jewish youth in Poland, including among the lower classes, and within Hasidic communities.[23] While many Yiddishists, Zionists, and traditionally religious Jews bemoaned this process and sought to ameliorate it or to slow it down, it was also increasingly recognized as an inevitability. Had it not been for the Holocaust, it seems inevitable that Polish would have replaced Yiddish within two to three generations as the new vernacular of that substantial portion of world Jewry that lived in Poland, including individuals in secular and religious, urban and provincial Jewish communities.

Few were more attuned to this process than Polish Catholic, right-nationalist literary and cultural critics, for whom it was seen as a corruption and a Judaizing of the Polish language. While powerless to influence the everyday linguistic reality on the Jewish street and in the courtyards of Polish towns and cities, critics could and did turn their attention to the writing class. Jewish poets and writers who chose to participate in the creation of a new and liberatory modern Polish writing, expressive of the spirit of a young, free, postwar generation whose slogan was a line from Jan Lechoń's 1920 poem "Herostrates": "*A wiosną - niechaj wiosnę, nie Polskę zobaczę*" ("In Spring, let it be spring, not Poland, that I see"), and who moved to the center of Polish culture as writers, publishers, and cabaret artists, became the targets of virulent antisemitic attacks. This attention included attacks on the Polish-language Jewish press, which was mocked for using the Polish language to promote Jewish nationalism. Most frequently, however, it was aimed at writers who did not limit themselves to Jewish topics, and who were in the process of creating instead a cosmopolitan and "universalist" literature directed at a broad Polish-language readership. Such writers were opening and actively transforming the Polish cultural imaginary of both Jewish and Polish readers. The writers associated with the *Skamander* group of poets and with Warsaw's weekly literary newspaper *Wiadomości Literackie* (Literary News, 1924–1939). As Joanna Michlic writes, "National Democracy [the nationalist right party *Narodowa Demokracja*] failed to extend its influence over the high culture of interwar Poland," and members of the liberal intelligentsia were the main creators and disseminators of the high culture of the interwar period."[24] Founded and edited by Mieczysław Grydzewski (b. Gretzhendler, 1894–1970), *Wiadomości Literackie* functioned as the leading producer and arbiter of modern Polish literature and culture and was openly opposed to the Endek politics of extrusionary ethnonationalism. It was considered by critics aligned with that party to be a Jewish journal. Other leading contributors to the paper included Julian Tuwim (1894–1953) and poet, journalist, and playwright Antoni Słonimski (1895–1976), grandson of the Hebrew publisher and astronomer Hayyim Selig Słonimski (1810–1904).[25]

These dynamics highlight the role of language as a metonym for the national body, and as the symbolic corollary of to the geographical space of the nation-state. The use of Polish as a literary language by non-Catholic, non-ethnically Polish writers represented for nationalist, Polish Catholic critics an invasion of and violation of the Polish cultural body. Jewish writers who brought their voices and forms of literary expression into the Polish cultural sphere, Schulz among them, were figured in the more extreme critiques as the reviled agents of a range of modern depravities: secularism and atheism, hyper-eroticism and sexual perversion, chaos and disorder, ethnic ambiguity. Understood as more egregious than the physical presence in Poland of traditional Jews who maintained their difference and engaged with ethnic Poles primarily in the economic sphere, the Jewish occupation of both Polish high culture and the sphere of Polish pedagogy, in the form of popular modern poetry, children's books, and theater and radio programming produced for children, was cast within nationalist critique as a spiritual and cultural infection aimed at the very spirit and consciousness of a new generation of ethnic Poles.

The enormously popular poet Julian Tuwim, who in his pre-WWII writing largely distanced himself in thematics and in his public statements from Jewish culture, was a particular focus of attacks from Polish nationalist critics.[26] He was accused of being "culturally alien to Poland," of "not understanding the spirit of the Polish language," and "of littering or defiling the Polish language." Even those who grudgingly acknowledged his virtuosity as a poet readily took up critic Władysław Rabski's claim: "*Tuwim nie pisze po polsku, tylko w polskim języku*"; "Tuwim does not write in Polish; he merely writes in the Polish language."[27] "A person who spent his childhood in the ghetto," wrote Tadeusz Kudliński, "cannot be a Polish poet. There is likely no one who believes that the language in which one creates testifies to one's belonging to that nation."[28] Scholarship has rightly treated statements of this kind with censure, studying them as examples of ethnonationalist discourse associated with the rise of extrusionary nationalism and proto-fascism in interwar Poland. But they can also be read as accurate, if tendentious and ideologically charged, reactions to what was nevertheless a real and characteristic dynamic of Polish and Jewish modernization. They record bigoted and also fearful reactions to a real linguistic and cultural shift that was underway in Poland, much like that taking place in the United States in the twenty-first century: the loss of control and hegemony over cultural resources by a previously dominant cultural group. Further study of this linguistic and cultural metamorphosis promises to change the ways that we understand and describe both Polish modernism and Jewish writing in the Polish language.[29] From the perspective of the multilingual Jewish polysystem that existed in interwar Poland and the emergence of Polish as a Jewish language, a range of Polish modernist texts can productively be read not only as cornerstones of the Polish modernist canon, but also as the work of early Polish Jewish pioneers and dissidents—willing or unwilling—who were paving the way for Polish-language literature to become a cosmopolitan, binational, and transnational cultural space.

Working at the intersection of modern Jewish philosophy and Polish literature, scholars Agata Bielik-Robson and Adam Lipszyc have initiated such a reevaluation of the modernist canon through the introduction of the paradigm of "marranism." Inspired by Hannah Arendt's 1948 text "Pariah and Jew," the marrano metaphor emphasizes the quality of hiddenness, and the encryption of Jewish content and identity that characterizes the work of many Jewish writers entering the Polish literary scene. Marranism becomes a discursive tool for contemporary critics to "explore the fruitful area of mixture and crossover which allowed modern thinkers, writers, and artists of the Jewish origin to enter the realm of universal communication—without, at the same time, making them relinquish their Jewishness, which they subsequently developed as a 'hidden tradition.'"[30] *Marranos of Polish Literature*, the first volume of essays to emerge from this project, rereads canonical Polish Jewish authors through the lens of marranism. In their introduction to the volume, entitled "In Esau's Skin," Bogalecki and Lipszyc explain that "in accordance with the historical source of the Marrano figure, it is an identity for which the element of hiding holds a fundamental significance. Taken nominally, that which is minor hides here within the substance of the majority. It is not what is hidden that determines the essence of this identity, however, but the very structure of secrecy itself."[31] In the case of Schulz, who embraced a Galician Jewish renaissance blending of Jewish and European content, another model emerges. Marrano hiddenness takes a back seat to two-track or multi-track polyphony, layered temporality, and intentional translationality. Yet each of these metaphors—marranism, two-track time, and a changing of masks—seeks to capture the rich complexity of a moment of dramatic change in which the Polish language and the sphere of Jewish cultural tradition collide with spectacular, yet-to-be unraveled results.

Skepticism about the central role the Polish Jewish writers and editors associated with *Wiadomości Literackie* were playing within Polish high and popular culture was not limited to Polish nationalist critics. Karolina Szymaniak, in her study "The Bootlickers' Bulletin," describes the resentment that existed within Yiddishist discourse surrounding acculturated Jews who were working at the center of Polish-language literary culture. The cultural politics of *Wiadomości Literackie* were also the subject of fierce debate on the pages of the Yiddish journal *Literarishe bleter*, where the editors and writers of the Polish-language *Wiadomości* were referred to as "literary Moyshkes," "*sruliks*," and "*zhidkes*," or "literary Jew-Boys."[32] As many Yiddish critics saw it, the editors and writers of *Wiadomości Literackie* had both the opportunity and responsibility, writing for the most respected and widely read Polish-language literary journal of interwar Poland, to play the role of cultural mediators—to accord recognition and respect to Yiddish works and writers, and to recognize the parallel development of both Yiddish and Polish modernist art. They not only failed to do so, but it was an editorial choice of the journal—which in general promoted a carefully curated cosmopolitan and antinationalist ethos—to demonstratively ignore Yiddish literature. Or, to treat the choice to devote oneself to writing poetry and literature in Yiddish as a decision in favor of narrow parochialism, as a decisively anticosmopolitan gesture. Within Bruno Schulz's Lwów-based, Polish-speaking intellectual milieu as well, skepticism regarding *Wiadomości Literackie*'s antinationalist but not openly Jewish posture can be found in evidence by the mid-1930s. "By introducing entirely new ways of experiencing the world," wrote Stanisława Blumenfeldowa in her article 'The Jewish Question in Poland' for *Sygnały*, "on the one hand we bring about an enrichment of the [Polish] cultural fabric, yet on the other, at least at the present time, we create a good deal of confusion. Perhaps the example of *Wiadomości Literackie* illustrates most clearly what I have in mind. . . . This group is playing an important role in the past 25 years, and is generating a good deal of dislike from both sides. . . . I believe that we could easily avoid this, were we to simply accept that in fact we are quite different from people who are natively Polish."[33]

It is true that many Polish Jewish modernists associated with *Skamander* and *Wiadomości Literackie*, including Tuwim, Słonimski, Schulz, and Leśmian, distanced themselves to varying degrees and through different poetic techniques from the use of openly Jewish subject matter, and all were interested to construct universalist/Europeanist, not exclusively Jewish themed literature. In some cases when Tuwim did address Jewish subjects directly, he cast himself in the role of conflicted onlooker, emotionally attached and yet separated by education, class, and culture from the non-assimilated Jewish masses.[34]

In response to this intentional occlusion, one option for post-WWII literary critics has been to respond in kind: if a writer chose to hide Jewishness and Jewish thematics in their work, it is respectful to leave it out of later discussions of that work. Yet such an approach tends to inadvertently reprise some of the original fears at the center of the Polish interwar literary world and within the *Wiadomości Literackie* milieu. In some cases it may speak to a perceived need to protect the universalism and the Enlightenment inheritance of Polish culture from the encroachment of parochialisms. It has also led critics to overlook the ways in which specifically Jewish writers, and Jewish entry into modern Polish society, were profoundly transforming Polish culture and language—both into spaces of secular Jewish expression and into non-ethnically-marked spaces—as well as to overlook the ways in which the discourses of cosmopolitanism and universalism have been studied as precisely characteristic of Jewish modernity.

"That Early Idyll": Baudouin de Courtenay's Politics of Pluralism

In post-WWI Poland, Schulz's evocation of a textual sanctuary beyond borders in a territory that was "no one's and God's," intentionally recovered and activated discourses of pluralism associated with the multicultural Habsburg Empire and the "Austrian Idea." But it also found its corollary in the discourse of inclusive pluralism advocated by progressive Polish intellectuals, stretching back to the Romantic thought of Adam Mickiewicz in the nineteenth century, and to earlier traditions of Jagiellonian Poland and the multicultural Polish-Lithuanian Commonwealth. In the early twentieth century, a politics of inclusive pluralism was passionately advocated by the noted linguist, Freethinker, and candidate for the Polish presidency Jan Niecisław Baudouin de Courtenay (1845–1929).[35] Baudouin, a Polish scholar of French aristocratic background, was a highly respected intellectual and public figure in Warsaw in the 1910s and '20s who both published and spoke publicly, before and after the First World War, on the subject of the Jewish Question.[36] A pacifist, feminist, environmentalist, and promoter of progressive education, Baudouin used his public inaugural lecture as a professor of linguistics at the University of Warsaw in 1918 to argue that "Poland had not been resurrected in order to swell the tally of imperialist hyena-states." He became the Minorities Bloc's candidate for president in independent Poland's first elections in 1922, earning 20 percent of the popular vote—and "in the discussions on educational reform [he] shocked many of his supporters by suggesting that Polish should be taught in all Jewish schools in Poland just as Yiddish ought to be taught in all Polish schools."[37] Opposed to the premise of national self-determination that emerged from Versailles, Baudouin argued that the nationalist ideology that undergirded emerging nation-states was supported by the "barbaric theory that a certain portion of the residents of a given country have the right to consider themselves its 'hosts,' and another can have pretensions at the very most to the role of tolerated 'guests.'" He imagined the logical outcome of this premise in sobering terms that predict the language Hannah Arendt would use in her later study of totalitarianism:

Of course people of other nationalities will be allowed to come to Poland, but only as temporary guests, humble guests, not as claimants with pretensions to any form of national distinction. The entire globe will be divided up into strictly separated national cages with only the purest fullbloods. These will be nationally-unblemished "fatherlands": The German will sit in his cage, the Frenchman in his, the Lithuanian in his and so on, and none is permitted to stick his nose outside the boundaries of his nationally-pure fatherland. Obviously, [Habsburg] Austria and Switzerland will be crossed off the list of allowable countries.[38]

Writing in 1911, the author used Galicia as a prime example of the impossibility and indefensibility of the nation-state premise: "But let's adapt these questions to the Jews of Galicia. In relation to which 'hosting' nationality should Galician Jews consider themselves the 'guests'? For example in eastern Galicia, who should be considered the 'hosts'? Are Jews there the 'guests' of Poles, or Rusyns, or maybe of Germans?[39] Or perhaps it would be most correct to allow each Jew, as an individual with full citizen's rights, to be what he wants. Let every person decide independently as to the nature of his or her national and religious belonging."[40]

Given Poland's history of partition and occupation, Baudouin's antinationalist stance, which could conceive of a reemergent Poland only as a pluralist civic polity, was a progressive minority view among the Polish intelligentsia, particularly in Warsaw and the Russian-controlled Congress Kingdom. Before Poland regained its independence, that intelligentsia had had to fight for cultural survival and the preservation of national narrative for over a century, with attendant periods of intense Russification and Germanicization aimed at the suppression of the Polish language and the eradication of Polish cultural identity. For this reason, in the early twentieth century even progressive members of the Polish intelligentsia felt that a Polish state, should it emerge, could not afford to be culturally and politically divided among ethnicities and nationalities with competing interests.[41] Eliza Orzeszkowa, one of the most influential and respected members of the progressive generation of Positivist Polish writers (1880s–1905), weighed in on the Jewish Question in the last year of her life. In her posthumously published notes on this subject, she reflected that "the organization of Jews on Polish land into a separate nationality, into a nationality indifferent to Polish struggles, aspirations and desires, to Polish ideas and culture—represents a serious and threatening danger for Polish society."[42] When Poland was granted independence following WWI, this prewar ethos was not without influence on the sense of caution surrounding treatment of Jewish subject matter displayed by Jewish writers who participated in Poland's leading literary movements. For many Galician Jews, however, acculturation in a Habsburg context looked very different: it had meant precisely embracing the civic, pluralist accommodation of cultural multiplicity and simultaneity—the "Austrian Idea"—and it did not engender the same degree of caution. Schulz's translational strategy of mythologizing is but one example of the modernist literary forms that owe their genesis to that multiethnic, post-Imperial context, so different from formerly Russian Warsaw.

In their firm commitment to pluralism and ethical individualism, Baudouin's acerbic formulations are quite similar to later nostalgic articulations of the "Austrian Idea" that were expressed by Galician Jewish contemporaries of Bruno Schulz, including Joseph Roth (1894–1939), Stefan Zweig (1881–1942), and Franz Werfel (1890–1945). For Habsburg scholar Claudio Magris, Zweig was "the classic *porte-parole* of the humanist cosmopolitan wave that the Habsburg civilization had produced," while Werfel was "the last voice of [its] impossible continuation."[43] Magris does not consider Polish-language voices, but Schulz's could easily be added. His two-track poetics brought the Austrian Idea to the center of Polish letters. The popular and also controversial playwright Werfel, who later converted to Christianity, described Austria as a "proud Empire," the mystery of whose success at joining so many diverse cultures and "racial stocks" "can be ignored only by the baldness and falsity of our modern theories, economic and biological" that "derive the history of mankind from the fortuitous meeting of races with particular portions of the earth's surface, from the symbiosis of blood and soil. . . . According to such theories the history of a people from its rise to its decline—follows one single primitive line, determined only by the material forces of earth, soil, and necessity. For the spirit there is no room."[44] Werfel wrote of the "indescribable richness and variety" of the former Austria in terms familiar from Schulz's prose: "The soil of Austria has a mysterious, humus-forming power. Whole peoples and races, whose footprints she bears, became like the fallen leaves of last year's autumn; she took them all into herself and changed them into something new."[45] Austria was "a home of humanity without regard to blood or confession, to origin or goal of its children," and "the Austrian born in old Austria has a home no longer."[46] Notwithstanding the complexity of his own relationship with Jewishness, the ethos that Werfel expresses in his essay on the "Austrian Idea" was shared by Jewish writers who remained strongly committed to their Jewish identity.[47] For some writers, this included viewing Jewishness precisely as a model for a culture and society that had transcended brute militarism. "Where's the pride for the Jew, who disarmed long ago, in proving once more that he is capable of a squad drill!" wrote Joseph Roth.[48] Many Jewish writers who praised the Austrian Idea did so nostalgically, mourning its passing, or with a sense of deep foreboding. "A chilly sort of family, this 'family of nations'!" wrote Roth in the 1937 afterword to the second edition of *Wandering Jews*: "The father is quite set on only sweeping outside his own door, while the stench from his son's room rises to high heaven."[49] In his 1936 essay "On the Meaning of Imperial Austria," Werfel contrasted triumphant nationalism with the higher (for him) spiritual and ethical idea represented by the former Austria, which could be compared to the melting pot of the United States. Referring to the Austrian "higher idea," he argued that those who agreed to "abjure all fanatical abandonment to the instincts of the blood" had been "destined by the higher idea to be a teacher of men" and a "light to the East."[50] "That world is gone forever," mused Franz Werfel.

> After the long twilight of its old age, it died; and its death was no gentle one, but an anguished struggle. Yet very many of its children still live. . . . They belong to two worlds: to that dead one which, living in them, is not yet quite dead; and to the world of its heirs, who took over the property like goods after a sale. But this belonging to two worlds, this embracing of two epochs within one soul, is a highly paradoxical state. . . . True, every soul born in the last century and alive today, wherever he may live belongs to two epochs. And to bestride them both he must stretch all his powers.[51]

A part of Schulz's two-track Polish-language poetics involved bringing the "Austrian Idea" into the center of Polish high modernism.

"In Our Own Sphere of Operations": Julian Tuwim's "Polish-Language Fatherland" and Schulz's "Dead End"

While it was only a small fraction of the literary production by Jewish writers in Poland, literature by Jewish writers who chose, to use Harshav's formulation, "to go to the center" of Polish culture—to contribute to the creation of modern Polish culture—was a defining feature of the cultural landscape of the Second Republic. However, the coming into existence of such integrally Polish/Jewish cultural spaces as *Wiadomości Literackie*, the studios of interwar Polish cinema, and the cafes, cabarets, and recording studios that became a focal point of modern Polish cultural life can again be understood not as evidence not of assimilation but as, but of a new phenomenon of Polish/Jewish cosmopolitan encounter. In this model, individuals of Polish and Jewish ethnicity and of differing class backgrounds became part of a developing and shifting stratum of secular, politically liberal intelligentsia taking shape in interwar Poland's cities and towns. The high concentration within the largest urban centers not only of large Jewish populations but also of a growing urban, socially liberal or at least tolerant non-Jewish population created a critical mass of cultural consumers to support publications, performances, and cultural spaces that were created by Jewish Poles and Polish Poles together.

Undoubtedly, there were some Polish Jewish families and individuals for whom acculturation into Polish high culture, and identification with Polish cultural heritage, was a clear and desirable goal. Many of those who contributed to the new Polish/Jewish cultural world developing in interwar Poland were of this ethos. Warsaw again had the critical mass to support an entire acculturated Polish Jewish community, in Moss's framing, "with its own *habitus* and communal values of 'Polishness,' 'good manners,' and 'civilized behavior,' that provided a supportive framework in which its offspring and (perhaps) newcomers to Polish culture could affirm these values even in the face of rising extrusion due to anti-Semitism and pointed doubt about the possibility of Jewish Polish fusion."[52] But the very existence of urban spaces that enabled Polish writers of Jewish background to feel themselves co-creators of modern Polish culture depended on the growth and maintenance of a liberal and cosmopolitan, multiethnic stratum of Polish society, and its ability to resist cooption by divisive nationalist tendencies. These dynamics of cultural production and exchange bear examination through the lens of "national indifference" introduced by Zahra, as well as within the category of cultural production in minor languages described by David Damrosch in his study of world literature—namely, uses of a minor national language (in this case, Polish) that represent a wholesale recreation of that national culture by minority users of the language.[53]

In her study of interwar Polish cabaret, Beth Holmgren focuses attention on the extent to which Polish cabaret was a joint Polish Polish/Polish Jewish[54] endeavor, and a cosmopolitan site of encounter that resisted nationalist calls for separation. "Polish Jews became the Polish-language literary cabaret's chief producers and consumers," she writes. "Most of the cabaret's writers, underwriters, composers, and musicians had a Jewish background and were very often the children of acculturated Jews who were established professionals (doctors, lawyers, academics, businessmen)."[55] Her study contributes to the archaeology of Polish Jewish modernism by undertaking to restore a nuanced picture of the cosmopolitan, multiethnic, and multilingual complexity of this interwar art form and artistic community. Stage performer Stefania Grodzieńska's memoir, *The Bluebird*, writes Holmgren, "vouches for a shared cabaret identity established between Jewish and Gentile artists in interwar Poland. The Polish-language cabaret functioned as an inclusive oasis, a site of Jewish–Gentile artistic collaboration between the world wars"; and "the producers and players in Warsaw's interwar Polish-language literary cabaret evinced many of the same attributes and attitudes of the interwar Polish cultural intelligentsia."[56]

The central role played by Jewish writers in the modern Polish cultural renewal also included the creation of a new, modern canon of children's literature, including works by Julian Tuwim (author of the beloved *Lokomotywa*), Jan Brzechwa, Janusz Korczak (*King Matt the First*), and Bolesław Leśmian (*The Adventures of Sinbad*); and the creation by Janusz Korczak (Henryk Goldszmit) of the immensely popular interwar radio program for children "*Gadaninki radiowe*," featuring the unnamed "Stary Doktor" (Old Doctor). With the rise of a diverse Polish-language Jewish press,[57] Warsaw's *Nasz Przegląd* (*Our Review*), though directed at a Jewish readership, also came to be relied on as a leading source of international news by both Jewish and non-Jewish readers. Polish Jewish poets, prose writers, critics, and songwriters not only wrote *within* the cosmopolitan contexts that flourished in independent Poland; their textual landscapes also *produced* those contexts, creating a new, aspirational symbolic imaginary in the Polish language.

Read from this perspective, many of what have become the canonical works of Polish poetry from the interwar period reveal an impetus to imagine de-ethnicized or deterritorialized linguistic and textual spaces of belonging—moveable and transnational homelands. Alternately, they record a tendency to fashion the modern literary work as a sanctuary text. For assimilating or acculturating Jewish artists, this involved developing distinctly modern, non-ethnically marked discourses and visual/verbal landscapes, whether avant-garde, socialist, mythical, or cosmopolitan. For Julian Tuwim, the Polish language became, famously, "*moja ojczyzna-polszczyzna*," "my Polish-language-fatherland," reimagined in Tuwim's poem "*Zieleń*" ("Greenery") as a linguistic landscape connected not to Polish ethnicity or to Poland's national literary tradition but to *zieleńczość*, or "greenness"—that is, to the racially and ethnically neutral natural world. His poems evoke an imagined physical territory identified not specifically with *polskość* (Polishness) but with organic growth, newness, and newly greenness. This gesture, that we might call the "greening of Polish literature," is central to the poetry of pioneering modern Polish poet Bolesław Leśmian as well. Fittingly, Leśmian changed his name when he entered Polish-language letters from Lesman, which he feared might take him out of the running in Polish writing competitions, to the polonized Leśmian, evocative of the forest, or *las* (the adjective *leśny* meaning "of the forest"). In both Leśmian's and Tuwim's work, the Polish language or language-heritage, "*polszczyzna*," is portrayed as an organic part of the natural world, available, like the grass, trees, and air of the region, to every person who grows into it.[58] Leśmian's "Meadow" ("*Łąka*") unfolds in such a de-ethnicized and primordial, or de-historicized, landscape:

Czy pamiętasz, jak głowę	Do you remember how
wynurzyłeś z boru,	from out the woods
Aby nazwać mnie Łąką	You raised your head of an
pewnego wieczoru?	evening to name me Meadow?
Zawołana po imieniu	Called by my name
Raz przejrzałam	I caught sight of myself
się w strumieniu—	in a stream—
I odtąd poznam siebie	And since then I can find myself, in the
wśród reszty przestworu.	great expanse.
Przyszły do mnie motyle,	Butterflies came to me
utrudzone lotem,	exhausted by their flight,
Przyszły pszczoły z	Bees came with
kadzidłem i mirrą i złotem,	incense and myrrh and gold,
Przyszła sama Nieskończoność,	Infinity herself came, to gaze on
By popatrzeć w mą zieloność -	my greenness—
Popatrzyła i odejść nie	She looked and didn't want
chciała z powrotem . . .	to take her leave.

Summarizing the interwar critic Ostap Ortwin's assessment of Leśmian's use of nature imagery, Michał Markowski writes that "his poetry is a 'poetry of primordial prehistoric nature, untouched by human foot, unblemished by human pupil.'"[59] Entering a similarly unblemished prehistoric terrain, Tuwim writes in "Greenery" ("*Zieleń*"):

> *Więc nie lepo-ż by nam zieleń ziemi / Opowiedzieć słowiesy staremi! / A poczniemy tę powieść—od spodu, / Od pierwizny, od lęgu, od rodu, / Od rdzennego zrodzenia, od jądra, / Tam gdzie wnętrze, gdzie nutro, gdzie jątra, / Od głębiny, gdzie szepnął w zawięzi / Pierwszy dźwięczek zielonej gałęzi.*

> But wouldn't it be just so much better, to tell us of earth's greenness in the ancient words! So we'll start this story—from the bottom . . . / from rooted begetting, from kernel . . . from the depths, where there whispered at the start / the first soundlet of a green limb.

In another poem, the lyric persona envisions himself being made of this same greenness—of grass—rather than of flesh and blood. In "Grass" ("*Trawa*"), the poet asks that, together with the word, the language of his poem, he be allowed to grow *into* the landscape, becoming interchangeable with the fresh grass:

Trawo, trawo do kolan!	Grass, grass up to my knees!
Podnieś mi się do czoła,	Up to my very brow,
Żeby myślom nie było	So my thoughts might know
Ani mnie, ani pola.	Neither self, nor the field
Żebym ja się uzielił,	That I might engreen myself,
Przekwiecił do rdzenia kości	And blossom to my bones' roots
I już się nie oddzielił	And no longer by words
Słowami od twej świeżości.	Be divided from your freshness.
Abym tobie i sobie	That you and myself
Jednym imieniem mówił:	I might name with one name:
Albo obojgu—trawa,	Either both of us—grass
Albo obojgu—tuwim	Or both of us—Tuwim.[60]

In treating language as a part of the organic landscape, Tuwim and Leśmian perform a self-fulfilling decoupling of language from the cultural and social history of the folk or nation that for Romantic-nationalist theorists of language was inextricably bound to the spirit or *geist* and the roots of a given language. An ironic lifting off or "transplantation," in Schulz's imagery, of a linguistic epidermis, onto one's own spiritual and metaphysical contents. The gesture of transforming the Polish language into a homeland or describing it as a homeland takes on additional resonance when compared with the discourse of "Yiddishland," which similarly figured the Yiddish language as a deterritorialized linguistic and textual homeland—but which precisely did *not*, in doing so, seek to dissociate it from Jewish ethnicity. Here we have in a sense a corollary but opposite gesture, but one that similarly reinscribes the concept of language and text as homelands that are "moveable," both geographically and metaphorically. As Jeffrey Shandler writes, "Yiddish poems written about the Yiddish language (a remarkably extensive subgenre of Yiddish *belles lettres*, apparently unparalleled in other literatures) frequently employ territorial images of Yiddish, explicitly or implicitly identified as Yiddishland."[61] "An empire of scattered, beautifully blossoming islands / is Yiddish culture," wrote the poet A. Almi in his 1930 poem "Yiddish," for example: "Its playful brooks and rivers / Cutting through the great oceans / Of peoples and cultures ... I would raise myself to the highest height / ... consider the scattered empire / Of Yiddish Culture / And see it stretch before my eyes / In a thousand colors and countless variations."[62] And Shandler cites Avrom Reizen's 1930 poem "Yiddish": "Yiddish, my language, my tongue / ... Among strangers here and there— / You are my home in every place. ... / And not just your word—books, too— / ... Peretz, Mendele, and all the others, / They've become my home— Yiddishland."[63] Read against the concept of Yiddishland, Tuwim's "*ojczyzna-polszczyzna*" ("Polish-language fatherland") becomes the sanctuary for a new form of modern and secular Polish Jewish subjectivity—one that did not belong to or associate itself with Yiddishland, but at the same time did not renounce its Jewishness. As a linguistic figure, Tuwim's metaphor marks both belonging and displacement—and records a period of transition for both the Polish language and the modern Jewish subjectivities that were emerging in independent Poland. Just as the publication of more Yiddish-language literature equaled the territorial expansion of Yiddishland, the more literature, song, cabaret, and criticism that were produced by Polish Jewish writers in the interwar period, the greater and greener became the territory of the Polish-language-fatherland.[64]

Further, while the emphasis on Polish as a part of the organic, natural world that is present in the work of Tuwim and Leśmian may seem to hint toward a Neo-Romantic imagery of blood-and-soil rootedness traditionally associated with ethno-nationalist discourse, its gesture in the case of both poets—as I propose it is in the case of Bruno Schulz—is precisely to coopt and subvert such discourse. If it is language in Tuwim's and Leśmian's poetry that defines the lyric persona's connection to fatherland, it is also language that, like the natural world, does not distinguish among speakers—or readers— on the basis of their ethnicity. As in Schulz's work, the specific linguistic forms of the Polish vernacular become points of access to the primordial linguistic sources of all language—the *majaczenie or* inchoate swirl of linguistic potentiality, Schulz's "pre-fatherland of the word."

David Damrosch in *What Is World Literature?* introduces a related dynamic in his discussion of the dissimilated author. "What might be called dissimilated authors . . . whether or not they have another language at their disposal, seek by every possible means to distance themselves from the dominant language, either by devising a distinctive (and therefore to some extent illegitimate) use of this language, or by creating—in some cases recreating—a new national (and potentially literary) language."[65]

The linguistically revolutionary Polish-language verse that Tuwim and Leśmian produced in the early twentieth century combined an unarticulated corollary to the Yiddish *doikeyt* through its insistence on belonging to place and its delight in the natural world, with universalizing references to classical, Renaissance Humanist, and Enlightenment traditions as well as to contemporary European philosophical developments. In addition to active distancing from Polish Catholic tradition, such "second-track" strategies also included cooptation of elements of that tradition, with the assignation of new, Jewish or more universal meanings. The adaptation, universalization, or Judaization of the image of Christ became a common trope in the landscapes of modern Jewish art and literature in Poland, in both Yiddish and Polish. In the poem "The Word and the Flesh" ("*Słowo i ciało*"), Tuwim adapts the image and trope of Christ as the word made flesh, secularizing it and using it as a figure for thinking the transformative relationship between poetry and the sensual, physical world.[66] The lengthy poem begins:

Słowo ciałem się stało	And the Word was made flesh
I mieszka między nami,	And it has dwelt among us,
Karmię zgłodniałe ciało	I feed the starving body
Słowami jak owocami;	With words as if they were fruit;
Pije jak zimną wodę	I drink the words with my mouth,
Słowa ustami, haustami,	Swallow them like cold water,
Wdycham je jak pogodę,	I breathe them like young leaves,
Gniotę jak listki młode,	I grind them with sweet odors
Rozcieram zapachami.	
Słowo jest winem i miodem,	The word is wine and honey,
Słowo jest mięsem i chlebem,	The word is meat and bread
Słowami oczy wiodę	It is the word that guides my eye
Po ścieżkach gwiezdnych niebem.	Along the starry sky.
Radości daru świętego,	O joy of the sacred gift,

O! wieczne umiłowanie!   O eternal fondness
Słowa mojego powszedniego   oh Lord, grant me today
Daj mi dziś, Panie!   my common word![67]

"That Christ figured in a number of poems in Tuwim's first collection, *Czyhanie na Boga (Lying in Wait for God)*," writes Antony Polonsky, "served merely to provoke the nationalist right, whose members saw it as another example of 'Jewish insolence.'"[68] Indeed, in the post-WWI context, the successful greening of modern Polish literature—its transformation into a supranational cultural space—acquires a quality of resistance and defiance.[69] In the face of vocal antisemitic cultural and literary criticism that aimed to divest Poland of its pluralist identity, for writers such as Leśmian, Tuwim, Brzechwa, Schulz, Vogel, Zuzanna Gińczanka, Aleksander Wat, or Bruno Schulz to continue to write and publish their literature in Polish, their native language—to write as if they were equally entitled to the Polish language and to determine the shape of Polish culture—can be viewed not only or primarily as an assimilatory gesture associated with suppression of identity and heritage but on the contrary, as an act of ownership, defiance, and also courage.[70]

To recover elements of the Jewishness of this Polish-language cultural landscape does not render it less culturally Polish, but it does indicate that the definition and shape of "culturally Polish" cultural production were changing as Jewish Poles moved to the center of Polish cultural production in independent Poland. Schulz's work in particular helps to constitute a category of modern Polish cultural production that, far from being invested in Polishness as an ethnic and national project, represented a Deleuzian *ligne de fuite* in a time of competition for control of literary Polishness. It effects a deterritorialization in the sense used by Deleuze and Guattari in their study of minor literatures, through which writing in the language of a dominant culture may introduce not assimilation but rather resistance to the dominant political and cultural discourses of that language.[71] Schulz provides a ready image for that gesture of escape in his repeated description of his Polish writing as a gradual movement, perhaps imperceptible for some, onto an illegal or suspect branch line. "Who knows? Perhaps even now, while we mention it, the doubtful maneuver [*nieczysta manipulacja*] is already behind us and we are, in fact, proceeding onto a blind track [*ślepy tor*]" (W, 30; O, 121). It was a blind track that would nevertheless blast a tunnel through to both mythic time and World literature, and would leave indelible traces in the landscape of Polish culture.

6

"WHAT HAVE YOU DONE WITH THE BOOK?"

Schulz's Exegetical Encounter from the Book of Idolatry to the "Mythologizing of Reality"

IN A 1934 PUBLIC "LETTER TO S. I. Witkiewicz," Schulz wrote that there are entrusted to the artist in childhood certain images that they will continue to ponder for the rest of their artistic lives:

> Such images amount to an agenda, establish an iron capital of the spirit, proffered to us very early in the form of forebodings and half-conscious experiences. These early images mark out to artists the boundaries of their creative powers.... They do not discover anything new after that, they only learn how to understand better and better the secret entrusted to them at the outset; their creative effort goes into an unending exegesis, a commentary on that one couplet of poetry assigned to them. It seems to me that all the rest of one's life is spent interpreting these insights, breaking them down to the last fragment of meaning we can master. They function like those threads in the solution around which the significance of the world crystallizes for us."[1]

For Schulz, one such couplet of poetry was the image of himself as a reader or exegete in a moment of productive encounter with a great book. This scene of reading passed through myriad iterations in Schulz's work, from the graphic works in the *Book of Idolatry* (*Xięga bałwochwalcza*) (1921) to the opening stories of *Sanatorium under the Sign of the Hourglass* (1936)— "The Book," "The Age of Genius," and "Spring"—and the 1937 essay "E. M. Lilien."[2] In closing, I consider a turn within the artist's treatment of this organizing theme of exegetical encounter, so defining for his modernist, diasporic aesthetic. I also situate this turn as a direct result of the real-world scene of reading that took place between Schulz and Debora

Figure 6.1. *Czytanie Księgi I* [*Reading the Book I*], c. 1933, pencil, courtesy of Muzeum Literatury, Warsaw.

Vogel: their mutual reading of the Galician landscape, of their historical moment, and of the relationship between the Jewish national and cultural continuity and modern Galician art.

Exegete and Child Reader

In discussions of his own work in the 1930s, the latter half of his short-lived period of creative productivity, Schulz placed the imagination of the child at the center of his artistic project. "The kind of art I care about is precisely a regression, childhood revisited," he wrote in a letter to Andrzej Pleśniewicz on March 4, 1936. "If it were possible to reverse development, to attain the state of childhood again, to have its abundance and limitlessness once more, that 'age of genius,' those 'messianic times' promised and sworn to us by all mythologies, would come to pass" (WE, 385). Here and throughout Schulz's literary landscapes of the '30s, the model for the individual not yet trapped in the prison of history was the child. His protagonist and alter ego Joseph was presented as an interpreter and exegete of the modern world, still able to discover messianic intimation and the potential for revelation in the streets and cityscapes through which he wanders, as through the pages of a text, and to slip onto an alternate temporality; an illegal sidetrack of time to which exegesis affords entry.

Using the paradigm of the child exegete, Schulz frequently described the vital, living substance of a book as being located in the commentary that the reader adds to it. "That's the best way to read," wrote Schulz to his close friend Romana Halpern in 1936, "—reading oneself, one's own book, between the lines. This is how we used to read in childhood, and that is why the same books, once so rich and full of pith, are like trees stripped bare of leaves when read in adulthood—stripped, that is of the commentary we used to putty over the gaps. . . . Whoever still has in him the memory and marrow of childhood should rewrite these books as he experienced them" (WE, 402).

The image of the vital, authentic, or original text (Schulz's "*oryginał*" and "*Autentyk*") as one that emerges spontaneously in the mind of the child or poet at the moment of reading appears in myriad iterations in Schulz's stories, essays, and letters. "Have you ever noticed swallows rising in flocks from between the lines of certain books," asks the narrator of "Spring," "whole stanzas of quivering pointed swallows? One should read the flight of these birds" (W, 167; O, 168). And later: "We're returning to the Authentic. We have never forsaken it [*wracamy do Autentyku. Ależ nie opuszczaliśmy go nigdy*]. . . . And here we will point out a strange characteristic of the Fragment [*Szpargału*], which by now no doubt has become clear to the reader: that it unfolds while it is being read [*rozwija się podczas czytania*], that from all sides its borders are open to every current and fluctuation." (O, 118). With this evocation of commentary and of living poetry as that which arises in the space between what has already been written, borderless and changing, and with the universalized image of the child reader, Schulz allowed his modern, secular writing to gesture toward its own indebtedness to the tradition of textual study defining for diasporic Jewish culture—to mark what could be called his text's scriptural impulse.[3] Walter Benjamin similarly harnessed the figure of a child exegete in a thought figure (*Denkbild*) that begins:

> Pretzel, Feather, Pause, Lament, Clowning. Such unconnected words are the starting point of a game that was very popular during the Biedermeier period. What you had to do was link them up meaningfully, without changing their order. . . . This game produced the most wonderful discoveries, especially among children. To children, words are still like caverns, with the strangest corridors connecting them. . . . And in fact the sentences that a child will compose from a group of words during a game really do have more in common with those in sacred texts than with the everyday language of grownups.[4]

French philosopher Emmanuel Levinas (1905–95), himself situated at the intersection of East European Jewish culture and secular European thought, offered a reading in which midrash and living commentary are figured as resistance to idolatry. "The reading or study of a text," he writes in *In the Time of Nations*, "protects itself from eventual idolatry of this very text, by renewing, through continual exegesis—and exegesis of that exegesis—the immutable letters, and hearing the breath of the living God in them. A God not incarnate, surely, but somehow inscribed . . . between the lines and in the exchange of ideas between the readers commenting upon them."[5] Schulz's artwork was closely tied to the idea of idolatry; and Levinas's image of commentary as an antidote to idolatry provides an intriguing frame through which to view a transition that took place within Schulz's own work, from his collection of graphic works *The Book of Idolatry* (*Xięga bałwochwalcza,* 1920–21) to his short story "The Book" ("*Księga,*" 1934), which reflects the maturation of his diasporic poetics and aesthetic philosophy.

Schulz's image of himself as reading/interpreting subject was already present in the graphic works of 1918–21 that make up *The Book of Idolatry*. In this period, following his return to Drohobycz from Vienna, the author's core scene of reading is rendered as a performance of idolatrous worship; and it is attached to Neo-Romantic self-portraiture in a psychological and erotic vein, characteristic of popular fin de siècle art in Vienna. Beginning, however, with the letters that Schulz wrote to Vogel a decade later, which became *Cinnamon Shops*, Schulz's treatment of this "iron capital"—the image of a redemptive exegetical encounter (or its ironic undermining)—changed dramatically. Schulz's real-life encounter with Vogel, their shared and parallel commentaries on the Galician cityscapes, and their debates on modernist forms of art that would adequately express their Galician historical moment, took his reflections on the Book out of the realm of parody, erotica, and sadomasochistic self-portraiture and into a new genre: a literary experiment in modernist midrash. With this shift, the author seems to give himself permission, as it were, to return to his sources, to ground his art in, and to pay homage to, his own childhood experience in Galicia. Here his art begins to validate the experiences of his Galician Jewish generation as a chapter, deserving of canonization, in the developing genealogy of the Jewish book. In my discussion of that transition, I will move backward from Schulz's mature poetics to consider his earlier experiments with the image of exegetical encounter: from commentary to idolatry.

In his study of the development of secular Jewish public culture in the late nineteenth and early twentieth centuries, Jeffrey Veidlinger draws attention to a distinguishing feature of the reading practices of Eastern European Jewish communities: the aspect of continuity that characterized movement from biblical and Talmudic exegesis to secular reading practices. As he recounts, "The autobiographies of the first generation to read modern *maskilic* literature reflect how individuals transplanted reverential forms of reading they had learned from Talmudic study onto secular literature, including memorization and ecstatic reading. Books were studied rather than read."⁶ For Naomi Seidman, "the study of modern literature by young men with traditional upbringings inevitably led to syncretic cultural practices, in which Schiller was parsed for shades of meaning in Talmudic singsong within a collective oral environment native to traditional rabbinic text study and foreign to the private reading practices of European modernity."⁷

Within Schulz's written work, the short story "The Book" (1935) offers his most direct engagement with the theme of Scripture and exegesis. The story's Polish title, "*Księga*" (as opposed to *książka*—book)—signals the translational poetics that will structure the story. In Polish the term indicates a large, weighty, and likely ancient book—a tome or book of Scripture. For Schulz's Yiddish-speaking readership, the difference between *książka* (book) and *księga* (tome) would also have resonated with a traditional dichotomy within East European Jewish culture between the Yiddish terms *bukh* and *seyfer*. "There was a visible and marked difference between the holy book and secular literature," writes Veidlinger. "The Yiddish language distinguishes between the two semantically, by leveraging two registers available to the speaker of the syncretic language of diaspora; *seyfer*, derived from the Hebrew, refers to a holy book, whereas the Germanic stock word *bukh* is used to refer to secular writings."⁸ Schulz's introduction of the term *Księga* transplants this distinction to his native, also diasporic, Polish and at the same time intentionally reverses the traditional hierarchy. In this story, which constitutes one of Schulz's modernist and diasporist poetic manifestoes, the Bible is rejected by the child protagonist, Joseph, as a "thousandth copy" and a fake—whereas the scraps of the advertising supplement being used by the maid Adela to wrap the fish appear to the child as "the dawn that flames up anew and continuously of its own accord" ("*zorzę, która wciąż na nowo od samej siebie się zapała*"), reminding him of the lost Original (O, 125).

Barefoot, wearing only a nightshirt and trembling with excitement, I rifled the books on Father's bookshelves, and, angry and disappointed, I tried to describe to a stunned audience that indescribable thing, which no words, no pictures . . . could evoke. I exhausted myself in endless explanations . . . and cried in helpless despair.

My parents towered over me, perplexed, ashamed of their helplessness. . . . They came up to me with various books and pressed them into my hands. . . . One of them, a thick and heavy tome, was again and again pushed toward me by my father. I opened it. It was the Bible. . . . I raised my reproachful eyes to Father. . . . "This book [*książka*] has given you away. Why are you giving me this tainted apocrypha [*skażony apokryf*], this thousandth copy, this incompetent forgery [*nieudolny falsifikat*]? What have you done with The Book [*Księga*]?" (L, 85).

Implied in Schulz's reversal is in one part the modern secular artist's substitution of the traditional practice of biblical and Talmudic study by a new exegetical practice focused on this-worldliness, on the artist's engagement with pieces of *tandeta*—unremarkable and disposable elements of the modern world that are figured in the story as containing fragments of the "Holy Original." The advertising supplement itself, in which Joseph finds the remnants of the Book, becomes a textual and iconographic equivalent of the "languages of everyday communication"—a commercial gospel in which human aspirations and desires, including the desire for an elusive redemption, have been translated into, rendered as, exchange value. The bipartite structure of the story models a movement across temporalities—from sacred, primordial time into profane, historical time, the time of the fragment (fig. 6.2). The shifting of temporalities that exegesis enables in the story is also a form of translation and recuperation. As he reads the Anna Csillag advertising emblem over Adela's shoulder ("So this was the Book, its final pages, its unofficial supplement, a rear annex full of waste and rubbish!"[L, 86]; see chap. 2), Joseph is shown to move kitsch/trash fragments from the golus of the vernacular and the commodity to the time of the Book; of "holidays and miracles."

Similarly, in the third story of *Sanatorium*, "Spring" (*Wiosna*), the Book (*Księga*) returns as a stamp album—a new "Book of Radiance" (*Księga blasku*) that the child exegete Joseph is uniquely qualified to decipher and thus recuperate. "I had reasons to believe the album was predestined for me. Many signs seemed to point to its holding a message and a personal commission for me." The young protagonist describes the album as "the true Book of Radiance" ("*prawdziwa księga blasku*")—the Polish translation of *Zohar*. Non-canonical, even heretical in its time, the *Zohar*,

Figure 6.2. *Xięga Bałchowalcza*. Title Page IV, 1920–22, pencil, courtesy of Muzeum Literatury, Warsaw.

published in the thirteenth century, consisted of a set of mystical commentaries on the Torah that would come to be treated as sacred. Moses de León (c. 1240–1305), later identified as the author of the commentaries gathered in the *Zohar*, presented them as recovered fragments of much older, second-century sacred commentary by Rabbi Simeon ben Yohai, which he claimed to have discovered. This historical detail, readily available for readers of Schulz's generation, contributes to the paradigm of textual recuperation upon which Schulz's modern, twentieth-century midrash could draw, and also to the playful, parodic tone of his texts' engagement with Jewish textual tradition. Rendered in Polish, the title *Księga blasku*, or Book of Radiance, functions as a shifter, a point of contact or tension, and also a formal signature of Schulz's diasporic writing. On the one hand, by translating *Zohar* "radiance," "splendor" into Polish, the phrase carries the "holy Original" down, across the translational boundary from sacred to vernacular, rendering it as a fragment or trace of Scripture trapped in or dispersed into the everyday language of communication. On the other hand, through the poetic function of allusion, the term raises or recuperates pieces of the Polish language text, or in Korn's formulation "leads them out of their golus"—in this case the terms *księga* and *blask*—by allowing them to "remember their home in (Jewish) myth," to resonate with, contain a memory of, or "reach out for" their mythical source—in this case the *Zohar*, and also the broader tradition of renewed and heretical interpretation. The title of Schulz's 1936 poetic manifesto "The Mythologizing of Reality" or "The Mythicization of Reality" is based on a similar translational trope. Here, the term *tikkun-olam*, "repair of the world," is translated or drawn down to the vernacular and rendered as *mityzacja rzeczywistości*. *Olam*—the world—becomes *rzeczywistość* ("reality") while Schulz proposes the work of *mityzacja* (mythicization or mythologization) as the poetic equivalent of *tikkun*—repair, and recuperation.

The gesture of attempting a profane or secular (and hence transgressive) recasting of both Scripture and exegetical engagement was again a familiar trope within the Jewish intellectual and artistic world of interwar Poland. Decades before Manger coined the genre of *literatoyre*, with poems that would become popular throughout Poland, Y. L. Peretz (1852–1915) had penned calls for a revival of the Jewish messianic spirit within Jewish letters. He argued that a renaissance of Jewish culture, of *Yidishkayt*, must combine the sources of Jewish textual tradition with the dynamism of modern secular culture. "A new Jewish life must flourish," he wrote. "A new Bible must be carried to the people as a seed, the Jewish folk [*folkstimlikhe*] symbols and legends rejuvenated as dew and rain!" Peretz, as Rachel Seelig writes, "demanded that the Jews take up 'new prophets and new books,' by which he meant secular European literature, without neglecting the [native] sources of Jewish culture found in Scripture and folklore."[9] Peretz went so far as to associate attachment to the fixed and unchangeable text as a form of idolatry. "You . . . who want thoroughly petrified ideas," he wrote in the 1911 essay *Vegn vos firn op fun yidishkayt* ("Paths That Diverge from Yidishkayt"): "Others want things of wood and stone, painted with brushes—you, children of the people of the book!—you satisfy yourself with the quill, with the word inscribed once and for all time—but these are all arrested, static forms! . . . The word is softer, more symbolic, but it is nevertheless—idol worship!"[10]

"Why shouldn't we put together and canonize a second Jewish Book of Books," wrote Galician Yiddish poet Melekh Ravitch, who had participated in creating the journal *Tsushtayer* together with Vogel and Auerbach in Lwów, and was a founding member of the Khaliastre group of avant-garde Yiddish poets. "Now the times are freer . . . more open to ideas about a second Bible which do keep coming up. . . . The canonized Bible is over two thousand years old, and a great deal has happened since then." Many modernist Jewish poets framed their projects, as Schulz did, as responses to a momentous task that lay before a new, secular generation of writers: to add their work to the lineage of Scripture, bringing it into the twentieth century—even as they broke with religious observance. Ravitch mused that an actual "second Jewish Book of Books" should include the works of Spinoza, Bergson, and Karl Marx, as well as the Parables of Jesus, the first reformer of Jewish law. "Who should put the second bible together?" he asks, "I don't know. I don't even dare to want to know. It would be best if someone suddenly appeared—a little-known man with a considerable knowledge. . . . No one may call the man and appoint him. He must do it on his own. He must be a man without a name, or at least a man whose name is of little concern to him."[11]

Through his focus on the secularization and relocation of the Book, Schulz too responded, like other members of his generation, to the calls initiated by Peretz—initially with parody, situating himself within a line of heretical inheritance associated with the *Zohar* with apocrypha, and also with Frankism. But his translational poetics of the "mythologizing of reality" would come to mark a dramatic change from his earlier graphic reflections on the artist as reading subject. In these first attempts, around 1920, Schulz began incorporating images of a book or large tome into his artwork—portraying it not as a "Holy Original" but as an idolatrous text, a profane parody of Scripture—and a substitute or alternate gospel. In these images—invariably self portraits—the modern artist is figured as worshipping prostrate at the foot of a woman, whose figure can also be taken to function as an allegory for profane form. They also invite interpretation as reflections on the situation of the modern Jewish artist as worshipper and supplicant before the altar of non-Jewish, European art.[12]

Idolatrous Gospel: Frankism as a Galician Trope

Self-portraits of Schulz kneeling before an open book feature prominently in a subset of the graphic works from approximately 1918 to 1921 that were included in editions of *The Book of Idolatry*.[13] Less openly masochistic

Figure 6.3. *Xięga Bałwochwalcza I*, 1920–1922, cliché-verre, courtesy of Muzeum Literatury, Warsaw.

than other works in the collection, these self-portraits combined themes of idolatrous worship with reflection on the place of Scripture or the Book in the modern, secular world. Visual essays or rehearsals of a subtheme, they were grafted onto the dominant genre of decadent fin-de-siècle self-portraiture in which Schulz was working at the time, influenced by Viennese erotica—itself strongly indebted to the work of Aubrey Beardsley—and by the popular texts of Galician author Leopold von Sacher-Masoch, author of *Venus in Furs* (*Venus im pelz*, 1870).[14] Using imagery that parodies the trope of the Word made flesh, Schulz situates himself in the self-portraiture of *The Book of Idolatry* as an apostle of a new faith, prostrate before an open tome from which a female form steps forth (fig. 6.3). On the title page of certain versions of *The Book of Idolatry*, Schulz's alter ego presents his texts to his readers as a scroll, perhaps an apocrypha, (fig. 6.4).[15] Lilien's influence is again present here: the use of the scroll as cover page echoes

"What Have You Done with the Book?" | 187

Figure 6.4. *Xięga Bałwochwalcza—frontispiece*, 1920–22, cliché-verre, courtesy of Muzeum Literatury, Warsaw.

the title page spread of *Die Bücher der Bibel*, for which Lilien provided the illustrations.

At the same time, in this frontispiece Schulz dresses himself in the white cassock of a bishop or pontiff, again suggesting that his scroll is a new gospel—one that will praise the female form, the subject of the artist's idolatrous exegesis. Schulz's parodic early works make liberal use of such a conscious mixing of Christian and Jewish imagery that lends strong support to interpretations by Panas and Lipszyc, who have examined Schulz's direct engagement with Frankist themes.[16] Paweł Maciejko, whose scholarship on the Frankist movement in Poland (*The Mixed Multitude: Jacob Frank and the Frankist Movement, 1755–1866*, 2011) has reenergized the field of Frank studies, explains that "in Frankism the true word of God descended into palpably material female flesh."[17] He refers here to a founding event in the eighteenth-century history of Frankism in which "participants in the [Frankist] Lanckorona ritual replaced the Torah with a naked woman," adding that "this trope also encompassed the seeds of Frankism's romance with Christianity and anticipated its later acceptance of the concept of incarnation."[18]

Like the themes and imagery in Sacher-Masoch's work, Frankist imagery and tropes were a part of the Galician Jewish imaginary, available to be used by modern artists of Schulz's generation. The history of Frankism, a Polish Jewish religious and social movement that emerged around the figure of the eighteenth-century "false messiah" Jacob Frank (1726–1791), and a continuation of seventeenth-century Sabbateanism in Polish lands, was strongly connected to Lwów and its environs. Trans-denominational, multilingual and antinomian, the movement itself provides a rich template for a poetics of heresy, Polish Jewish hybridity, and the blasphemous hijacking of Scripture in the creation of a new gospel.[19] All were themes that became central to Schulz's work. Frank and Frankism were a regular feature within Polish Jewish literary and scholarly discourse of the interwar period, in Galicia and throughout Poland, both as an object of historical study and fascination, and for the richly suggestive metaphorical raw material that they afforded writers. Lwów's *Chwila* regularly ran articles on the state of Frank historiography, including a lengthy 1932 article by Meir Bałaban, one of the Galician founders of the field of Polish Jewish historiography. In it, Bałaban announces his own forthcoming publication of a multi-volume study of Frank and Frankism, "years in the making" and based on extensive archival research, that would dramatically expand upon the earlier work of Aleksander Kraushar (*Frank and the Polish Frankists, 1726–1816*, 1895), but take a decidedly less "objective" approach. Exposing Frank as a "simpleton and a psychopath" and emphasizing his sexual depravity and lack of education, Bałaban also critiques Kraushar for failing to understand "the connections between a sectarian religion based on the Zohar and Christian dogma."[20] In the same year, Bałaban also delivered a lecture in Lwów on the theme of "Jacob Leibowicz Frank, the Last Pseudo-Messiah in Poland—New Historical Research." In another *Chwila* article from 1934, "Eva Frank and Casanova," Oswald Wandel updates readers on "unknown details about Frank and the Frankists" based on new research into archival sources at the Vatican.[21] Thus for an artist from the Lwów region to incorporate Frankist themes, particularly in modern works that explore the boundaries and tensions between Jewish and non-Jewish culture, and between sacred and profane categories of existence, was to participate directly in the Galician Jewish cultural imaginary of the interwar period.

Schulz's contemporaries beyond Galicia, Yiddish poets and playwrights Moyshe Kulbak (1896–1937) and Aaron Zeitlin (1898–1973), each devoted a full play to the topic of Frank in the interwar period (*Yankev Frank* [1922] and *Yaakov Frank* [1929], respectively).[22] As a false messiah, at times ruthless and capable of attracting a fanatical and in many cases disenfranchised following, Frank functioned within Yiddish literature in part as a symbol of real-world political programs in which the Jewish population had placed its faith in a time attuned to secular messianic promises, which may include revolution, political Zionism, or the promise of Polish-Jewish brotherhood. The Polish Romantic poet Adam Mickiewicz (1798–1855), Poland's national poet and perhaps the first to canonize an imagined literary territory of messianic Polish Jewish brotherhood, was also widely recognized by Polish Jewish readership in the interwar period to have been of Frankist background. This fact carried enormous symbolic weight in discourses on the possibility or impossibility of a shared Polish Jewish future, and the potential for a Polish-language literature and culture woven from the contributions of both Polish and Jewish authors.[23]

Frank's teachings, which garnered a following of thousands or tens of thousands of Polish Jews in the eighteenth century, had also circulated in the form of an idolatrous pseudo-gospel: a fragmentary collection of pronouncements entitled *Księga Słów Pańskich* (*The Book of the Words of Our Lord*).[24] Drawing back to Schulz's *Book of Idolatry*: among the nods Schulz's imagery makes here is a gesture to Frank's belief that the messiah was a woman—his own daughter Eva. Among its opponents the Frankist movement had become infamous early on for transgressive rituals in which a female member of the community, partially or fully undressed, was honored or worshipped in place of or as an incarnation of the Torah.[25] Renewed scholarly and literary treatments, including Maciejko's study and Olga Tokarczuk's 2014 historical novel *The Books of Jacob* (*Księgi Jakubowe*), have provided ample material to enable further exploration of Schulz's engagement with Frankist and Sabbatean themes, a line of analysis initially undertaken by Władysław Panas.[26]

Of key importance for Panas was Debora Vogel's 1930 short discussion of Schulz's graphic work published in *Judisk Tidskrift*, the Swedish Jewish literary journal edited by Vogel's uncle, Markus Ehrenpreis (originally published in *Tsushtayer* in 1930). Vogel makes mention in her note of a subset of

Figure 6.5. *Xięga Bałwochwalcza—Procesja*, 1920–21, cliché-verre, courtesy of Muzeum Literatury, Warsaw.

Schulz's "works on the themes of Messianic times [*Meshiakh-tsaytn*]." "Even these," she writes, "are given an erotic coloring." For Panas, her reference to this subset confirms that Schulz was working in his early graphics with a constellation of messianic, kabbalistic, and also specifically Frankist images and themes, including the idea of a female messiah and the combination linking antinomian sexual transgression with messianic times. Ubiquitous in Schulz's graphic works from *The Book of Idolatry*, as in Frankist thought, are images that employ a strategy of hybridity, a conscious mixing of Jewish and Christian imagery that resists full legibility within any one cultural framework, and which is also mapped onto the double-faced trope of sacred/profane. In his use of Frankist imagery, Schulz seems also to strive for shock value, seeking his own Galician idiom for the modernist "slap in the face of public taste."

In one such image entitled "Procession" (fig. 6.5), Schulz offers a parodic nod to Rembrandt's portrayals of Christ before his followers, including "Christ Presented to the People" (1655) and "Christ Preaching" ("*La Petite Tombe*," 1652, fig. 6.6).[27]

Figure 6.6. *Christ Preaching (La petite Tombe)*, c. 1652, etching, engraving, and drypoint. Gift of W. G. Russell Allen. Courtesy National Gallery of Art.

Here, a young woman is presented to a group of worshippers, critics, or potential apostles assembled for the procession, her body revealed before them, while a man—one of several self-portraits of Schulz in this graphic—holds the robe or covering that he has taken off to present her. This scene of profane reading, as it were, takes place in front of a house of worship conspicuously lacking in denominational markings.[28] A banner showing a high-heeled shoe mocks and also translates the pageantry associated both with Catholic holidays, and with the procession on the Jewish holiday of Simchat Torah (Rejoicing of the Torah). Provocatively exploring the concept of idolatry in relation to both Jewish and Christian theological traditions, the image makes reference simultaneously to the Word made flesh, but also to the Torah as the bride of Israel that on Simchat Torah is brought out of the synagogue in procession, undressed, read and interpreted, and covered once again; and finally to the history of Frankist ritual. Placing himself throughout the image as the revealer, the worshipper, and the infant who turns away indifferently, Schulz also interrogates the modern artist's relationship to form and inherited tradition. The gesture simultaneously elevates the interpretative engagement of the artist with the material world of form as a new and heretical gospel, and finds idolatry in both Christian and Jewish worship of the objectified, fixed sacred word.

In connection with the central role played by idolatry in Schulz's work—the sources of which are unknown—it is intriguing to note that his birthday, July 12, 1892, falls on 17 Tammuz in the Hebrew calendar, a date with significant connections to the theme of idolatry. A fast day, 17 Tammuz initiates a three-week period of mourning leading up to Tisha B'Av, marking the double destruction of the Holy Temple in Jerusalem. In a widely referenced portion of Mishna or Oral Law, the date became associated with five tragic events, among them three of note: "On the seventeenth of Tammuz the tablets were broken by Moses when he saw that the Jews had made the golden calf"; the general "Apostemos burned a Torah scroll"; and Menasseh "placed an idol in the Sanctuary."[29] In the story "Night of the Great Season" from *Cinnamon Shops*, analyzed by David Goldfarb in one of the first studies to elaborate Schulz's direct engagement with the tradition of biblical and Talmudic exegesis, the cloth shop of the author's childhood becomes a "fantastic Canaan" in which "the people were gesticulating, cursing and worshipping Baal, and trading" (L, 76; O, 99) while "increased in stature by his anger, [my Father would] thunder from on high at the idolaters with his mighty words" (O, 100).[30] If Schulz did have a bar mitzvah, if he prepared it for the week of his actual thirteenth birthday, and if he prepared a d'var Torah for it, it may well have been in that formative period of young exegesis that the image joining idolatry with the study of the book added itself to the iron capital of the artist's imagination.

In another image from the *Book of Idolatry* that references Titian's *Venus of Urbino*, Schulz's doppelganger kneels before the reclining, partly nude figure of a woman, holding a large book open in his hands (fig. 6.7). An equation is suggested between her body and the book, the album or volume he is studying: two texts that he encounters in the scene of reading and presumably subjects to exegesis. The artist's devoted attention to the gospel of the female form is portrayed here as a form of profane prayer, while the tradition of scriptural exegesis is again treated as its own form of idolatry. Schulz's erotic images become available as permutations in an extended exegesis on the artist who devotes himself to the study, even the worship, of the material, embodied world of form: the text projected into the modern cityscape that lies available to interpretation.

"What Have You Done with the Book?" | 193

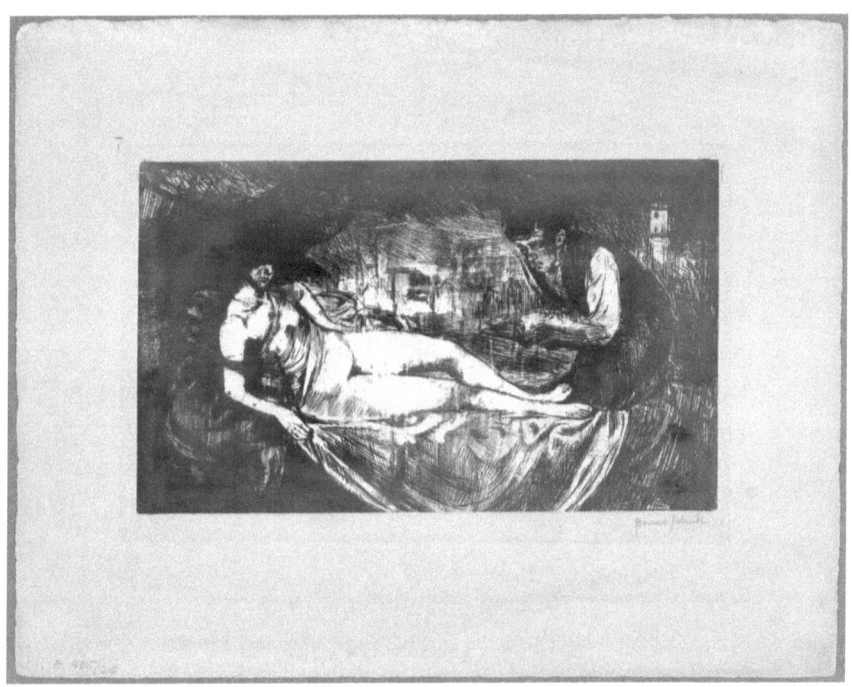

Figure 6.7. *Xięga Bałwochwalcza II*, 1920–22, cliché-verre, courtesy of Muzeum Literatury, Warsaw.

Yet another subset of sketches is set on the streets of a town. In one, as two young Jewish students walk together engaged in conversation, they pass—or encounter—the nude form of a woman posing mannequin-like, positioned as if to suggest that her body or form is the object of their shared commentary and contemplation. This is but one instance of an extensive series of variations that Schulz produced on the theme of the street encounter. He would continue to do so up until the illustrations for Sanatorium, that include an encounter of two young mean with the character Bianca. The most striking example has gained fame as the only surviving oil painting by Schulz. Entitled *"Spotkanie"* ("The Encounter"), it has been dated at to 1920 (fig. 6.9).

Here, the boundary between sacred and profane is foregrounded by the inclusion of a seemingly ancient stone wall that cuts a line through the painting's center. A young man in a full-length capote and peyes observes two women in elegant modern dress as they pass and also turn back to glance at the male gazer in a mutual exchange of readings. They occupy

Figure 6.8. *Kobieta i dwaj chłopcy* [*Woman and Two Boys*], after 1933, kredka, 1920–22, courtesy of Muzeum Literatury, Warsaw. (Title assigned posthumously.)

Figure 6.9. *Spotkanie* (*Encounter*), 1930, courtesy of Muzeum Literatury, Warsaw.

Figure 6.10. *Spotkanie* (*Encounter*)—self-potrait, two women and Stanisław Weingarten, c. 1922. Ink and pencil on cardboard. Courtesy of the Galeria Obrazów we Lwowie.

the twin temporalities of exegetical/mythical and historical/weekday time characteristic of Schulz's written narratives. In *Looking Jewish*, Carol Zemel describes the painting as a "sunset encounter between the traditional Jew and modern women" that "in contrast to the happy modernity of loving family and prospering town and countryside in Chagall's *The Promenade* (1917) . . . presents only sexual tension and social anxiety."[31] In another iteration of the same encounter, dated to the early 1920s, the set and costumes are not yet Jewishly marked, but the encounter is similar the men are portraits of Schulz and his close friend Stanisław Weingarten (fig. 6.10). The traditional dress of *The Encounter* has been traded here for the long, elegant wool coat that Schulz's persona wears over a jacket and tie, and both men are bareheaded. Elements of a cityscape sharply rendered in light and shadow suggest an expressionist stage or film set. Positioned similarly to the Jewish subject in his 1930 painting, Schulz's alter ego is here not separated by a wall or barrier from the passing women but occupies the same spatial and cultural imaginary, while Weingarten seems to direct his "study" to the hand of one of the pair of passing women.

Throughout these and other versions of the "encounter," Schulz's female figures are rendered as mannequin-like, sexualized objects of the male gaze and of male evaluation. This is certainly true in the print from the encounter series that Vogel and Auerbach chose to include in the second issue of *Tsushtayer* (see chap. 3, fig. 3.1). The piece portrays two young Jewish men engaged in conversation, approaching or discussing—reading as it were—two women who pose in the street, dressed in lingerie, suggesting that they are sex workers. How might Vogel, who helped to promote Schulz's work, have evaluated his use of this subject matter? She chose to feature and to review this piece in the journal, and her review is not a critical one. But given her own treatment of the theme of the mannequin in this period, there can be little doubt that the writer and keen cultural critic would also have criticized, perhaps quite forcefully, the easy objectification contained in Schulz's images, and his recurring use of the female figure as an idol, and allegory for the profane modern world. Vogel would not have been the only critic to do so. The Lwów paper *Wiek Nowy* contained a review of Schulz's work displayed in the 1930 Spring Salon art exhibition in Lwów. The reviewer wrote that Schulz's graphic works follow in a path already well trodden by "two excellent representatives of erotic art: Rops and Beardsley, who could boast of true triumphs in their works of eroticism," and even before them by a rich tradition of erotic art that had flourished in both the Renaissance and Rococo periods. Thus, "what Mr. Schulz gives us is not something new. . . . Beardsley also presented processions of men, degenerate slaves of their passions, dragging themselves toward their masters—women. But," the critic continued, "Beardsley's woman is a demon, conscious of her power—while the female figures of Mr. Schulz are portrayed as thoughtless, almost identically smiling dolls."[32]

In their debates of the same year, Vogel and Schulz would have touched on the question of the sexist objectification of the female figure upon which the landscape of his messianic-erotic imaginary in *The Book of Idolatry* depends. Indeed, the results of their discussions can already be seen in the text of Schulz's four-part "Tractate on Mannequins" which makes up a substantial portion of *Cinnamon Shops* (1934). It is possible to read the stories that make up the "Tractate on Mannequins" as a direct acknowledgement of, and engagement with, the kind of critique Vogel would certainly have made of Schulz's objectifying imagery—itself a form of visual *tandeta* or *shund*. Schulz's stories, which were written in letters to Vogel during their discussions, stage precisely a conversation about the process by which the artist presses individuals and souls into the hard, fixed shapes of his fantasy. These reflections unfold in the dining room of the protagonist's apartment, above his father's cloth shop, in the presence of an actual mannequin—its necessity to the plot now differently from that of the mannequin-like women in *The Book of Idolatry*, by the fact that it is a tailor's dummy used by the living and creative dressmakers Polda and Polina in the protagonist's father's cloth shop: "Carried on their shoulders, a silent immobile lady had entered the room, a lady of oakum and canvas, with a black wooden knob instead of a head" (W, 28; O, 29). "That Moloch . . . sent them back to work again and again, . . . they manipulated with deft fingers (*zgrabnymi ruchami*) the piles of silk and wool, cut with noisy scissors into its colorful mass (W, 28; O, 29). The craft of these female artists is portrayed as a form of poetry, in which mannequin-existence and the colorfulness of untamed matter form a dialectical thought-figure or *obraz-talisman*. What is living in this poetry, the work of the female assistants, resides in the detritus of the commercial world and in what exceeds or cannot be contained within the commodity: "Their hearts, and the quick magic of their fingers, were not in the boring dresses which remained on the table, but in the thousand scraps, the frivolous and fickle trimmings . . . the rubbish of a possible carnival, in the storeroom for some great unrealized masquerade" (W, 28; O, 29).

Also in the "Tractate on Mannequins" stories, Schulz's own dubious treatment of the "pliable matter" at his disposal in the *Book of Idolatry* is notably displaced onto the figure of an Heresiarch Father—Jacob, of an older generation. The premise that an artist holds the power to impose on helpless matter the forms that he wills is foregrounded in the text, and made available to critique. Objectification of the subject by the artist is portrayed as a form of both alchemy and sadism: "Here is the starting point for a new apologia for sadism" (W, 31; O, 33). Jacob elaborates a program of Second Demiurgy, proposing that matter, with its "seductive power of temptation," is a territory "'open to all kinds of charlatans and dilettanti, a domain of abuses and of dubious demiurgical manipulations. . . . Anyone can mold it and shape it; it obeys everybody.' . . . My father never tired of glorifying this extraordinary element—matter" (W, 31; O, 33). Continues Jacob:

> we openly admit: our creations will be temporary, to serve for a single occasion. If they be human beings, we shall give them . . . only one profile, one hand, one leg. . . . Their backs can be made of canvas or simply whitewashed. . . . Such is our whim, and the world will be run according to our pleasure"; "our creatures will not be heroes of romances. Their roles will be short . . . their characters—without a background. . . . The Demiurge was in love with consummate, superb, and complicated materials; we shall give priority to trash" (W, 33; O, 35).

In the same story, Schulz's young narrator (and porte-parole) Joseph, adds, "As for us, we did not share these demiurgical aspirations" (W, 32; O, 35).[33]

As scholars of Vogel have explored, her poetry from the same period focuses on a reclaimed female subjectivity, alternately rejecting and refiguring the objectification to which women are subjected, and to which they subject themselves, in a commodified modern world. Anna Torres observes that "Fogel explores complex identification with mannequins, with the 'male gaze' largely absent." Where Vogel does, like Schulz, reference "that perennial subject of painting, the nude upon the sofa," her poems "reverse the usual logic of animacy."[34] Thus in "Ballad of a Street Walker I," the subjectivity, sensations, and memories belong to the street walker, "Dressed in a black scarf": "the scarf is very much like satin—/ . . . and black was her color of choice . . . / Days pass by on the plush red sofa / the sofa can be like a beloved / she had a lover in a bright coat / he forgot her, maybe it should be like that."[35] Not an allegorical stage piece or a product of male fantasy, Vogel's sex-worker is a woman with emotions and desires—and, as Torres also notes, in Vogel's collection *Manekinen*, sex workers are the only poetic speakers to address the reader.

The very different treatments that each artist gives to the image of the sex worker, mannequin, or reclining female nude allow us again to infer the type of critique that Vogel would have brought to Schulz's use of erotic imagery. In a 1936 essay, Vogel herself was drily critical and dismissive of erotica, associating it with "the grotesque split of an artist degraded by his petit bourgeois origins." Such artists come in two types, she wrote: "the programmatically proletarian personality," and a second, "no more 'intellectual' than the first, the boring and sentimental-bourgeois sensibility. The latter is expressed independently from the first one, mainly through eroticism."[36] The recent archival discovery of the previously unknown story "Undula" invites additional reflection both on the influence that Vogel's critiques may have had on Schulz's developing aesthetic program, and on his shifting treatment of the organizing theme of the exegetical encounter.

"Undula" by Marceli Weron

In 2019, Ukrainian researcher Lesya Khomych discovered the short story entitled entitled "Undula," published in 1922 under the pen name of Marceli Weron, twelve years before Schulz published *Cinnamon Shops* with Rój.[37] The story appeared in a local biweekly paper entitled *Świt* (*Dawn*), published in Borysław and directed at executives within the oil and gas industry—including the directorship of the POLMIN oil and gas company where Schulz's elder brother Izydor Schulz was employed.[38] The physical and psychic landscape of the story is immediately recognizable as a literary corollary to Schulz's erotically themed graphic works published as the portfolio *Book of Idolatry*—the period of his association with the artistic group Kalleia.[39] The name "Undula" itself appears in several images from that collection, including "Undula, the Eternal Ideal" (1920) and "Undula on Her Walk."[40] Khomych uncovered a direct correspondence between Schulz's first exhibition of graphics, organized in Borysław by members of the artistic group Kalleia, and the story's publication in *Świt* nine months later, and was able to establish with confidence that Schulz authored the work.[41] Indeed, the story allows readers to glimpse characteristically Schulzian images that would reappear in the later stories of *Cinnamon Shops*: looming wooden credenzas; lurking cockroaches; the heavy, rhythmic breathing of bedridden sleepers; the dark interiors of a somewhat labyrinthine house, through which the protagonist moves in a dreamlike state; and the figure of the narrator's maid, Adela. "I sleep, wake, and then doze off again, patiently pushing my way through sickly thickets of phantoms and dreams. . . . Sometimes I recognize the oversized furniture that stretches up to the ceiling, these plain oak wardrobes bristling with dust-covered junk. . . . The floor and the old wardrobe will creak and groan. . . . Great, black cockroaches stand motionless, staring vacantly into the light. They seem dead. All of a sudden, those flat, headless bodies take off in an uncanny crablike run, cutting diagonally across the floor. . . ." But in *"Undula,"* the stage that is set with these elements is painted, as it were, with a different semiotic pallet: that of Viennese erotica, psychoanalysis, and the works of Leopold von Sacher-Masoch—and, most notably, without the characteristic later emphasis on Jewish myth as a key point of reference.[42]

Prior to Khomych's discovery, Jerzy Ficowski and other scholars working with available information had concluded that while Schulz had tried his hand at writing short stories before he met Vogel, the prose that emerged in his postscripts to her were in fact the first texts that made it into print.[43] It was also observed that Schulz had intentionally protected his prose, as it were, from the directly erotic, self-deprecating, and masochistic themes present in his early graphics. The 1922 story "Undula" disrupts both of these assumptions—yet in doing so it also testifies to an even more seminal role played by Vogel in shaping the themes in Schulz's mature work. In his encounter with her, his energies turn noticeably toward a committed engagement with the project of modern Jewish literature and culture. Because Khomych's discovery enables us to contrast Schulz's first literary attempts of the 1920s—the erotically and masochistically themed text of "Undula" that corresponds in time and subject matter to Schulz's *Book of Idolatry*—with the genre and thematics of the stories that emerged after 1930 in his letters to Vogel, it becomes possible to reevaluate the significance of Schulz's encounter with Vogel. That period of encounter and debate becomes visible as a defining turning point in his emergence as a modern Jewish writer.

Schulz's story "Undula" turns the reader's attention not to childhood sources—the organizing premise that would later structure both *Cinnamon Shops* and *Sanatorium*—but to the object of the adult narrator's fantasies—"Undula, languid and leaning enticingly in black gauze and panties; Undula, her eyes afire behind the black lace of a fan."

> Through what pale nights of revelry, through what moonlit suburban parks did I not fly after them, like a moth bewitched by Undula's smile. And everywhere I saw her in the shoulders of the dancers . . .
>
> Undula, Undula, o sigh of the soul for the land of the happy and perfect! How my soul expanded in that light, when I stood, a humble Lazarus, at your bright threshold. Through you, in a feverish shiver, I came to know my own misery and ugliness in the light of your perfection. How sweet it was to read from a single glance the sentence condemning me forever, and to obey with the deepest humility the gesture of your hand, spurning me from your banqueting tables. I would have doubted your perfection had you done anything else. Now it's time for me to return to the furnace from which I came, botched and misshapen.[44]

While individual thematic elements found in "Undula" are also present in the later *Cinnamon Shops*, a character by this name is not. Schulz folds some of her characteristics into the character of Adela—who does make an appearance in the earlier story—but it is notable that Adela's existence as an allegorical device and a projection of male fantasy is tempered in the later stories by images that remind the reader of the centrality of her labor. She "liquidates the few hours remaining until dusk [*likwidowała z energią tych parę godzin do zmierzchu*] . . . amid the clatter of saucepans and splashing of cold water" (W, 27; O, 29); grinds coffee before the family awakes; returns from the market to unload fruit and sides of meat; and her destruction of Jacob's empire of poetry unfolds as an act of cleaning. The character of Adela still functions as a central allegorical device, representative of the world of sensual materiality, but she no longer wields redemptive power, in a landscape that has moved away from the image of the idolatrous gospel. Instead, Schulz's texts in *Cinnamon Shops* and *Sanatorium* internalize the redemptive function, proposing to transfer it to the poetic practice itself—as they turn toward the poetic and aesthetic work of redeeming fragments of an idyllic Galician childhood.

A discussion of "Undula" warrants a brief aside on pseudonyms. For Schulz scholars, the emergence of the story opens additional areas of inquiry: Why did Schulz choose the name Marceli Weron?[45] Do other stories remain to be excavated, salvaged from the ephemera of interwar Drohobycz and Borysław, published under the name Marceli Weron? Might Schulz also have published stories, critical essays, or articles under other pseudonyms, male or female? The adoption of pen names has a long history within Jewish writing, both religious and secular. It was common for Yiddish writers of the nineteenth and early twentieth centuries to publish under meaningful pseudonyms, such as Sholem Aleichem ("How do you do?")—the pen-name of Solomon Rabinovitch, Pinchus Kahanovich's choice of Der Nister, "the Hidden One"; Isidor [Yisroel] Eliashev's pseudonym Bal-Makhshoves ("Man of Thoughts"); and literary critic Shmuel Tsharni's choice to translate his last name from the Russian Tsharni ("Black") to Niger. As Sharon Bar-Kochva writes in her study of Hebrew-derived pseudonyms, in many cases such pseudonyms "were utilized to form and represent the author's imagined identity," to express "different aspects of the author's work and the way he wished to be perceived by the public," and that "the linguistic origin of the adopted name plays an important role, for both cultural and political reasons."[46]

Responding to different but adjacent motivations, Polish Jewish writers who entered the Polish literary world often took pseudonyms that disguised their Jewishness, so as to circumvent potentially antisemitic obstacles to entry into the literary world in Poland. Jan Wiktor Lesman (1898–1966), renowned author of Polish-language children's poetry and prose (including the much loved postwar *Akademia Pana Kleksa*/*Professor Inkblot's Academy*) adopted the last name Brzechwa—referring to the feathered end of an arrow.[47] Jan Brzechwa in turn recommended to his cousin Bolesław Lesman, who would later be considered one of the founders of modern Polish poetry, that he submit his early poems to a contest using a polonized pen name as well. He helped him to settle on the surname Leśmian. The pen name under which Schulz published "Undula" in *Świt*, Marceli Weron, might play on both motivations. It both hides Jewishness and also gestures toward it meaningfully: the name brings to mind the Italian city of Verona and the popular and influential 1850 novel *The Jew of Verona* by the Italian Jesuit priest Antoni Bresciani, which gave narrative fuel to religious antisemitism in Italy and Europe. Not a traditionally Polish name, the Latinate Weron (pronounced "Veron"; common in French and Spanish, and meaning "of truth" in Esperanto), is suggestive of foreign origin or adaptation. Thus, even as the choice of name marks Schulz's refusal to be polonized or to adopt the mask or pretense of Polishness, it may contain a veiled commentary on the situation of the Jewish writer in the Polish language. Further questions arise and remain to be solved: Did Vogel convince Schulz of the importance of his coming out, as it were, as a Jewish writer and urge him to publish *Cinnamon Shops* under his own name? Was that decision occasioned by a shift within his own relationship to the Jewishness of his work, which developed in the period of his discussions with her on aesthetics and the responsibility of the artist to Jewish cultural continuity?[48]

In terms of genre, the shift from the graphic works in *The Book of Idolatry* to "The Book" (*"Księga"*) can be mapped as a move from a visual medium of parodic iconography toward a textual medium of commentary that negotiates a relationship to Jewish exegetical tradition. Erotic imagery by no means disappeared from Schulz's graphic art. In the 1930s, female figures continued to hold a central place here. But in the stories his prose work in *Sanatorium*, Schulz's exploration of the theme of exegetical encounter— of a reader who encounters the profane text of the modern world—develops in a new direction, away from idolatry and toward commentary, as the textual medium of an imagined redemption. What the two approaches share is, first, an interrogation of modern art as both an encounter between the artist and the material world of form that is charged with redemptive significance and, second, their attempt to find a a profane or vernacular "translation" of the Book or Scripture. In *The Book of Idolatry*, Schulz's iconography suggests that it is the artist, a "humble Lazarus," who seeks elusive redemption as a supplicant at the altar of European and now Polish art. That which redeems, these images imply, lies outside the artist and holds dominion over him, perhaps as the world of European culture beckons the acculturating Jewish artist. In the latter, Lurianically inspired model of Schulz's mature poetics, the artist, poet, or exegete is refigured as a medium and a conduit, while it is language itself that longs for return—together with authentic mosaic fragments of a Jewish life, community, and era—and that desires or needs to be redeemed. The reading artist is refigured not as supplicant but as exegete and agent in the process of repair. In *Cinnamon Shops*, Schulz introduces his father, cast as both prophet and heresiarch, as a central character in the stories. The sources of the author's own specifically Galician Jewish imaginary, his parents' cloth shop and his childhood in a Drohobycz that belonged to the Habsburg Empire, become the primary raw material for his mythologizing experiments. And elements of Jewish tradition, drawn from kabbalah, Frankism, Hasidic storytelling, and the post-WWI Polish Jewish experience substantially inform the thematics of the stories.[49] While for Schulz the self-portrait will remain at the center of the scene of reading, the perspective in *Cinnamon Shops* and later *Sanatorium* has shifted to that of the child. Schulz recasts his reading subject not as a man, a supplicant, and a victim but as a child attuned to clues that only he can decipher, and that he rushes to recuperate, and as an artist compelled to recapture Scripture in his own medium of translation. "Wake up!" cries Joseph in "The Wondrous Era" from *Sanatorium*. "Come and help me! How can I face this flood alone, how can I deal with this inundation? How can I, all by myself, answer the million dazzling questions with which God is inundating me?" (L, 96).

> I set among those papers, blinded by the radiance, my eyes full of explosions, rockets, and colors, and I drew . . . my colored pencils flew across columns of illegible texts, raced in brilliant scrawls . . . knitting into anagrams of visions, into rebuses of luminous revelations. . . . As in the days of Noah these colorful parades flowed past, these rivers of fur and manes, these undulating spines and tails . . . And when I reached for the azure paint . . . the panes trembled, one after the other, full of azure and heavenly fire; curtains waved as if alerted; and a joyful draft rose in that lane between muslin curtains and oleanders on the empty balconies, as if on the other end of this long bright avenue someone had appeared in the distance and was approaching—radiant, preceded by new, by a presentiment, portended by the flight of swallows, by fiery runners scattered from mile to mile. (L, 96–99; O, 123–126)

"One could say," comments the petty criminal Shloma in the same story, "that the world had passed through your hands in order to renew itself. . . . Ah, Joseph, you should have been born earlier." "To you, Shloma," Joseph replies, "I can reveal the secret of these drawings. . . . I must confess to you," I added quietly, looking into his eyes, "I have discovered the Authentic" (L, 102). Here, the utopian and liberatory potential of both art and literature is envisioned not only as a slight adjustment that allows the historical present to activate the temporality of myth and exegesis, but also as a return to or recovery of the imaginative and spiritual reality of the child, with the attendant freedom, the transgression or obviation of social, linguistic, and perceptual boundaries, and the state of immunity from history and law that that return implies.

"It is then that the revelation took place," proclaims Joseph in the next story in the collection, "Spring," upon encountering the stamp album that serves as one of several shifting metonymies in Schulz's stories for the living text: "the secret message of good tidings, the special announcement of the limitless possibilities of being. Bright, fierce, and breathtaking horizons opened wide, the world trembled and shook in its joints, leaning dangerously, threatening to break out from its rules and habits" (W, 150). In its exclamatory mode of address, its unbridled pronouncements of revelation, Schulz's language in the early stories of *Sanatorium* reminds of the emotive-ecstatic writing of Y. L. Peretz. No longer based on parodic bravura or self-abnegation, however, these stories represent instead a conscious engagement with the challenge of Jewish cultural and literary continuity, and they develop a repertoire of recognizable images and organizing themes that have helped to establish Schulz's literary landscape as a boundary territory between materialism and theology. "How empty the world is today," comments Shloma in "The Wondrous Era" ("*Genialna epoka*") as he and Joseph stand alone on the market square of their town. "We could divide it and give it a new name; it's lying there so open defenseless and ownerless," answers Joseph.

> On such a day the Messiah approaches the very edge of the horizon and from there looks down on the earth. And when he sees it so white and silent, with its azures and pensiveness, it can happen that in his eyes it loses its boundary, the bluish bands of clouds lie down to form a passageway, and, not knowing himself what he is doing, he descends to earth. And in its reverie the earth will not even notice the one who has descended onto its paths, and people will awaken from their afternoon naps and remember nothing. (L, 101; O, 130)

Already with the stories in *Cinnamon Shops* that developed out of his letters to Vogel, Schulz moved the concept of a redemptive exegetical encounter away from the Frankist-erotic-idolatrous configuration characteristic of his graphic work at the time that she met him and toward a Lurianic-inspired constellation premised on the idea of the redeemable linguistic/material fragment. Whether this shift came as a result of her direct suggestion that he experiment more directly with the abundance of Jewish sources that he had available to him, and that had shaped him; or that as a Galician artist he could do better than to rehearse a trite erotica imported to the provinces from Vienna; or through principled objection to the lack of imagination displayed in his opportunistic objectification of women, Vogel undoubtedly influenced Schulz's movement from the parodic bravura of a heretical-idolatrous gospel to a translational, diasporic poetics of mythologized reality.

Through the introduction of his child narrator Joseph, beginning in 1930, Schulz was able to allow the "iron capital of his imagination," the image of the Encounter, to crystallize around a narrative of a child exegete tasked with deciphering and redeeming the fragmented world, filled with clues and messianic promise. These stories also place a new emphasis on the possibilities for escape that a modernist poetics affords: of movement through the historical-material realm and up into the alternate temporality of holiday and miracle, or onto a sidetrack of time where myth resides at all times, accompanying the idolatrous present of commodified dreams.

Schulz was a metaphysical modernist, interested in substance or spirit and the processes by which that substance enters into and moves through form, adopting masks, and donning the changing garb of reality and history. His stories accept a challenge, as it were, and offer a proposal that the Polish language was a form, a medium, capable of giving profound expression to the modern Galician Jewish experience. They harness the pliable material of that language, doubling down stubbornly on the fact that for Schulz, this was the raw material most adequate to both his personal experience, and the experience of the community and the milieu out of which he came. On the one hand, through two volumes of short stories written in post-WWI Poland, he left in the center of Polish modernism a legacy and a testament to his own and his generation's experience that would forever change the Polish literary and cultural imaginary. On the other, he left a commentary in his twentieth-century Polish Jewish vernacular in the post-theological margins of the Jewish Book. By the mid-1930s, as his aesthetic philosophy matured, he had leveraged the fact of his writing in Polish to develop a luminous poetics of golus or diaspora, and of redemptive exegesis.

In this sense, Schulz's ontological-poetic project is a conversation about the limits that historical exigencies place on the human soul. A poetics of memory, recuperation, escape, and also messianic anticipation, it speaks very specifically to the experience of finding oneself a Polish-speaking

Polish Jew at a moment when history was turning. Viewed as a reflection on and literary engagement with the experiences of diaspora and exile, Schulz's work becomes an argument that the human spirit will never be limited by the exigencies of history, and a meditation on language as the enduring vehicle that carries the human soul, and the spirit of a people and its culture, beyond the confines of that history.

NOTES

Introduction

1. Schulz was murdered on November 19, 1942, during an SS killing spree in which more than one hundred Jews were shot dead in the streets of Drohobycz.

2. Rachel Auerbach [Rokhl Oyerbakh], *"Nisht-oysgeshpunene fedem"* ("Un-Spun Threads"), *Di goldene keyt* 50 (1964), 137. Writer, art critic, and philosopher of aesthetics Debora Vogel (1900–42) was an author of poetry (the volumes *Tog-figurn* [*Day Figures*, 1930] and *Manekinen* [*Mannequins*, 1934]), prose (*Akatsyes blien. Montazhn* [*The Acacias Are Blooming. Montages*, 1935]), and critical essays in Polish and Yiddish, and a founding editor with Auerbach of the journal of Yiddish culture *Tsushtayer* in Lwów. Yiddish and Polish author, historian, essayist and editor Rachel Auerbach (1901–1976) was close friends with Debora Vogel at the time she met Schulz. A survivor of the Warsaw Ghetto and writer for the underground war-time *Oyneg Shabes* archive, she would devote her later life to documenting the Warsaw Ghetto, in her own diaries, in articles, and through the collection of survivor testimonials. See Auerbach, *Pisma z Getta Warszawskiego*, ed. and trans. by Karolina Szymaniak (Warsaw: Żydowski Instytut Historyczny, 2016).

3. Auerbach provides an account of Schulz's death based on her conversations with survivors, as does Polish Jewish author Henryk Grynberg in his collection of Holocaust memoirs, *Drohobycz, Drohobycz and Other Stories: True Tales from the Holocaust and Life After*, trans. Alicia Nitecki (New York: Penguin Books, 2002), 23–24. See also the first biographical source on Schulz's life, a work that defined the field of Schulzology: Jerzy Ficowski, *Regions of the Great Heresy: Bruno Schulz, a Biographical Portrait*, trans. Theodosia Robertson (New York: W. W. Norton & Company, 2003), 165–68; and Anna Kaszuba-Dębska, *Bruno. Epoka genialna* (Kraków: Wydawnictwo Znak, 2020), which draws extensively on archival materials not available to Ficowski.

4. For a detailed discussion of the controversy surrounding the discovery and removal of Schulz's frescoes from the walls of the wartime Landau residence in 2001, and the debate surrounding responsibility to and ownership of Schulz's artistic legacy within Poland, Israel, and Ukraine, see Benjamin Paloff, "Who Owns Bruno Schulz?" *Boston Review* 29, (December 2004/January 2005): 22–25. For Adam Zachary Newton, the events surrounding this rediscovery invite reflection on the palimpsestuous nature of narratives of Jewish culture in Eastern Europe more broadly. See Adam Zachary Newton, "A Queen, Jesters, Horse-and-Carriage, and Self Portrait: Marginocentric Afterlives of Bruno Schulz and the Migration of Forms," in *Eastern Europe Unmapped: Beyond Borders and Peripheries*, eds. Irene Kacandes and Yuliya Komska (New York: Berghahn Books, 2017).

5. See Jerzy Jarzębski, "Schulz uniwersalny," *Schulz/Forum* 6 (2015): 5–16 for a discussion of the extent to which, as he writes, the "Holocaust theme reduces the meanings of Schulz's prose" (12), obscuring, among other things, its defining universality. Michał Paweł Markowski had expressed a similar frustration earlier in his *Powszechna rozwiązłość. Schulz, egzystencja, literatura* (Kraków: Wydawnictwo Uniwersytetu Jagiellońskiego, 2012): "The

West's recent excitement concerning the figure of Bruno Schulz was connected not with his works, but with the scandal that exploded after the theft of his frescoes from Drohobycz" (29).

6. Including such canonical Polish-language writers as Bolesław Leśmian (born Bolesław Lesman, 1877–1937) and Janusz Korczak (Henryk Goldszmit, 1878–1942); futurists Aleksander Wat (Aleksander Chwat, 1900–1967), Bruno Jasieński (Wiktor Zysman, 1901–1938), and Anatol Stern (1899–1968), and the writers affiliated with the Skamander group and with Poland's leading interwar literary journal, *Wiadomości Literackie* (*Literary News*): Julian Tuwim (1894–1953), Antoni Słonimski (1895–1976), Józef Wittlin (1896–1976), Jan Brzechwa (Jan Wiktor Lesman, 1898–1966), and Bruno Schulz, among others.

7. Scholars have addressed a parallel phenomenon within German Jewish literature, focusing in particular on the dynamics surrounding reception of Franz Kafka's work. See in particular David Suchoff, *Kafka's Jewish Languages: The Hidden Openness of Tradition* (Philadelphia: University of Pennsylvania Press, 2012).

8. Mikhail Krutikov, *From Kabbalah to Class Struggle: Expressionism, Marxism, and Yiddish Literature in the Life and Work of Meir Wiener* (Stanford, CA: Stanford University Press, 2011), 4.

9. Szymaniak has detailed the reception of Polish literature within Yiddish literary criticism and the lack of corresponding attention to Yiddish literature by Polish critics. This history helps to identify a genealogy of erasure and forgetting that continued in the postwar period. See Monika Adamczyk-Garbowska, "'I Know Who You Are, but Who I Am—You Do Not Know . . .': Reading Yiddish Writers in a Polish Literary Context," *Shofar* 29 (Spring 2011), 83–104; and Karolina Szymaniak, "The Bootlickers' Bulletin: *Wiadomości Literackie* and Discursive Figures of Domination and Exclusion in Jewish-Polish Cultural Relations in the Interwar Period" unpublished manuscript (2019).

10. Kamil Kijek, *Dzieci modernizmu. Świadomość, kultura i socjalizacja polityczna młodzieży żydowskiej w II Rzeczypospolitej* (Wrocław: Wydawnictwo Uniwersytetu Wrocławskiego, 2017).

11. Chana Kronfeld and Robert Adler Peckerar, "Tongue-Twisted: Itzik Manger between *Mame-Loshn* and *Loshn-Koydesh*," In geveb: A Journal of Yiddish Studies, 2015, http://ingeveb .org/articles/tongue-twisted-itzik-manger-between-mame-loshn-and-loshn-koydesh.

12. Harriet Murav, *Music from a Speeding Train: Jewish Literature in Post-Revolution Russia* (Stanford, CA: Stanford University Press, 2011), 3. Murav's study reads the work of Russian Jewish authors including Isaac Babel, David Bergelson, Osip Mandelshtam, Peretz Markish, and Der Nister not only within the historical contexts of revolution and catastrophe, and in relation to attendant modernist and social realist literary responses, but also within the transhistorical framework of Jewish textual tradition, including in relation to the Hebrew Bible, liturgy, and classic rabbinic texts that contributed vitally to the "framework for creativity" (3) of these Jewish writers in the Russian language.

13. The ongoing project of archival research and recovery taking place within Schulz studies is currently concentrated around two primary initiatives: the research and editorial team of *Schulz/Forum*, based at the University of Gdańsk, and the biannual Schulz Festival organized by Wiera Meniok in Drohobych, Ukraine, and accompanying year-long cultural events organized by Grzegorz Józefczuk in Lublin (see information on the Stowarzyszenie Festiwal Brunona Schulza [Bruno Schulz Festival Society] at https://brunoschulzfestival.org).

14. In addition to the definitive critical editions of Schulz's prose, graphic work, and correspondence in seven volumes, Słowo/obraz has published a series of invaluable studies of the contexts surrounding Schulz's work and reception that await much-needed translation

into English. See, among others, Jerzy Jarzębski, *Schulzowskie miejsca i znaki* (*Schulzian Places and Signs*, 2016); Anna Kaszuba-Dębska, *Kobiety i Schulz* (*Women and Schulz*, 2016), which expands substantially on Ficowski's initial findings, incorporating in particular new research into the lives of women who were less present in Ficowski's original biography; Piotr Sitkiewicz, *Bruno Schulz w oczach współczesnych. Antologia tekstów krytycznych i publicystycznych lat 1920–1939* [*Bruno Schulz in the Eyes of his Contemporarires: An Anthology of Periodical and Critical Writings, 1920–1939*], 2021); Serge Fauchereau, *Fantazmatyczny świat Brunona Schulza*, 2018); Katarzyna Warska, *Schulz w kanonie. Recepcja szkolna w latach 1945–2018* [*Schulz in the Canon: Reception in Schools from 1945–2018*], 2021); and Stanisław Rosiek, *Odcięcie. Szkice wokół Brunona Schulza* [*Fragments. Sketches on Bruno Schulz*], 2022). See also Kaszuba-Dębska's full biography, *Schulz: Epoka genialna* [*Schulz: The Wondrous Era*], Kraków: Znak, 2020), which assimilates new archival research and details drawn from the letters of Schulz's surviving fiancé, Józefina Szelińska.

15. See Stanisław Rosiek, "O projekcie—tu i teraz. Wersja beta." https://schulzforum.pl/pl/strona/o-projekcie.

16. For discussion of the initial discovery of this article by Ukrainian researcher Bohdan Lazorak in Drohobych and Poznań-based Piotr Sitkiewicz, of the research team of Stanisław Rosiek, see Lazorak, "'Trzon galerii miejskiej' i 'mój ślub mistyczny ze sztuką': zapomniane teksty Brunona Schulza o malarstwie drohobyckich artystów, Feliksa Lachowicza i Efraima Mojżesza Liliena." *Bruno Schulz tesksty i konteksty. Materiały VI Międzynarodowego Festiwalu Brunona Schulza w Drohobyczu*, ed. Wiera Meniok (Drohobycz: Polonistyczne Centrum Naukowo-Informacyjne im. Igora Menioka, 2016), 521–570; and Piotr Sitkiewicz, "Ocalony przez mit. Schulz i Lilien," *Schulz/Forum* 6 (2015): 97–104.

17. *Golus*—the Yiddish term for both "exile" and "diaspora." Bruno Schulz, "E. M. Lilien," *Schulz/Forum* 6 (2015): 88. Translations from the essay are my own. Page citations using "SF6" within the text refer the reader to the full Polish-language text of the 8-part article, compiled and published in *Schulz/Forum* in 2015.

18. See Karen Underhill, "Bruno Schulz, E. M. Lilien i archeologia polsko-żydowskiego modernizmu," *Ruch Literacki* 2016, no. 6: 655–80.

19. In the 1936 essay "The Mythologizing of Reality," which is treated by critics as a poetic manifesto, Schulz describes his poetic approach as a process of transforming the mundane and transient realia of everyday life into myth: responding to a "reverse longing" of the smallest, fragmented "mosaic pieces" of everyday language and experience to return to the primordial home or "pre-fatherland of the word." Bruno Schulz, *Opowiadania. Wybór esejów i listów*, ed. Jerzy Jarzębski (Wrocław: *Zakład Narodowy im. Ossolińskich*, 1989), 365–68.

20. Bruno Schulz, "Pod Belwederem," *Tygodnik Illustrowany* (Warsaw: Gebethner i Wolff), July 26, 1936, 571.

21. See chapter 2, fn 1 and 5, for full bibliographical information on Schulz's 8-part essay entitled "E. M. Lilien," published in *Przegląd Podkarpacia* in 1937–8.

22. David Goldfarb explored the centrality of exegesis to Schulz's literary landscape in "A Living Schulz: 'Noc Wielkiego Sezonu' ('The Night of the Great Season')," *Prooftexts* 14, no. 1 (1994): 25–47. See also Alfred Sproede, "Bruno Schulz: Between Avant-Garde and Hasidic Redemption," in *(Un)masking Bruno Schulz: New Combinations, Further Fragmentations, Ultimate Reintegrations* (Amsterdam: Rodopi, 2009). Among the first critics to draw attention to the Kabbalistic paradigms in play in Schulz's *Sanatorium* and to read its stories as a form of "neo-Kabbalistic" writing were Władysław Panas and Bożena Shallcross.

Drawing on Gershom Scholem's *Major Trends in Jewish Mysticism*, Panas examined messianic and kabbalistic tropes in Schulz's work in his seminal study *Księga blasku: traktat o kabale w prozie Brunona Schulza* [*The Book of Splendor: A Tractate on the Kabbalah in the Prose of Bruno Schulz*] (Lublin: Towarzystwo Naukowe KUL, 1997) and a number of articles analyzing Schulz's graphic and prose works. He was able to establish that the paradigms of *tzimtzum* (contraction), emanation, *shevirat ha-kelim* (shattering of the vessels), and *tikkun-olam* (repair of the world) represent a coherent subtext and organizing structure for Schulz's stories. Bożena Shallcross, in her article "Fragments of a Broken Mirror: Bruno Schulz's Retextualization of the Kabbalah" (1997), situated Schulz's allusions to Neoplatonic Lurianic cosmogony within a modernist context in which the use of a kabbalistic model of redemption becomes material for Schulz's own examinations into the nature of language and "the ontological status of the word in the modern world." She reads Schulz as a modernist writer who "ingeniously retextualized" these elements of Jewish tradition and myth that he had at his disposal to express and extend his modern investigations. See also the first postwar text to approach Schulz's work in relation to Jewish tradition: Artur Sandauer, "Rzeczywistość zdegradowana," in *Proza* by Bruno Schulz (Kraków: Wydawnictwo Literackie, 1973). For Sandauer, Schulz is a contradiction: a progressive writer who has "nothing in common with progress," whose literary imagination is informed instead by ritual, tradition, and an "Old Testament subconscious."

23. See Henri Lewi, *Bruno Schulz, ou, Les stratégies messianiques* (Paris: Table rond, 1989); Panas, *Księga blasku*; Bożena Shallcross, "Fragments of a Broken Mirror: Bruno Schulz's Retextualization of the Kabbalah," *East European Politics and Societies* 11, no. 2 (1997): 270–81; Agata Bielik-Robson, "Życie na marginesach: Kabała Brunona Schulza," in *Cienie pod czerwoną skałą. Eseje o literaturze* (Gdańsk: Fundacja Terytoria Książki, 2015). See also my earlier treatment in Karen Underhill, *Bruno Schulz and Jewish Modernity*, University of Chicago, ProQuest Dissertations Publishing, 2011, 3460247.

24. Kenneth Moss, *An Unchosen People: Jewish Political Reckoning in Interwar Poland* (Cambridge, MA: Harvard University Press, 2021).

25. On the history of the oil industry and its development in the Borysław-Drohobycz region, see Schatzker (2015); and Moskalets (2017). On the rise of Jewish nationalisms in Galicia and in Drohobycz specifically, see Joshua Shanes, *Diaspora Nationalism and Jewish Identity in Habsburg Galicia* (Cambridge: Cambridge University Press, 2012). On the changing nature and influence of Hasidism in twentieth century Poland see David Biale, et al., eds. *Hasidism: A New History* (Princeton, NJ: Princeton University Press, 2018).

26. Nationalities previously recognized within the Austrian Empire included Croats, Czechs, Germans, Italians, Magyars, Poles, Ruthenians (Ukrainians), and Slovenians. Jewish residents and later citizens of the empire made up approximately 10% of the population, with Galicia's Jewish population at 11.1% in 1900. See Paul Robert Magocsi, *Historical Atlas of East Central Europe* (Seattle and London: University of Washington Press, 1993), 108–9.

27. As Joshua Shanes details: "Besides the power of the Polish-controlled Diet, buttressed by the Polish gentry's political domination at the district level, in 1867, Galicia's formerly German-oriented schools were Polonized through the formation of a Polish-dominated school board; in 1869, an imperial decree made Polish the language of the bureaucracy and courts in Galicia; and in 1870–71, Polish became the official language of instruction for Galicia's two universities in Cracow and Lemberg. In 1871 a permanent cabinet ministry without portfolio was created to oversee Galician affairs, a post held continuously in Polish hands." Shanes, *Diaspora Nationalism*, 37 (fn 95). Shanes cites James Shedel, "Austria and Its

Polish Subjects, 1866–1914: A Relationship of Interests," *Austrian History Yearbook*, 19–20, part 2 (1983–84): 23–42.

28. "After Galicia gained autonomy in 1867 on terms favorable to the Poles," writes Timothy Snyder, "Jews learned Polish in Austrian schools. The decline of Austrian liberalism after the financial crash of 1873 undermined the political option of choice of secular Jews" (Snyder, *The Reconstruction of Nations: Poland, Ukraine, Lithuania, Belarus, 1569–1999*, 136).

29. Martin Buber, who was raised on an estate outside of Lwów/Lemberg with his grandparents (1878–1965), attended the gimnazjum im. Franciszka Józefa in Lwów. Schulz himself attended the C. K. Gimnazjum im. Franciszka Józefa in Drohobycz.

30. Letter to Romana Halpern, February 21, 1938 [WE, 430; KL, 166]. On the centrality of and politics of translation in the creation of "world literature," see Pascale Casanova, *The World Republic of Letters* (Cambridge, MA: Harvard University Press, 2004); and David Damrosch, *What Is World Literature?* (Princeton, NJ: Princeton University Press, 2003). "The 'choices' made by dominated writers with regard to language . . . do not consist, as in the great literary nations, in docile submission to a national form, even if they largely depend upon national linguistic politics. For these writers the dilemma of language is complex, and the solutions that they devise are varied" (Damrosch, 256).

31. Nathan Birnbaum (1864–1937), the son of Galician immigrants to Vienna, is credited with being the first writer to use this phrase in his 1902 article entitled "Jewish Renaissance Movement" for the magazine *Ost und West*. See Mathias Acher [Nathan Birnbaum], "Die Judische Renaissance-Bewegung," *Ost und West* (September 1902), 576–84.

32. Shanes, *Diaspora Nationalism*, 36. As Shanes notes, within Polish lands as a whole there had also been an unprecedented and short-lived period of Polish-Jewish cooperation "that climaxed, and abruptly ended, during the failed January Uprising in Russian Poland in 1863" (36). In Galicia, however, acculturation, political cooperation, and sympathy on the part of Jews toward the Polish national cause was relatively high among Jewish intelligentsia of what would be Schulz's parents' pre-WWI generation. See Magdalena M. Opalski and Israel Bartal, *Poles and Jews: A Failed Brotherhood* (Waltham, MA: Brandeis University Press, 1992).

33. A note on translations: in this study I use a number of translations, drawn from three published editions of Schulz's work in English: the 2019 edition of Schulz's *Collected Stories* translated by Madeline Levine, cited within the text using the abbreviation "L." (Evanston, IL: Northwestern University Press, 2019); the 2008 Penguin edition published under the title *Street of Crocodiles and Other Stories*, in the translation of Celina Wieniewska (New York: Penguin Books, 2008), abbreviated within the text as "W"; and the 1998 Picador edition of *The Collected Works of Bruno Schulz*, also in Wieniewska's translation, that makes a selection of Schulz's essays and letters available to English-language readers, abbreviated as "WE." Where no abbreviation is given, the translations are my own. When I have modified the translations used, a note has been added. The abbreviation "O" refers readers to the Polish-language original, in the Ossolineum edition: *Opowiadania, Wybór esejów i listów*. ed. Jerzy Jarzębski (Wrocław: Zakład Narodowy im. Ossolińskich, 1989).

34. Shanes, *Diaspora Nationalism*, 5.

35. On the Jewish experience in pre- and post-WWI Galicia see: Marsha L. Rozenblit, *Reconstructing a National Identity: The Jews of Habsburg Austria during World War I* (New York: Oxford University Press, 2001); Samuel Kassow, *Who Will Write Our History? Rediscovering a Hidden Archive from the Warsaw Ghetto* (Bloomington: Indiana University Press, 2007); Timothy Snyder, *The Reconstruction of Nations: Poland, Ukraine, Lithuania,*

Belarus, 1569–1999 (New Haven, CT: Yale University Press, 2004); Antony Polonsky and Israel Bartal, eds., *Polin: Studies in Polish Jewry. Galicia: Jews, Poles and Ukrainians 1772–1918* (Oxford: Littman Library of Jewish Civilization, 1999); and Larry Wolff's 2010 intellectual history of the "Idea of Galicia" (Larry Wolff, *The Idea of Galicia: History and Fantasy in Habsburg Political Culture* [Stanford, CA: Stanford University Press, 2010]). Russian Jewish writer, ethnographer, and Yiddishist S. Ansky offered one of the first glimpses of the Jewish experience during WWI in his 1914 *The Enemy at His Pleasure: A Journey through the Jewish Pale of Settlement during World War I*, which was republished in English translation in a 2003 edition edited by Joachim Neugroschel. In the 1920s, Austrian Jewish novelist Joseph Roth turned his attention to the plight of WWI Galician Jewish refugees in his portrait of Galician Jewish culture, *The Wandering Jews*. For scholarship that explores the history of competing nationalisms in the region and relations among Ukrainians, Poles, and Jews, see, among others, Paul Robert Magocsi, *Galicia: A Multicultured Land* (Toronto: University of Toronto Press, 2005); Keely Stauter-Halsted, *The Nation in the Village: The Genesis of Peasant National Identity in Austrian Poland, 1848–1914* (Ithaca, NY: Cornell University Press, 2001); and Shanes, *Diaspora Nationalism*. On the rise of the oil industry in Schulz's town of Drohobycz and neighboring Borysław, see Allison F. Frank, *Oil Empire: Visions of Prosperity in Austrian Galicia* (Cambridge, MA: Harvard University Press, 2005) and Valerie Schatzker, *The Jewish Oil Magnates of Galicia: A History, 1853–1945* (Montreal and Kingston: McGill-Queen's University Press, 2015).

36. See, in addition to those titles mentioned above, Natalia Aleksiun, "Salo Baron and Jewish Historiography in Galicia," in *The Enduring Legacy of Salo W. Baron*, ed. Tirosh-Samuelson and Edward Dabrowa (Kraków: Jagiellonian University Press, 2017); Rachel Manekin, "Being Jewish in Fin De Siècle Galicia—the View from Salo Baron's Memoir," ibid.; Ela Bauer, "The Intellectual and the City. Lvov (Lwów, Lemberg, Lviv) and Yehoshua Ozjasz Thon," in *A Romantic Polish Jew: Rabbi Ozjasz Thon from Various Perspectives*, ed. Michał Galas and Shoshana Ronen (Kraków: Jagiellonian University Press, 2015).

37. While treating Schulz's literary landscapes as an imaginary forged at the periphery or margin of the Warsaw cultural "center," scholarship has by no means ignored the rich dynamism of his multicultural Galician context. To describe and explore the liminal positionality of Schulz's Galician Jewish writing, critics have engaged theoretical discourses of hybridity, marginality, and peripherality, and of the "Galician melting pot" or cultural borderlands. Studies have also drawn on the concepts of occultation or cultural "marranism"—and on images of the palimpsestuous text and of culturally hybrid literature as a productive "third space," in the sense introduced by Homi Bhabha. See Eugenia Prokop-Janiec, "Schulz a galicyjski tygiel kultury," *Czytanie Schulza. Materiały międzynarodowej sesji naukowej Bruno Schulz – w stulecie urodzin i w pięćdziesięciolecie śmierci*, ed. Jerzy Jarzębski (Kraków: TIC, Nakładem Instytutu Filologii Polskiej UJ, 1994), 95–107; Jerzy Jarzębski, *Prowincja centrum. Przypisy do Schulza* (Kraków: Wydawnictwo Literackie, 2005); George Gasyna, "Tandeta: Schulz and the Micropolitics of Everyday Life," *Slavic Review* 74, no. 4 (2015). See, among others, Dorota Wojda, "Schulzowskie reprezentacje pogranicza kulturowego w perspektywie postkolonialne," *Teksty Drugie* 2007, no. 4: 233–47; Karen Underhill, "'What Have You Done with the Book?' The Exegetical Encounter in Bruno Schulz's Graphic Works," *Polin* 28 (2015): 323–49; Stanley Bill, "Schulz a znikająca granica," *Bruno Schulz: teksty i konteksty. Materiał VI Międzynarodowego festiwalu Brunona Schulza w Drohobyczu*, ed. Wiera Meniok (Drohobycz: Polonistyczne Centrum Naukowo-Informacyjne im. Igora Menioka, 2016), 219–31; and, for a discussion of Schulz's literary

treatment of Jewish marginality as a trope of vitality and creative potential, Agata Bielik-Robson, "Życie na marginesach: Kabała Brunona Schulza," *Cienie pod czerwoną skałą* (Gdańsk: Fundacja Terytoria Książki, 2015), 209–24. The present study aims to enable a reading in which diaspora itself forms the center of Schulz's literary imaginary.

38. Stanisław Rosiek, *Schulz/Forum*. "Schulz," writes Michal Pawel Markowski, "nie służy żadnej sprawie, nie krzepi, nie zagrzewa i nawet jego eseje o Piłsudskim rozczarowują starych legionistów." Markowski, *Powszechna rozwiązłość*, 28. George Gasyna elaborates, "In an era when Polish creative artists were frequently courted by various agencies of the resurrected state, and leaned on to reify its visions and ambitions through their work, Schulz remained relatively neutral: no pamphlets staunchly advocating nationalist causes, patiently explicating the social democratic ones, or stridently justifying the communist ones' historical necessity . . . can be traced back to his pen. (Similarly, no dizzying visions of a luminous future Poland can be tracked to his paintbrush and easel.)" George Gasyna, "Tandeta: Schulz and the Micropolitics of Everyday Life," *Slavic Review* 74, no. 4 (2015).

39. "His literary heroes," Newton continues, "were contemporary, to be found across Poland's western border." Adam Zachary Newton, *The Elsewhere: On Belonging at a Near Distance* (Madison: University of Wisconsin Press, 2005), 108.

40. Bruno Schulz, *Księga listow. Dzieła zebrane, Tom 5*, ed. Jerzy Ficowski and Stanisław Danecki (Gdańsk: Słowo/obraz terytoria, 2002), 63. Cited within the text using the abbreviation "KL."

41. *Wiadomości Literackie* (*Literary News*): Poland's leading, Warsaw-based weekly literary newspaper. Edited for the full 15-year period of its publication (1924–1939) by the Polish Jewish editor Mieczysław Grydzewski (neé Grecendler), the paper was initially modeled on the French weekly *Les nouvelles littéraires*. It became the leading forum for Poland's liberal, left-leaning intelligentsia of the interwar period, and a space for the discussion of not only literary but also social, political, economic, and moral problems.

42. This group included, among others, the poets Roman Brandstaetter, Maurycy Szymel, Henryk Adler, and Jakub Appenszlak. See Eugenia Prokop-Janiec, *Międzywojenna literatura polsko-żydowska jako zjawisko kulturowe i artystyczne* (Kraków: Universitas, 1992); in English translation: Prokop-Janiec, *Polish-Jewish Literature in the Interwar Years*, trans. Abe Shenitzer (Syracuse, NY: Syracuse University Press, 2003).

43. Jews represented between 10 and 11 percent of the population of interwar Poland and, due to demographic concentrations, between 30 and 60 percent of the population of most towns and cities.

44. See Prokop-Janiec, *Polish-Jewish Literature*; Joanna Beata Michlic, *Poland's Threatening Other: The Image of the Jew from 1880 to the Present* (Lincoln: University of Nebraska Press, 2006); Shore, *Caviar and Ashes*; and Antony Polonsky, "Why Did They Hate Tuwim and Boy So Much? Jews and Artificial Jews in the Literary Polemics of the Second Polish Republic," in *Antisemitism and Its Opponents in Modern Poland*, ed. Robert Blobaum (Ithaca, NY: Cornell University Press, 2005), 189–209.

45. Benjamin Harshav, *Language in Time of Revolution* (Berkeley: University of California Press, 1993). Chone Shmeruk, "Hebrew-Yiddish-Polish: A Trilingual Jewish Culture," in *The Jews of Poland between Two World Wars*, ed. Yisrael Gutman, Ezra Mendelsohn, Jehuda Reinharz, and Chone Shmeruk (Hanover: Published for Brandeis University Press by University Press of New England, 1989), 285–311.

46. In the US, the National Origins Quota of 1924 introduced strict limits on immigration from Eastern Europe.

47. As cited by Jonathan Frankel, *Prophecy and Politics: Socialism, Nationalism, and the Russian Jews, 1862–1917* (Cambridge: Cambridge University Press, 1981), 304.

48. On Warsaw's Polish Jewish intellectual milieu in the interwar and post-WWII periods, see Marci Shore, *Caviar and Ashes: A Warsaw Generation's Life and Death in Marxism, 1918–1968* (New Haven, CT: Yale University Press, 2006).

49. The title, translated by Celina Wieniewska as "The Mythologizing of Reality," is alternately rendered as "The Mythicization of Reality."

50. Kassow, *Who Will Write Our History?*, 19.

51. Kamil Kijek, *Dzieci modernizmu: Świadomość, kultura i socjalizacja polityczna młodzieży żydowskiej w II Rzeczypospolitej* (Wrocław: Wydawnictwo Uniwersytetu Wrocławskiego, 2017).

52. Bałaban produced the first histories of the Jews of Lwów and Kraków, Schiper of economic relations in the Commonwealth. Both historians moved to Warsaw in 1918, in effect bringing the Galician "head start"—Jewish historiography in the Polish language—to the intellectual center when Poland gained independence.

53. "Mesjasz rośnie pomału" (*"The Messiah* is growing, little by little") he wrote to Kazimierz Truchanowski in a letter of 1936, calling the work by the title he had chosen by that time (KL, 168).

54. It is also true that the project was never realized. Despite Jerzy Ficowski's speculation that Schulz had completed the manuscript of the novel *Mesjasz* and that it may yet be found, the correspondence that remains is ambiguous and suggests the work was likely never completed.

55. On what Benjamin Harshav has called the "Modern Jewish Revolution" and the choices made by Jewish writers in post-WWI Central and Eastern Europe, see Kenneth Moss, *Jewish Renaissance in the Russian Revolution* (2009); Benjamin Harshav, *Language in Time of Revolution* (1993); Mikhail Krutikov, *Yiddish Fiction and the Crisis of Modernity 1905–1914* (2001); Shanes (2012); Joshua Fishman, *The Rise of Modern Yiddish Literature* (2010); Joshua Karlip (2013).

56. Or, in Schulz's case, who *continued* to write in Polish, rather than switching to Hebrew or Yiddish for ideological reasons. See Prokop-Janiec, *Polish-Jewish Literature*, 74–82. Addressing the "problem" of multilingualism in Jewish literature, leading Yiddish literary critic H. Leivick wrote, "I will be even clearer: should our Yiddish-Hebrew literature exist only through, for example, a Bialik or a Peretz, no one else—we would have the full right to say that we have a national literature; however, should we not have any literature in Yiddish or in Hebrew, even were we to have 50 Heines and 50 Werfels, we would have nothing from a national standpoint." H. Leivick, *Iz undzer literatur a tzvey-oder fil-shprachike literatur?* "Is our literature a bi- or a multilingual literature?" in *Eseyen un Redes* (Congress for Jewish Culture: New York, 1963). Originally published in 1944.

57. Krutikov, *From Kabbalah to Class Struggle*, 4.

58. Marci Shore, *Caviar and Ashes: A Warsaw Generation's Life and Death in Marxism, 1918–1968* (New Haven, CT: Yale University Press, 2006), 5. The subjects of Shore's intellectual history include, among others, Antoni Słonimski, Aleksander and Ola Wat, Anatol Stern, Bruno Jasieński, Julian Tuwim, Mieczysław Braun, and Mieczysław Grydzewski.

59. Schulz did not express support for the Soviet project until the Soviet occupation of his hometown during World War II, at which time he applied for and accepted employment with the local Soviet authorities. See a discussion of artwork for the Ukrainian-Soviet newspaper *Bilshevitska Pravda* in Bogdan Lazorak and Leonid Timoshenko, *Vidomij i nievidomij Bruno*

Schulz (Koło, 2016); and Stanley Bill, "Propaganda on the Margins: Bruno Schulz's Soviet Illustrations, 1940–41, *The Slavonic and East European Review* 96, no. 3 (July 2018): 432–468.

60. In the second half of the 1930s, while other Polish Jewish writers increased their political engagement (Antoni Słonimski turned his acerbic wit in essays for *Wiadomości Literackie* from disparagement of traditional, unassimilated Polish Jewry toward attacks on Endek ideology and policy; Aleksander Wat, who had been jailed for editing the Marxist journal *Miesięcznik Literacki* (*Literary Monthly*) considered founding a new communist literary organ, and Bruno Jasieński, already in the Soviet Union, was "dispatched to Tadzhikistan as an agitator for higher cotton production") (Shore, *Caviar and Ashes*, 107). Schulz sought time to work on his new novel, entitled *Messiah*.

61. *Ost und West* (East and West), also the title of the Berlin-based German-language Jewish magazine (1901–1923) that sought to bridge German Jewish and East European Jewish cultures in the construction of an affirmative modern Jewish identity. E. M. Lilien's graphic art gave the magazine its signature secessionist style.

62. "Undula" appeared in *Świt* (*Dawn*), a newspaper published in Borysław and directed primarily toward oil executives, on January 15, 1922.

63. Additionally, while references to Jewish and classical Greek mythologies abound in the stories, allusions to Polish-Catholic literary tradition are largely absent. In an interesting note from what remains of his correspondence, Schulz responded to an invitation from Zenon Waśniewski (1891–1945), founder and editor of the progressive monthly literary journal *Kamena* (Chełm Lubelski), to contribute something to the 1934 anniversary issue on Polish national poet Adam Mickiewicz: "For the Mickiewicz number I can give you nothing. What I know of Mickiewicz I have from grade school" (letter to Zenon Waśniewski, April 24, 1934 [KL, 68]).

64. Marc Caplan, *How Strange the Change Language, Temporality, and Narrative Form in Peripheral Modernisms* (Stanford, CA: Stanford University Press, 2011); Schachter, Allison, *Diasporic Modernisms: Hebrew and Yiddish Literature in the Twentieth Century* (Oxford: Oxford University Press, 2012).

65. Schachter, *Diasporic Modernisms*, 15.

66. Ibid., 15.

67. Murav cites Dan Miron (2000), 40. See Harriet Murav, *Music from a Speeding Train: Jewish Literature in Post-Revolution Russia*, 7.

68. Schachter, *Diasporic Modernisms*, 15.

69. Tara Zahra, "Imagined Noncommunities: National Indifference as a Category of Analysis," *Slavic Review* 69(1): 93–119.

70. Ibid., 98.

71. It can be pointed out that many of the actors in Zahra's study of national indifference are individuals, including children and refugees, whose "indifference" to national affiliation was passive, and determined more by questions of expediency and survival in the tumultuous post-WWI environment of Central Europe than by intentional ideological resistance. However, Zahra's identification of indifference as an understudied category of analysis offers a wedge with which to open up fields of scholarship—historical, literary, and cultural—that have for generations been structured along ethno-national lines. In the context of central European Modernist literature and art, then, it may provide an additional language with which to discuss and identify writers who, not passively but quite intentionally, resisted participation in the nationalist political and literary projects of the period.

72. Schulz might be interestingly compared to the actors in Zahra's discussion of national indifference who continue to privilege affiliation on the basis of faith rather than nationality, though as a secular writer, Schulz emphasizes his connection with the aggadic and hermeneutic, rather than halakhic aspects of Jewish tradition—seeking modern and modernist, secular corollaries to the concepts of scripture and exegesis.

73. Bruno Schulz, *Street of Crocodiles and Other Stories*, trans. Celina Wieniewska (New York: Penguin, 2008), 224.

74. Schulz, "E. M. Lilien," *Schulz/Forum 6*, 2015, Stanisław Rosiek, ed. (Gdańsk: Fundacja Terytoria Książki), 83–96.

75. David Suchoff, *Kafka's Jewish Languages: The Hidden Openness of Tradition* (Philadelphia: University of Pennsylvania Press, 2012).

76. Marc Caplan has described Yiddish as a "spectral language," arguing that from the perspective of contemporary scholarship, Yiddish can be considered "the language of the dead, the spectral, the thwarted possibility." I would argue that such a spectral fate applies more readily to the emergent interwar Polish Jewish language than it does to the Yiddish language, whose connections to prewar Yiddish culture are thriving today. Marc Caplan, *How Strange the Change Language, Temporality, and Narrative Form in Peripheral Modernisms* (Stanford, CA: Stanford University Press, 2011), 7.

77. I propose this term "Spectral Polin" in connection with reemergent discourse surrounding the Jewish past and culture of Poland, with attendant dynamics of memory, longing, and responsibility, in "Toward a Diasporic Poland/Polin: Zeitlin, Sutzkever, and the Ghost Dance with Jewish Poland," in *Poland and Polin: New Interpretations in Polish-Jewish Studies*, ed. Irena Grudzińska-Gross and Iwa Nawrocki. *Eastern European Culture, Politics and Societies*, Vol. 10 (Frankfurt am Main, New York: Peter Lang, 2016), 181–96.

78. Polish Jewish novelist and publisher Piotr Paziński argues that one of the most marginalized discourses within contemporary Poland is precisely that of Jewish *continuity* in Poland, both after '68, and after '89: the emphasis within discussion of the post-1989 period being placed exclusively on Jewish "revival." This perspective in fact reaffirms the assignation of "spectrality." Because they belong to a still unrecognized discourse, present-day uses of Polish as a Jewish language are effectively "spectralized" in the sense used by Gayatri Spivak. See also Paziński, Piotr, "Ku żydowskiej polszczyźnie. Julian Stryjkowski i językowy palimpsest Austerii." *Marani literatury polskiej*. Lipszyc, Adam and Piotr Bogalecki, eds. (Kraków: Wydawnictwo Austeria, 2020), 523–541.

79. Gayatri Chakravorty Spivak, "Ghostwriting." *Diacritics* 25, no. 2 (1995): 65–84.

80. Ibid.

81. Mikhail Krutikov, *From Kabbalah to Class Struggle: Expressionism, Marxism, and Yiddish Literature in the Life and Work of Meir Wiener* (Stanford, CA: Stanford University Press, 2011), 2.

82. Arnold M. Eisen, *Galut: Modern Jewish Reflection on Homelessness and Homecoming* (Bloomington: Indiana University Press, 1986), 117.

1. Leading the Word Out of Its Golus

1. Chone Shmeruk, "Hebrew-Yiddish-Polish: A Trilingual Jewish Culture" in *The Jews of Poland between Two World Wars*, eds. Yisrael Gutman, Ezra Mendelsohn, Jehuda Reinharz, and Chone Shmeruk (Hanover, NH: University Press of New England, 1989), 285–311.

2. On the rise of the Jewish public sphere, see Scott Ury, *Barricades and Banners: The Revolution of 1905 and the Transformation of Warsaw Jewry* (Stanford, CA: Stanford University Press, 2012); Jeffrey Veidlinger, *Jewish Public Culture in the Late Russian Empire* (Bloomington: Indiana University Press, 2009); Joshua M. Karlip, *The Tragedy of a Generation: The Rise and Fall of Jewish Nationalism in Eastern Europe* (Cambridge, MA: Harvard University Press, 2013); Shachar Pinsker, *A Rich Brew: How Cafés Created Modern Jewish Culture* (New York: New York University Press, 2018).

3. Pinsker, 2018.

4. Benjamin Harshav, *Language in Time of Revolution* (Berkeley: University of California Press, 1993), 5. Harshav interestingly does not mention Polish here, testifying to the fraught nature of scholarship's engagement with the Polish Jewish past. On the dynamics of resistance to exploring the Jewish resonances and sources of Polish-language literature within the fields of both Polish and Jewish literary studies, see also introduction.

5. Ibid., 14.

6. See, for example, Deleuze and Guattari, whose *Kafka: Toward a Minor Literature* (Gilles Deleuze and Felix Guattari, *Kafka: Toward a Minor Literature*, trans. Dana Polan, vol. 30, Theory and History of Literature [Minneapolis: University of Minnesota Press, 1986]) marked the beginning of a paradigm shift; and later Damrosch, *What Is World Literature?* (Princeton: Princeton University Press, 2003), 187–205; Vivian Liska, *When Kafka Says We: Uncommon Communities in German-Jewish Literature* (Bloomington: Indiana University Press, 2009); and David Suchoff, *Kafka's Jewish Languages: The Hidden Openness of Tradition* (Philadelphia: University of Pennsylvania Press, 2012). See also Kronfeld and Peckerar, "Tongue-Twisted" (2015). For Kronfeld and Peckerar in their study of Itzik Manger "the rhetorical practices typical of Jewish modernisms are often Janus-faced: they exhibit a simultaneous affiliation with intra- and extra Jewish trends, and they offer a 'dual motivation' for the same poetic choices" (87–92).

7. As Benjamin Paloff demonstrates, this polyphony finds its equivalent in the spatial imaginary of Schulz's texts as well, "in what Schulz . . . calls, in a chance echo of Bakhtin, its 'manifold architectonic polyphony'—that is, narrative dimensions layered on top of one another." For Paloff, Schulz's layered treatment of the spatial landscape also challenges the binary paradigm of center and periphery, suggestive of social and cultural hierarchies, introducing a less fixable model of "noncenter." Benjamin Paloff, *Lost in the Shadow of the Word: Space, Time, and Freedom in Interwar Eastern Europe* (Evanston, IL: Northwestern University Press, 2016), 37.

8. See especially Monika Adamczyk-Garbowska, Eugenia Prokop-Janiec, Sławomir Żurek, and Antony Polonsky, eds., *Polin: Studies in Polish Jewry Volume 28: Jewish Writing in Poland* (London: Basil Blackwell for The Institute for Jewish Studies, 2016); A. Molisak and S. Ronen, eds., *The Trilingual Literature of Polish Jews from Different Perspectives* (Cambridge Scholars Publisher, 2017); and Adam Lipszyc and Piotr Bogalecki, *Marani literatury polskiej* (Kraków: Austeria, 2020).

9. Schulz, "Bruno Schulz do St. I. Witkiewicz." *Tygodnik Illustrowany* 1935, no. 17, 322.

10. Ibid.

11. Benjamin Harshav, *Language in Time of Revolution* (Berkeley: University of California Press, 1993).

12. Ibid., 16.

13. The collection *Cinnamon Shops* was first published in English under the title *Street of Crocodiles and Other Stories*.

14. Bruno Schulz, *Collected Stories*, translated by Madeline Levine (Evanston, IL: Northwestern University Press, 2012), 47. Henceforth "L," cited within the text.

15. *"Dlatego wszelka poezja jest mitologizowaniem, dąży do odtworzenia mitów o świecie. Umitycznienie świata nie jest zakończone . . . gdyż mit leży już w samych elementach i poza mit nie możemy w ogóle wyjść."* Bruno Schulz, "Mityzacja rzeczywistości," *Studio*, no. 3–4 (1936): 32–34. Schulz uses a variety of terms in his writing for the poetic activation of and reconnection with myth, including "mitologizowanie" (mythologizing), "umitycznienie" (en-myth-ening), and "mityzacja" (mythicization). In English these have been used by translators and critics interchangeably, most often as "mythologizing."

16. Schulz, "E. M. Lilien." Translation my own.

17. Allison Schachter, *Diasporic Modernisms: Hebrew and Yiddish Literature in the Twentieth Century* (Oxford: Oxford University Press, 2012).

18. Shachar Pinsker, "The Urban Literary Café and the Geography of Hebrew and Yiddish Modernism in Europe," in Mark Wollaeger, (ed.), *The Oxford Handbook of Global Modernisms*, (Oxford: Oxford University Press, 2012), 436.

19. Rokhl Korn, "'*Tzimring gevelber*' fun Bruno Schulz," *Literarishe bleter* 16, no. 519 (1934): 248.

20. In 1938, Rachel Auerbach wrote to Schulz expressing her interest in translating his prose into Yiddish. "Have I already written to you from Przemyśl about how very pleased I am about your attempts to write in German, or to translate your things into German? . . . If you can't be for the community from which you came," she wrote, "may you at least be for the world. I, for one, would like to try translating your work into Yiddish" (*KL*, 294). With the onset of the war, Auerbach did not return to undertake this project. Separately, Debora Vogel recommended Schulz to her friend the publisher Mendel Neugroschel, and Schulz responded to this opportunity with interest; but this project, too, did not come to fruition.

21. Waïl S. Hassan, "Translational Literature and the Pleasures of Exile," *PMLA*, vol. 131, no. 5 (2016): 1435–43. At the same time, Korn's reading may be treated as a form of appropriation or "domestication" of Schulz's intentionally universalist text, which reincorporates or repackages it for the Jewish reader: a kind of apologia. As Hassan writes, "This way of thinking dictates that the foreign text must be domesticated, shorn of the quality that makes it foreign; its strangeness" (1436). This tendency to domesticate is equally present within Polish or "non-Jewish" readings. Hassan's approach speaks to the review of *Cinnamon Shops* written by S. I. Witkiewicz discussed earlier. If in Korn's review Schulz's book gains resonance with its Jewish context and the difficult experiences of Jews in interwar Poland, in Witkacy's it becomes part of a dialogue on madness, perversion, and breaking through to new levels of consciousness.

22. Hassan, "Translational Literature," 1442.

23. Ibid., 1437.

24. For example, "seder" becomes "*kolejność*" ("order"); "Zohar" becomes "*Księga blasku*" ("Book of Radiance"); "High Holidays": "Wielki sezon" ("Great Season"); Torah, Bible or Scripture: "*Księga*," "*Oryginał*" or "*Autentyk*" ("The Book," "The Original," or "The Authentic"); "Hasidim": "*brodaci*" (bearded ones)"; "Pesach": "*tydzień świąteczny*" ("the holiday week"); and as I will argue in chapter 6, "*tikkun-olam*" becomes "*mityzacja rzeczywistości*" ("mythologizing of reality").

25. Kronfeld and Peckerar contribute the argument that within a Jewish context, the translational model "has great cultural resonance precisely because it builds upon discursive

practices such as midrash and exegetical translation that are at the very core of Yiddish—and, more generally, Jewish—textual culture." They explore a key formal characteristic of the work of modern writers in Yiddish and Hebrew—"what linguists call 'component awareness': a metalinguistic consciousness of the source languages (in the case of Yiddish) or the historical layers (in the case of Hebrew), and of the cultural class and gender hierarchies that go along with those sources and layers [that] informs all discursive practices in these languages." Chana Kronfeld and Robert Adler Peckerar, "Tongue-Twisted: Itzik Manger between *Mame-Loshn* and *Loshn-Koydesh,*" *In geveb: A Journal of Yiddish Studies* (2015): 21.

26. I thank Michael Wex for suggesting this translation of Korn's phrase.
27. Rokhl Korn, "Tzimring gevelber," *Literarishe bleter*, 80.
28. Ibid. *"ofnbarung"* from German, *"Offenbarung."*
29. The narrator in "Tailors' Dummies" refers to his father as an "inspired Heresiarch" (W, 34), portraying him as a prophet or proponent of "heretical" creative acts and a "metaphysical conjurer" "defending the lost cause of poetry" (W, 25).

30. In Schulz's Polish: *"Kto wie ile jest cierpiących, okaleczonych, fragmentarycznych postaci życia, jak sztucznie sklecone, gwoździami na gwałt zbite życie szaf i stołów, ukrzyżowanego drzewa, cichych męczenników okrutnej pomysłowości ludzkiej"* (O, 44). I have modified the English translation from Wieniewska's: "merging into one misbegotten personality" (W, 39). This section of Schulz's "Treatise" goes on to draw a direct connection—which Korn also cites—between the forms of wooden furniture and the speaker himself, the protagonist's aging Jewish father: "'How much ancient suffering is there in the varnished grain, in the veins and knots of our old familiar wardrobes? Who would recognize in them the old features, smiles and glances, almost planed and polished out of all recognition?' My father's face, when he said that, dissolved into a thoughtful net of wrinkles, began to resemble an old plank full of knots and veins, from which all memories had been planed away" (W, 39).

31. The event was the largest and most widely known of pogroms that took place within the newly formed Polish state. The same period saw a much larger and sustained pattern of anti-Jewish violence throughout Eastern Ukraine during the Ukrainian Civil War of 1917–21, during which between 60,000 and 200,000 Jews were murdered and 200,000 children orphaned in 1,300 separate events (Anthony Polonsky, *The Jews in Russia and Poland, Vol. II* (Liverpool: Littman Library of Jewish Civilization, 2012), 200. For discussion of the scale and nature of the pogroms that influenced the demographics and cultural climate of the Soviet Union and also Interwar Poland, see Elissa Bemporad, *Legacy of Blood: Jews, Pogroms, and Ritual Murder in the Lands of the Soviets* (New York: Oxford University Press, 2019) and Jeffrey Veidlinger, *In the Midst of Civilized Europe: The Pogroms of 1918–1921 and the Onset of the Holocaust* (New York: Metropolitan Books, Henry Holt, 2021).

32. Tara Zahra, *Kidnapped Souls: National Indifference and the Battle for Children in the Bohemian Lands, 1900–1948* (Ithaca, NY: Cornell University Press, 2009).

33. Korn, "Tzimring gevelber."

34. The dynamic took similar forms across the countries of Central Europe following WWI. In his study *German as a Jewish Problem*, Marc Volovici explores "the growing political pressure on German Jews to address their national and linguistic loyalties." As he writes, "This pressure was generated by effective agitation coming from Eastern European Zionists and was part of a broader current among European Nationalist movements to advocate linguistic uniformity within a confined territory." Marc Volovici, *German as a Jewish Problem: The Language Politics of Jewish Nationalism* (Redwood City, CA: Stanford University Press, 2020).

35. Chaim Löw, "Żydzi w poezji odrodzonej Polski," *Miesięcznik Żydowski* vol. 3, no. 2 (7–12) (1933): 27–35.
36. The leading Polish literary journal out of Warsaw, granter of the annual *Wiadomości Literackie* award that would confer canonical status on contemporary Polish-language writers.
37. Staff writer. "Setny numer *Wiadomości Literackie*" *Przegląd Poranny* (Poznań) Dec. 1, 1925. Cited by Löw, "Żydzi w poezji odrodzonej Polski," 31.
38. Hersz Buchman, "The Rebirth of Language," *Chwila*, June 5, 1932, no. 4740 (9).
39. Ibid.
40. Ibid.
41. Ibid.
42. "*Genialna epoka*:" the title of the second story that would appear in Schulz's second volume, *Sanatorium under the Sign of the Hourglass*.
43. In 1908 Czernowitz was the site of the first international conference on the Yiddish language, organized at the initiative of Nathanial Birnbaum and attracting delegates from across wide political spectrum. Joshua M. Karlip, *The Tragedy of a Generation: The Rise and Fall of Jewish Nationalism in Eastern Europe* (Cambridge, MA: Harvard University Press, 2013).
44. Buchman, "The Rebirth of Language."
45. Uri Zvi Grinberg, interview with Benzion Zangen, *Chwila*, January 29, 1938. In line with Grinberg's emphasis on a Hebrew rhythm, Raisa Shapiro has drawn attention in Schulz's writing to strategies of repetition that align with the theory of translation articulated by Franz Rosenzweig and Martin Buber, developed during their translation of the Bible into German. "Linguistically unconventional repetition is a hallmark of Schulz's style," writes Shapiro. This includes the use of keywords, or *Leitwerte*: "By *Leitwort* we mean a word or a word-root that repeats meaningfully within a text," producing a "measured repetition that corresponds to the inner rhythm of the text, or, better yet, pours out from it." See Martin Buber, "Leitwort Style in Pentateuch Narrative," in *Scripture in Translation*, eds. Rosenwald and Fox (Bloomington: Indiana University Press, 1994), 114. See also: Leora Batnitzky, "Translation as Transcendence: A Glimpse into the Workshop of the Buber-Rosenzweig Bible Translation." *New German Critique*, no. 70 (1997): 87–116. For David Goldfarb, in Schulz "the effect is anaphoric and elevates the tone to the level of epic" (Goldfarb, "Night of the Great Season," 33). Michal Paweł Markowski builds his 2012 study *Powszechna rozwiązłość* around the elaboration of Schulz's use of the prefix *roz-*. Here, repetition can be seen to provide an overarching semantic rhythm, pointing in Schulz's work to an ontological principle of dissolution that inheres in matter and being.
46. See Benjamin Harshav, *Language in Time of Revolution* (Berkeley: University of California Press, 1993).
47. This was true for many Polish Jewish writers more assimilated than Schulz as well. Julian Tuwim explained in an interview with the poet S. L. Shneiderman for *Literarishe bleter* that, though "I myself can't read in Yiddish, when someone reads it to me, I can understand what it's all about." He continues, "I don't know Yiddish well enough to be able to do translations freely. If you were to help me with it, I would compile a small anthology of new Yiddish poetry. First, I would publish it in 'Skamander,' and then in book form. . . . Let this quickly put an end to the perception of my negative . . . attitude towards Yiddish literature." "Bay Julian Tuwim," *Literarishe bleter* 132: 748.
48. Letter of December 7, 1938 (KL, 267).

49. Letter to Romana Halpern, February 21, 1938 (WE, 430; KL, 166).
50. Born in a Polish Jewish farming family outside of Lwów, Korn published her first volume of Yiddish language poems, entitled *Dorf*, in 1927.
51. Melech Ravitch, *Mayn Leksikon* (Montreal: 1945).
52. A result of the partial administrative autonomy granted by the Habsburg monarchy to Galician province in the 1860s and the attendant Polonization of administrative bodies and the public education system.
53. Kathryn Hellerstein, *A Question of Tradition: Women Poets in Yiddish, 1586–1987* (Stanford: Stanford University Press, 2014), 155. On the influence of the 1918 pogrom on Jewish identity, see Albert Lichtblau and Michael John, "Jewries in Galicia and Bukovina," *Jewries at the Frontier: Accommodation, Identity, Conflict*, ed. Sander L. Gilman and Milton Shain (Urbana: University of Illinois Press, 1999). "As to the question of the identity of the Jews of Lemberg and Galicia, Jewish national consciousness and self-confidence had gained increasing influence. This had its roots in the highly problematic relations between Jews and Poles, whose strongest manifestation was the Lemberg pogrom" (40). In the face of continued antisemitic policies in the interwar period, such as the introduction of restrictive university admissions policies, "a majority of Jews oriented themselves toward those outlooks in which their own national identity played an increasingly prominent role. To a certain extent, however, religious orthodoxy and Chassidism along with the rejection of Zionism continued to dominate rural Jewish communities" (40).
54. Hellerstein, *A Question of Tradition*, 168.
55. Ibid., 156.
56. The details of their relationship are not known. That the two maintained contact and visited one another in Drohobycz is suggested by Schulz's letter to Ostap Ortwin of May 1921.
57. Herman Sternbach, "Sklepy cynamonowe," *Miesięcznik Żydowski* (1934), 384.
58. Schulz's linguistic cosmogony laid out in the manifesto shares much with Benjamin's formulations in "On Language as Such and on the Language of Man," and "The Task of the Translator," in Marcus Bullock and Michael W. Jennings, eds., *Selected Writings, Vol. 1, 1913–1926* (Cambridge, MA: Belknap Press of Harvard University, 1996).
59. Schulz, "Mityzacja rzeczywistości," *Studio*, No. 3-4 (June 1936): 32–34.
60. This gesture creates a metonymic skid that joins (raw) matter to (pure) language to human being or spirit—the living material that in each case is trapped in form, longing for release.
61. Schulz's "mythologizing" essay notably avoids naming his Jewish textual sources directly, as Benjamin does here, replacing Jewish theological vocabulary with the word *sens* (meaning), and also the Romantic language of primordial "myth." This form of translation belongs to the gesture of translational concealment or inversion characteristic of Schulz's textual strategies. In both cases Schulz, like Benjamin, "follows" Jewish theological tradition in "presupposing language as an ultimate reality, perceptible only in its manifestation, inexplicable and mystical" (Benjamin, "On Language as Such").
62. Schulz's antinomy between two language spheres, associated as well with two temporalities, within and beyond history, also bears comparison with the language theories of Benjamin, as he formulated them in his early mystical essays on language. In "On Language as Such and on the Language of Man," he maps a similar distinction between the "language of everyday use" and the primordial "language as such," which Benjamin also describes as the Name. The Name, which is "the innermost nature of language," stands in contrast to "the bourgeois conception of language" as a means of everyday communication.

Similarly to Schulz, here again an originary fragmentation or Fall leads to "the enslavement of language in prattle." "The life of man in pure language-mind was blissful.... In the Fall, man abandoned immediacy in the communication of the concrete, name, and fell into the abyss of the mediateness of all communication, of the word as means, of the empty word, into the abyss of prattle" (Walter Benjamin, "On Language as Such"). Further, in order to grasp the idiosyncratic way that Schulz uses the term *integral mythology* here, we may again draw on Benjamin's early mystical essays on linguistics. While the terminology—specifically Schulz's use of the term *myth*—would seem directly anti-Benjaminian, his conception of integral mythology here matches quite closely Benjamin's concept of translation: the "universal meaning" corresponds to Benjamin's concept of a source "language" of which all other languages represent translations.

63. Hillel Zeitlin, "Book One," *Hasidic Spirituality for a New Era: The Religious Writings of Hillel Zeitlin*, ed. Arthur Green, trans. Joel Rosenberg (Mahwah, NJ: Paulist Press, 2012), 88.

64. Hillel Zeitlin, *Hasidic Spirituality*, 88.

65. Korn, "'Tzimring gevelber,'" 248.

66. Ahad Ha'am, "The Spiritual Revival," in *Selected Essays of Ahad Ha'am*. Translated and edited by Leon Simon (Philadelphia: The Jewish Publication Society of America, 1962), 264.

67. Prepared as the afterword to the Polish-language translation of *The Trial*—a translation that, though attributed to Schulz, was the work of his fiancée, Józefina Szelińska.

68. "Sklepy cynamonowe," 384.

69. Ibid.

70. Rachel Auerbach, "*Nisht-oysgeshpunene fedem*," *Di goldene keyt* 50 (1964): 131–43

71. Ibid.

72. For an extensive review of the critical reception of Schulz's work, see Piotr Sitkiewicz, *Bruno Schulz i krytycy* (Gdańsk: Słowo/obraz terytoria, 2018).

73. S. I. Witkiewicz, "Twórczość literacka Brunona Schulza," *Pion*, no. 34(99) (1935):2.

74. Stefan Chwin suggests the possibility that Schulz may have quite consciously curated the version of his artistic output—and, we may add, by extension, of his aesthetic views—that he shared with Witkacy: "It is notable that Witkacy did not notice even a shade of Jewishness in his graphic works, locating the Schulzian vision near that of the goy, and certainly not placing it in the context of the Biblical iconography of the Hasidic world—which leads one to suspect that Schulz simply did not show him anything of his graphic work aside from *Xięga* (KL, 163–64)." Stefan Chwin, "Dlaczego Bruno Schulz nie chciał być pisarzem żydowskim (O 'wymazywaniu' żydowskości w *Sanatorium pod klepsydrą* i *Sklepach cynamonowych*)," *Schulz Forum* 4 (2014): 5–21, 10.

75. Stanisław Ignacy Witkiewicz, "Twórczość literacka Brunona Schulza," *Pion* (Warsaw), no. 34–35, 1935. Translation modified from that available in: "Bruno Schulz's Literary Work," in *The Witkiewicz Reader*, ed. Daniel Gerould, trans. Daniel Gerould (Evanston, IL: Northwestern University Press, 1992), 308. It should be stressed that one would be hard pressed to find a more complementary text written by Witkacy about any artist. The language employed identifies Schulz's project with states of consciousness and artistic perception that Witkacy sought to achieve in his own artistic practice.

76. Leading modernist Witold Gombrowicz (1904–69) wrote after the war of his highly publicized relationship with Schulz: "It would be hard to call it friendship—in the years we became acquainted we were both still unborn. In this film, 'flickering onto the screen of memory,' I see him as someone almost completely unknown to me, but then I see myself that way, too—it was not us, but the introduction to us, an overture, prologue." His reflections

continue, "He first showed up at my place, on Służewska, after the publication of *Cinnamon Shops*—I had just published my *Memoir from Adolescence*. He was small, strange, chimerical, focused, intense, almost feverish—and this is how our conversations got started, usually on walks. . . . That we truly needed each other is indisputable. We found ourselves in a vacuum, our literary situations were permeated with a void, our admirers were spectral. . . . we both roamed Polish literature like a flourish, ornament, chimera, griffin." But Gombrowicz uses the entry to confess, "His extended hand did not meet my own. I did not return his regard, I gave him abysmally little, almost nothing, of myself, our relationship was a fiasco . . . but perhaps even this secretly worked to our advantage. Perhaps he and I needed fiasco rather than happy symbiosis." Translated by Lillian Vallee. Witold Gombrowicz, "Diary 1961–1966," *New York Times Book Review*, April 13, 1989. A notable review in 1939 of Schulz's second volume, *Sanatorium*, by two of interwar Poland's leading literary critics once again emphasized what seemed to them the unbridgeable distance between Schulz's reality and the lived experiences of a new interwar generation: "*Sanatorium under the Sign of the Hourglass*, even were it burned at the stake, would strike no chord with the younger generation, for the coincidence in its time of publication is in no way indicative of a coincidence in essence: none of the characteristics of this book is a characteristic of a future that it would be worth fighting for" (Kazimierz Wyka, Stefan Napierski, "Dwugłos o Schulzu," *Ateneum* 1 ([1939]) In Kazimierz Wyka, *Stara szuflada i inne szkice z lat 1932–1939*. Ed. Maciej Urbanowski (Kraków: Wydawnictwo Literackie, 2000), 419–427.

77. Thomas Anessi, "The Great Heresy of the Varsovian Center," in Heuckelom and de Bruyn, eds., 2009, 397–418; and Stefan Chwin, "Dlaczego Bruno Schulz nie chciał być pisarzem żydowskim," 2014.

78. Bruno Schulz, "Wiosna," *Kamena* (Chełm Lubelski) 1935 (VI), 10: 191–193. (Translation my own). Following the three paragraph fragment translated here, the text printed in *Kamena* aligns with the text that was later published as chapter 13 of "Wiosna" in *Sanatorium under the Sign of the Hourglass* (O, 150–152).

79. Walter Benjamin, "On The Concept of History," in Walter Benjamin, *Selected Writings, 4: 1938–1940*. Ed. Howard Eiland, Michael W. Jennings (Cambridge, MA: Harvard University Press, 2006), 397.

2. "A Creation Born of the Longing of Golus"

1. Bruno Schulz, "E. M. Lilien," *Przegląd Podkarpacia*, no. 71: 2. The Lilien article in its entirety was first recompiled and reprinted in Drohobycz in November 2015 as part of the bilingual *Acta Schulziana: Artyści z Drohobycza, Lilien i Lachowicz*, edited by Wiera Meniok and Grzegorz Józefczuk (*Acta Schulziana* 2015, no. 1). A second publication of the full article followed in *Schulz/Forum* 6, 2015, edited by Stanisław Rosiek (Gdańsk: Fundacja Terytoria Książki), 83–96. Citations of the article's text here are my own translation. The page numbers provided refer the reader to the Polish-language version of the fully reconstructed essay that was published in *Schulz/Forum 6* (henceforth abbreviated as SF6).

2. Michael Stanislawski, *Zionism and the Fin de Siècle: Cosmopolitanism and Nationalism from Nordau to Jabotinsky* (Berkeley: University of California Press, 2001).

3. Erotic themes were prominent in both artists' work. As David Biale writes of Lilien's liberal choice of imagery, here in reference to the illustrated version of the Bible that began

work on in 1907: "This was not a Bible to be brought to synagogue! It was intended for an audience that appreciated art and would not be aghast when it encountered Lilien's ploys and designs.... Lilien's Bible is filled with daring allusions and dramatically original interpretations, capped by a celebration of masculinity and strength, eroticism and nudity" (David Biale et al., *Cultures of the Jews: A New History* (New York: Schocken Books, 2002), 781.

4. Continuing in a self-referential vein, Schulz writes:

> The contents of this creation are, speaking in the most general terms, a certain romantic lyricism, a certain romantic longing that had taken hold within the intellectual classes of Europe.... One longed for what was most distant and most inaccessible to the contemporary mentality; one was carried in one's imagination to an epoque with a hot spiritual climate; one conjured up times in which the rhythm of life flowed on a more sublime, more wonderful and more colorful wave, called forth a vision of a future of heightened emotion, more colorful and more abundant than the gray present. (SF6, 91)

5. "*Przegląd Podkarpacia*," 1937, nr 71, s. 2; 1937, nr 72, s. 2; 1937, nr 73–74, s. 3; 1938, nr 75–76, s. 4; 1938, nr 77, s. 3; 1938, nr 78–79, s. 3; 1938, nr 80, s. 4, 1938, nr 81–82, s. 3–4. See Piotr Sitkiewicz's introductory article on the Lilien essay, published in *Schulz/Forum 6* (March 2016, 97–104) for additional details on both *Przegląd Podkarpacia* and its editor, Henryk Springer.

6. In his book *Crypto-Jewish Poetry*, published by the publishing house National Thought (*Myśl Narodowa*) in 1926, Pieńkowski wrote of Polish Jewish avant-garde and expressionist writers that they "dig around in the urban trash-pile, while artistry based on themes drawn from nature they treat as anachronistic and deserving of scorn" (*Myśl Narodowa* [Warsaw] no. 41). Together with other resonances, Schulz's formulation here offers a humorous rebuff of such criticisms made by right-wing Polish nationalist critics about the "un-Polish" Polish-language literature written by Jews. I have translated *wyklęta* here as "exiled one" to highlight resonances between Schulz's image and that of the Shekhinah, the Divine spirit in feminine form, in its state of exile in the physical world.

7. Hillel Zeitlin, from "Book One" (Warsaw, 1910), translated and collected in Arthur Green, ed., *The Religious Writings of Hillel Zeitlin* (New York: Paulist Press, 2012), 81–84.

8. In the *Zohar*'s commentary on *Be-reshit* (Genesis 1:1): "At the head of potency of the King, He engraved engravings in luster on high ... a cluster of vapor forming in formlessness, thrust in a ring, not white, not black, not red, not green, no color at all. As a cord surveyed, it yielded radiant colors. Deep within the spark gushed a flow, splaying colors below, concealed within the concealed of the mystery of *Ein Sof*." Daniel Chanan Matt, trans. and Ed. *The Zohar* (Stanford, CA: Stanford University Press, 2006), 7.

9. The Polish pronoun *on*, which I have changed here to "them," refers to the word *reader* and as such is non-gendered.

10. Martin Buber, "My Way to Hasidism," *Hasidism and Modern Man* (Atlantic Highlands: Humanities Press International, Inc., 1958), 47.

11. Paul Mendes-Flohr, *Divided Passions: Jewish Intellectuals and the Experience of Modernity* (Detroit, MI: Wayne State University Press, 1991), 107.

12. Martin Buber, *Die Legende des Baal-schem* (Frankfurt am Main: Rütten und Loening, 1908).

13. Grete Schaeder, *The Hebrew Humanism of Martin Buber*, trans. N.J. Jacobs (Detroit, MI: Wayne State University Press, 1973), 51.

14. Mendes-Flohr, *Passions*, 107.
15. Ibid., 14.
16. Ibid., 80.
17. Ibid., 83.
18. Martin Buber, *On Judaism*, N. M. Glatzer, ed. (New York: Schocken Books, 1967), 78.
19. Ehrenpreis, Markus. *Die Entwickelung der Emanationslehre in Der Kabbala des XIII. Jahrhunderts* (Frankfurt am Mainz: J. Kaufmann, 1895).
20. Martin Buber, "*Jüdische Renaissance*," *Ost und West* 1, no. 1 (January 1901): cols. 7–10. Quoted in English translation in "Jewish Renaissance," in *The First Buber: Youthful Zionist Writings of Martin Buber*, ed. and trans. Gilya G. Schmidt (Syracuse, NY: Syracuse University Press, 1999), 33.
21. Ibid., 33. Introducing the now familiar tropes that Schulz would draw on in his later essay, Buber saw the Jewish Renaissance as a struggle that would "transform latent energies into active ones, qualities of our tribe" and "present them to our modern life as its form.... No return, [but] creation from ancient material" (33).
22. Ahad Ha'am: the pen name of Asher Zvi Hirsch Ginsberg (b. 1856, Kiev—d. 1927, Tel Aviv), considered the founder of Cultural or spiritual Zionism.
23. Buber, "*Jüdische Renaissance*," 30.
24. Martin Buber, "Address on Jewish Art," *The First Buber*, 57. Lilien was one of a number of Jewish artists invited to take part in an exhibition at the congress. He also designed the mass-produced postcard announcing the Fifth Congress, which became perhaps the single most iconic piece of Jewish national art.
25. Ibid., 57.
26. Referring to Binjamin Segel (1867–1931), the main editorialist of *Ost und West*, David Brenner writes that "having been raised in the multiethnic Hapsburg Empire . . . [he] favored Jewish cultural autonomy on a nonterritorial basis. To call for state-sanctioned Jewish particularism may have been possible in Austro-Hungary, but it was virtually unheard of in the *Kaiserreich*" (David A. Brenner, *Marketing Identities: The Invention of Jewish Ethnicity in Ost und West* [Detroit, MI: Wayne State University Press, 2019], 29).
27. Jess Olson, *Nathan Birnbaum and Jewish Modernity: Architect of Zionism, Yiddishism, and Orthodoxy* (Stanford, CA: Stanford University Press, 2013).
28. *Judisk Tidskrift*, founded in 1928.
29. As cited in Martina Urban, "The Jewish Library Reconfigured: Buber and the Zionist Anthology Discourse," in *New Perspectives on Martin Buber*, ed. Michael Zank (Tübingen: Mohr Siebeck, 2006), 31–60.
30. Urban, "The Jewish Library Reconfigured," 52.
31. He presented this vision in a speech to the Zionist Congress in 1897, entitled "The New Hebrew Literature." Markus Ehrenpreis, "Min livsväg," *Judisk Tidskrift* (1939): 6, 186; as cited in Stephen Fruitman, *Creating a New Heart: Marcus Ehrenpreis on Jewry and Judaism* (Umea: Umea Institute for Historical Studies, 2001), 126.
32. Fruitman, *Creating a New Heart*, 73.
33. Markus Ehrenpreis, *Die Entwickelung der Emanationslehre in der Kabbala Des XIII. Jahrhunderts* (Rome, 1895).
34. Buber, "Address on Jewish Art," 30.
35. David A. Brenner, *Marketing Identities: The Invention of Jewish Ethnicity in Ost und West* (Detroit, MI: Wayne State University Press, 1998), 35.

36. Ahad Ha'am, "The Spiritual Revival," in *Selected Essays of Ahad Ha'am*. Translated and edited by Leon Simon (Philadelphia: The Jewish Publication Society of America, 1962), 293.

37. "Od Redakcji," in Achad Haam, *O sjonizmie duchowym* (Warsaw: Akademicka Korporacja Sjonistyczna, 1928), 37-42. The "Biblioteka Sjonistyczna," created by "Zelotia-Kanaim" to address the situation would include texts on cultural problems, by Buber and Sokołów, on the theory and practice of Zionism by Ahad Ha'am, Ozjasz Thon, Theodor Herzl, Max Nordau, Klaczkin, Jabotinsky and others; and, and on economic questions in Palestine. Writing in 1928, the editors distinguish "political Zionism" as a subcategory of Zionist thought.

38. Buber, "Address on Jewish Art," 50.

39. Olson, *Nathan Birnbaum*, 69.

40. Nathan Birnbaum, "Jüdische Renaissance Bewegung," *Ost und West* 2, no.9 (September 1902): 577–84. English translation in Olson, *Nathan Birnbaum*, 130.

41. Fruitman, *Creating a New Heart*, 129.

42. Buber, "Address on Jewish Art," 32.

43. Ibid., 32.

44. Fruitman, *Creating a New Heart*, 129.

45. Paul Mendes-Flohr, "The Berlin Jew as Cosmopolitan," in *Berlin Metropolis: Jews and the New Culture, 1890–1918* (Berkeley: University of California Press, 1999).

46. Buber, "Address on Jewish Art," 51.

47. Ibid., 98.

48. Ibid., 63.

49. Jacob Lestschinsky, "Jewish Autonomy Yesterday and Today," trans. Anna Fishman Gonshor and Esther Frank, *Jews and Diaspora Nationalism*, ed. Simon Rabinovitch (Waltham, MA: Brandeis University Press, 2012), 127. Originally published as: *Di Yidishe avtonomye amol un haynt.* (Kyiv, 1918).

50. Hillel Zeitlin, "The Great Call of the Hour (Part 1)," *In geveb*, March 2016, http://ingeveb.org/texts-and-translations/the-great-call-of-the-hour-part-1.

51. Lestschinsky, "Jewish Autonomy Yesterday and Today," 128.

52. Zeitlin, Aaron. *"Der kult fun gornisht, un kunst vi zi darf zayn: protest un ani-maymin"* ["The Cult of Nothing, and Art as It Should Be: Protest and Credo"]. *Varshever Shriftn* [*Warsaw Writings*], Literatn klub baym farayn fun yidishe literatn un zhurnalistn in Varshe, 1926-1927, 1-9.

53. Jerzy Ficowski, "Henrietta i Jakub," *Regiony wielkiej herezji i okolice* (Sejny: Fundacja Pogranicza, 2002), 123.

54. SF, 87.

55. Kaszuba-Dębska, *Bruno. Epoka genialna*, 474.

56. Schulz, "E. M. Lilien," 71:2.

57. Schulz's language in this part of the essay recalls his discussion from the 1936 "Essay for S. I. Witkiewicz": "The role of art is to be a probe sunk into the nameless. The artist is an apparatus for registering processes in that deep stratum where value is formed" (O, 445–46).

58. Zeitlin, "The Great Call of the Hour (Part 1)."

59. Jerzy Ficowski, *Bruno Schulz: Listy, fragmenty, wspomnienia o pisarzu* (Kraków: Wydawnictwo Literackie, 1984), 70.

60. Ahad Ha'am, "The Jewish State and the Jewish Problem." Arthur Herzberg, Editor. *The Zionist Idea: A Historical Analysis and Reader* (Philadelphia: The Jewish Publication Society,

1997), 266. See also: Achad Haam. *O sjonizmie duchowym* (Warsaw: Akademicka Korporacja Sjonistyczna, 1928), 37-42.

61. Michael Brenner, *Prophets of the Past: Interpreters of Jewish History* (Princeton, NJ: Princeton University Press, 2010), 157.

62. "Schulz Bruno, professor, received paid leave for the period from 1 January 1936 to 30 June 1936 with the aim of enabling his literary work" (Letters from Bruno Schulz to the school administration, KL, 224).

63. Stefan Zweig, "Introduction," in *E. M. Lilien: Sein Werk, mit einer Einleitung von Stefan Zweig* (Berlin: Schuster & Loeffler, 1903), 12.

64. The text was originally published as Bruno Schulz, "*Republika marzeń*," *Tygodnik Illustrowany*, no. 29 (1936): 554.

65. In his introduction to *Lieder des Ghetto*, the editor Berthold Feiwel quickly departs from a discussion of the poet Morris Rosenfeld, and of the Yiddish language in which the poems were written, to focus in his essay on a vision of the urban ghettos of Russia and Galicia: "How much horror one street alone reveals!" His text combines both exoticizing and sympathetic elements of West European Jewish discourse surrounding Galician Jews. See Berthold Feiwel, "Vorrede," *Lieder des Ghetto* (Berlin: S. Calvary, 1903).

66. "Sometimes the daring, or the tortured restlessness, chases these Ghetto people individually, in the hundreds or the thousands, across the borders. Work, work for any price—it is nothing but this that they seek. Poor dreamers! Wherever they set their foot, the Ghetto grows. They plant it on the military roads, under the bridge arches, at the harbor squares, on board the ships and finally across the sea, insofar as the new world has any empathy to take them in." Feiwel, "Vorrede," *Lieder des Ghetto*, 1903.

67. Ibid.
68. Ibid.
69. SF, 86.
70. Auerbach, letter to Schulz, July 25, 1938 (KL, 294).

3. The Sunday Seminars of Bruno Schulz and Debora Vogel

1. See: Rachel Auerbach, *Varsheve tsavoes: bagegenishn, aktivitetn, goyroles: 1933–1943* [*Warsaw Testaments: Encounters, Activities, Fates 1933–1943*] (Tel Aviv: Yisroel-bukh, 1974).

2. Stanisław Ignacy Witkiewicz (1885–1939), known as "Witkacy," was a leading modernist innovator and theorist of interwar Poland: playwright, painter, philosopher of art, a defining figure of Polish modernism. Witkacy was raised in the town of Zakopane in the Tatra mountains, which became at the turn of the century a resort community and cultural center frequented by poets and artists of the Young Poland movement, a national-secessionist style of Polish art that drew on folk themes. Due in part to the presence of Witkacy and the theater he later created there, Zakopane continued to be an important center of culture, theater, and visual arts throughout the interwar period.

3. Jerzy Ficowski proposed early on that "a confrontation of *Tractate on Mannequins* from *Cinnamon Shops* with the book *Acacias Are Blooming* seems to reveal traces of the correspondence between Debora Vogel and Schulz . . . that suffered destruction: in Lwów and in Drohobycz" (Ficowski, *Księga listów*, 169). This correspondence had included dozens if not

hundreds of letters from Schulz to Vogel that were left at her last apartment in Lwów during the war. Ficowski discovered that these letters had survived well into the 1950s, only to be thrown out or destroyed as part of building maintenance, together with piles of papers that had been left in the basement of the building.

4. Vogel's short story by this name was published in 1919 in *Nowa Młodzież*, the magazine of the Left Zionist youth organization *Hashomer Hatzair*, of which she was a council member.

5. See Karolina Szymaniak, *Agent of an Eternal Idea: Transformations in the Aesthetic Beliefs of Debora Vogel* (*Być agentem wiecznej idei. Przemiany poglądów estetycznych Debory Vogel*; Kraków: Universitas, 2006); Annette Werberger, "Nür Eine Muse? Die Jiddische Schriftstellerin Debora Vogel und Bruno Schulz," in *Ins Wort Gesetzt, Ins Bild Gesetzt: Gender in Wissenschaft, Kunst Und Literatur*, ed. Ingrid Hotz-Davies and Schamma Schahadat (Bielefeld: Transcript Verlag, 2009); Kathryn Hellerstein, *A Question of Tradition: Women Poets in Yiddish, 1586–1987* (Stanford: Stanford University Press, 2014); Anna Elena Torres, "Circular Landscapes: Montage and Myth in Dvoyre Fogel's Yiddish Poetry," *Nashim: A Journal of Jewish Women's Studies & Gender Issues* 35 (2019): 40–73; and Anastasiya Lyubas, *Blooming Spaces: The Collected Poetry, Prose, Critical Writing, and Letters of Debora Vogel* (Boston: Academic Studies, 2020); Sylwia Werner, "Between Philosophy and Art: The Avant-Garde Work of Debora Vogel," *East European Jewish Affairs*, No. 49:1 (2019): 20–41; and Anna Maja Misiak, "Reading as the Shaping Force of Life: Debora Vogel's Contributions to Education." Trans. Matthew Johnson. *In geveb* (October 2021). See also the 2021 special issue of *In Geveb* devoted to the Vogel's work: Anna Torres, Kathryn Hellerstein, and Anastasiya Lyubas. "Walking with Vogel: New Perspectives on Debora Vogel." *In geveb*, October 2021: https://ingeveb.org/articles/walking-with-vogel-new-perspectives-on-debora-vogel.

6. See in particular the 2017 volume *Montages: Debora Vogel and the New Legend of the City*, prepared in connection with a the multimedia exhibition on Vogel's work in the context of multilingual interwar Lwów, prepared for the Łódź Museum of Art: *Montaże. Debora Vogel i nowa legenda miasta*, ed. and with texts by Andrij Bojarov, Paweł Polit, and Karolina Szymaniak (Łódź: Muzeum Sztuki w Łodzi, 2017).

7. Adamczyk-Garbowska, Monika. "I Know Who You Are, but Who I Am—You Do Not Know ...": Reading Yiddish Writers in a Polish Literary Context," *Shofar* 29, no. 3 (2011): 83–104, 84. Adamczyk-Garbowska's pioneering effort in this area places pairs of literary works, Polish and Yiddish, in conversation: Reymont and I. J. Singer's Lodz novels, *The Promised Land* and *The Brothers Ashkenazi*; and Avrom Sutzkever and Polish Romantic poets, in particular Cyprian Kamil Norwid. See also Justin Cammy and Marta Figlerowicz, "Translating History into Art: The Influences of Cyprian Kamil Norwid in Abraham Sutzkever's Poetry," *Prooftexts* 27 (2007): 427–73.

8. Justin Cammy and Marta Figlerowicz, "Translating History into Art: The Influences of Cyprian Kamil Norwid in Abraham Sutzkever's Poetry," *Prooftexts* 27 (2007): 427–73, 428.

9. During this period, Schulz also likely deepened his familiarity with Markus Ehrenpreis's work on kabbalah. In a letter to Schulz in 1938, Vogel uses language that indicates that in their private conversations about aesthetics the two had together adapted the kabbalistic language of contraction and emanation—the subject of her uncle Ehrenpreis's dissertation—to speak about the artist's creative process. She writes of her own "content," at a moment preceding creativity, as being in "a state that one can describe as 'withdrawing

from circulation,' withdrawing from intellect (*wycofanie z intelektu*), withdrawing into the body, from which it can emanate into the intellect (*promieniuje w intelekt*) in appropriate, provoked situations that throw themselves forward associatively" (KL, 264).

10. According to Szymaniak, "Vogel was very closely connected with her uncles [Ehrenpreis and Malz] and they had an strong influence on the shape of her early creative work." The first monograph on Vogel's philosophy of aesthetics, Szymaniak's 2006 study *Agent of an Eternal Idea*, also represents the most complete repository to date of biographical information on Vogel, her family background, and her publication history. It serves as a basis for the biographical information provided here. Among other things, Szymaniak clarifies Vogel's year of birth as 1900 (Vogel had given 1902). Vogel's mother, Lea, who ran a trade school of handcrafts for girls, was, in Rachel Auerbach's words, "of Lemberger *yikhes*." In addition to being the niece of Markus Ehrenpreis, with whom she was very close, she was also related to the Zionist activist David Malz, who was married to her mother's sister, Mariem Ettel. Malz and Ehrenpreis, among their many activities to promote Zionism in Galicia, were founders of the organization Zion, whose aim was to educate a new generation of youth and prepare them for emigration to Palestine.

11. The Drohobycz election of 1911, which resulted in a massacre of local residents by Austrian military forces, was one of the most infamous political events in the history of the Austrian Empire. In his fascinating study of this rare case of Jewish-on-Jewish violence, historian Joshua Shanes explains, "On June 19, 1911, Austrian military forces in Drohobycz, East Galicia opened fire on a group of unarmed citizens, killing dozens—including women, children and elderly. The massacre shocked Austrian and foreign public opinion, but rarely noted at the time was its incredible Jewish character. The election was being rigged in favor of the Jewish candidate of the Polish faction by the town's most powerful politician, also Jewish, against a Zionist attempting to unseat him." See Joshua Shanes, "The 'Bloody Election' in Drohobycz: Violence, Urban Politics, and National Memory in an Imperial Borderland," *Austrian History Yearbook*, Vol. 53, May 2022, 121–149; and Wiesław Budzyński, *Miasto Schulza* (Warsaw: Prószyński i S-ka, 2005), 22–35.

12. See biographical detail on this topic uncovered by Anna Kaszuba-Dębska in her study of women influential in Schulz's life, whose biographies, like Vogel's, had been almost entirely overlooked within Schulz scholarship. Anna Kaszuba-Dębska, *Kobiety i Schulz* (Gdańsk: Słowo/obraz terytoria, 2016).

13. Izydor Schulz funded the publication of Schulz's first book by the Rój publishing house.

14. Vogel spent the entire period of the war in Vienna with her parents. The exact amount of time that Schulz lived in Vienna is not known. His residence cards show him to have lived for varying lengths of time in three different apartments in Vienna between 1914 and 1918 and to have spent time again in 1923. See Paolo Caneppele, "Bruno Schulz w Wiedniu," *W ułamkach zwierciadła*, ed. M. Kitowskiej-Łysiak and Panas Władysław (Stowarzystwo Naukowe KUL, 2003), 533–45. As Caneppele writes "It remains a secret what Schulz did in Vienna. But it is certain that this 'student' and later 'painter' [these titles from his visa applications] did not miss the opportunity to learn, feel and hear all that the cultural laboratory of Vienna had to offer in these decisive years" (537).

15. The phrase cited in the subtitle is Vogel's—"*Potrzebna nam jest wielość*"—and appears in a letter that she wrote to Schulz on May 21, 1938.

16. Auerbach, *Nisht-oysgeshpunene fedem*, 135.

17. Karolina Szymaniak, *Być agentem wiecznej idei*, 45. Polish philosopher, aesthetician, and art historian Kremer was a leading proponent of Hegelianism in Poland.

18. See: Adam Stepnowski, "Debora Vogel w galicyjskim jidyszlandzie. Czasopismo 'Cusztajer,'" Schulz/Forum 16 (2020): 176–90; and Szymaniak, *Być agentem wiecznej idei*.

19. "Fun undz," *Tsushtayer* 1, no. 2 (June 1930): 2.

20. Panas had drawn initial attention to this dynamic in his study *Pismo i rana*, writing that Vogel "put enormous effort into being a bilingual writer." Władysław Panas, *Pismo i rana* (Lublin: Wydawnictwo KUL, 1999, 64). It is also true that this combination was difficult for Vogel to sustain, and it is clear in a letter she wrote to Schulz in 1938 that, even as her frustration with the Yiddish cultural context in Lemberg grew, her participation within the Polish literary world had taken a back seat.

21. Vogel's article "The Position of St. I. Witkiewicz in contemporary Polish Culture," published in 1931 (*Pomost*, no. 1 (1935): 1–5), may represent a part of that polemic.

22. Auerbach, *Nisht-oysgeshpunene fedem*, 135. Witkacy supported himself with his famous "Portrait-Painting Firm," painting boldly colored expressionist portraits in which he experimented with altered states of consciousness and artistic perception. Each portrait was painted while under the influence of a cocktail of narcotics, the formulae for which were sometimes included at the base of each panting, forming an integral element of the work of art. Clients who elected to sit for such a portrait were asked to sign a contract agreeing to accept the results, which could be less than flattering, and to refrain from requesting a refund. To view his portrait of Debora Vogel, visit https://commons.wikimedia.org/wiki/File:Stanis%C5%82aw_Ignacy_Witkiewicz_-_Portret_Debory_Vogel.jpg.

23. KL, 265.

24. Ogród Jezuicki, today Ivan Franko Park in Lviv.

25. Auerbach, *Nisht-oysgeshpunene fedem*, 135.

26. Schulz's Polish first name is not used here, only the initial B.

27. The Yiddishist Mendel Neugroschel, born in Nowy Sącz, lived in Vienna and was the editor of an anthology of translations from Polish poetry into Yiddish. A letter to Neugroschel on November 4, 1936, indicates that Schulz sent him a copy of *Cinnamon Shops* in response to his expressed interest in translating the work (KL, 126).

28. "Fun der kunstler-velt," *Tsushtayer* 1, no. 2 (June 1930): 53.

29. Ibid, 53.

30. Novelist, columnist, and activist Zofia Nałkowska (1884–1954), the host of Warsaw's most influential Polish-language literary salon, played a leading role in shaping literary developments in interwar Poland and in helping to bring recognition to emerging talents in the Polish language. Her own "psychological novels," which treated themes of women's emancipation, psychological relations among individuals, and challenges of modernist aesthetics, were considered groundbreaking for Polish letters. Author of, among other works, *Cudzoziemca* (*The Foreigner*), Nałkowska was a member of the left-leaning *Przedmieście* literary group, vice chairman and later chairman of the Polish Pen-Club, and the only female member of the Polish Academy of Literature. After the war, in her capacity as a member of the Central Commission for the Investigation of the Nazi War Crimes, she was witness to the shocking evidence that she would bring to public knowledge through a collection of short sketches entitled *Medallions* (*Medaliony*, 1946), a milestone of Holocaust literature in the Polish language. After their meeting and Nałkowska's strong support for the publication of *Cinnamon Shops*, Schulz and Nałkowska became close friends and occasional lovers—events

that Nałkowska recorded in her extensive diaries. One of Schulz's most extensive works of literary criticism is a lengthy 1936 essay, highly laudatory, on Nałkowska's *Cudzoziemca* (*The Foreigner*).

31. The question of who first recognized the brilliance of Schulz's stories and encouraged him to send them, or bring them, to Nałkowska, remains open-ended. Other individuals have claimed to have played an integral role as well.

32. Auerbach, *Nisht-oysgeshpunene fedem*, 137.

33. Letter to Romana Halpern, November 15, 1936 (KL, 142).

34. A biographical corollary to the traditional visage of the female muse that Vogel acquired within Polish literary scholarship can be found in comments from a letter she wrote to the Yiddish poet A. Leyeles in 1939, on the challenges she faced as a woman writer:

> Yiddish literature needs such people as yourself. I am amazed by your constant preparedness, your responsibility. This feeling results partly from the fact that I also possess such a talent, but it cannot so easily find expression, because . . . I would venture such a verdict: because of the unhappy fortune that it is to be a woman. The "metaphysical" role of the woman flows in a stream of crippling frivolities. Professional work absorbs me as well, though it is very poorly compensated. . . . But after all, competition from men does not permit a woman to obtain a position. It is accepted in a number of magazines that men, even scribblers and those who have nothing to say, receive honoraria, while women—the opposite—the only honor they receive is respect" (Letter to A. Leyeles, May 23, 1939, as cited in Szymaniak, 2006, 50).

35. Debora Vogel, Forward to *Tog-figurn* [*Day Figures*] (Lwów: Tsushtayer, 1930), I.

36. As Kathryn Hellerstein notes, "[Vogel's] diction omits virtually all Hebraic words and, instead, imports from French, German, and Greek such word as *Manekene*, *rekhtek* (rectangle), and *tors* (torso)" (Hellerstein, *A Question of Tradition*, 144).

37. Ibid., 185.

38. On Ehrenpreis, see also Chapter 2. Markus [Mordechai] Ehrenpreis was a leading Galician proponent of the Cultural Zionism that exerted a formative influence on Schulz, who may have had the opportunity to meet and speak with him through his relationship with Vogel. While he was Chief Rabbi of Sweden, Ehrenpreis visited Lwów to much fanfare in 1930, in the period during which Schulz was visiting Vogel regularly. See D. M., "Grand-Rabin Szwecji Dr. M. Ehrenpreis przybył do Polski," *Chwila*, June 14, 1930: 7.

39. Yiddish, the "folk" vernacular.

40. Auerbach, *Nisht-oysgeshpunene fedem*, 132.

41. Auerbach describes them as "*fremdartiker*."

42. Auerbach, *Nisht-oysgeshpunene fedem*, 132.

43. Szymaniak, *Być agentem wiecznej idei*, 212.

44. Auerbach, *Nisht-oysgeshpunene fedem*, 132.

45. Ibid., 132–33.

46. Szymaniak, *Być agentem wiecznej idei*, 211.

47. Letter to Schulz of December 7, 1938 (KL, 267).

48. Vogel published her volume of montage works both in Yiddish (*Akatsyes blien*, 1935) and Polish (*Akacje kwitną*, 1936) at Rój publishing house, in her own translation with significant modifications. For a comparison of these two versions, see: Lyubas, *Blooming Spaces*, 2020.

49. Debora Vogel-Barenbluth, "Ludzkie egzotyki," *Przegląd Społeczny*, no. 7-8 (1934): 150-59, 151.
50. Ibid., 151.
51. Bruno Schulz, "Akacje kwitną," *Nasza opinia* no. 72 (1936): 9.
52. Italics are Vogel's.
53. Vogel-Barenbluth, "Ludzkie Egzotyki," 153-54.
54. Debora Vogel, "Lwowska Juderia. (Ekspozycja do monografii żydowskiego Lwowa)," *Almanach i leksykon Żydowstwa Polskiego* [Lwów] 1 (1937): 89-98.
55. Auerbach, *Nisht-oysgeshpunene fedem*, 132.
56. On Schulz's relationship with Józefina Szelińska, see Agata Tuszyńska's biography, based on access to previously unresearched letters: Agata Tuszyńska, *Narzeczona Schulza* (Kraków: Wydawnictwo Literackie, 2015).
57. "My fiancée is Catholic (her parents converted). There are certain reasons that she cannot resign from the Catholic faith. I however do not want to convert. For her I was able to make only the concession of withdrawing my registration in the Jewish *gmina* [officially registered body of the Jewish community of Drohobycz]. Under these conditions it is only possible for us to marry according to the German laws that obtain in the former Prussian partition, for example in Katowice" (letter to Romana Halpern of November 19, 1936, KL, 135).
58. After the war, a former student and friend of Schulz's, an engineer named Schreyer who contacted Ficowski, had returned to the house on Floriańska that Schulz had lived in with his family before they were moved to the ghetto—the house at which he had paid visits to Schulz—to see if any of Schulz's papers or artwork remained. Incredibly, he found in the attic of that home a box with the damaged remains of several letters. Among them were several letters written to Schulz in the years 1938 and '39 by Vogel. The letters offer a rare chance to hear how certain literary tropes familiar from both writers' texts sound when used between them in everyday speech. These include the concept of "*kolorowość*," the "colorfulness" of the landscape that emerges as poetic distillation or extract; and the kabbalistic paradigm of *tzimtzum*, contraction or withdrawal and emanation, adapted as a metaphor for the artistic process.
59. Bruno Schulz, *Księga listów / Bruno Schulz* (Gdańsk: Słowo/obraz terytoria, 2002).
60. Bruno Schulz, "Akacje kwitną," Nasza Opinia (1936, No. 72): 9.
61. Letter to Schulz of September 1, 1938 (KL, 264).
62. Letter to Schulz of November 21, 1938 (KL, 265).
63. Ibid.
64. Bruno Schulz, "Akacje kwitną," 9.
65. Werberger, "Nür Eine Muse?" 280.
66. Ibid., 282.
67. Vogel, Debora Vogel, "'Vayse verter' in der dikhtung" ["White Words in Poetry"], *Tsushtayer* (April 1931, no. 3): 42-48, 43.
68. Ibid., 43.
69. Vogel, Ibid., 43.
70. Ibid., 43.
71. Ibid., 43.
72. His style and choices, only ostensibly positioned as "outdated" here, can also be compared with contemporary (interwar) developments in Jewish "futurism" and expressionism: n.b. Zeitlin's proposal of a "Zohar-plastic" aesthetic. See Nathan Wolski, "The Secret of Yiddish: Zoharic Composition in the Poetry of Aaron Zeitlin," *Kabbalah: Journal for the Study of Jewish Mystical Texts* no. 20 (2009): 147-80.

73. Schulz, "Akacje kwitną," 9.
74. Ibid., 9. Schulz's language here is similar to Zeitlin's proposal for an "idea image" that is arrived at by a process of condensation, as well as to the *Denkbild* that became a central device in writing of the Frankfurt School. "Such an 'abstract image' does not yet exist," wrote Zeitlin in 1926. "This is the visual arts in their highest condensation." Aaron Zeitlin, "Der kult fun gornisht," 7.
75. Schulz, "Akacje kwitną," 9.
76. Schulz's protagonist says in the opening of "The Book": "Besides, any true reader—and this story is only addressed to him—will understand me anyway when I look him straight in the eye. [. . .] For, under the imaginary table that separates me from my readers, don't we secretly clasp each other's hands?" (W, 115).
77. Schulz, "Akacje kwitną," 9.
78. Debora Vogel, "Kilka uwag o współczesnej inteligencji," *Przegląd Społeczny* 10, no. 6 (1936): 114–22, 120.
79. Ibid., 121.
80. Ibid., 120.
81. Ibid., 120.
82. "We need multiplicity" (*"Potrzebna nam jest wielość"*), she wrote in one of her last letters to Schulz, from May 21, 1938 (KL, 261).
83. "In man, otherness, which he shares with everything that is, and distinctness, which he shares with everything alive, become uniqueness, and human plurality is the paradoxical plurality of unique beings." Hannah Arendt, *The Human Condition* (Chicago: University of Chicago Press, 1998), 176.
84. Jan Baudouin de Courtenay, *Kwestja żydowska w Państwie Polskiem* (Warszawa: Biblioteka Wolnomyśliciela, 1923).
85. Vogel-Barenbluth, "Ludzkie egzotyki," 157.
86. Hannah Arendt, *The Origins of Totalitarianism* (New York: Houghton Mifflin Harcourt, 1985).
87. Kruczkowski, Andrzej. "Do krytyków." *Sygnały*, no. 14 (1936): 3.
88. Ibid.
89. Ibid.
90. Stefan Chwin reminds us that "in 1938 he even feared that he might simply be fired from his job at the Drohobycz school, 'should the currents now flowing through our country become law' (letter of 31 March 1938 to Romana Halpern [KL, 172])." Stefan Chwin, "Dlaczego Bruno Schulz nie chciał być pisarzem żydowskim (O 'wymazywaniu' żydowskości w *Sanatorium pod klepsydrą* i *Sklepach cynamonowych*)," *Schulz Forum* 4 (2014): 12.
91. Edmund Löwenthal, recollections in *Bruno Schulz: Listy, fragmenty, wspomniena o pisarzu*, ed. Jerzy Ficowski (Kraków: Wydawnictwo Literackie, 1984), 56–57. Published before the discovery of Schulz's Lilien article, Chwin's discussion, which considers the strategies of concealment present in Schulz's work, provides a catalogue of references to Jewish subject matter and also tracks the notable absence of such references in Schulz's work.
92. Translation from the original: Zeitlin, Aaron. "Fir strofn." *Globus* no. 18 (December 1933): 60.
93. Blumenfeldowa, Stanisława. "Zagadnienie żydowskie w Polsce," *Sygnały* no. 14 (1936): 4–5.
94. Kenneth Moss, *An Unchosen People*, 319.

4. Sanatorium under the Sign of the Hourglass

1. For exploration of Józefina Szelińska's biography and relationship to Schulz, see Agata Tuszyńska, *Narzeczona Schulza. Apokryf* (Kraków: Wydawnictwo Literackie, 2015); and Anna Kaszuba-Dębska, *Kobiety i Schulz* (Gdańsk: Słowo/obraz terytoria, 2016) and *Bruno. Epoka genialna* (Kraków: Znak, 2020).
2. Bruno Schulz, "Posłowie," in Franciszek Kafka, *Proces* (Warsaw: Rój, 1936), 279–284.
3. See Bruno Schulz, "Powstają legendy," *Tygodnik Illustrowany* no 22 (1935): 425; "Wolność tragiczna," *Tygodnik Illustrowany*, July 5, 1936, 510–511; and "Pod Belwederem," *Tygodnik Illustrowany* (Warszawa), July 26, 1936, 571.
4. Bruno Schulz, "Jesień," *Sygnały* (Lwów), no. 17, May 1, 1936: 4; Bruno Schulz, "Republika marzeń," *Tygodnik Illustrowany*, no. 29, July 19, 1936: 554–56. and Schulz, *Powstają legendy. Trzy szkice wokól Piłsudskiego*, edited by Stanisław Rosiek (Kraków: Oficyna Literacka, 1993).
5. Ficowski, *Regions of the Great Heresy*, 156.
6. Bruno Schulz, "Genjalna epoka" ["Fragment z powieści Mesjasz"], *Wiadomości literackie* 13 (April 1, 1934): 4.
7. Bruno Schulz [Illustrator: Bruno Schulz], "*Sanatorjum pod Klepsydrą*," Bruno *Wiadomości literackie* 16 (April 21, 1935): 4–5.
8. This translation has been changed from Wieniewska's original to capture the repetition and resonance that joins "father" and "fatherland" throughout the story.
9. Leo Pinsker, "Auto-Emancipation: An Appeal to His People by a Russian Jew," in *Road to Freedom: Writings and Addresses by Leo Pinsker*, trans. David S. Blondheim (New York, 1944), 94. Originally published as Leo Pinsker, *"Autoemancipation!" Mahnruf an seine Stammesgenossen von einem russischen Juden* (Berlin: Issleib, 1882). Pinsker continues: "this spectral form without precedence in history, unlike anything that preceded or followed it, could but strangely affect the imagination of the nations." Dmitry Shumsky argues that the "'from assimilation to nationalism' paradigm" in which Pinsker's essay had long been read, as a precursor to Herzl's thought, has "in recent decades lost much of its analytic and interpretational capacity to explain modern Jewish history." Instead, he emphasizes Pinsker's early thinking on multinational citizenship and points out that in fact "Pinsker dissociated himself from the idea of 'reestablishing the political independence of the Jews in Palestine'" (Dmitri Shumsky, "Leon Pinsker and 'Autoemancipation!': A Reevaluation," *Jewish Social Studies: History, Culture, Society* 18, no. 1 [Fall 2011]: 36–49).
10. Elsewhere in Schulz's work, Jewish tradition becomes one instantiation of the ubiquitous *pałuba*-cadaver. The perception, not uncommon in Schulz's acculturating Jewish generation, that vital Jewish tradition had been emptied out and replaced by hollow display became a central trope in Franz Kafka's *Letter to His Father*. In Schulz's "Birds," the father's dispersed collection of birds, previously exiled and responding to his final conjuring gesture, return to him as "blind, paper birds," "that fake progeny;" emptied out and deformed shells of their former selves: "And soon the sky came out in a colored rash . . . and was filled with a strange tribe of birds, circling and revolving. . . . Their lofty flight, the movement of their wings, formed majestic scrolls that filled the silent sky" (W, 91). And yet: "The birds were empty and lifeless inside. . . . They were like exhibits of extinct species in a museum, the lumber room of a birds' paradise" (W, 92). The story reflects a sense of melancholy about the

fate in particular of Jewish prophetic and literary tradition, including Hasidic storytelling tradition, of which Schulz's father figure represents a last epigone.

11. Sholem Aleichem,"*A konsilium fun doktoyrim,*" *Felietonen* (Beth Sholem Aleichem I. L. Peretz Publishing House, 1976 [originally Warsaw, 1903]), 74–85.

12. In 1903, Rabbi Akiva Rabinowitz of Poltava called a meeting of rabbis to strategize against Zionism.

13. Sholem Aleichem, "*A konsilium fun doktoyrim,*" 77. In Herzl's words, "Zionism is a kind of new Jewish care for the sick. We have stepped in as volunteer nurses, and we want to cure the patients—the poor, sick, Jewish people—by means of a healthful way of life in our own ancestral soil" (Theodor Herzl, "The Family Affliction" (1899), *Zionist Writings* 2, 1898–1904 (New York: Herzl Press, 1975), 45.

14. Y. L. Peretz, "Escaping Jewishness," in *Peretz*, trans. and ed. Sol Liptzin (New York: YIVO, 1947), 363–64. Originally published in 1911 as "*Vegn vos firn op fun yidishkayt.*" See *Di verk fun Yitzchok Leybush Peretz. Tsuzamen geshtelt unter der redaktsion fun Dovid Pinski* (New York: Farlag "Yidish," 1920), 44–88. The translation of the title as "Paths which Divert from Yidishkayt" is offered by Michael Steinlauf. See: "Hope and Fear: Y. L. Peretz and the Dialectics of Diaspora Nationalism, 1905–12." In Dynner, Glenn, François Guesnet, and Antony Polonsky. *Warsaw. the Jewish Metropolis: Essays in Honor of the 75th Birthday of Professor Antony Polonsky* (Boston: Brill, 2015), 227–251.

15. Sholem Aleichem, "*A konsilium,*" 83.

16. Ibid., 83. "*Vey iz tzum khole! Vey iz tzu undzer Isroylikn! . . . A sheyne khasene hobn zey ongearbet mit zeyere refues! A khurbn beyshamikdesh! Der driter khurbn! Frier tzionizm, haynt Uganda! A hilel-hashem far laytn!*" In an Austro-Hungarian context, the views of Sholem Aleichem's Rabbi Akiva were also shared by Dr. Moriz Güdemann, Chief Rabbi of Vienna. In his 1897 work "*National-Judenthum,*" Gudemann argued that the historical task of Israel, since its dispersion, lay in opposing the idea of nationalism. He equated efforts to reawaken Jewish desire for secular nationhood to committing suicide and insisted that the image of a return to Zion was a rhetorical figure to be treated allegorically—as a symbol of future justice that referred not only to Jews but to all mankind. With regard to the operations of contemporary political solutions that cut into the spiritual heritage of Jewishness, Y. L. Peretz offered, in "Escaping Jewishness," cited above, "So one operation after another is performed. Surgeons cut into dead cells and not a drop of blood appears. Not a groan is heard. Perhaps there is a moaning of the divine spirit in some ruin or other, but nobody pays attention" (Peretz, "Escaping Jewishness," 364).

17. The story was first published in *Tygodnik Illustrowany* in 1935.

18. While the thematics Schulz engages allegorically in "Sanatorium" would have been familiar and accessible to a majority of his readers within Polish Jewish intellectual milieux at the time that he was writing, already by the 1980s, when criticism of Schulz reemerged in a post-Holocaust context, the prewar debates on the Jewish Question with which Schulz engages in this story were largely unknown, or avoided for the antisemitic context to which they attest. Filling this lacuna in the case of Polish Jewish writing constitutes a part of the archaeology of Polish Jewish modernism that this study seeks to encourage and to model.

19. *The Holy Scriptures, Vol. 1* (Philadelphia: The Jewish Publication Society of America, 1955), 383. Or "Not near": *Harper Collins Study Bible. New Revised Standard Edition* (New York: Harper Collins, 1993), 248. Ahad Ha'am, "This Is Not the Way," *Essential Texts of Zionism*, trans. Leon Simon (Philadelphia: Jewish Publication Society of America, 1912).

Writes Dowty (2000), "His first important publication, the article 'This Is Not the Way;' . . . established him as a severe critic of the prevailing mode of settlement during the first decade of Zionist (or proto-Zionist) activity."

20. As Michlic writes, "Jews were the only large minority in Poland without any irredentist territorial aspirations, but the OZN nevertheless endorsed the ethno-nationalist project of reducing Polish Jewry through emigration." OZN: Obóz Zjednoczenia Narodowego (Camp of National Unity), or OZON, formed in 1937 from the far-right wing of Sanacja. Joanna Beata Michlic, *Poland's Threatening Other: The Image of the Jew from 1880 to the Present* (Lincoln: University of Nebraska Press, 2006), 74.

21. The "Madagascar Plan," though of older providence, was introduced in Poland in 1936. Writes Timothy Snyder, "[Minister of Foreign Affairs] Beck proposed the emigration of Polish Jews to Madagascar to French prime minister Léon Blum in October 1936, and Blum allowed the Poles to send a three-man exploratory delegation to the island. . . . Warsaw wanted both massive emigration of Jews from Europe and a Jewish state in Palestine" (Timothy Snyder, *Black Earth: The Holocaust as History and Warning* [New York:Penguin Random House, 2015]), 60.

22. Nachman's protagonist in some of his best-known tales is a "Viceroy" in search of the exiled Shekhinah. See Nachman of Bratslav, "The Loss of the Princess," in *Nachman of Bratslav: The Tales*, trans. Arnold J. Band (New York: Paulist Press, 1978), 51–62.

23. The story's references to night and to sleep—"The Sanatorium was in deep sleep. All the windows were shuttered in black"—evoke the language of *"nachtasyl,"* or "night shelter," coined by Max Nordau to describe Herzl's conception of the role Uganda would play as a temporary asylum, particularly for East European Jews: "Herzl believed that mass Jewish settlement in the British colony of Uganda would provide the beleaguered Jews, especially of Czarist Russia, with a temporary but secure 'shelter' until such time as Palestine (Zion) would be open to unrestricted Jewish immigration." Nahum Glatzer and Paul Mendes Flohr, Eds. *The Letters of Martin Buber*, (New York: Knopf Doubleday Publishing Group, 2013), fn 85.

24. Translation modified.

25. And for his Polish-language readership, versed in the literature of the *Wiadomości Literackie* milieu, it would have brought to mind Julian Tuwim's poem *"Żydek"* ("Little Jew" or "Yid"), in which the assimilated Polish-language poet identifies with a poor Jewish boy "wrapped up in rags," whom he watches dance in his courtyard:

> Where has fate carried us, where have we strayed
> in an alien world /
> The Gentleman from the first floor, who's a poet, alas! /
> will wrap up his heart like a coin and thus /
> throw it through the window and on to the street /
> to be trampled upon till it ceases to beat. /
> Thereafter we'll go on our different ways, /
> we'll never find peace and a haven of rest, /
> we singing Jews, we Jews possessed.
> Translated by Jacob Sonntag, *Jewish Quarterly* 30, no. 4 (1983): 36.

26. Franz Kafka, "The Hunter Gracchus," *The Great Wall of China: Stories and Reflections* (New York: Schocken Books), 1946.

27. Bruno Schulz, "Sanatorium pod klepsydrą," *Wiadomości Literackie*, no. 16 (April 21, 1935): 4–5.

28. As cited in Kaszuba-Dębska (2020), 474. Szelińska refers to the 1931 publication of *The Great Wall of China*, which would have been available to Schulz: Franz Kafka and Max Brod, *Beim Bau Der Chinesischen Mauer: Erzaehlungen und Prosa aus dem Nachlass* (Berlin: Kiepenheuer, 1931).

29. Kafka, "The Hunter Gracchus."

30. It also finds its present-day inheritors among proponents of post-Zionism and what has been called the "new diasporism." In their 1993 article "Diaspora," the Boyarins write, for example, "The solution of Zionism—that is, Jewish state hegemony, except insofar as it represented an emergency and temporary rescue operation—seems to us the subversion of Jewish culture and not its culmination. It represents the substitution of a European, Western cultural political formation for traditional Jewish one that has been based on a sharing, at best, of political power with others and that takes on entirely other meanings when combined with political hegemony." Daniel Boyarin and Jonathan Boyarin, "Diaspora: Generation and the Ground of Jewish Identity," *Critical Inquiry* 19, no. 4 (1993): 693–725.

31. Y. L. Peretz, "Natsionalizm un tsionizm," *Ale werk fun Y.L. Peretz* 11 (1925), 272–76. If Schulz's work shows strong affinity with Peretz's ethos, his golus was less a battlefield than a citadel, a sidetrack, or a secret detour. Peretz, an inheritor of the Haskalah and of Polish Positivism, was also strongly opposed to Orthodoxy while Schulz was formed by the Neo-Romantic spirit of fin-de-siècle Orientalism that surrounds Buber's formulation of a neo-Hasidic spirituality.

32. Baruch Spinoza, *Works of Spinoza: Theological Political Treatise*, trans. R. H. M. Elwes (New York: Dover Publications, 1951), 176.

33. Spinoza's work and legacy received significant attention within the Polish Jewish world on both occasions, and throughout the interwar period. In 1918 Yiddish poet Melech Ravitch had published the poem cycle *Spinoza: poetishe pruven*, and in 1927 in connection with the 250th anniversary Ravitch he offered a lead article in *Literarishe bleter* entitled "Benedikt d'Espinoza *Sub Specie Poesia*." In 1932, the Association of Jewish Writers and Journalists in Warsaw sent representatives to the international conference on Spinoza that took place at the Hague, and that year also saw the publication of the *Spinoza Book*, a compilation of scholarly essays and a translation into Yiddish of Spinoza's *Tractate on the Emendation of the Intellect*: Shatzky, Jacob, and Benedictus de Spinoza. *Spinoza bukh: tsum drayhundertstn geboyrnyor fun Benediktus de Spinoza: 1632–1932* (New York: Spinoza Institut in Amerike, 1932).

34. David G. Roskies, *A Bridge of Longing: The Lost Art of Yiddish Storytelling* (Cambridge, MA: Harvard University Press, 1995).

35. Ibid., 234.

36. Efrat Gal-Ed, "*Poezye Un Lebn*: A Note on Manger's Self Concept," ed. A. Molisak and S. Ronen, *The Trilingual Literature of Polish Jews from Different Perspectives: In Memory of I. L. Peretz* (Newcastle upon Tyne, UK: Cambridge Scholars, 2017), 45. See also Efrat Gal-Ed, *Niemandssprache: Itzik Manger—ein europäischer Dichter* (Berlin: Jüdischer im Suhrkamp, 2016), 149–51, 169–93 and "The Local and the European: Itzik Manger and His Autumn Landscape," *Prooftexts* 31 (2011): 31–59.

37. Efrat Gal-Ed, "*Poezye Un Lebn*," 45.

38. In an earlier statement, Manger connected his commitment to Jewish textual tradition with the work of his predecessor Y. L. Peretz: "My major work will firstly be the *folkstimlekhe baladn*, containing balladic motifs and characters from the Bible down to our time, from Cain down to Naftoli Botwin. It will be an attempt to create a second Yiddish folk epic, after the *folkstimlekhe* stories of Peretz." As cited in Gal-Ed, ibid., 45. See: Itzik Manger, *Khumesh lider* (Warsaw: Farlag Aleynenin, 1935).

39. Itzik Manger, *The World According to Itzik: Selected Poetry and Prose*, ed. and trans. Leonard Wolf (New Haven, CT: Yale University Press, 2002).

40. Itzik Manger, "Introduction, Itzik's Midrash," in *The World According to Itzik: Selected Poetry and Prose*, ed. and trans. Leonard Wolf (New Haven, CT: Yale University Press, 2002), 3.

41. Ibid., "Hagar's Last Night in Abraham's House," 13.

42. Ibid., "Abraham Takes Itzik to the Sacrifice," 17.

43. The most well-known of these Jewish legends of origin that was passed down for centuries within Polish-Jewish communities is the legend that interprets the name of Poland through reference to two Hebrew words, *Po-lin*, meaning "here rest." According to this legend, when Jewish settlers fleeing persecution in Germany in the fourteenth century arrived on Polish lands, they found tractates of the Gemara hanging as leaves on the trees, or carved in the trunks of the trees, and received messages telling them they had found their resting place. A version of this story was printed by Gershom Bader in 1927:

> "If you want to know how it suddenly occurred to these Jews in Germany to seek refuge in Poland, legend has it that after the Jews had decreed a fast and beseeched God to save them from the murderers, a slip of paper fell from heaven. On it was written: 'Go to Poland, for there you will find rest.' . . . The Jews set out for Poland. When they reached it, the birds in the forest chirped to greet them: 'Po lin! Po lin!' The travelers translated this into Hebrew, as if the birds were saying: 'Here you should lodge.' . . . Afterwards, when they looked closely at the trees, it seemed to them that a leaf from the Gemara was hanging on every branch. At once they understood that here a new place had been revealed to them, where they should settle and continue to develop the Jewish spirit and the age-old Jewish learning."

English translation from Haya Bar-Itzhak, *Jewish Poland: Legends of Origin* (Detroit: Wayne State University Press, 2001), 34

44. Roskies, *A Bridge of Longing*, 233.

45. Ibid.

46. See Simon Dubnow, "Autonomism," in *Nationalism and History: Essays on Old and New Judaism*, ed. Koppel S. Pinson (Philadelphia: Jewish Publication Society of America, 1958).

47. Samuel Kassow, "Travel and Local History as a National Mission: Polish Jews and the Landkentenish Movement in the 1920s and 1930s," in *Jewish Topographies: Visions of Space, Traditions of Place*, ed. Julia Brauch et al. (New York: Routledge, 2016), 241–64.

48. Joshua Shanes, "Yiddish and Jewish Diaspora Nationalism," *Monatshefte* 90, no. 2 (summer 1998): 179.

49. Rokhl Korn, "'*Tzimring gevelber*' fun Bruno Schulz," *Literarishe bleter* 16, no. 519 (April 20, 1934): 248.

50. See also Goldfarb's detailed reading of the story "Noc Wielkiego Sezonu" as an intentional engagement by Schulz with the tradition of biblical exegesis, and as instruction manual for the reader into how to approach the reading of his texts through that lens: David A. Goldfarb, "A Living Schulz: '*Noc Wielkiego Sezonu*' ('The Night of the Great Season')," *Prooftexts* 14 (1994): 25.

51. Triply disenfranchised: as a woman, a servant, and a Gentile.

52. Manger, *The World According to Itzik*, 12–13.

53. Ibid., 16–17.

54. Schulz uses here the term *kmiotek*, which implies a foolish or uneducated peasant and can be used as a disparaging term: a yokel, a country bumpkin.

55. It has been established that Schulz spent a significant portion of the war years in Vienna, with other members of this family. While little is known about this period in his life, his level of education and fluency in German place him in an intermediate and ambivalent position with regard to the East-West Jewish dichotomy in the period.

56. Baruch Spinoza, *Theologico-Political Tractate*, Chapter XIII, "Of the Simplicity of Scripture," Proposition 5, 186. Spinoza's radical treatments of biblical texts as historically grounded works of literature can be seen to have provided Schulz's generation a kind of originary model for a writing at the intersection of theology and materialism.

57. Bruno Schulz, "Ojczyzna," *Sygnały* no. 59 (1938): 7.

58. The author Stanisław Jerzy Lec also reports that Schulz sent a copy of this story for consideration to the Russian journal *Inoizdat* in Moscow (KL). Two sections of Lothar Brieger's 1922 album *E. M. Lilien* are thematically related to the content of Schulz's *Fatherland* and "E.M. Lilien": the sections entitled *"Die Heimat"* ("Homeland") and *"Das gelobte land"* ("The Promised Land"). In the latter, Brieger discusses specifically the realistic style to which Lilien turned in his art once he moved to Palestine, as well as the economic and social realities that Lilien encountered when he moved there.

59. Moss, *An Unchosen People*, 2021.

60. Ahad Ha'am, "Truth from Eretz Israel," trans. Alan Dowry, *Israel Studies* 5, no. 2: 160. Writes Dowry: "'Truth' originally appeared as a series of articles in the Hebrew daily newspaper *Hamelitz* (St. Petersburg), 13–24 Sivan, 5651 (19–30 June 1891), following Ahad Ha'am's first visit to Eretz Israel, 26 February-17 May 1891. . . . One of early Zionism's most cited references . . . it is regarded as a milestone in Zionist thought and in Ahad Ha'am's own role in the movement, and even, more notably, as the first serious analysis of the Arab issue" (Dowry, 154). Seminal to debates about Cultural and political Zionism, the essay was widely read within the Jewish world. It appeared in German translation in *Der Jude*, edited by Martin Buber: "Die Wahrheit aus Palastine," *Der Jude: Eine Monatsschrift* 7 (1923): 257–268; and that same year in a volume of essays by the author, published by Jüdischer Verlag: Achad Haam, *"Am Scheidewege. Gesammelte Aufsatze*, vol. I," trans. Israel Friedlander (Berlin: Jüdischer Verlag, 1923), 86–87.

61. Walter Benjamin, "On The Concept of History," in *Walter Benjamin: Selected Writings, 4: 1938–1940*. Ed. Howard Eiland, Michael W. Jennings (Cambridge, MA: Harvard University Press, 2006), 395.

62. The mulberry had also played a prominent role in Ahad Ha'am's essay "The Truth from Israel," as a symbol for unverified promises of material comfort and opportunity that, for the author, were driving a materially and not spiritually based emigration to Palestine.

63. Within Yiddish literature contemporary with "Sanatorium," a similar theme appears in Aaron Zeitlin's play *Der yidisher melukhe, oder Vaytsman der tsveyter* (The Jewish Kingdom, or Weizmann the Second), published in his Warsaw journal *Globus*. Aaron Zeitlin, *"Di Yidishe melukhe, oder: Weizmann der tsveyter," Globus* 3, no. 21–22 (March-April 1934): 3–53. A central theme of Zeitlin's play is the contrast between the quest for authentic Jewish spiritual renewal, on the one hand, represented in the play by the "Eternal Jew" and a small group of characters in the play led by Ben-Horin, whose scenes are treated with gravitas, and the nonspiritual, "realistic" fate of the majority of Jews in the play, who bring with them to their new state materialistic and bourgeois values acquired during their lives in the United

States, Germany, France, and Poland. This split—sacred/profane—is highlighted by the juxtaposition of contrasting dramatic genres within a single play.

64. Schulz's Lilien essay, discussed earlier, had traced that artist's development and metamorphosis from his beginnings in Galician Drohobycz, through participation in the Jewish Renaissance Movement and Buber's *Der Jude*, toward political Zionism and emigration to Palestine. Here Schulz moves toward a conversation with his inspiration Franz Kafka, and the mood of his story resonates with Kafka's possibly apocryphal comment, cited by Brod "Yes, there is hope, but not for us."

65. Familiarity with some kabbalistic and Zoharic tropes was widespread for Schulz's generation, but the texts of "*Księga*" and "*Wiosna*" suggest that he had likely read either fragments of the *Zohar* or writings about it. As a reader of German he would have had access to the translation of the *Zohar* in German, that came out in 1932—*Der Sohar—Das heilige Buch der Kabbala. Nach dem Urtext*. Translated by Ernst Müller (Wien: Glanz, 1932) as well as to German-language secondary literature on the Zohar and on Jewish mysticism. In addition to Martin Buber's writings on Hasidic philosophy, a point of reference for German-language readers before the work of Gershom Scholem was Joël, David. *Die Religionsphilosophie Des Sohar und ihr Verhältnis zur Allgemeinen Jüdischen Theologie: Zugleich Eine Kritische Beleuchtung der Franck'schen "Kabbla"* [The Religious Philosophy of the Zohar and its Relationship to General Jewish Theology: at the same time a critical examination of Franck's "Kabbla"]. (Leipzig: O.L. Fritzsche, 1849). Joël's study included a response to the French-language study of Kabbalah by Adolphe Franck: Franck, Adolphe. *La Kabbale: Ou, La Philosophie Religieuse Des Hébreux*. [1. éd.]. (Paris: L. Hachette, 1843).

66. *Die Bücher der Bibel*. Illustrated by E. M. Lilien, edited by F. Rahlwes (Braunschweig: G. Westermann, 1908). Only three volumes of the planned complete edition were published—volumes 1, 6, and 7. [VOL.I]: Überlieferung und Gesetz—das Fünfbuch Mose und das Buch Josua / [VOL.VI]: Die Liederdichtung—Die Psalmen, Die Klagelieder, Das Hohelied / [VOL. VII]: Die Lehrdichtung—Die Sprüche, Hiob, Der Prediger, Ruth, Jona, Esther, Daniel.

67. See: Genesis 4:1–16.

68. SF6, 88.

5. Acculturation without Assimilation

1. "*Załatwimy to po cichu we własnym zakresie działania*" (O, 121). This translation is changed from that offered by Wieniewska: "We can settle it all calmly within our own terms of reference."

2. "*Genialna epoka*," also "The Wondrous Er", W, 129–130; O, 121.

3. Gershon David Hundert, *Jews in Poland-Lithuania in the Eighteenth Century* (Berkeley: University of California Press, 2004), 11.

4. As the editors of *Ab Imperio* argue in "From Nationalizing Empire to Postcolonial Nation," the cultural and political contexts of hybridity have been insufficiently studied, as nationalities studies typically "perceive empire largely as a redundant category: a form of underdeveloped nation or a nation abusing the 'natural' mandate of nation-state." They propose instead a "hypothesis of the imperial regime's hybridity" that "problematizes the normative postcolonial theory of empire and deconstructs the teleological concept of a

nation as a natural group." This shift of perspective is invaluable for a reading that would attempt to tease Galician Jewish Polish-language cultural forms with roots in the Habsburg Empire apart from a relation of simple marginality with respect to the new Polish nation-state, or to the Polish cultural center in Warsaw. "From the Editors," *Ab Imperio 3/2020*, 11.

5. Ibid., 11.

6. S. M. Dubnov, *"Evreistvo, kak dukhovnaia (lul'turno-istoricheskaia) natsiia sredi politicheskikh natsii"* ("Jews as a Spiritual [Cultural-Historical] Nation among Political Nations"), in *Pis'ma o starom i novom evreistve* (1897–1907) (St. Petersburg: Obschchestvennaia Pol'za, 1907).

7. Kenneth B. Moss, *Jewish Renaissance in the Russian Revolution* (Cambridge, MA: Harvard University Press, 2009), 10–11.

8. Jacob Lestschinsky, "Jewish Autonomy Yesterday and Today," in *Jews and Diaspora Nationalism*, ed. Simon Rabinovitch (Waltham, MA: Brandeis University Press, 2012), 125–39. Originally published as: Yakov Lestschinsky, *Di Yidishe avtonomye amol un haynt*. Kiev: Central Committee of the Faraynikte Yidishe Sotsyalistishe Arbeter Partey, 1918.

9. Hundert, *Jews in Poland-Lithuania*, 11.

10. Hundert, *Jews in Poland-Lithuania*, 21–22. As has been observed in criticism on Yiddish-language literature of the shtetl, the literary imagination exaggerated this historical reality, creating narrative landscapes devoid of non-Jews. See Dan Miron, *The Image of the Shtetl and Other Studies of Modern Jewish Literary Imagination* (Syracuse, NY: Syracuse University Press, 2001); and Jeffrey Shandler, *Shtetl: A Vernacular Intellectual History* (New Brunswick, NJ: Rutgers University Press, 2014).

11. For additional discussion and analysis of the economic relations that produced this demographic within the Polish Lithuanian Commonwealth, see M. J. Rosman, *The Lord's Jews: Magnate-Jewish Relations in the Polish-Lithuanian Commonwealth in the 18th Century* (Cambridge, MA: Harvard University Press, 1990); Antony Polonsky, *The Jews in Poland and Russia. Volume 1: 1350–1881* (Oxford; Portland, OR: Littman Library of Jewish Civilization, 2010); Jeffrey Shandler, *Shtetl: A Vernacular Intellectual History* (New Brunswick, NJ: Rutgers University Press, 2014); Yuri Slezkine, *The Jewish Century* (Princeton University Press, 2004).

12. On the emergence of the Jewish public sphere in the Russian territories of the former Polish Lithuanian Commonwealth, and in Congress Poland, see Jeffrey Veidlinger, *Jewish Public Culture in the Late Russian Empire* (Bloomington: Indiana University Press, 2009); Scott Ury, *Barricades and Banners: The Revolution of 1905 and the Transformation of Warsaw Jewry* (Stanford, CA: Stanford University Press, 2012).

13. Kenneth B. Moss, *Jewish Renaissance in the Russian Revolution* (Cambridge, MA: Harvard University Press, 2009), 10.

14. This dynamic of Jewish territorial concentration on the lands of the former Polish-Lithuanian Commonwealth was a building block of developing diaspora nationalist narratives already at the turn of the century. Galician activist and theorist of Jewish nationalism Nathan Birnbaum, for example, wrote that "it is arbitrary to regard all cultural beginnings in the Golus simply as valuable cultural manure for just one potential culture on a soil which is not yet ours. Territorial concentration is not to be understood in too narrow a sense, it must not be confused with the establishment of a single territorial center." Nathan Birnbaum, *"Iberblik iber mayn lebn," Yubileum-Bikh*, 1925, 10. As cited in Emanuel S. Goldsmith, *Modern Yiddish Culture: The Story of the Yiddish Language Movement* (New York: Fordham University Press, 1987), 106.

15. Alfred Nossig, *Jan Prorok: Opowieść na tle Galicyjskim z 1880 r.* Nakład Funduszu Konkursowego im. H. Wawelberga, 1892, 108. As cited in: Albert Lichtblau and Michael John, "Jewries in Galicia and Bukovina," in *Jewries at the Frontier: Accommodation, Identity, Conflict*, ed. Sander L. Gilman and Milton Shain (Urbana: University of Illinois Press, 1999), 34.

16. On the shift from German to Polish in the Lemberg/Lwów/Lviv region following the granting in 1867 of autonomous status to Galicia, see also Albert Lichtblau and Michael John, "Jewries in Galicia and Bukovina," 1999.

17. On the complex negotiations surrounding the question of Jewish schooling and language, and the negotiations during and following WWI, see Marcos Silber, "Yiddish Language Rights in Congress Poland," *Polin* 27 (2015): 335–65. In Congress Poland (formerly under Russian control, including Warsaw), as Silber writes, "official recognition for the Yiddish vernacular was sacrificed on the altar of a political compromise. The final regulation declared that Jews were solely a religious minority and that the state would establish parallel classes for Jews within Polish schools or in parallel schools where the day of rest would be Saturday. The *cheders* and *talmudei torah* were to be recognized as *private* institutions that would be required to provide a general elementary education in the Polish language. Public funding was to be provided for the classes taught in Polish" (355).

18. Ela Bauer, "The Intellectual and the City. Lvov (Lwów, Lemberg, Lviv) and Yehoshua Ozjasz Thon," *A Romantic Polish Jew: Rabbi Ozjasz Thon from Various Perspectives*, ed. Michał Galas and Shoshana Ronen (Kraków: Jagiellonian University Press, 2015).

19. Nathan Cohen, "Reading Polish among Young Jewish People," *Polin Studies in Polish Jewry* 28 (2016): 173–86.

20. Kassow, *Who Will Write Our History?*, 19.

21. Kamil Kijek, *Dzieci modernizmu. Świadomość, kultura i socjalizacja polityczna młodzieży żydowskiej w II Rzeczypospolitej*, (Wrocław: Wydawnictwo Uniwersytetu Wrocławskiego, 2017), 260.

22. Kijek, *Dzieci modernizmu*, 2017.

23. Cohen, "Reading Polish among Young Jewish People," 173–86. Cohen examines studies of language use among Jewish youth that were conducted in the interwar period by engaged Yiddishists whose goal was to sustain Yiddish-language use into the next generation.

24. Joanna Michlic, *Poland's Threatening Other: The Image of the Jew from 1880 to the Present* (Lincoln: University of Nebraska Press, 2006).

25. Szymaniak details that "responding to anti-Semitic attacks, the *Wiadomości Literackie* editors published a special satirical issue in 1926 entitled *Jadą Mośki Literackie* [Here Come the Literary Jew-Boys], which was a play on the sound of the journal's actual title (*Wiadomości* and *Jadą Mośki* sound similar). "The Bootlickers' Bulletin," 2019. See also Magdalena M. Opalski, "*Wiadomości Literackie*: Polemics on the Jewish Question, 1924–1939," in *The Jews of Poland between Two World Wars*, ed. Israel Gutman et al. (Hanover, NH: University Press of New England, 1989). Słonimski's father converted to Christianity for marriage, and Słonimski was raised as a Christian.

26. An interesting source on Tuwim are the memoirs of Yiddishist S. L. Shneiderman, poet and publisher of the trilingual (Polish-Yiddish-Hebrew) literary journal *Trybuna Akademicka*, who was invested in facilitating ties between the Yiddish and Polish-language poets in the interwar period. He writes of Tuwim that, despite his distancing himself from Jewish thematics in his own writing, the poet had expressed to him an interest in developments in Yiddish poetry and in working with Shneiderman on an anthology of new Yiddish poetry translated into Polish. Said Tuwim, "I can't read the writing, but if you read

the poems to me, I can understand what they're about." "Bay Julian Tuwim," *Literarishe bleter* 132 (November 12, 1926).

27. J. Stradecki "Notes," *Julian Tuwim: Jarmark Rymów* (Warsaw: Czytelnik, 1958), 680.

28. Piotr Matywiecki, *Twarz Tuwima*. (Warsaw: W.A.B., 2007) 298. Matywiecki cites Tadeusz Kudliński, whose comments capture the spirit of this line of criticism: "Should *Wiadomości* put Tuwim at the head of Polish poetry—we can't agree to this. Tuwim is an excellent poet—agreed. Tuwim writes in Polish—agreed. But he also writes in jargon for Jewish journals" (Matywiecki, 298). (Note: this is inaccurate. Tuwim did not write or publish in Yiddish.) By comparison, Sitkiewicz, whose *Bruno Schulz i krytycy* examines Schulz's reception across shifting generations, writes that "occurrences of antisemitism among prewar critics of Schulz's work . . . were isolated voices, and lacking in the type of poisonous aggression that met the work of Skamander poets such as Tuwim and Słonimski." Piotr Sitkiewicz, *Bruno Schulz i krytycy: Recepcja twórczości Brunona Schulza w latach 1921–1939* (Gdansk: Fundacja terytoria ksiazki, 2018), 204.

29. In his essay "Ku żydowskiej polszczyźnie. Julian Stryjkowski i językowy palimpsest," Piotr Paziński considers the emergence of or experimentation with a "Jewish Polish" literary language in the post-WWII writing of Julian Stryjkowski who, as he argues, "did not fear a language that was far removed from the purism of the neophyte, but on the contrary . . . systematically created his own idiolect, a Jewish-Polish linguistic fabric rich with sounds and meanings, phraseology and borrowings; and even a number of registers, which in postwar Polish literature appears to be a phenomenon without precedent." In *Marani literatury polskiej*, ed. Adam Lipszyc and Piotr Bogalecki (Kraków: Wydawnictwo Austeria, 2020), 528.

30. Agata Bielik-Robson, ed., "Preface," in *The Marrano Phenomenon: Jewish Hidden Tradition and Modernity*, Special Issue of *Religions* (Basel: MDPI, 2019), 9. See Hannah Arendt, "The Jew as Pariah: A Hidden Tradition," in *Jewish Writings*, ed. Jerome Kohn and Ron H. Feldman (New York: Schocken Books, 2007).

31. Piotr Bogalecki and Adam Lipszyc, eds., *Marani literatury polskiej*, 2020, 15. Their collection *Marranos of Polish Literature* inaugurates a project to apply the Marrano metaphor as a tool for opening texts by Polish Jewish authors, or with strongly Jewish content, from the eighteenth century Enlightenment author Jan Potocki, through interwar and postwar writers Aleksander Wat, Leo Lipski, and Julian Stryjkowski, to contemporary writers Piotr Sommer and Zenon Fajfer.

32. Karolina Szymaniak, "The Bootlickers' Bulletin: *Wiadomości literackie* and Discursive Figures of Domination and Exclusion in Jewish-Polish Cultural Relations in the Interwar Period," unpublished manuscript, 2019. By focusing on previously unstudied Yiddish cultural critique of Polish-language writers, Szymaniak engages in the archaeology of Jewish Polish modernism by seeking to correct an existing imbalance within liberal historiography that in her view has "neglected to document and theorize more broadly Jewish voice and agency" (6).

33. Stanisława Blumenfeldowa, "*Zagadnienie żydowskie w Polsce*," *Sygnały* no. 14 (1936): 4–5.

34. Tuwim's poem "Żydek," ("Little Jew") is an iconic example of such a positioning of the lyric persona. In this poem the lyric persona looking at a young Jewish boy playing in his courtyard, empathizes and identifies with the child and also uses the space of the poem to emphasize the unbridgeable cultural and social chasm that divides him from the poor, unassimilated Polish Jews and from the traditional Jewish culture from which he is estranged.

35. Jan Niecisław Baudouin de Courtenay, a Polish philologist of French aristocratic background, taught in Kazan (1875), Dorpat, Kraków (1894–98), and Petersburg before the war, and in Warsaw from 1918 on. He had been unable to keep a position at either Warsaw University or Jagiellonian University before the war due to his support for minorities in both regions. Founder of the Kazan school of linguistics, he published numerous works of linguistic theory and history, was active in Polish political and social life, and became a leading spokesman for the rights of the many minority groups that were brought under Polish rule with the emergence of the Second Polish Republic—including but not limited to Belorussians, Ukrainians, Jews, Sorbians, Kashubians, Roma, Łemko, Bojko, Silesians, and Germans. "From his fieldwork researching the dialects of the 'minor' Slav such as the Sorbs, the Silesians, and the Slovenes," writes Davies, "he was perfectly well aware that the individual's right to a cultural identity of his own was no less threatened by the modern nationalist movements than by the imperialist regimes" (Davies, 44).

36. Jan Baudouin de Courtenay, *Kwestja żydowska w państwie polskiem*. Stowarzyszenie wolnomyślicieli polskich, 1923.

37. Norman Davies, *God's Playground: A History of Poland, Vol. I: 1795 to the Present* (Oxford: Oxford University Press, 2005), 44.

38. Hannah Arendt, *The Origins of Totalitarianism* (New York: HBJ, 1973).

39. Jan Baudouin de Courtenay, *W sprawie "antysemityzmu postępowego"* (Kraków: Nakładem autora, 1911), 31. Baudouin's scorn for the project that would find fulfillment in the post-WWI peace predicts the language used by Hannah Arendt in *The Origins of Totalitarianism* (1948), where she describes as "simply preposterous" the attempt to regulate the nationality problem in Eastern and Southern Europe through the establishment of nation-states and the introduction of minority treaties. "The treaties lumped together many peoples in single states, called some of them 'state people' and entrusted them with the government, silently assumed that others ... were equal partners in the government, which of course they were not, and with equal arbitrariness created out of the remnant a third group of nationalities called 'minorities,' thereby adding to the many burdens of the new states the trouble of observing special regulations for part of the population." Hannah Arendt, *The Origins of Totalitarianism* (New York: Houghton Mifflin Harcourt, 1985), 270.

40. Baudouin de Courtenay, ibid., 32. Schulz, in a letter to Maria Kasprowicz in 1934, echoes the extreme ethical individualism expressed here by Baudouin: "The very word 'human being' is a brilliant fiction whose beautiful and consoling lie covers all those abysses, those worlds, those hermetically sealed cosmoses that are individual human beings. There is no human being; there are only infinitely distant from each other sovereign modes of existence which cannot be contained in one coherent formula or reduced to a common denominator.... Passing from one face to another we have to undergo a fundamental restructuring, we have to change all our measures and assumptions" (*KL*, 47–48).

41. Jerzy Jedlicki, "Resisting the Wave: Intellectuals against Antisemitism in the Last Years of the 'Polish Kingdom,'" in *Antisemitism and Its Opponents in Modern Poland*, ed. Robert Blobaum (Ithaca, NY: Cornell University Press, 2005), 60–80.

42. Eliza Orzeszkowa, *O Żydach i kwestyi żydowskiej*, (Warsaw: Gebethner i Wolff, 1913). Translation in Jedlicki, "Resisting the Wave," 68.

43. Claudio Magris, *Le Mythe et L'Empire* (Paris: Gallimard, 1991), 326–27.

44. F. V. Werfel, "Prologue. An Essay upon the Meaning of Imperial Austria," in *Twilight of a World*, trans. H. T. Lowe-Porter (New York: Viking Press1937), 3–40, 3.

45. Werfel, ibid., 11.

46. Ibid., 40

47. A proponent of diversity of the empire, Werfel also converted to Catholicism and wrote Catholic-themed plays that made him the subject of severe critiques within the Jewish literary world.

48. Joseph Roth, *The Wandering Jews*, trans. Michael Hoffman (New York: W. W. Norton, 2001), 19. According to Roth's biographer, David Vronsen, he liked to tell this story that epitomized the Jewish relationship with the empire: "An old caftaned Jewish refugee, sitting in a train compartment, shows his ticket to the inspector. The Inspector, suspicious, thinking that perhaps he is hiding a child in his caftan to save the rice of a ticket, asks the Jew what he has in there. The Jew produces a framed portrait of Emperor Franz Joseph." Cited in Joseph Roth, "Translator's Preface," ibid., xviii.

49. Roth, *The Wandering Jews*, 137.

50. Franz Werfel, "Prologue," 4.

51. Ibid., 4.

52. Kenneth B. Moss, "Negotiating Jewish Nationalism in Interwar Warsaw," in *Warsaw. The Jewish Metropolis: Essays in Honor of the 75th Birthday of Professor Antony Polonsky*, ed. Glenn Dynner and François Guesnet (Leiden: Brill, 2015), 406.

53. Damrosch, *What Is World Literature?*, 256.

54. This slashed formulation is introduced to ameliorate the problematic use of the hyphen in "Polish-Jewish relations," which, often inadvertently, posits Jews as non-Poles or opposes them to Poles, rather than highlighting their shared identity as citizens in the multiethnic Polish state.

55. Beth Holmgren, "Cabaret Identity: How Best to Play a Jew or Pass as a Gentile in Wartime Poland," *Journal of Jewish Identities* (July 2014): 7(2), 18. And as Holmgren writes of Shore's *Caviar and Ashes*: "In . . . her generational study of Warsaw intellectuals' varied engagement with Marxism, Marci Shore acknowledges that, 'in a sense, my whole book is about . . . the "Jewish question" in Poland,' for so many of these intellectuals 'were first- and second-generation assimilated Jews, Polish patriots and cosmopolitans, their families often split apart by differing responses to a modernity that had arrived somewhat later in Europe's east'" (16).

56. Holmgren, "Cabaret Identity," 18.

57. Including three daily newspapers, Lwów's *Chwila* (*Moment*), Kraków's *Nowy Dziennik* (*New Daily*), and Warsaw's *Nasz Przegląd* (*Our Review*).

58. See also discussions of *landkentenish* by Samuel Kassow. Sam Kassow, "Travel and Local History as a National Mission: Polish Jews and the Landkentenish Movement in the 1920s and 1930s," in *Jewish Topographies: Visions of Space, Traditions of Place*, ed. Julia Brauch et al. (New York: Routledge, 2016): 241–64; and J. Hoberman's discussion of what he termed "The Greening of Yiddish Film" in a play on both Joseph Green's *Yidl mitn Fidl* (1937) and Edgar G. Ulmer's 1937 *Grine Felder* (*Green Fields*). Writes Hoberman, "Theirs were the first sound films to 'green' the Yiddish screen with extensive exteriors; the lyrical optimism of their movies [produced and set in interwar Poland] stands in marked contrast to the sanctimonious guilt of the American generational melodramas as well as to the morbid fatalism of later Polish films." J. Hoberman, *Bridge of Light: Yiddish Film between Two Worlds* (Hanover, NH: Dartmouth College Press, 2010).

59. Going on to problematize this assessment, which he considers a myth that "attached itself irreversibly to Leśmian," and to which he himself "submitted" in speaking of his work, Markowski emphasizes again the fundamentally *linguistic* nature of the "primordial" natural

landscapes and energies evoked in Leśmian's poems: "For Leśmian this seeing—of colors, and of foliage—is of a linguistic nature"; and that it is not a specific and concrete natural world, but rather the source of existence itself, that this imagery serves to evoke: "'nature' as a metaphor for timeless, ungraspable and unfathomable existence, out of which man arises," and to which he returns. Michał Paweł Markowski, *Polska literatura nowoczesna. Leśmian, Schulz, Witkacy* (Kraków: Universitas, 2007), 114.

60. Translated by Lawrence Davis. As cited in Czesław Miłosz, *A History of Polish Literature* (Berkeley: University of California Press, 1983).

61. Jeffrey Shandler, *Adventures in Yiddishland: Postvernacular Language and Culture* (Berkeley: University of California Press, 2006), 134.

62. A. Almi, "Yidish," *Far yidish: a zamlbukh*, ed. S. Erdberg (New York: 1930). As cited in translation in Emanuel S. Goldsmith, *Modern Yiddish Culture: The Story of the Yiddish Language Movement* (New York: Fordham University Press, 1987), 21.

63. Shandler, *Adventures in Yiddishland*, 134.

64. The multiethnic Polish-language homeland imagined in the pages of Polish Jewish modernist writing gained an evanescent, half-materialized nature that is discernable still today. Its territories can be entered through the pages of that literature bristling with hope and a strangely visceral, organic consistency.

65. Damrosch, *What Is World Literature?*, 256.

66. A similar adaptation of the trope of the Word made flesh informs Bruno Schulz's imagery from the folio of graphic works entitled *Book of Idolatry*, discussed later in this study.

67. English-language translation in Antony Polonsky, "'Why Did They Hate Tuwim and Boy So Much?' Jews and Artificial Jews in the Literary Polemics of the Second Polish Republic," in *Antisemitism and Its Opponents in Modern Poland*, ed. Robert Blobaum (Ithaca, NY: Cornell University Press, 2005), 189–209, 24.

68. Ibid., 24.

69. On Tuwim's staunch defense of humanist principles and his war of words with the right-wing critics who attacked him in this period, see Polonsky, ibid.; and Joanna B. Michlic, "The Culture of Ethno-Nationalism and the Identity of Jews in Inter-War Poland: Some Responses to 'The Aces of Purebred Race,'" in *Insiders and Outsiders: Dilemmas of East European Jewry*, ed. R. Cohen, J. Frankel, and S. Hoffman (Oxford: Littman Library of Jewish Civilization, 2010).

70. Writes Joanna Michlic, "The defining feature of interwar Polish ethno-nationalism was the quest for achieving both ethnic and cultural sameness within the nation. This was the main goal of National Democracy, the core ethno-nationalistic party in interwar Poland, and its offshoot radical organizations.... Thus 'dejudaization' of culture and society was the only viable strategy of 'improving the ethnic Poles,' of helping them to re-discover their 'real identity and collective destiny." Joanna Michlic, ibid., 72.

71. See Gilles Deleuze and Felix Guattari, *Kafka: Toward a Minor Literature*, trans. Dana Polan (Minneapolis: University of Minnesota Press, 1986). Approaching Schulz's writing from an ontological rather than a political perspective, George Gasyna reads *Cinnamon Shops* "as a case study of mythopoeia that recuperates the topos of resistance (to the authority of reality as such—that is, against the related problems of automatized perception and that of assimilation or acceptance of reality) in the practice of everyday life." George Gasyna, "Tandeta: Schulz and the Micropolitics of Everyday Life," *Slavic Review* 74, no. 4 (2015): 762.

6. "What Have You Done with the Book?"

1. Schulz, "Letter to S. I. Witkiewicz" (WE, 367–68).
2. This image was also central to E. M. Lilien's work. A 1922 collection of Lilien's work by Lothar Brieger, published by Verlag Benjamin Harz Berlin/Wien entitled *E. M. Lilien: Eine kunstlerische entwickelung um die jahrhundertwende* (*E. M. Lilien: A Turn of the Century Artistic Development*) opens with an introduction entitled "*Das Volk des Buches*," that brings together a collection of Lilien's images of Jewish men absorbed in study. Scenes of men reading, either alone or in pairs, were also a subcategory of Schulz's graphic works. Often containing erotic elements they could be seen to offer a profane commentary on or riposte to Lilien's reverential images of traditional exegesis. See also Kris Van Heuckelom, "In Defense of Idolatrous Creativity: Bruno Schulz's *Xięga Bałwochwalcza* and the *Traktat o manekinach albo Wtóra Księga Rodzaju*," in *Bruno Schulz: New Readings, New Meanings*, ed. Stanislaw Latek (Montreal: Polish Academy of Arts and Sciences, 2009).
3. For Robert Alter, writing on Kafka, "the use of biblical materials in a modern setting, at once playful and thematically serious, reflects both the afterlife of authority and the altered standing of the Bible in modernist writing." Robert Alter, "Wrenching Scripture," *New England Review* 21, no. 3 (Summer 2000): 7–19.
4. Walter Benjamin, excerpt from "Thought Figures," in Walter Benjamin, Marcus Paul Bullock, Michael William Jennings, Howard Eiland, and Gary Smith. *Selected Writings, Vol. 2*. (Cambridge, MA: Belknap Press, 1996), 726–727. Originally published in *Die literarische Welt*, November 1933, under the pseudonym Detlef Holz. Translated by Rodney Livingstone.
5. Emmanuel Levinas, *In the Time of Nations*, trans. Michael B. Smith (Bloomington: Indiana University Press, 1994), 59.
6. Jeffrey Veidlinger, *Jewish Public Culture in the Late Russian Empire* (Bloomington: Indiana University Press, 2009), 70.
7. Naomi Seidman, *The Marriage Plot: Or, How Jews Fell in Love with Love, and with Literature* (Stanford, CA: Stanford University Press, 2016), 4.
8. Ibid., 69.
9. Rachel Seelig, "A Yiddish Bard in Berlin: Moyshe Kulbak and the Flourishing of Yiddish Poetry in Exile," *The Jewish Quarterly Review* 102, no. 1 (January 2012): 19–48, 26.
10. Y. L. Peretz, "Escaping Jewishness," in *Peretz*, trans. and ed. Sol Liptzin (New York: YIVO, 1947). Originally published in 1911 as "*Vegn vos firn op fun yidishkayt*." See *Di verk fun Yitzchok Leybush Peretz*, ed. Dovid Pinski (New York: Farlag "Yidish," 1920).
11. Melech Ravitch, "Why Not Canonise a Second Book of Books?" in *Anthology of Yiddish Literature*, ed. Joseph Leftwich (The Hague: Mouton & Co., 1974), 165.
12. In his essay "Reality Degraded," Artur Sandauer, who knew Schulz personally, reads Schulz's imagery of prostration as a visualization of the generational and historical divide that he straddled in his own time and work: when his characters fall to their knees before indifferent or wrathful women, argues Sandauer, "it is a bow from nineteenth-century poetry to the brutal reality of the new age; the bow of Schulz's Arcadian childhood to the experiences of his manhood. The antithesis of the two worlds takes on a chronological shade here; his life is divided into two halves." Artur Sandauer, "Rzeczywistość zdegradowana," in *Proza* by Bruno Schulz (Kraków: Wydawnictwo Literackie, 1973). Schulz valued Sandauer's perception of his work and ethos. "That Sandauer . . . is my good friend, a young man of 23," he wrote to Romana Halpern in a letter of January 23, 1938 (KL, 163).

13. The exact dates of these works are not known. Schulz began to compile *The Book of Idolatry* and sell it in versions that contained differing selections of his prints in 1920.

14. Both Ariko Kato and Ewa Kuryluk discuss Schulz's imagery in connection with Sacher-Masoch's *Venus in Furs*. See Ariko Kato, "The Early Graphic Works of Bruno Schulz and Sacher-Masoch's *Venus in Furs: Schulz as Modernist*," in *(Un)masking Bruno Schulz: New Combinations, Further Fragmentations, Ultimate Reintegrations*, ed. Dieter de Bruyn and Kris Van Heuckelom (Amsterdam: Rodopi, 2009), 219–50; and Ewa Kuryluk, "The Caterpillar Car, or Bruno Schulz's Drive into the Future Past," in *The Drawings of Bruno Schulz* (Evanston: Northwestern University Press, 1990). Kuryluk draws attention to the use and objectification of the female figure in Schulz's works: "women represent a physical threat and an irresistible temptation. Each of them is a potential Eve and whore—a medium of debasement men want to use in order to escape from the law and order of the public world." She also reads the masochistic gestures of self-debasement within Schulz's erotica within a context of post-WWI political and historical change. Schulz's "reveling in degradation and apocalypse" signals a "crisis of civilization" and testifies, like Sacher-Masoch's work, to the "masochism of late-nineteenth century Europe." It indicates for her a "collective desire for submission and regressions" associated with "the end of Empire and of the power of traditional centralized male authority" (Kuryluk, "The Caterpillar Car," 34).

15. *Xięga bałchowalcza* was produced in a limited edition—the exact number is not known—and with variable contents. The portfolio contained approximately twenty graphic works bound in board covers, and Schulz created a different title page for each copy of the portfolio that he produced. This formal choice increased the thematic variability and allusive potential available for the collection of graphics as a whole. I refer here to one instance of these title pages among those that survive, which allows for strong resonance with the themes of Scripture and exegesis.

16. Adam Lipszyc, *Czerwone listy. Eseje frankistowskie o literaturze polskiej* (Kraków: Wydawnictwo Austeria, 2018). Władysław Panas, *Bruno od Mesjasza. Rzecz o dwóch ekslibrisach oraz jednym obrazie i kilkudziesięciu rysunkach Brunona Schulza* (Lublin: Wydawnictwo Uniwersytetu Marii Curie-Skłodowskiej, 2001). For Lipszyc, Schulz's recourse to Frankism strengthens his commitment to the hybrid Jewish/Modern pose: "Thus, perhaps it is Frankism as a borderline but very clearly Messianic form that can indeed be used as a chemical reagent which—preserving both what is modern in Schulz *and* what might be traditionally Jewish—reveals a more interesting profile of his Messianism?"

17. Paweł Maciejko, *The Mixed Multitude: Jacob Frank and the Frankist Movement 1755–1816* (Philadelphia: University of Pennsylvania Press, 2011).

18. Paweł Maciejko, *The Mixed Multitude*, 27.

19. On Frankism, in addition to Maciejko see Olga Tokarczuk's monumental treatment of Frank and Frankism in the Polish-Lithuanian Commonwealth in *Księgi Jakubowe* (Kraków: Wydawnictwo Literackie, 2015). *The Books of Jacob*, trans. Jennifer Croft (New York: Penguin, 2022).

20. Majer Bałaban, Le-Toldot ha-tenuʻah ha-Frankit (Tel Aviv, 1935); Bałaban's study would deepen the research Aleksander Kraushar had begun with his study *Frank i frankiści polscy, 1726–1816* in Kraków in 1895.

21. Public notice. *Chwila*, No. 2188 (April 10, 1925): 10. Wandel mentions the German-language publication of "*Studien und Quellen zur Frankistenbewegung in Polen*" by Bałaban, "the doyen of scholarship on Frankism in Poland." Oswald Wandel, "Eva Frank and

Casanova (Unknown Details about Frank and the Frankists. A delegate of the Podolian Jews in Rome, from archival sources at the Vatican)," *Chwila* (November 16, 1934).

22. See Moyshe Kulbak's drama *Yankev Frank, Ale verk fun Moyshe Kulbak, Vol. 3* (Vilna: B. Kletskin, 1929); and his modernist prose work *Meshiekh ben efrayim* (Buenos-Aires, 1958); and Aaron Zeitlin, *Yaakov Frank: Drama in zeks bilder* (Vilna: B. Kletskin, 1929).

23. On Mickiewicz's Frankist background and the place of kabbalistic and Frankist thought in his literature and his messianic thought see Roman Brandstaetter, "Legjon Żydowski Adama Mickiewicza," *Miesięcznik Żydowski*. Łódź, vol. 2, no. 1 (January 1932): 20–43; no. 2, (February 1932): 112–32; and no. 3, (March 1932): 225–48. See also Duker (1962); Maurer (1990); Janion (1998).

24. See *Księga Słów Pańskich. Ezoteryczne wykłady Jakuba Franka* 1-2. Edited and with commentary by Jan Doktór (Warszawa: Semper, 1997).

25. As Maciejko writes, the earliest account of the "Lanckorona ritual" was given by Rabbi Jacob Emden in his *Sefer shimush* (1760): "And they took the wife of the local rabbi . . . a woman beautiful but lacking discretion, they undressed her naked and placed the Crown of the Torah on her head, sat her under the canopy like a bride, and danced around her. . . . In dance they fell upon her kissing her, and called her 'mezuzah,' as if they were kissing a mezuzah." Maciejko, *Mixed Multitude*, 23.

26. Władysław Panas, *Bruno od Mesjasza*. (Lublin Wydawnictwo Uniwersytetu Marii Curie-Skłodowskiej, 2001).

27. Modern Jewish art and literature that engaged with or appropriated the figure of Christ, some in far less parodic forms, was common in Poland. Maurycy Gottlieb, considered by many the father of Jewish painting, also Schulz's Drohobyczan predecessor and likely an inspiration, produced the well-known works *Christ before his Judges* (1877–79) and *Christ Preaching at Capernaum* (1878–79). Schulz's lecture on Gottlieb, delivered in Drohobycz, has not yet been discovered but certainly contained revealing details on Schulz's thinking about the modern renaissance of Jewish art. On Gottlieb, see Ezra Mendelsohn, *Painting a People: Maurycy Gottlieb and Jewish Art* (Hanover, NH: University Press of New England, 2002). "The figure of Jesus has played a surprisingly important role in the formation of modern Jewish culture," writes Julian Levinson; a phenomenon that "scholars such as Matthew Hoffman have termed the 'Jewish reclamation of Jesus.'" In the work of Yiddish poets and novelists, including—Itzik Manger, Aaron Zeitlin, Moyshe-Leyb Halpern, and Sholem Asch, the figure of Christ serves as a metaphor for both universal human suffering and present-day Jewish suffering, for martyrdom, exile, and redemption. "Never before has there been an intersection of so many symbols," wrote Yiddish poet Itzik Manger in 1929. "Hamlet's tousled head floats through our sleepless nights. Blood has pictured the agony of our generation and scattered crucifixes over all the road of the world. Christ's head sobs symbolically in our dreams." In the Polish Jewish transcultural imaginary, such imagery functioned along a kind of metonymic skid: a series of layered and interchangeable allegorical readings. See also Matthew Hoffman, *From Rebel to Rabbi: Reclaiming Jesus and the Making of Modern Jewish Culture* (Palo Alto, CA: Stanford University Press, 2007); Julian Levinson, "A Yiddish Modernist Speaks of Jesus," *Michigan Quarterly Review* 51, no. 1 (Winter 2012).

28. The architecture of the building in this print resembles part of the Holy Trinity Church in Schulz's Drohobycz, but framed so as to remove the crosses that top it.

29. Mishnah Ta'anit 4:3.

30. "In '"Noc wielkiego sezonu,"' writes Goldfarb, "Father stands over a mercantile Baal worship, asking . . . 'Where were the shop assistants?' while watching 'the shop assistants

chasing Adela' [*gonitwa subiektów za Adelą*], as Moses asked, Where was Aaron? Here Adela is an isomorphism of the Golden Calf, the whole scene resembling the 'Procession' from Schulz's collection of drawings, *The Book of Idolatry*." David A. Goldfarb, "A Living Schulz: '*Noc wielkiego sezonu*' ['The Night of the Great Season']," *Prooftexts* 14 (1994): 37. On Schulz's unorthodox modernist treatment of idolatry in "Night of the Great Season" and the "Tractate on Mannequins," see also Kris Van Heuckelom, "In Defense of Idolatrous Creativity," 69–83.

31. Carol Zemel, "Bruno Schulz's *Book of Idolatry*: Making Jewish Art in the Diaspora," in *Jewish Artists and Central Eastern Europe*, ed. Jerzy Malinowski, Renata Piątkowska, and Tamara Sztyma-Knasiecka (Warsaw: Wydawnictwo DiG, 2010), 276. Republished and modified in Carol Zemel, *Looking Jewish: Visual Culture and Modern Diaspora* (Bloomington: Indiana University Press, 2015), 57.

32. M. K., "*Ze sztuki. Salon Wiosenny. Maj 1930. Wystawa ogólna*," *Wiek nowy*, May 21, 1930: 4–5. Schulz, like many artists of his generation in Vienna, was particularly interested in the art of Aubrey Beardsley and strongly influenced by his themes and imagery. As Szelińska recounts, Oscar Wilde's *Salome*, with illustrations by Beardsley (1893–1894), was one of his favorite books. Examining the critical reception of Beardsley's artwork in fin de siècle Austria, Nathan Timpano notes that "Beardsley's exploration of erotic or grotesque imagery profoundly affected the visual culture generated by artists affiliated with the Secession." Meir-Graefe's book *Entwicklungsgeschichte der modernen Kunst* (*Modern Art*, 1904) in particular "did much to popularize Beardsley's art in the German-speaking art world," as did the transnational pornographic publications of Franz Blei, which "demonstrate that a market for obscene literature and illustrations existed in German-speaking Europe at the *fin-de-siècle*." See Nathan J. Timpano, "'His Wretched Hand': Aubrey Beardsley, the Grotesque Body, and Viennese Modern Art," *Art History* (June 2017): 554–81.

33. Schulz employs a similar alibi in the later story "The Age of Genius" from *Sanatorium*. Here, worship or fetishization of the female shoe that figures centrally in *The Book of Idolatry* is shifted from the child narrator to the character of Shloma: "Lifting up with awe Adela's slim shoe, he spoke as if seduced by the lustrous eloquence of that empty shell of patent leather" while the child narrator asks, "What are you doing, Shloma?"

34. Anna Elena Torres, "Circular Landscapes: Montage and Myth in Dvoyre Fogel's Yiddish Poetry," *Nashim: A Journal of Jewish Women's Studies & Gender Issues* no. 35 (fall 5780/2019): 54.

35. Debora Vogel, "Ballad of a Street Walker I," in *Blooming Spaces: The Collected Poetry, Prose, Critical Writing, and Letters of Debora Vogel*, trans. and ed. and with an introduction by Anastasiya Lyubas (Boston: Academic Studies Press, 2020), 209.

36. Debora Vogel, "A Few Remarks on the Contemporary Intellectual Elite" (1936), in *Blooming Spaces*, ed. Anastasiya Lyubas, 117.

37. Lesya Khomycz, "Wokół wystawy w Borysławiu: o dwóch debiutach Brunona Schulza," *Schulz/Forum* 14 (2019): 13–33.

38. Marceli Weron, "Undula," *Świt. Organ urzędników naftowych w Borysławiu*, no. 25–26 (January 15, 1922): 2–5. Republished in *Schulz/Forum* 14 (2019), ed. Piotr Sitkiewicz. See in English translation: Marceli Weron [Bruno Schulz], "Undula," trans. Stanley Bill, Notes from Poland, July 11, 2020, https://notesfrompoland.com/2020/07/11/undula-a-newly-discovered-story-by-bruno-schulz/.

39. On the artistic group Kalleia, see especially "*Bruno Schulz i drohobycka twórcza śpiłka 'Kalleja*,'" B. Lazorak, L. Tymoszenko, L. Chomycz, I. Czawa, *Widomyj i niewidomyj Bruno Schulz (sociokulturnyj portret Drohobycza)*, ed. L. Tymoszenko (Drohobycz, 2016): 234–66. For comparison of motifs in "Undula" and other stories by Schulz, see also Lesya

Khomycz, "*Wokół wystawy w Borysławiu. O dwóch debiutach Brunona Schulza*," trans. Adam Pomorski, *Schulz/Forum* 14 (2019): 13–32; Ariko Kato, "Is Marceli Weron Bruno Schulz? The Newly Discovered Short Story 'Undula'" *The Polish Review* 66, no. 4 (2021): 106–14; Juliette Bretan, "Between Sleep & Awaking: Analyzing Schulz's 'Undula,'" Culture.pl, January 26, 2021; Piotr Policht, "Buried Treasure: A New Story by Bruno Schulz Unearthed," Culture.pl, July 28, 2020; Frank Garrett, "Translator's Afterword," in Bruno Schulz, "Undula," trans. Frank Garrett (Seattle, WA: Sublunary Editions, 2020), 15–24. Interestingly, Serge Faucherau seems to be alone among critics prior to Khomych's discovery in having identified Schulz's prints featuring "Undula" as illustrations that were meant to accompany a text—or vice versa. He wrote in his introduction to the French volume *Le Livre d'Idolâtre*: "The text that the *Book of Idolatry* presupposes never appeared, and should we want to imagine the story of this Undula, who made a regular appearance on its pages, we would subject ourselves to conjectures of the most fantastic kind." B. Schulz, *Le Livre d'Idolâtre*, préface de S. Fauchereau (Zurich: Quimper, 1983).

40. Vogel later included "Undula on Her Walk" as "*Undula afn shpatsir*" in the 1930 *Tsushtayer* issue that presented Schulz as part of an emerging cohort of Jewish artists in Galicia.

41. Among the editors of *Świt* was Klemens Funkenstein, also president of the Koło Naukowo-Literackie, a later iteration of the group Kalleia. See Khomycz, "Wokół wystawy," 1. As Khomych identifies, this debut Borysław exhibit was reviewed in *Świt* as well, nine months before the publication of "Undula."

42. Ariko Kato has demonstrated that "some of Schulz's cliché-verre works correspond closely to descriptions in the novel *Venus im Pelz* [*Venus in Furs*], 1870) by Leopold von Sacher-Masoch," and certain of his cliché-verre works imitate the composition of images reprinted in *Die Weiberherrschaft in der Geschichte der Menschheit* [*Female Domination in the History of Mankind*], a publication that included a supplementary volume of masochistic images, edited by the renowned art collector Eduard Fuchs. Kato, "Is Marceli Weron Bruno Schulz?" (2021), 113. See also Ariko Kato, *Eduard Fuchs i Bruno Schulz*, *Schulz/Forum* (2016): 7, 240–44. Kato notes that the very description of the "furry" darkness that gathers up Undula's "white, velvety limbs" in the story "Undula" may itself be inspired by the cliché-verre technique used by Schulz, in a direct translation from image to text.

43. That Schulz had written stories "*do szuflady*," or for himself and friends, in the 1920s had already been established by Ficowski.

44. Bill, "Undula. A Newly Discovered Story by Bruno Schulz."

45. Stanley Bill suggests in his translator's preface that "Schulz's elder brother, Izydor, who worked in the oil business that dominated the Drohobycz area . . . could have facilitated the publication, with the pseudonym necessitated by his (or Bruno's) embarrassment at the story's candidly sexual content." For Kato, Schulz "may have been reluctant to risk compromising his reputation as an artist by publishing a first writing attempt under his own name before knowing if he was capable of success" (114).

46. Sharon Bar-Kochva, "Some Reflections on Hebrew Pseudonyms of Yiddish Writers: Meaning of the (Seemingly) Meaningless," in *The Trilingual Literature of Polish Jews from Different Perspectives*, ed. A. Molisak and S. Ronen (Newcastle-upon-Tyne: Cambridge Scholars Publisher, 2017), 205–16.

47. For a reading that explores the Jewish subtext of "The Academy of Pan Kleks," placing Brzechwa's work in the category of Marranist Polish Jewish writing, see Lipszyc (2020).

48. Goldfarb, "A Living Schulz," 21.

49. On the absence of the father, Jacob, in "Undula," see Kato, "Is Marceli Weron Bruno Schulz?" 106–14.

BIBLIOGRAPHY

Ab Imperio. "From Nationalizing Empire to Postcolonial Nation. From the Editors." Ab Imperio 3/2020: 9–19.
Acher, Mathias [Nathan Birnbaum]. "Die Jüdische Renaissance-Bewegung." Ost und West (September 1902): 576–84.
Adamczyk-Garbowska, Monika. "'I Know Who You Are, but Who I Am—You Do Not Know': Reading Yiddish Writers in a Polish Literary Context." Shofar 29, no. 3 (2011): 83–104.
Agamben, Giorgio. The Time That Remains. Translated by Patricia Dailey. Stanford, CA: Stanford University Press, 2005.
Ahad Ha'am [Asher Zvi Hirsch Ginsberg]. O Sjonizmie duchowym. Warsaw: Akademicka Korporacja Sjonistyczna, 1928, 37–42.
———. "The Jewish State and the Jewish Problem." In The Zionist Idea: A Historical Analysis and Reader, edited by Arthur Herzberg. Philadelphia: The Jewish Publication Society, 1997.
———. "The Spiritual Revival." In Selected Essays of Ahad Ha'am, translated and edited by Leon Simon. Philadelphia: The Jewish Publication Society of America, 1962.
———. "This Is Not the Way." In Essential Texts of Zionism. Translated by Leon Simon. Philadelphia: Jewish Publication Society of America, 1912.
———. "Truth from Eretz Israel." Translated by Alan Dowry. Israel Studies 5, no. 2 (Fall 2000).
Aleksiun, Natalia. "Salo Baron and Jewish Historiography in Galicia." In The Enduring Legacy of Salo W. Baron, edited by Tirosh-Samuelson and Edward Dabrowa. Kraków: Jagiellonian University Press, 2017.
Alter, Robert. "Wrenching Scripture." New England Review 21, no. 3 (Summer 2000): 7–19.
Anessi, Thomas. "The Great Heresy of the Varsovian Center." In (Un)masking Bruno Schulz: New Combinations, Further Fragmentations, Ultimate Reintegrations, edited by Dieter de Bruyn and Kris van Heuckelom. Amsterdam: Rodopi, 2009.
An-sky, S. [Shloyme-Zanvl Rappoport]. The Enemy at His Pleasure: A Journey through the Jewish Pale of Settlement during World War I. Edited and translated by Joachim Neugroschel. New York: Metropolitan Books, 2002.
Arendt, Hannah. The Origins of Totalitarianism. Boston: Houghton Mifflin Harcourt, 1985.
Arkush, Allan. "From Diaspora Nationalism to Radical Diasporism." Modern Judaism—A Journal of Jewish Ideas and Experience 29, no. 3 (2009): 326–50.
Auerbach, Rachel [Rokhl Oyerbakh]. Dziennik i inne pisma z getta. Translated by Karolina Szymaniak. Warszawa: Żydowski Instytut Historyczny, 2016.
———. "Nisht-oysgeshpunene fedem" ("Un-Spun Threads"). Tel Aviv: Di goldene keyt 50 (1964): 137.
Bałaban, Majer. Le-Toldot ha-tenu'ah ha-Frankit. Tel Aviv, 1935

Bar-Itzhak, Haya. *Jewish Poland: Legends of Origin*. Detroit, MI: Wayne State University Press, 2001.

Bar-Kochva, Sharon. "Some Reflections on Hebrew Pseudonyms of Yiddish Writers: Meaning of the (Seemingly) Meaningless." In *The Trilingual Literature of Polish Jews from Different Perspectives*, edited by A. Molisak and S. Ronen, 205–16. Newcastle upon Tyne: Cambridge Scholars, 2017.

Batnitzky, Leora. *Idolatry and Representation: The Philosophy of Franz Rosenzweig Reconsidered*. Princeton, NJ: Princeton University Press, 2009.

———. "Translation as Transcendence: A Glimpse into the Workshop of the Buber-Rosenzweig Bible Translation." *New German Critique*, no. 70 (1997): 87–116.

Baudouin de Courtenay, Jan. *Kwestja żydowska w państwie polskiem*. Stowarzyszenie Wolnomyślicieli Polskich, 1923.

———. *W sprawie "antysemityzmu postępowego."* Kraków: Nakładem autora, 1911.

Bauer, Ela. "The Intellectual and the City. Lvov (Lwów, Lemberg, Lviv) and Yehoshua Ozjasz Thon." In *A Romantic Polish Jew: Rabbi Ozjasz Thon from Various Perspectives*, edited by Michał Galas and Shoshana Ronen. Kraków: Jagiellonian University Press, 2015.

Bemporad, Elissa. *Legacy of Blood: Jews, Pogroms, and Ritual Murder in the Lands of the Soviets*. New York: Oxford University Press, 2019.

Benjamin, Walter. "On Language as Such and On the Language of Man." In *Selected Writings, Vol. 1, 1913–1926*, edited by Marcus Bullock and Michael W. Jennings. Cambridge, MA: Belknap Press of Harvard University, 1996.

———. "On the Concept of History." *Selected Writings, Vol. 4, 1938–1940*. Cambridge, MA: Belknap Press of Harvard University, 2006.

———. *The Origin of German Tragic Drama*. Translated by John Osborne. New York: Verso, 2003.

———. "Thought Figures." In *Selected Writings, Vol. 2*, edited by Marcus Paul Bullock, Michael William Jennings, Howard Eiland, and Gary Smith, 726–27. Cambridge, MA: Belknap Press, 1996.

Benjamin, Walter, and Gershom Scholem. *The Correspondence of Walter Benjamin and Gershom Scholem 1932–1940*. Translated by Andre Lefevre and Gary Smith. New York: Schocken Books, 1989.

Biale, David. *Cultures of the Jews*. New York: Schocken Books, 2002.

Bielik-Robson, Agata. "Burzliwy żywot amureca, czyli jak Jakub Pannę zdobywał. *Słowo Pańskie* Jakuba Franka jako powieść łotrzykowska." *Marani literatury polskiej*, edited by Adam Lipszyc and Piotr Bogalecki. Kraków: Wydawnictwo Austeria, 2020.

———. "Fenomen maranizmu." In *Marani literatury polskiej*, edited by Adam Lipszyc and Piotr Bogalecki. Kraków: Wydawnictwo Austeria, 2020.

———. *Jewish Cryptotheologies of Late Modernity: Philosophical Marranos*. Abingdon: Routledge, 2014.

———. "Życie na marginesach: Kabała Brunona Schulza." In *Cienie pod czerwoną skałą. Eseje o literaturze*. Gdańsk: Fundacja Terytoria Książki, 2015.

Bill, Stanley. "Propaganda on the Margins: Bruno Schulz's Soviet Illustrations, 1940–41." *The Slavonic and East European Review* 96, no. 3 (July 2018): 432–68.

———. "Schulz a znikająca granica." In *Bruno Schulz: teksty i konteksty. Materiał VI Międzynarodowego Festiwalu Brunona Schulza w Drohobyczu*, edited by Wiera Meniok. Drohobycz: Polonistyczne Centrum Naukowo-Informacyjne im. Igora Menioka, 2016.

——— "Undula: A Newly Discovered Story by Bruno Schulz." *Notes from Poland.* https://notesfrompoland.com/2020/07/11/undula-a-newly-discovered-story-by-bruno-schulz.
Birnbaum, Nathan. "Iberblik iber mayn lebn." *Yubileum-bikh*, 1925.
———. "Jüdische Renaissance Bewegung." *Ost und West* 2, no. 9 (September 1902): 577–84.
Blumenfeldowa, Stanisława. "Zagadnienie żydowskie w Polsce." *Sygnały* no. 14 (1936): 4–5.
Bolecki, Włodzimierz et al., eds. *Słownik Schulzowski: Opracowanie i redakcja.* 2nd ed. Gdańsk: Słowo/obraz terytoria, 2006.
Boyarin, Daniel, and Jonathan Boyarin. "Diaspora: Generation and the Ground of Jewish Identity." *Critical Inquiry* 19, no. 4 (1993): 693–725.
Boyarin, Jonathan. *A Traveling Homeland: The Babylonian Homeland as Diaspora.* Philadelphia: University of Pennsylvania Press, 2015.
Brandstaetter, Roman. "Legjon Żydowski Adama Mickiewicza." *Miesięcznik Żydowski* Łódź, vol. II, no. 1, January 1932, 20–43; no. 2, February, 112–32; and no. 3, March, 225–48.
Brenner, David A. *Marketing Identities: The Invention of Jewish Ethnicity in Ost und West.* Detroit, MI: Wayne State University Press, 1998.
Brenner, Michael. *Prophets of the Past: Interpreters of Jewish History.* Princeton, NJ: Princeton University Press, 2010.
Bretan, Juliette. "Between Sleep & Awaking: Analyzing Schulz's 'Undula.'" Culture.pl. January 26, 2021. https://culture.pl/en/article/between-sleep-awakening-analysing-schulzs-undula.
Brieger, Lothar. *E. M. Lilien: eine kunstlerische Entwickelung um die Jahrhundertwende.* Berlin/Wien: Benjamin Harz, 1922.
Buber, Martin. "The Bible as Storyteller." In *The First Buber: Youthful Zionist Writings of Martin Buber*, edited and translated by Gilya G. Schmidt. Syracuse, NY: Syracuse University Press, 1999.
———. *Die Legende des Baal-schem.* Frankfurt am Main: Rütten und Loening, 1908.
———. *The First Buber: Youthful Zionist Writings of Martin Buber.* Edited and translated by Gilya G. Schmidt. Syracuse, NY: Syracuse University Press, 1999.
———. *Hasidism and Modern Man.* Atlantic Highlands, NJ: Humanities Press International, 1958.
———. "Leitwort Style in Pentateuch Narrative." In *Scripture in Translation*, edited and translated by Lawrence Alan Rosenwald and Everett Fox. Bloomington: Indiana University Press, 1994.
———. *The Letters of Martin Buber.* Edited by Nahum Glatzer and Paul Mendes Flohr. New York: Knopf Doubleday Publishing Group, 2013,
———. *On Judaism.* Edited and translated by Nahum N. Glatzer. New York: Schocken Books, 1967.
Buchman, Hersz. "Odrodzenia języka." *Chwila*, no. 4740 (June 5, 1932): 9.
Budick, Emily Miller. *The Subject of Holocaust Fiction.* Bloomington: Indiana University Press, 2015.
Budzyński, Wiesław. *Miasto Schulza.* Warsaw: Prószyński i S-ka, 2005.
Butler, Judith. *Parting Ways: Jewishness and the Critique of Zionism.* New York: Columbia University Press, 2013.
Cammy, Justin, and Marta Figlerowicz. "Translating History into Art: The Influences of Cyprian Kamil Norwid in Abraham Sutzkever's Poetry." *Prooftexts* 27 (2007): 427–73.

Caneppele, Paolo. "Bruno Schulz w Wiedniu." In *W ułamkach zwierciadła*. Edited by M. Kitowskiej-Łysiak and Władysław Panas. Lublin: Towarzystwo Naukowe KUL, 2003.
Caplan, Marc. *How Strange the Change: Language, Temporality, and Narrative Form in Peripheral Modernisms*. Stanford, CA: Stanford University Press, 2011.
Casanova, Pascale. *The World Republic of Letters*. Cambridge, MA: Harvard University Press, 2004.
Chwin, Stefan. "Dlaczego Bruno Schulz nie chciał być pisarzem żydowskim (O 'wymazywaniu' żydowskości w *Sanatorium pod klepsydrą* i *Sklepach cynamonowych*)." *Schulz/Forum* 4 (2014): 5–21.
Cohen, Nathan. "Reading Polish among Young Jewish People." *Polin* 28 (January 2016): 173–86.
Cooper, Julie E. "A Diasporic Critique of Diasporism: The Question of Jewish Political Agency." *Political Theory* 43, no. 1 (2015): 80–110.
Damrosch, David. *What Is World Literature?* Princeton, NJ: Princeton University Press, 2003.
Davies, Norman. *God's Playground: A History of Poland, Vol. II: 1795 to the Present*. Oxford: Oxford University Press, 2005.
Deleuze, Gilles, and Felix Guattari. *Kafka: Toward a Minor Literature*. Translated by Dana Polan. Minneapolis: University of Minnesota Press, 1986.
Derrida, Jacques. "The Eyes of Language: The Abyss and the Volcano." In *Acts of Religion*. Edited and translated by Gil Anidjar. Abingdon: Routledge, 2002.
D. M. "Grand-Rabin Szwecji Dr. M. Ehrenpreis przybył do Polski." *Chwila* (June 14, 1930): 7.
Doktór, Jan. *Księga Słów Pańskich. Ezoteryczne wykłady Jakuba Franka* 1–2. Edited and with commentary by Jan Doktór. Warszawa: Semper, 1997.
Dowty, Alan. "Much Ado about Little: Ahad Ha'am's 'Truth from Eretz Yisrael,' Zionism, and the Arabs." *Israel Studies* 5, no. 2 (fall 2000): 154–81.
Dubnow, Simon. "Autonomism." In *Nationalism and History: Essays on Old and New Judaism*, edited by Koppel S. Pinson. Philadelphia: Jewish Publication Society of America, 1958.
———. "Evreistvo, kak dukhovnaia (lul'turno-istoricheskaia) natsiia sredi politicheskikh natsii" (Jews as a Spiritual [Cultural-Historical] Nation among Political Nations). In *Pis'ma o starom i novom evreistve (1897–1907)*. St. Petersburg: Obschchestvennaia Pol'za, 1907.
Duker, Abraham G. *The Mystery of the Jews in Mickiewicz's Towianist Lectures on Slav Literature*. The Polish Review Vol. 7, no. 3 (Summer 1962), 40–66.
Dynes, Ofer. "Polish Whiskers and the Jewish Tongue: On Y. L. Peretz Not Becoming a Polish Writer." *Polin* 28 (2015): 107–19.
Ehrenpreis, Markus. *Die Entwickelung der Emanationslehre in der Kabbala Des XIII. Jahrhunderts*. 1895.
———. "Min livsväg." *Judisk Tidskrift* 6 (1939): 186.
Eisen, Arnold M. *Galut: Modern Jewish Reflection on Homelessness and Homecoming*. Bloomington: Indiana University Press, 1986.
Fauchereau, S. *Fantazmatyczny świat Brunona Schulza*. Gdańsk: Słowo/obraz terytoria, 2018.
———. "Preface." In *B. Schulz, Le Livre Idolâtre*. Quimper: Caligrammes, 1983.
Feiwel, Berthold. "Vorrede." *Lieder des Ghetto*. Berlin: S. Calvary, 1903.
Ficowski, Jerzy. *Regions of the Great Heresy: Bruno Schulz, a Biographical Portrait*. Translated by Theodosia Robertson. New York: Norton, 2003.
———. *Regiony wielkiej herezji i okolice*. Sejny: Fundacja Pogranicza, 2002.

Finkin, Jordan D. *Exile as Home: The Cosmopolitan Poetics of Leyb Najdus*. Pittsburgh: University of Pittsburgh Press, 2017.
Fishman, Joshua. *The Rise of Modern Yiddish Literature*. Pittsburgh: University of Pittsburgh Press, 2005.
Franck, Adolphe. *La Kabbale: Ou, La Philosophie Religieuse des Hebreux*. Paris: L. Hachette, 1843.
Frank, Allison F. *Oil Empire: Visions of Prosperity in Austrian Galicia*. Cambridge, MA: Harvard University Press, 2005.
Frankel, Jonathan. *Prophecy and Politics: Socialism, Nationalism, and the Russian Jews, 1862–1917*. Cambridge: Cambridge University Press, 1981.
Fruitman, Stephen. *Creating a New Heart: Marcus Ehrenpreis on Jewry and Judaism*. Umeå: Umeå University Institute for Historical Studies, 2001.
Gal-Ed, Efrat. "The Local and the European: Itzik Manger and His Autumn Landscape." *Prooftexts* 31 (2011): 31–59.
———. *Niemandssprache: Itzik Manger—ein europäischer Dichter*. Berlin: Jüdischer im Suhrkamp, 2016.
———. "*Poezye Un Lebn*: A Note on Manger's Self Concept." In *The Trilingual Literature of Polish Jews from Different Perspectives: In Memory of I. L. Peretz*, edited by A. Molisak and S. Ronen. Newcastle upon Tyne, UK: Cambridge Scholars, 2017.
Garrett, Frank. Afterword to "Undula" by Bruno Schulz, 15–24. Translated by Frank Garrett. Seattle, WA: Sublunary Editions, 2020.
Gasyna, George. "Tandeta: Schulz and the Micropolitics of Everyday Life." *Slavic Review* 74, no. 4 (2015): 760–84.
Goldfarb, David A. "A Living Schulz: 'Noc wielkiego sezonu' ('The Night of the Great Season')." *Prooftexts* 14 (1994): 25–47.
Goldsmith, Emanuel S. *Modern Yiddish Culture: The Story of the Yiddish Language Movement*. Fordham, NY: Fordham University Press, 1987.
Gombrowicz, Witold. "On Bruno Schulz." Translated by Lillian Vallee. *New York Times Book Review*, April 13, 1989.
Grinberg, Uri Zvi. Interview with Benzion Zangen. *Chwila* 17, no. 5762 (April 6, 1935): 9.
Grynberg, Henryk. *Drohobycz, Drohobycz and Other Stories: True Tales from the Holocaust and Life After*. Translated by Alicia Nitecki. New York: Penguin Books, 2002.
Gutman, Yisrael et al., eds. *The Jews of Poland between Two World Wars*. Lebanon, NH: University Press of New England, 1989.
Harper Collins Study Bible. New Revised Standard Edition. New York: Harper Collins, 1993.
Harshav, Benjamin. *Language in Time of Revolution*. Berkeley: University of California Press, 1993.
Hassan, Waïl S. "Translational Literature and the Pleasures of Exile." *PMLA* 131, no. 5 (2016): 1435–43.
Hellerstein, Kathryn. *A Question of Tradition: Women Poets in Yiddish, 1586–1987*. Stanford, CA: Stanford University Press, 2014.
Hoberman, J. *Bridge of Light: Yiddish Film between Two Worlds*. Hanover, NH: Dartmouth College Press, 2010.
Hoffman, Matthew. *From Rebel to Rabbi: Reclaiming Jesus and the Making of Modern Jewish Culture*. Palo Alto, CA: Stanford University Press, 2007.
Hoffman, Michael. Preface to *The Wandering Jews* by Joseph Roth. Translated by Michael Hoffman. New York: Norton, 2001.

Holmgren, Beth. "Cabaret Identity: How Best to Play a Jew or Pass as a Gentile in Wartime Poland." *Journal of Jewish Identities* 7, no. 2 (2014): 17–33.
The Holy Scriptures, Vol. 1. Philadelphia: The Jewish Publication Society of America, 1955.
Janion, Maria. "Tematy żydowskie u Mickiewicza." *Tajemnice Mickiewicza*. Edited by Marta Zielińska. Warsaw: Instytut Badań Literackich, 1998, 79–110.
Jarzębski, Jerzy, ed. *Czytanie Schulza: Materiały międzynarodowej sesji naukowej Bruno Schulz - w stulecie urodzin i w pięćdziesięciolecie śmierci*. Kraków: TiC—Instytut Filologii Polskiej UJ, 1994.
———. *Schulzowskie miejsca i znaki*. Gdańsk: Słowo/obraz terytoria, 2016.
———. "Schulz uniwersalny." *Schulz/Forum* 6 (2015): 5–16.
———. "Wstęp." *Bruno Schulz: Opowiadania, wybór esejów i listów*. Edited by Jerzy Jarzębski. Wrocław: Zakład Narodowy im. Ossolińskich, 1989.
Jedlicki, Jerzy. "Resisting the Wave: Intellectuals against Antisemitism in the Last Years of the 'Polish Kingdom,'" In *Antisemitism and Its Opponents in Modern Poland*, edited by Robert Blobaum. Ithaca, NY: Cornell University Press, 2005.
Joël, David. *Die Religionsphilosophie Des Sohar und ihr Verhältnis zur Allgemeinen Jüdischen Theologie: Zugleich Eine Kritische Beleuchtung der Franck'schen "Kabbla."* Leipzig: O.L. Fritzsche, 1849.
Kafka, Franz. *Diaries, 1910–1923*. Translated by Joseph Kresh and Martin Greenberg. Edited by Max Brod. New York: Schocken, 1948.
———. "The Hunter Gracchus." In *The Complete Stories*, edited by Nahum N. Glatzer, translated by Willa and Edwin Muir. New York: Schocken, 1995.
Kafka, Franz, and Max Brod. *Beim Bau Der Chinesischen Mauer: Erzaehlungen und Prosa aus dem Nachlass*. Berlin: Kiepenheuer, 1931.
Karlip, Joshua M. *The Tragedy of a Generation: The Rise and Fall of Jewish Nationalism in Eastern Europe*. Cambridge, MA: Harvard University Press, 2013.
Kassow, Samuel. "Travel and Local History as a National Mission: Polish Jews and the Landkentenish Movement in the 1920s and 1930s." In *Jewish Topographies: Visions of Space, Traditions of Place*, edited by Julia Brauch et al. Abingdon: Routledge, 2016.
———. *Who Will Write Our History?: Emanuel Ringelblum, the Warsaw Ghetto, and the Oyneg Shabes Archive*. Bloomington: Indiana University Press, 2018.
Kaszuba-Dębska, Anna. *Bruno. Epoka genialna*. Kraków: Wydawnictwo Znak, 2020.
———. *Kobiety i Schulz*. Gdańsk: Słowo/obraz terytoria, 2016.
Kato, Ariko. "The Early Graphic Works of Bruno Schulz and Sacher-Masoch's Venus in Furs: Schulz as Modernist." In *(Un)masking Bruno Schulz: New Combinations, Further Fragmentations, Ultimate Reintegrations*, edited by Dieter de Bruyn and Kris van Heuckelom. Amsterdam: Rodopi, 2009.
———. "Eduard Fuchs i Bruno Schulz." *Schulz/Forum* (2016): 7, 240–44.
———. "Is Marceli Weron Bruno Schulz? The Newly Discovered Short Story 'Undula.'" *The Polish Review* 66 no. 4 (2021): 106–14.
Kaye/Kantrowitz, Melanie. *The Colors of Jews*. Bloomington: Indiana University Press, 2007.
Khomych, Lesya. "Wokół wystawy w Borysławiu : o dwóch debiutach Brunona Schulza." Translated by Adam Pomorski. *Schulz/Forum* 14 (2019): 13–33.
Kijek, Kamil. *Dzieci modernizmu. Świadomość, kultura i socjalizacja polityczna młodzieży żydowskiej w II Rzeczypospolitej*. Wrocław: Wydawnictwo Uniwersytetu Wrocławskiego, 2017.
Korn, Rokhl. "'Tzimring gevelber' fun Bruno Schulz." *Literarishe bleter* 16, no. 519 (1934): 248.

Kraushar, Aleksander. *Frank i frankiści polscy, 1726–1816.* Kraków, 1895.
Kronfeld, Chana, and Robert Adler Peckerar. "Tongue-Twisted: Itzik Manger between *Mame-Loshn* and *Loshn-Koydesh*." *In geveb: A Journal of Yiddish Studies* (2015). https://ingeveb.org/articles/tongue-twisted-itzik-manger-between-mame-loshn-and-loshn-koydesh.
Kruczkowski, Andrzej. "Do krytyków." *Sygnały* no. 14 (1936): 3.
Krutikov, Mikhail. *From Kabbalah to Class Struggle: Expressionism, Marxism, and Yiddish Literature in the Life and Work of Meir Wiener.* Stanford, CA: Stanford University Press, 2011.
———. *Yiddish Fiction and the Crisis of Modernity 1905–1914.* Stanford, CA: Stanford University Press, 2001.
Kulbak, Moyshe. *Ale verk fun Moyshe Kulbak, Vol. 3.* Vilna: B. Kletskin, 1929.
———. *Meshiekh Ben-Efraim & Montag.* Buenos-Aires: Farlag Dovid Lerman, 1958.
Kuryluk, Ewa. "The Caterpillar Car, or Bruno Schulz's Drive into the Future Past." In *The Drawings of Bruno Schulz*, edited by Jerzy Ficowski. Evanston, IL: Northwestern University Press, 1990.
Lauterhahn, Artur. "Salon Wiosenny." *Chwila* 21 (May 1930): 16.
Lazorak, Bogdan. "'Trzon galerii miejskiej' i 'mój ślub mistyczny ze sztuką': zapomniane teksty Brunona Schulza o malarstwie drohobyckich artystów, Feliksa Lachowicza i Efraima Mojżesza Liliena." In *Bruno Schulz teksty i konteksty. Materiały VI Międzynarodowego Festiwalu Brunona Schulza w Drohobyczu*, edited by Wiera Meniok. Drohobycz: Polonistyczne Centrum Naukowo-Informacyjne im. Igora Menioka, 2016.
———. *Wpływowy brat Izydor (Baruch, Izrael) Schulz. Schulz/Forum* 2014, nr 3, s. 89–104.
Lazorak, Bogdan, L. Timoshenko, L. Khomych, and I. Czawa. *Vidomij i nievidomij Bruno Schulz: (sociokulturnyj portret Drohobycza).* Drohobych, 2016.
Leder, Andrzej. *Prześniona rewolucja. Ćwiczenia z logiki historycznej.* Warsaw: Wydawnictwo Krytyki Politycznej, 2015.
Leivick, H. "Iz undzer literatur a tzvey- oder fil-shprakhike literatur?" ("Is Our Literature a Bi- or a Multilingual Literature?"). In *Eseyen un redes.* New York: Congress for Jewish Culture, 1963.
Lestschinsky, Jacob. "Jewish Autonomy Yesterday and Today." In *Jews and Diaspora Nationalism: Writings on Jewish Peoplehood in Europe and the United States*, edited by Simon Rabinovitch, 125–39. Waltham, MA: Brandeis University Press, 2012.
Levinas, Emmanuel. *In the Time of Nations.* Translated by Michael B. Smith. Bloomington: Indiana University Press, 1994, 59.
Levinson, Julian. "A Yiddish Modernist Speaks of Jesus." *Michigan Quarterly Review* 51, no. 1 (Winter 2012). http://hdl.handle.net/2027/spo.act2080.0051.109.
Lichtblau, Albert, and Michael John. "Jewries in Galicia and Bukovina." In *Jewries at the Frontier: Accommodation, Identity, Conflict*, edited by Sander L. Gilman and Milton Shain. Champaign: University of Illinois Press, 1999.
Lilien, E. M. *Die bücher der Bibel.* Illustrated by E. M. Lilien. Edited by F. Rahlwes. Braunschweig: G. Westermann, 1908.
Lipszyc, Adam. *Czerwone listy. Eseje frankistowskie o literaturze polskiej.* Krakow: Wydawnictwo Austeria, 2018.
Lipszyc, Adam, and Piotr Bogalecki, eds. *Marani literatury polskiej.* Kraków: Wydawnictwo Austeria, 2020.
Liska, Vivian. *When Kafka Says We: Uncommon Communities in German-Jewish Literature.* Bloomington: Indiana University Press, 2009.

Löw, Chaim. "Żydzi w poezji odrodzonej Polski." *Miesięcznik Żydowski* 3, no. 2:7/12 (1933): 27–35.
Lyubas, Anastasiya. *Blooming Spaces: The Collected Poetry, Prose, Critical Writing, and Letters of Debora Vogel*. Boston: Academic Studies Press, 2020.
Maciejko, Paweł. *The Mixed Multitude: Jacob Frank and the Frankist Movement 1755–1816*. Philadelphia: University of Pennsylvania Press, 2011.
Magocsi, Paul Robert. *Galicia: A Multicultured Land*. Toronto: University of Toronto Press, 2005.
———. *Historical Atlas of East Central Europe*. Seattle: University of Washington Press, 1993.
Magris, Claudio. *Le Mythe et L'Empire dans la littérature autrichienne moderne*. Paris: Éditions Gallimard, 1991.
Manekin, Rachel. "Being Jewish in Fin de Siècle Galicia—the View from Salo Baron's Memoir." In *The Enduring Legacy of Salo W. Baron*, edited by Tirosh-Samuelson and Edward Dabrowa. Kraków: Jagiellonian University Press, 2017.
Manger, Itzik. *The World According to Itzik: Selected Poetry and Prose*. Edited and translated by Leonard Wolf. New Haven, CT: Yale University Press, 2002.
Mann, Thomas. *Joseph and His Brothers*. Translated by H. T. Lowe-Porter. London: Vintage, 1999.
Markowski, Michał Paweł. *Polska literatura nowoczesna. Leśmian, Schulz, Witkacy*. Kraków: Universitas, 2007.
———. *Powszechna rozwiązłość. Schulz, egzystencja, literatura*. Kraków: Wydawnictwo Uniwersytetu Jagiellońskiego, 2012.
Matt, Daniel Chanan, ed. *The Zohar*. Stanford, CA: Stanford University Press, 2006.
Matywiecki, Piotr. *Twarz Tuwima*. Warsaw: W.A.B., 2007.
Maurer, Jadwiga. *"Z matki obcej . . .": Szkice o powiązaniach Mickiewicza ze swiatem Żydów*. London: Polska Fundacja Kulturalna, 1990.
Mendelsohn, Ezra. *The Jews of East and Central Europe between the World Wars*. Bloomington: Indiana University Press, 1983.
Mendes-Flohr, Paul. "The Berlin Jew as Cosmopolitan." In *Berlin Metropolis: Jews and the New Culture 1890–1918*, edited by Emily D. Bilski, 14–31. Berkeley: University of California Press, 2000.
———. *Divided Passions: Jewish Intellectuals and the Experience of Modernity*. Detroit, MI: Wayne State University Press, 1991.
Michlic, Joanna Beata. "The Culture of Ethno-Nationalism and the Identity of Jews in Inter-War Poland: Some Responses to 'The Aces of Purebred Race.'" In *Insiders and Outsiders: Dilemmas of East European Jewry*, edited by R. Cohen et al. Littman Library of Jewish Civilization. Liverpool: Liverpool University Press, 2010.
———. *Poland's Threatening Other: The Image of the Jew from 1880 to the Present*. Lincoln: University of Nebraska Press, 2006.
Miller, Michael L., and Scott Ury. "Cosmopolitanism: The End of Jewishness?" In *Cosmopolitanism, Nationalism and the Jews of East Central Europe*, edited by Michael L. Miller and Scott Ury. Abingdon: Routledge, 2014.
Miron, Dan. *The Image of the Shtetl and Other Studies of Modern Jewish Literary Imagination*. Syracuse, NY: Syracuse University Press, 2001.
M. K. "Ze sztuki. Salon Wiosenny. Maj 1930. Wystawa ogólna." *Wiek nowy* (May 21, 1930).
Molisak, Alina, and Shoshana Ronen, eds. *The Trilingual Literature of Polish Jews from Different Perspectives*. Cambridge: Cambridge Scholars Publisher, 2017.

Moskalets, Vladislava. *Jewish Industrial Elites in Drohobych and Boryslav, 1860–1900.* Dissertation, Jagiellonian University, Kraków, 2017.
Moss, Kenneth B. *Jewish Renaissance in the Russian Revolution.* Cambridge, MA: Harvard University Press, 2009.
———. "Negotiating Jewish Nationalism in Interwar Warsaw." In *Warsaw. The Jewish Metropolis: Essays in Honor of the 75th Birthday of Professor Antony Polonsky,* edited by Glenn Dynner and François Guesnet, 390–434. Leiden: Brill, 2015.
———. "Polish Jewish Political Culture in the Shadow of a Polish Jewish Condition: Renegotiating Minorityhood, Diaspora, Zionism, and Home in the 1930s." Keynote, Third International Polish Jewish Studies Workshop, Chicago, IL, April 12, 2016.
———. *An Unchosen People: Jewish Political Reckoning in Interwar Poland.* Cambridge, MA: Harvard University Press, 2021.
Mosse, George L. *German Jews beyond Judaism.* Cincinnati: Hebrew Union College—Jewish Institute of Religion, 1985.
Müller, Ernst, trans. *Der Sohar—Das heilige Buch der Kabbala. Nach dem Urtext.* Wien: Glanz, 1932.
Murav, Harriet. *Music from a Speeding Train: Jewish Literature in Post-Revolution Russia.* Stanford, CA: Stanford University Press, 2011.
Nachman of Bratslav. "The Loss of the Princess." In *Nachman of Bratslav: The Tales,* edited and translated by Arnold J. Band, 51–62. New York: Paulist Press, 1978.
Newton, Adam Zachary. "A Queen, Jesters, Horse-and-Carriage, and Self-Portrait: Marginocentric Afterlives of Bruno Schulz and the Migration of Forms." In *Eastern Europe Unmapped: Beyond Borders and Peripheries,* edited by Irene Kacandes and Yuliya Komska. New York: Berghahn Books, 2017.
———. *The Elsewhere: On Belonging at a Near Distance.* Madison: University of Wisconsin Press, 2005.
Nossig, Alfred. *Jan Prorok: Opowieść na tle Galicyjskim z 1880 r.* Lwów: Nakład Funduszu Konkursowego im. H. Wawelberga, 1892.
Olson, Jess. *Nathan Birnbaum and Jewish Modernity: Architect of Zionism, Yiddishism, and Orthodoxy.* Stanford, CA: Stanford University Press, 2013.
Opalski, Magdalena M. "*Wiadomości Literackie*: Polemics on the Jewish Question, 1924–1939." In *The Jews of Poland between Two World Wars,* edited by Israel Gutman et al. Lebanon, NH: University Press of New England, 1989.
Opalski, Magdalena, and Israel Bartal. *Poles and Jews: A Failed Brotherhood.* Waltham, MA: Brandeis University Press, 1992.
Orzeszkowa, Eliza. *O Żydach i kwestyi żydowskiej.* Warsaw: Gebethner i Wolff, 1913.
Paloff, Benjamin. *Lost in the Shadow of the Word: Space, Time, and Freedom in Interwar Eastern Europe.* Evanston, IL: Northwestern University Press, 2016.
———. "Who Owns Bruno Schulz?" *Boston Review* 29, no. 6 (December 2004/January 2005): 22–25
Panas, Władysław. *Bruno od Mesjasza.* Lublin: Wydawnictwo Uniwersytetu Marii Curie-Skłodowskiej, 2001.
———. *Księga blasku: traktat o kabale w prozie Brunona Schulza.* Lublin: Towarzystwo Naukowe Katolickiego Uniwersytetu Lubelskiego, 1997.
———. *Pismo i rana.* Lublin: KUL, 1996.
Paziński, Piotr. "Ku żydowskiej polszczyźnie. Julian Stryjkowski i językowy palimpsest Austerii." In *Marani literatury polskiej,* edited by Adam Lipszyc and Piotr Bogalecki, 523–41. Kraków: Wydawnictwo Austeria, 2020.

Peretz, Y. L. "Escaping Jewishness." In *Peretz*, translated and edited by Sol Liptzin. New York: YIVO, 1947.

———. "Vegn vos firn op fun yidishkayt." *Di verk fun Yitzchok Leybush Peretz. Tsuzamen geshtelt unter der redaktsion fun Dovid Pinski*. New York: Farlag "Yidish," 1920.

Pieńkowski, S. "Poezja kryptożydowska."*Myśl Narodowa* , no. 41 (1926).

Pinsker, Leo. *"Autoemancipation!" Mahnruf an seine Stammesgenossen von einem russischen Juden*. Berlin: Issleib, 1882.

Pinsker, Shachar. *A Rich Brew: How Cafés Created Modern Jewish Culture*. New York: New York University Press, 2018.

Policht, Piotr. "Buried Treasure: A New Story by Bruno Schulz Unearthed." Culture.pl, July 28, 2020. https://culture.pl/en/article/buried-treasure-a-new-story-by-bruno-schulz-unearthed.

Polonsky, Antony. *The Jews in Poland and Russia. Volume 1: 1350–1881*. Littman Library of Jewish Civilization. Liverpool: Liverpool University Press, 2010.

———. *The Jews in Poland and Russia. Volume 2: 1881–1914*. Littman Library of Jewish Civilization. Liverpool: Liverpool University Press, 2012.

———. "'Why Did They Hate Tuwim and Boy So Much?' Jews and Artificial Jews in the Literary Polemics of the Second Polish Republic." In *Antisemitism and Its Opponents in Modern Poland*, edited by Robert Blobaum. Ithaca, NY: Cornell University Press, 2005.

Polonsky, Antony, and Israel Bartal, eds. *Polin 12: Studies in Polish Jewry. Galicia: Jews, Poles and Ukrainians 1772–1918*. Littman Library of Jewish Civilization. Liverpool: Liverpool University Press, 1999.

Presner, Todd Samuel. *Mobile Modernity: Germans, Jews, Trains*. New York: Columbia University Press, 2007.

Prokop-Janiec, Eugenia. *Międzywojenna literatura polsko-żydowska jako zjawisko kulturowe i artystyczne*. Kraków: Universitas, 1992.

———. *Polish-Jewish Literature in the Interwar Years*. Translated by Abe Shenitzer. Syracuse, NY: Syracuse University Press, 2003.

———. "Schulz a galicyjski tygiel kultury." In *Czytanie Schulza. Materiały międzynarodowej sesji naukowej Bruno Schulz—w stulecie urodzin i w pięćdziesięciolecie śmierci*, edited by Jerzy Jarzębski. Kraków: TIC, Nakładem Instytutu Filologii Polskiej UJ, 1994.

Ravitch, Melech. *Mayn leksikon*. Montreal: Yiddish Book Center, 1945.

———. "Why Not Canonise a Second Book of Books?" In *Anthology of Yiddish Literature*, edited and translated by Joseph Leftwich. The Hague: Mouton, 1974.

Rosiek, Stanisław. *Odcięcie. Szkice wokół Brunona Schulza (Fragments. Sketches on Bruno Schulz)*. Gdańsk: Słowo/obraz terytoria, 2022.

Roskies, David G. *A Bridge of Longing: The Lost Art of Yiddish Storytelling*. Cambridge, MA: Harvard University Press, 1995.

———. *The Jewish Search for a Usable Past*. Bloomington: Indiana University Press, 1999.

Rosman, M. J. *The Lord's Jews: Magnate-Jewish Relations in the Polish-Lithuanian Commonwealth in the 18th Century*. Cambridge, MA: Harvard University Press, 1990.

Roth, Joseph. *The Wandering Jews*. Translated by Michael Hoffman. New York: Norton, 2001.

Roth, Philip. *Operation Shylock: A Confession*. New York: Simon & Schuster, 1993.

Rozenblit, Marsha L. *Reconstructing a National Identity: The Jews of Habsburg Austria during World War I*. Oxford: Oxford University Press, 2001.

Sandauer, Artur. "Bruno Schulz i Romantycy." *Chwila* July 10, 1937: 9
———. *O sytuacji pisarza polskiego pochodzenia żydowskiego w XX wieku: (Rzecz, która nie Ja powinienem był napisać . . .)*. Warsaw: Wydawnictwo Czytelnik, 1982.
———. "Rzeczywistość zdegradowana." In *Proza* by Bruno Schulz. Kraków: Wydawnictwo Literackie, 1973.
Schachter, Allison. *Diasporic Modernisms: Hebrew and Yiddish Literature in the Twentieth Century*. Oxford: Oxford University Press, 2012.
Schaeder, Grete. *The Hebrew Humanism of Martin Buber*. Translated by N. J. Jacobs. Detroit, MI: Wayne State University Press, 1973.
Schatzker, Valerie. *The Jewish Oil Magnates of Galicia: A History, 1853–1945*. Montreal: McGill-Queen's University Press, 2015.
Scholem, Gershom G. *Major Trends in Jewish Mysticism*. New York: Schocken, 1954.
Schulz, Bruno. "Akacje kwitną." *Nasza Opinia*, no. 72 (1936): 9.
———. *Bruno Schulz: Opowiadania, wybór esejów i listów*. Edited by Jerzy Jarzębski. Wrocław: Zakład Narodowy im. Ossolińskich, 1989.
———. *Collected Stories*. Translated by Madeline G. Levine. Evanston, IL: Northwestern University Press, 2018.
———. *The Collected Works of Bruno Schulz*. Edited by Jerzy Ficowski. Translated by Celina Wieniewska. London: Picador, 1998.
———. "E. M. Lilien." Edited by Stanisław Rosiek. *Schulz/Forum* 6 (2015): 83–96. Gdańsk: Fundacja Terytoria Książki.
———. "'Genjalna epoka' ['Fragment z powieści Mesjasz']," *Wiadomości Literackie* 13 (April 1, 1934): 4.
———. "Jesień." *Sygnały*, no. 17 (May 1936): 425.
———. *Księga listów. Dzieła zebrane, Vol. 5*. Edited by Jerzy Ficowski and Stanisław Danecki. Gdańsk: Słowo/obraz terytoria, 2002.
———. "Mityzacja rzeczywistości." *Studio*, no. 3–4 (June 1936): 32–34.
———. "Ojczyzna." *Sygnały* no. 59 (1938): 7.
———. *Opowiadania, Wybór esejów i listów*. Edited by Jerzy Jarzębski. Wrocław: Zakład Narodowy im. Ossolińskich, 1989.
———. "Pod Belwederem." *Tygodnik Illustrowany*. July 26 (1936): 571.
———. "Posłowie." In *Proces* by Franciszek Kafka, 279–84. Warsaw: Rój, 1936.
———. "Powstają legendy." *Tygodnik Illustrowany*, no. 22 (1935): 425.
———. "Republika marzeń." *Tygodnik Illustrowany*, no. 29 (1936): 554–56.
———. "Sanatorium pod klepsydrą." *Wiadomości literackie*, no. 16 (April 21, 1935).
———. *Street of Crocodiles and Other Stories*. Translated by Celina Wieniewska. New York: Penguin Books, 2008.
———. "Wiosna." *Kamena*, no. 10 (June 1935): 191–93.
———. "Wolność tragiczna." *Tygodnik Illustrowany*. July 5 (1936): 510–11.
Seelig, Rachel. "A Yiddish Bard in Berlin: Moyshe Kulbak and the Flourishing of Yiddish Poetry in Exile." *Jewish Quarterly Review* 102, no. 1 (January 2012): 19–48.
Seidman, Naomi. *The Marriage Plot: Or, How Jews Fell in Love with Love, and with Literature*. Stanford, CA: Stanford University Press, 2016.
Shallcross, Bożena. "Fragments of a Broken Mirror: Bruno Schulz's Retextualization of the Kabbalah." *East European Politics and Societies* 11, no. 2 (1997): 270–81.
Shandler, Jeffrey. *Adventures in Yiddishland: Postvernacular Language and Culture*. Berkeley, CA: University of California Press, 2006.

———. *Shtetl: A Vernacular Intellectual History*. New Brunswick, NJ: Rutgers University Press, 2014.
Shanes, Joshua. "The 'Bloody Election' in Drohobycz: Violence, Urban Politics, and National Memory in an Imperial Borderland." *Austrian History Yearbook* 53 (May 2022): 121–49.
———. *Diaspora Nationalism and Jewish Identity in Habsburg Galicia*. Cambridge: Cambridge University Press, 2012.
———. "Yiddish and Jewish Diaspora Nationalism." *Monatshefte* 90, no. 2. (Summer 1998): 178–88.
Shapiro, Raisa. "Buber-Rosenzweig *Leitwort* Style and the Task of Translating Bruno Schulz." Unpublished conference paper, In/Between Conference, March 2019, Chicago, IL.
Shatzky, Jacob, and Benedictus de Spinoza. *Spinoza bukh: tsum drayhundertstn geboyrnyor fun Benediḳtus de Spinoza: 1632-1932*. New York: Spinoza Institut in Amerike, 1932.
Shedel, James. "Austria and Its Polish Subjects, 1866–1914: A Relationship of Interests." *Austrian History Yearbook*, 19–20, Part 2 (1983–1984): 23–42.
Shmeruk, Chone. "Hebrew-Yiddish-Polish: A Trilingual Jewish Culture." In *The Jews of Poland between Two World Wars*, edited by Yisrael Gutman, Ezra Mendelsohn, Jehuda Reinharz, and Chone Shmeruk. Lebanon, NH: University Press of New England, 1989.
Shneiderman, Shmuel Leyb. "Bay Julian Tuwim." *Literarishe bleter* 132 (November 12, 1926).
Sholem Aleichem. "*A konsilium fun doktoyrim*." In *Felietonen*. Tel Aviv: Beth Sholem Aleichem I. L. Peretz Publishing House, 1976 (originally 1903).
Shore, Marci. *Caviar and Ashes: A Warsaw Generation's Life and Death in Marxism, 1918-1968*. New Haven, CT: Yale University Press, 2006.
Shumsky, Dmitri. "Leon Pinsker and 'Autoemancipation!': A Reevaluation." *Jewish Social Studies: History, Culture, Society* 18, no. 1 (Fall 2011): 36–49.
Silber, Marcos. "Yiddish Language Rights in Congress Poland." *Polin* 27 (2015): 335–65.
Sitkiewicz, Piotr. *Bruno Schulz i krytycy: Recepcja twórczości Brunona Schulza w latach 1921–1939*. Gdańsk: Słowo/obraz terytoria, 2018.
———. *Bruno Schulz w oczach współczesnych. Antologia tekstów krytycznych i publicystycznych lat 1920–1939*. Gdańsk: Słowo/obraz terytoria, 2021.
———. "Ocalony przez mit. Schulz i Lilien." *Schulz/Forum* 6 (2015): 97–104.
Slezkine, Yuri. *The Jewish Century*. Princeton, NJ: Princeton University Press, 2004.
Snyder, Timothy. *Black Earth: The Holocaust as History and Warning*. New York: Penguin Random House, 2015.
———. *The Reconstruction of Nations: Poland, Ukraine, Lithuania, Belarus, 1569–1999*. New Haven, CT: Yale University Press, 2003.
Spinoza, Baruch. *Works of Spinoza: Theological Political Treatise*. Translated by R. H. M. Elwes. New York: Dover Publications, 1951.
Spivak, Gayatri Chakhravorty. "Ghostwriting." *Diacritics* 25, no. 2 (1995): 65–84.
Sproede, Alfred. "Bruno Schulz: Between Avant-Garde and Hasidic Redemption." In *(Un)masking Bruno Schulz: New Combinations, Further Fragmentations, Ultimate Reintegrations*, edited by Dieter de Bruyn and Kris van Heuckelom. Amsterdam: Rodopi, 2009.
Stanislawski, Michael. *Zionism and the Fin de Siècle: Cosmopolitanism and Nationalism from Nordau to Jabotinsky*. Berkeley: University of California Press, 2001.
Stauter-Halsted, Keely. *The Nation in the Village: The Genesis of Peasant National Identity in Austrian Poland, 1848–1914*. Ithaca, NY: Cornell University Press, 2001.

Steinlauf, Michael. "Hope and Fear: Y. L. Peretz and the Dialectics of Diaspora Nationalism, 1905–12." In *Warsaw. The Jewish Metropolis: Essays in Honor of the 75th Birthday of Professor Antony Polonsky*, edited by Glenn Dynner, François Guesnet, and Antony Polonsky, 227–251. Boston: Brill, 2015.
Sternbach, Herman. "Sklepy cynamonowe." *Miesięcznik Żydowski* (1934): 384.
Stradecki, Janusz. "Notes." In *Julian Tuwim: Jarmark rymów*. Warsaw: Wydawnictwo Czytelnik, 1958.
Suchoff, David. *Kafka's Jewish Languages: The Hidden Openness of Tradition*. Philadelphia: University of Pennsylvania Press, 2012.
Sutzkever, Avrom. "Tzu Poyln." In *Yidishe gas*. New York: Farlag Matones, 1948.
Szymaniak, Karolina. "The Bootlickers' Bulletin: *Wiadomości Literackie* and Discursive Figures of Domination and Exclusion in Jewish-Polish Cultural Relations in the Interwar Period." Unpublished article, March 2019.
———. *Być agentem wiecznej idei. Przemiany poglądów estetycznych Debory Vogel*. Kraków: Universitas, 2006.
Timpano, Nathan J. "'His Wretched Hand': Aubrey Beardsley, the Grotesque Body, and Viennese Modern Art." *Art History* (June 2017): 554–81.
Tokarczuk, Olga. *Ksiegi Jakubowe*. Kraków: Wydawnictwo Literackie, 2015.
Torres, Anna Elena. "Circular Landscapes: Montage and Myth in Dvoyre Fogel's Yiddish Poetry." *Nashim: A Journal of Jewish Women's Studies & Gender Issues* 35 (2019): 40–73.
Tuszyńska, Agata. *Narzeczona Schulza*. Kraków: Wydawnictwo Literackie, 2015.
Underhill, Karen. "Bruno Schulz, E. M. Lilien i archeologia polsko-żydowskiego modernizmu" ("Bruno Schulz, E. M. Lilien, and the Archaeology of Polish Jewish Modernism"). *Ruch Literacki* 6, no. 339 (2016): 655–80.
———. "Toward a Diasporic Poland/Polin: Zeitlin, Sutzkever, and the Ghost Dance with Jewish Poland." In *Poland and Polin: New Interpretations in Polish-Jewish Studies*, edited by Irena Grudzińska-Gross and Iwa Nawrocki. Eastern European Culture, Politics and Societies, Vol. 10. Frankfurt am Main, New York: Peter Lang, 2016.
———. "'What Have You Done with the Book?' The Exegetical Encounter in Bruno Schulz's Graphic Works." *POLIN* 28 (2015): 323–49.
———. "Writing in the Third Language: Between Theology and Materialism in Gershom Scholem and Jacques Derrida." In *The Effect of Palimpsest*, edited by Bożena Shallcross and Ryszard Nycz. Frankfurt am Main: Peter Lang, 2011.
Urban, Martina. "The Jewish Library Reconfigured: Buber and the Zionist Anthology Discourse." In *New Perspectives on Martin Buber*, edited by Michael Zank. Tübingen: Mohr Siebeck, 2006.
Ury, Scott. *Barricades and Banners: The Revolution of 1905 and the Transformation of Warsaw Jewry*. Stanford, CA: Stanford University Press, 2012.
Van Heuckelom, Kris. "In Defense of Idolatrous Creativity. Bruno Schulz's *Xięga Bałwochwalcza* and *Traktat o manekinach albo wtóra Księga Rodzaju*." In *Bruno Schulz: New Readings, New Meanings*, edited by Stanisław Latek et al. Montreal: Polish Academy of Arts and Sciences, 2009.
Veidlinger, Jeffrey. *Jewish Public Culture in the Late Russian Empire*. Bloomington: Indiana University Press, 2009.
———. *In the Midst of Civilized Europe: The Pogroms of 1918-1921 and the Onset of the Holocaust*. New York: Metropolitan Books, Henry Holt, 2021.
Vogel-Barenbluth, Debora. "Ludzkie egzotyki." *Przegląd Społeczny* (1934): 150–59.

Vogel, Debora. *Akacje kwitną. Montaże*. Warsaw: Towarzystwo Wydawnicze "Rój," 1936.
———. *Akatsyes blien. Montazhn*. Varshe-Lemberg, 1935.
———. *Blooming Spaces: The Collected Poetry, Prose, Critical Writing, and Letters of Debora Vogel*. Translated, edited, and with an introduction by Anastasiya Lyubas. Boston: Academic Studies Press, 2020.
———. "Kilka uwag o współczesnej inteligencji." *Przegląd Społeczny* 10, no. 6 (1936): 114–22.
———. *Manekinen: lider*. Lwów: Tsushtayer, 1934.
———. *Tog-figurn: lider*. Lwów: Tsushtayer, 1930.
———. "'Vayse verter' in dichtung." *Tsushtayer* no. 3 (1931): 42–47.
Volovici, Marc. *German as a Jewish Problem: The Language Politics of Jewish Nationalism*. Redwood City, CA: Stanford University Press, 2020.
Wandel, Oswald. "Eva Frank and Casanova (Unknown Details about Frank and the Frankists. A delegate of the Podolian Jews in Rome, from archival sources at the Vatican)." *Chwila* (November 16,1934).
Warska, Katarzyna. *Schulz w kanonie. Recepcja szkolna w latach 1945–2018*. 2021.
Wat, Aleksander. *My Century*. With Czesław Miłosz. Edited by Richard Lourie. New York: New York Review of Books, 2003.
Werberger, Annette. "Nür eine Muse? Die Jiddische Schriftshtellerin Debora Vogel und Bruno Schulz." *Ins Wort gesetzt, ins Bild gesetzt: Gender in Wissenschaft, Kunst und Literatur*. Edited by Ingrid Hotz-Davies and Schamma Schahadat. Bielefeld: Transcript, 2009.
Werfel, F. V. "An Essay upon the Meaning of Imperial Austria." In *Twilight of a World*, translated by H. T. Lowe-Porter. New York: Viking, 1937.
Weron, Marceli (Bruno Schulz). "Undula." *Świt: Organ Urzędników Naftowych w Borysławiu (Dawn: Organ of the Oil Executives in Borysław)* no. 25–26 (January 15, 1922): 2–5. In English translation: Stanley Bill, "Undula," Notes from Poland, July 11, 2020. https://notesfrompoland.com/2020/07/11/undula-a-newly.
Wisse, Ruth R. *The Modern Jewish Canon*. Chicago: University of Chicago Press, 2000.
Witkiewicz, S. I. "Bruno Schulz's Literary Work." In *The Witkiewicz Reader*, edited and translated by Daniel Gerould. Evanston, IL: Northwestern University Press, 1992.
———. "Twórczość literacka Brunona Schulza." *Pion* no. 34/35 (1935): 2.
Wojda, Dorota. "Schulzowskie reprezentacje pogranicza kulturowego w perspektywie postkolonialne." *Teksty Drugie* 4 (2007): 233–47.
Wolff, Larry. *The Idea of Galicia: History and Fantasy in Habsburg Political Culture*. Stanford, CA: Stanford University Press, 2010.
Wolin, Richard. "Reflections on Jewish Secular Messianism." In *Jews and Messianism in the Modern Era: Metaphor and Meaning*, edited by Jonathan Frankel. Studies in Contemporary Jewry. Oxford: Oxford University Press, 1991.
Wolski, Nathan. "The Secret of Yiddish: Zoharic Composition in the Poetry of Aaron Zeitlin." *Kabbalah: Journal for the Study of Jewish Mystical Texts* no. 20 (2009): 147–80.
Wyka, Kazimierz, and Napierski. "Dwugłos o Schulzu." *Ateneum*, no. 1 (1939). In *Stara szuflada i inne szkice z lat 1932–1939*, edited by M. Urbanowski, 419–23. Kraków: Universitas, 2000.
Zahra, Tara. "Imagined Noncommunities: National Indifference as a Category of Analysis." *Slavic Review* 69, no. 1 (2010): 93–119.
———. *Kidnapped Souls: National Indifference and the Battle for Children in the Bohemian Lands, 1900–1948*. Ithaca, NY: Cornell University Press, 2009.

Zeitlin, Aaron. "*Der kult fun gornisht, un kunst vi zi darf zayn: Protest un ani-maamin (The Cult of Nothing, and Art as It Should Be: Protest and Credo)*." *Varshever Shriftn (Warsaw Writings)*. Warsaw: Literatn klub baym farayn fun yidishe literatn un zhurnalistn in Varshe, 1926–27.

———. "Di yidishe melukhe, oder: Weizmann der tsveyter." *Globus* 3, no. 21–22 (March-April 1934): 3–53.

———. "Fir strofn." *Globus* no. 18 (December 1933): 60.

———. *Yaakov Frank*. Vilna, 1924.

Zeitlin, Hillel. "The Great Call of the Hour (Part 1)." In *geveb* (March 2016). http://ingeveb.org/texts-and-translations/the-great-call-of-the-hour-part-1.

———. *Hasidic Spirituality for a New Era: The Religious Writings of Hillel Zeitlin*. Edited by Arthur Green. Translated by Joel Rosenberg. Mahwah, NJ: Paulist Press, 2012.

Zemel, Carol. *Looking Jewish: Visual Culture and Modern Diaspora*. Bloomington: Indiana University Press, 2015.

Zweig, Arnold. *The Face of East European Jewry*. Berkeley: University of California Press, 2004.

Zweig, Stefan. "Introduction." In *E. M. Lilien: Sein Werk, mit einer Einleitung von Stefan Zweig*. Berlin: Schuster & Loeffler, 1903.

INDEX

Acacias Are Blooming (*Akatsjes blien, Akacje kwitną*), 100, 102, 106, 108, 112–114, 116, 207n2, 227n3. *See also* Vogel, Debora
Adamczyk-Garbowska, Monika, 94, 208n9, 217n8, 228n7, 253
Ahad Ha'am (Asher Zvi Hirsch Ginsberg), 16–17, 23, 38, 67, 147–148, 225n22, 226n37, 239n60; and Cultural or spiritual Zionism, 45–46, 67, 69, 71–72, 79, 81–82, 89, 130–132; and Jewish languages, 38, 45
Aleksiun, Natalia, 212n36
Alter, Robert, 247n3
Almi, A. 174, 246n62
Anessi, Thomas, 51
Ansky, Sh., 212n35
antisemitism, 12–13, 35, 41, 120, 202, 221n53; literary reactions to, 120, 235n18; Polish-language acquisition by Jews despite, 13, 159, 94; in Polish schools, 159; rising in Interwar Poland, 12–13, 120, 221n53; and Schulz, 123, 243; and Zionism, 57, 71, 82. *See also* National Democracy (*Narodowa Demokracja*); pogroms: Lwów pogrom of 1918; language, Polish; Tuwim, Julian
Arendt, Hannah, 119, 120, 163–164, 166, 233, 244
Asch, Sholem, 249n27
Assimilation, 28, 45, 63, 141, 246n71; acculturation without, 14, 154, 159; assimilationists, 30, 95, 170; German-Jewish model of, 24, 156; as impediment to Jewish cultural renaissance, 74; problematized, 155–158, 170, 176, 234n9; rejection of, 67, 72, 141; Schulz on, 72, 75–76, 129; Vogel on, 108–109, 119–120. *See also* language, Polish
Auerbach, Rachel (Rokhl Oyerbakh), 3, 25, 90, 139, 207n3; friendship with Vogel, 32, 48, 97, 102–103, 185, 207; and Schulz's work, 48, 50, 87, 100, 154, 218n20, and *Tsushtayer*, 98–99, 185, 196, 207n1, 230n18; "Un-Spun Threads" ("*Nisht-oysgeshpunene fedem*"), 1, 18, 48, 90–91, 96, 110, 207n2; yiddishism and, 18, 25, 49, 87–88, 90, 102

Ba'al Shem Tov, 58
Bader, Gershom, 238n43
Bałaban, Majer (Meir Balaban), 14, 188, 214n52, 248nn20–21
Bal-Makshoves (Isidor [Yisroel] Eliashev), 201
Barenblüt, Szulim, 98
Bar-Kochva, Sharon, 201
Baudouin de Courtenay, Jan Niecisław, 119–120, 166, 244
Beardsley, Aubrey, 78–79, 186, 196, 250n32
Benjamin, Walter, 52, 60, 148, 179, 221n58, 221nn61–62,
Bergson, Henri, 44, 185
Birobidzhian Autonomous Region, 132
Blei, Franz, 250n32
Brieger, Lothar, 239n58, 247n2
Brzechwa, Jan (Jan Wiktor Lesman), 160, 171, 176, 201, 208n6, 251n47
Buber, Martin, 7, 16, 17, 38, 75, 87–88, 148, 211n29, 220n45, 225n21, 226n37, 254–55, 263–65; *Drei Reden über das Judenthum* (*Three Lectures on Judaism*), 63–66; and Fifth Zionist Congress, 70–74; and fin de siècle Orientalism, 62–67; and E. M. Lilien, 68; and Jewish Renaissance Movement, 9, 67, 240n64; Neo-Hasidism of, 17
Buber, Paula (née Winkler), 63
Buber, Salomon, 63
Buchman, Hersz, 37–39

cabaret, 162,170
Cammy, Justin, 94

269

Caneppele, Paolo, 229n14
Caplan, Marc, 19, 216n76
Carpathian Mountains, 35, 60, 83, 140–141
Chagall, Marc, 195
Chavannes, de, Puvis, 78
childhood, 148, 163, 177–178; and exegesis, 23, 179–182, 205; in Korn, 41, 45–46; and messianic times, 124, 178; Schulz's, in Galicia, xi, 7, 13, 15, 31, 34, 39–40, 45, 142, 180, 192, 200–201, 203, 247n12
Chirico, de, Giorgio, 101
Christian imagery, in modern Jewish art and literature, 185, 249n27; in Schulz's graphic work, 187–192, 187, 190, 191; in Tuwim's poetry, 175–176
Chwila, 24, 37–39, 57, 70, 188, 220n45, 231n38, 245n57, 248–249n21
Chwin, Stefan, 51, 222n74, 233nn90–91
Cohen, Nathan, 161, 242n23,
Csillag, Anna, *60*, 60–61, 182
Cultural Zionism. *See* Zionism

Damrosch, David, 170, 175
Daytsher, Itzhak, 160
Deleuze, Gilles, 176, 217n6
Der Nister, 201
Derrida, Jacques, 25
Diaspora Nationalism, 9, 12, 18, 28–29, 68, 72, 141, 210n25, 235n14, 238n48, 241n8. *See also* Manger, Itzik; Peretz, Yitzhok Leybush
Diedrichs, Eugen, 65
Di goldene keyt, 18, 90, 207n2, 222n70
Dix, Otto, 99
doikeyt, 141, 175. *See also* Diaspora Nationalism
Dowry, Alan, 239n60
Dubnow, Simon, 130, 141, 156
Dürer, Albrecht, 78

Ehrenpreis, Lea, 95, 111, 229n10
Ehrenpreis, Markus, 9, 21, 72–75, 231n38; as editor of *Judisk Tidskrift*, 189; Jewish Cultural Renaissance and, 67–70; and kabbalah, 66, 228n9; Schulz and, 70, 228n9; 231n38; uncle of Debora Vogel, 15, 69, 95, 102, 229n10; and Zionism, 102, 225n31, 229n10
Eisen, Arnold, 26

Emden, Jacob, 249n25
encounter, 177–180, 198; exegetical, 24, 150, 177–205, *193*, *194*, 202; Frankism as, 186–189; Galician modernity as, 21–22; in graphic work of Schulz, 91, 113, 186, 193, *194*, 196; and interwar Polish culture, 24, 96, 154–166, 169–176; between Jewish particularity and European universalism, 21–22, 31, 68–70, 72–74, 142, 153, 165–166; between Schulz and Vogel, 23, 90–120; 180, 200; between Schulz and work of E. M. Lilien, 23, 54–62, 74–89. *See also* picture-riddle; under Schulz, "A bagegenish," ("An Encounter,"), "*Encounter*" ("*Spotkanie*"), "Dead Season" ("*Martwy Sezon*"), "E. M. Lilien," "Woman and Two Boys" (*Kobieta i dwaj chłopcy*)

Faucherau, Serge, 251n39
Fayering, Max, 98
Feiwel, Berthold, 9, 54–55, 74, 85–87, 227nn65–66
Ficowski, Jerzy, 5, 47, 93, 94, 136, 199, 209n14, 214n54, 251n43; interviews with Drohobycz residents, 77, 81, 122; on Vogel, 93, 100, 227n3, 228n3, 232n58
Figlerowicz, Marta, 94, 255
fin de siecle Orientalism, 62–67. *See also* Buber, Martin; Hasidism
Folk und land, 103
Frank, Eva, 188. *See also* Frankism
Frank, Jacob Leibowicz. *See* Frankism
Frankism, 185–191, 203–204, 248nn16–19; 249n21; in Yiddish literature, 189; 249n22
Franzos, Karl Emil, 65
Funkenstein, Klemens, 251n41

Gal-Ed, Efrat, 140, 237n36
Gasyna, George, 213n38
Genesis, Book of, 33–34, 43, 49, 151, 223n3, 224n8; in Manger's *Bible Songs* (*Khumesh-lider*), 140–144; in "Night of the Great Season," 144, 146; in "Tractate on Mannequins, or the Second Book of Genesis," 106
Ginsberg, Asher Hirsch. *See* Ahad Ha'am
Giżycki, Jerzy, 107
Globus, 233n92, 239n63

Goldfarb, David, 192, 209n22, 220n45, 238n50, 249–250n30
Goldszmit, Henryk. *See* Korczak, Jan
golus (exile, diaspora, *galut*), x, 37, 44, 72, 86; 241n14; as condition of language, 25, 43; Golus-Nationalism, 141; in Korn's review of *Cinnamon Shops*, 33–37, 42, 44–49, 184; in "E. M. Lilien," 4, 18, 80, 87–89; existence, 13, 18, 29, 47, 82, 85, 91, 107, 108, 110, 135; as ontological condition, 35–36, 43; in Schulz's aesthetic philosophy, 24, 48, 95, 124, 127, 137, 149, 182, 205, 237n31; in Vogel, 107–108, 110. *See also* language, Polish; Korn, Rokhl: review of *Cinnamon Shops*; Schulz, Bruno: "Tractate on Mannequins"
Gombrowicz, Witold, 10, 47–48, 57, 125, 22–23n76
Gottlieb, Maurycy, 249n27
Górski, Emil, 81
Goya, Francisco, 99
Grinberg Uri Tvi (Tsevi), 39, 220n45
Grodzieńska, Stefania, 171
Grosz, George, 99
Grydzewski, Mieczysław, 162, 213n41, 214n58
Grynberg, Henryk, 207n3
Guattari, Felix, 176

Habsburg Empire, 6, 9, 61, 101, 137, 139, 203, 241n4; and Austrian Idea, 167–169; emancipation of Jews in, 7; end of, 11, 36; and Jewish Enlightenment, 7, 15; multiethnicity of, 120, 155, 167–168, 225n26; Schulz's art as product of, 62, 78, 95; 119, 150, 152
haggadot, 76, 78–79
Halpern, Moyshe Leyb, 249n27
Halpern, Romana, 8, 40, 100, 111, 122, 179, 232n57, 233n90, 247n12, 249n27
Harshav, Benjamin, 12, 29–30, 169, 214n55, 217n4
Hasidism, 62, 153, 222n74; Buber and, 63–67, 69, 237n31; Ehrenpreis and, 69; and fin de siècle Orientalism, 63–67; in Galician Region, 7, 17, 131–132, 138; Manger and, 141; modern, 39, 61, 161, 210n25; in Polish-Lithuanian Commonwealth, 157; tales and storytelling tradition, 8, 19, 63–64, 66, 203, 235n10; Zeitlin (Hillel) and, 17, 44, 75. *See also* Buber, Martin; Kabbalah; Nachman of Bratslav; Neo-Hasidism; Hillel Zeitlin
Hassan, Waïl, 33–34, 218n21
Hegel, G. W., 96–97, 102, 114, 120
Heine, Heinrich, 38–39, 214n56
Hellerstein, Kathryn, 41, 93, 228n5, 231n36
Herzl, Theodor, 70–71, 130, 226n37, 235n13, 236n23
Hesse, Herman, 139
Hoberman, J., 245n58
Hoffman, Zygmunt, 122
Holbein, Hans the Younger, 78
Holmgren, Beth, 170–171, 245n55
Hundert, Gershon, 156–157

idolatry, 153, 180, 190–192, 202–205; and Frankism, 185–189; in Peretz, 18. *See also* under Schulz, *Book of Idolatry*

Jarzębski, Jerzy, 207n5, 209n14, 211n33, 212n37
Jaworski, Kazimierz Andrzej, 51
Jewish Question in Poland, 11, 119, 123, 125, 165–167, 178, 235n18, 242n25, 245n55
Job, Book of, 60
John, Michael, 158
Józefczuk, Grzegorz, 208, 223n1
Jüdische Verlag, 71, 73–74, 239n60
Judisk Tidskrift, 69, 189, 225n28, 225n31

Kabbalah, 6, 24, 53, 62, 66–67, 76, 85; 101; Lurianic, 6, 17, 44, 58, 153, 202–204, 240n65; in Schulz criticism, 6, 209n22, 210n22; *shevirat ha-kelim*, 44, 58, 70, 210n22; *tikkun-olam*, 6, 24, 44, 53, 153, 184, 210n22, 218n24; *tzimtzum*, 210n22, 228n9, 232n58. *See also* Buber; Ehrenpreis; Hasidism; Schulz, Bruno: "The Book," and "Mythologizing of Reality;" Zeitlin (Aaron); Zeitlin (Hillel); *Zohar*
Kafka, Franz, v, 25, 29, 32, 49, 63, 125; "Afterword to Kafka's *The Trial*" (Schulz), 46–47; and German literary modernism, 137; "The Hunter Gracchus," 135–136, 237n28; influence on Schulz, 11, 15–16, 23, 32, 38, 46, 49, 53, 86, 101, 124, 129, 136, 240n64; as a Jewish writer, 208n7, 217n6, 234n10; and Scripture, 247n3

Kahanovich, Pinchus. *See* Der Nister
Kalleia, 199
Kalmanovich, Zelig, 39
Kamena, 51–52, 126, 215n63, 223n78
Karlip, Joshua, 39, 220n43
Kassow, Samuel, 14, 159, 160, 245n58
Kaszuba-Dębska, Anna, 207n3, 209n14, 229n12, 237n28
Kato, Ariko, 248n14, 251n39, 251n42, 251n45, 251n49
Khaliastre, 185
Khomych, Lesya, 18, 95, 98, 198–200, 251n39
Kijek, Kamil, *Children of Modernism* (*Dzieci modernizmu*), 3, 160–61
Kleiner, Juliusz, 103
Kleinmann, Fritz, 98
Kleist, Heinrich von, 139
Klimt, Gustav, 78, 101
Korczak, Jan (Henryk Goldszmit), 171, 228n6
Korn, Rokhl (Rachel Haring Korn), 8, 142, 184; life, 41, 221n50; multilingualism and language choice, 39–41, 45–46; "*Tzimring gevelber' fun Bruno Schulz*" ("Review of 'Cinnamon Shops'"), 23, 33–37, 40–50, 80, 91–92, 142, 218n21, 219n30
Krasiński, Zygmunt, 160
Kraushar, Aleksander, 188, 248n20
Kremer, Józef, 96–97, 230n17
Kronfeld, Chana, 3, 217n6, 218–219n25
Kruczkowski, Andrzej, 120–121
Krutikov, Mikhail, 3, 16, 26
Kudliński, Tadeusz, 162, 243n28
Kuhmerker, Henrietta. *See* Schulz, Henrietta
Kulbak, Moyshe, 189, 249n22
Kuryluk, Ewa, 248n14

Landauer, Gustav, 63–64
language, 23, 101, 129, 138, 149, 179; choice, 12–13, 29–30, 36–42, 102–104; as deterritorialized homeland, 173–174; of everyday communication, x, 44, 51, 181, 184; in exile, x, 4, 18, 23, 33–37, 43–44, 152; linguistic universalization, 149, 164, 175; as mask or form, 30, 102, 205; minor, 169, 176; as raw material, 92, 206; wars, Jewish, 28–30. *See also* multilingualism; individual languages

language, German: Buber and, 17, 62–67, 219n45; and Galicia, 7–8, 10, 28, 41, 158, 242n16; and language choice, 28–29, 31; *Lieder des Ghetto*, 54, 77, 80, 83–86; and Manger, 139–140; as modern Jewish literary language, 15–16, 26, 29, 39, 137, 208n7, 219n34 (*See also* Kafka); and modern Jewish renaissance, 9, 17, 29, 62–67, 70–71, 122, 215n61, 239n60; Schulz and, 7–10, 25, 95, 139, 147, 218n20, 239n55, 240n65 (*See also* "Homecoming" ["*Heimkehr*"]); Vogel and, 95–96, 102–103, 231n36
language, Hebrew, 17, 44, 63, 162, 192, 201, 238n43; as component of Yiddish, 181, 219n25; as deterritorialized, 20; and Ehrenpreis, 69–70, 225n31; and language choice, x, 28–31, 213n56; modernism, literary, 3, 19, 26, 29, 33; within multilingual Jewish polysystem, 8, 28, 147, 159–60, 213n45, 242n26; and Vogel, 25, 95, 102–103; and Zionism, 12, 37–39, 72. *See also* diasporic modernism; multilingualism; individual author names
language, Polish, 7, 167, 172–173; and diasporic modernism, 15–16, 18–20, 33, 102; as fatherland (*ojczyzna-polszczyzna*), 45, 173; Galician Jews and, 8, 10, 96; golus and, 4, 33–37, 45, 127, 151–152, 173, 184, 203; Jewish culture and publishing in, 2, 17–19, 24, 33, 38–40, 49, 95, 129, 162–165, 169–176, 189, 201–202, 205; Jewish literary modernism in, 9–11, 15, 152–155, 158; as Jewish vernacular, 13–14, 16, 155, 158–162; schools, 41, 159–160. *See also Chwila*; *Miesięcznik Żydowski*; multilingualism; National Democracy; *Nasz Przegląd*
language, Yiddish, x, 2–3, 8, 15, 18–19, 33–39, 41, 63, 93–95, 103, 159–161, 181, 184, 201, 228n7; as deterritorialized, 20, 35, 173–174; and Diaspora Nationalism, 12, 18, 29, 68, 70, 175; film, 245n58; and language choice, x, 8, 30–31, 41, 102–104, 213n56; literary modernism, 3, 19, 33, 62, 76, 91, 102, 139–144 (*See also* individual author names); and multilingual Jewish culture in Poland, 2, 12, 16, 28, 72,

159–160; as national Jewish language, 13, 16, 29, 35, 46, 129, 138, 153, 155, 220n43, 242n17; Polish-language writers and, 208n9, 219n47, 242n26; in schools, 166; Schulz and, 6, 8, 18, 33–35, 40, 87, 95, 218n20, 230n27; Spinoza in, 237n33; and *Wiadomości literackie*, 164–165, 208n9, 243n32; yiddishism, 12, 18, 29, 68, 159 (*see also* Auerbach: friendship with Vogel); yiddishland, 173–174. *See also* individual periodical titles; under Korn, "Review of *'Cinnamon Shops'*"

Lasker-Schüler, Else, 39
Lazorak, Bogdan, ix, 4, 209n16, 214n59
Lec, Stanisław Jerzy, 239n58
Lechoń, Jan, 161
Léger, Fernand, 101
Leivick, H., 123, 214n56
Leon, Moses de, 183
Lemkin, Raphael, 160
Lesman, Bolesław. *See* Leśmian, Bolesław
Leśmian, Bolesław, 121, 160, 165, 171–176, 208n6, 245–246n59,
Lestschinsky, Jacob, 74–75, 156, 241n8
Levinas, Emmanuel, 180
Levinson, Julian, 249n27
Levitan, Seymour, 41
Lewi, Henri, 6, 210n23
Leyeles, Aaron-Glanz, 103, 120, 231n34
Lichtblau, Albert, 158
Lieder des Ghetto (*Songs of the Ghetto*). *See* under Lilien, Ephraim Moses.
Lilien, Ephraim Moses, 9, 18, 130, 186–187; Brieger album, 239n58, 247n2; Buber on , 68, 73–74; "The Creation of Man," 79; *Die Bücher der Bibel* (*The Books of the Bible*), 151, 187, 240n66; and erotic themes, 223–24n3; Fifth Zionist Congress and, 55, 58, 73, 84, 225n24; influence on Schulz, 53, 55, 96, 101, 150, 186; and Jewish cultural renaissance, 9, 55–56, 67–75, 79, 148; "Jewish May," 85; *Juda*, 4, 57, 77–78, 80, 153; Jüdischer Verlag and, 74; *Lieder des Ghetto* (*Songs of the Ghetto*), 4, 53–58, 55, 67–89, 74, 77, 153, 227n66; and *Ost und West*, 68, 215n61; "Passover," 82, 83; and Secessionist art, 55–56, 96, 215n61; Zweig

(Stefan) on, 83–86. *See also* Brieger; Buber; Palestine; Schulz, Bruno: "E. M. Lilien": Zionism; Zweig
Lipski, Leo, 243n31
Lipszyc, Adam, 163–64, 187, 243n31, 248n16, 251n46
Literarishe bleter, 12, 32, 164, 220n47, 237n33
Loeffler, James, 160
Löw, Chaim, 37, 122
Löwenthal, Edmund, 122–123
Lurianic kabbalah. *See* Kabbalah
Lyubas, Anastasiya, 93, 228n5, 231n48

Maciejko, Paweł, 187, 249n25,
Magris, Claudio, 168
Malz, Dovid, 95, 229n10
Mandelshtam, Max Emmanuel, 130
Manger, Itzik, 3, 23, 138–146, 184, 217n6, 219n25, 237n36, 237n38, 249n27; *Khumesh-lider* (*Bible Songs*), 139–145
Mann, Thomas, 8, 11, 101
Markowski, Michał Paweł, 173, 207n5; *Powszechna rozwiązłość*, 213n38, 220n45; 246n59
Marranism in literature, 29, 163–164, 212n37, 243n30, 243n31
Meltzer, Nosen, 103
Meltzer, Wanda, 107–108
Meir-Grafe, 250n32
Mendes-Flohr, Paul, 64, 73
Meniok, Wiera, 208
messianism, 4, 22, 61, 69, 80, 89, 129, 138, 205; 248n16; in Benjamin, 51; and *Book of Idolatry*, 99, 153, 190, 196; in "E. M. Lilien," 4, 10, 22, 58, 61, 80–81; in Peretz, 184; messianic tropes in Schulz, 15, 17, 39, 53, 87, 124, 178, 210; secular, in modern politics, 12, 56, 87, 149, 189. *See also* Frankism; time: messianic
Michlic, Joanna, 162, 236n20, 246n69, 246n70
Mickiewicz, Adam, 155, 160–161, 166, 189, 215n63, 249n23
Miesięcznik żydowski, 42, 57
Mikulka, Anatol, 121
Misiak, Anna Maja, 93

modernism, diasporic, 15, 19–20, 32–34, 51,142; diasporist poetics, 11,18, 20, 26, 48, 95, 137, 177–181 (as distinct from Diaspora Nationalism, 18); and Galicia, 6, 9, 11, 19, 95, 102; Kafka and, 136–137; Manger and, 139–142; multilingualism and 19, 33–34, 153; in the Polish language, 11, 15–18, 102, 181; and scripture, 142, 179, 183; and translationality, 9, 11, 20, 27, 51–52, 183, 205; universalizing strategies in, 52, 139; of Vogel, 103, 108–110, 119. *See also* golus; multilingualism; time

Molodowsky, Kadya, 41

Morris, William, 78

Moskalets, Ladyslava, 210n25

Moss, Kenneth, 6, 124, 147, 156–158, 170, 214n55

multilingualism, 3–4, 8, 19–20, 24, 29, 94, 214n56, 228n6; of Habsburg Galicia, 2, 6, 30, 120, 155; of interwar Poland, 28, 30, 97, 171; and Jewish modernity, 2, 28, 33, 153, 214n56; as Jewish polysystem, 3, 28, 163; as "multiplicity" ("*wielość*"), 119–20, 152; of Polish-Lithuanian Commonwealth, 155, 188. *See also* language; individual languages

Murav, Harriet, 3, 20, 208n12

Mussa, Alberto, 33–34

Mythologizing, of reality, as poetic practice, 5, 42–43, 52, 150, 153 177, 185, 203; and temporality, 52–53, as translational, 168, 185. *See also* Kabbalah: *tikkun-olam*; Schulz, Bruno: "Mythologizing of Reality"; time

Nachman of Bratslav, 67, 133, 152, 236n22

Nałkowska, Zofia, 47, 100, 230n30, 231nn30–31

National Democracy (*Narodowa Demokracja*), 12, 132, 162, 215n60, 246n70

Nasza Opinia, 125

Nasz Przegląd, 57, 171, 245n57

Naye morgn, 103

Neo-Hasidism, 17, 44, 62, 75. *See also* Buber, Martin; Hasidism; Zeitlin (Hillel)

Neugroeschel, Mendel (Naygreshel), 98, 218n20, 230n27

Newton, Adam Zachary, 207, 213n39

Niger, Shmuel (Tsharni), 201

Nisht-oysgeshpunene fedem. *See* Auerbach, Rachel

Nordau, Max, 71, 73, 130, 226n37, 236n23

Norwid, Cyprian Kamil, 94, 228nn7–8

Nossig, Alfred, 159

obraz-talisman. *See* thought figure

obraz-zagadka. *See* thought figure

Olson, Jess, 72

Ortwin, Ostap, 173

Orzeszkowa, Eliza, 167

Ost und West, 9, 67–68, 70, 211, 225n26

Ottenbreit, Rudolf, 11

Palestine, 4, 28–29, 56, 71–72, 80, 88, 127, 131–132, 137, 147–150, 229n10, 234n9, 236n21, 239n58, 240n64. *See also* Lilien; Schulz, Bruno: "E. M. Lilien"; Zionism

Paloff, Benjamin, 207n4, 217n7

Panas, Władysław, 6, 187, 189, 190, 209n22, 210n22, 230n20

Paziński, Piotr, 216n78, 243n29

Peckerar, Robert Adler, 3, 217n6, 218–219n25

Peiper, Tadeusz, 10

Peretz, Yitzhok Leybush, 23, 67, 98, 140, 174, 185, 204, 214n56, 237n31; and diasporism, 138, 141; on Jewish cultural continuity, 16, 67, 184; Itzik Manger on, 237n38; *Vegn vos firn op fun yidishkayt* ("Escaping Jewishness"), 130, 235n14, 235n16

Picture-riddle (*obraz-zagadka*), 21–22, 144–145. *See also* thought figure

Pilpul, Mundek, 8

Pinsker, Leon, 128–29, 234n9

Pinsker, Shachar, 33

Pion, 49, 125

Pleśniewicz, Andrzej, 178

pogroms, 41; Lwów pogrom of 1918, 35, 103, 219n31, 221n53; and Ukrainian Civil War, 219n31

Polish-Lithuanian Commonwealth, 7, 155–157, 166, 241n11, 248n19

Polonsky, Anthony, 176, 246n67, 246n69

Prokop-Janiec, Eugenia, 11, 214n56

Przegląd Podkarpacia (*The Subcarpathian Review*), ix, 54, 57–58, 59, 61, 83, 223n1, 224n5
Przegląd Społeczny (The Social Review), 107, 117, 119

Rabski, Władysław, 162
Ravitch, Melech (Meylekh), 41, 97, 184–185, 237n33
refugees, 143, 146, 148, 245; during WWI, 143, 212n35. *See also* sanctuary
Reizen, Avrom, 174
Rembrandt, 190
Rilke, Rainer Maria, 11, 101, 115, 139, 140
Rój publishing house, 31, 125, 198, 229n13, 231n48
Rops, Félicien, 196
Rosenfeld, Morris, 54, 55, 86–87, 227n65; See also Lilien: *Lieder des Ghetto*
Rosenzweig, Franz, 220n45
Rosiek, Stanisław, 4, 209nn14–16, 223n1
Roskies, David, 139, 141
Roth, Joseph, 7, 40, 168–169, 212n35, 245nn48–49
Rothschild, Baron, 150
Rozenblit, Marsha L., 211n35

Sacher-Masoch, Leopold von, 186, 188, 199, 248n14, 251n42. *See also* Schulz, Bruno: *Book of Idolatry*
sanctuary, 87, 129; citadel, 13, 81, 237n31; fortress, 13, 81–82; refuge, 71, 122, 147–149, 238. *See also* Palestine; time: second track; Schulz, Bruno: "Republic of Dreams" and "Sanatorium under the Sign of the Hourglass"; Vienna
Sandauer, Artur, 91, 210n22, 247n12
Schachter, Allison, 19, 20, 32, 93, 215nn64–66
Schiper, Yitzhak, 14
Schorr, Mojżesz (Moses), 14
Schulz, Bruno, works of: "The Age of Genius" ("*Genialna epoka*," "Wondrous Era"), 77, 101, 177; childhood and, 124, 203; included in *Sanatorium*, 53, 126, 150–51, 220n42; messianic themes in, 204; publication of, 126; two-track time in, 154; "August" ("*Sierpień*"), 115; "Book, The"

("*Księga*"), 5, 38, 53–54, 56, 126, 135–136, 177, 233; compared to Lilien article, 5, 54, 58–62; exegetical tropes in, 24, 138, 178–184; and Jewish artistic renaissance, 76–77; sacred/profane dichotomy in, 182–83; Schulz's changing aesthetics and, 180, 202; title as translational, 181, 218n24; in *Sanatorium*, 53; 126; and *Zohar*, 150–151, 183, 185, 240n65; *Book of Idolatry* (*Xięga bałwochwalcza*), 24, 177, 180–202, 183, 186–187, 190, 193, 248n13, 250n30, 250n33, 251n39; *See also* idolatry, "Undula"; *Cinnamon Shops* (volume of stories), 22, 51, 53, 75, 93, 126, 132, 153, 180, 192, 203–204, 198; 229n27, 246n71; Auberbach on, 100; Korn review of, 23, 28, 32–36, 40–48, 91, 142, 217n21; metaphoric style in, 114–116, 136; publication of, 31, 198, 202, 223n76, 231n30; "Undula" compared to, 199–201; as arising through Schulz's encounter with Vogel, 18–19, 98, 100, 113, 180, 196, 227n3; idolatry in, 192; "Cinnamon Shops" ("*Sklepy cynamonowe*") (story), 93–94, 136; "Dead Season, The" ("*Martwy sezon*"), 21–22, 144–146, 153; "E. M. Lilien," ix–x, 4–5, 9, 18, 22–23, 34, 47, 51–57, 89, 116–117, 121, 125, 177; arc of resignation traced in, 57, 147–151, 240n64; and "The Book" ("*Księga*"), 150–151, 251n64; delivered as public lecture, 75; discovery of, ix, 4–5, 57, 209n16, 233n91; and demythologization, 34, 53, 76, 149; publishing of, 23, 53, 57–58, 87, 223n1, 224n5; and Jewish cultural renaissance, 67–89; and Jewish messianic tradition, 58, 80; and Schulz's diasporist poetics, 86–89, 109–110, 121, 142, 152–153; and "Fatherland," 147–150; and "Republic of Dreams," 82–85; and *Sanatorium*, 106, 150–153; and "Spring," 87; and Schulz's biography, 57, 86–87; in *Subcarpathian Review* (*Przegląd podkarpacia*), 57–61, 209n21; *See also* Lilien, Ephraim Moses; "Encounter, An" (*A bagegenish*), 39, 53, 77, 99, 101, 126, 177, 203–204, 220n42, 234; "Encounter" ("*Spotkanie*"), 193–195, 194 "Fatherland" ("*Ojczyzna*"), 53, 121–124, 129, 146–150, 239; "Homecoming" ("*Heimkehr*"), 8, 40, 53,

Schulz, Bruno, works of (cont.) 121; "Letter to S. I. Witkiewicz," 177, 217, 247; *Messiah, The* (*Mesjasz*), 4, 15, 126, 214nn53–54; "Mythologizing of Reality" (*Mityzacja rzeczywistości*), 22, 43, 47, 125, 137, 209n19, 214n49, 218n15; and Korn's review of *Cinnamon Shops*, 42–43; and Lurianic kabbalah, 44, 184; 218n24; "Reading the Book I" ("*Czytanie Księgi I*"), *178*; "Republic of Dreams" ("*Republika marzeń*"), 13, 16, 53, 121, 126, 227n64; and essay "E. M. Lilien," 81–85; *Sanatorium under the Sign of the Hourglass* (*Sanatorium pod klepsydrą*) (volume), 19, 22, 38, 51, 53, 58,122, 154, structure of, 126, 147, 150–153; childhood in, 100, 200, compared to "E. M. Lilien," 5, 88, 106; exegesis in, 177, 182, 201–204; messianic themes in, 202–205; publication of, 53, 125–126; reception, 235n18, 223n76; self-illustrated, 79; "Sanatorium under the Sign of the Hourglass" ("*Sanatorium pod klepsydrą*") (story), 23, 53, 125–138, 147–49, 236n23; illustrated by Schulz, *127*, *128*, *134*; on Jewish culture as dying, 129–131; and Kafka's "Hunter Gracchus," 135–37; man-dog in, 133–134, *134*; "Spring" ("*Wiosna*"), 58, 113, 124, 138, 150–151, 182, 240; and "E. M. Lilien," 77, 88; and *Messiah* (*Mesjasz*), 126; Pesach in original publication of, 51–53, 223n78; "Tractate on Mannequins" (4-part) (*Manekiny, Wtóra Księga Rodzaju, Ciąg dalszy, Dokończenie*), 113, 196–197, 250n30; Korn's translation and reading of, 35–36; and Vogel's *Manekinen*, 93, 100, 104–106; originating in letters to Vogel, 106, 196, 227n3; "Undula," 19, 95; discovery of, 18, 198, 251n39; publication of, 215n62, 250n38, 250n39, 251n41, 251n45; and Schulz's graphic work, 98, 251n40, 251n42; *See also* Weron, Marceli; "Woman and Two Boys" ("*Kobieta i dwaj chłopcy*"), *194*
Schulz, Henrietta (née Kuhmerker), 7, 77
Schulz, Izydor, 8, 54, 96, 199, 229n13, 251n45
Schulz, Jacob, 7, 144
Schulz/Forum, 4, 208n13, 209nn16–17, 213n38
Seelig, Rachel, 184

Segel, Binjamin, 225n26
Seidman, Naomi, 181
Shallcross, Bożena, 6, 209n22, 210nn22–23
Shandler, Jeffrey, 174
Shanes, Joshua, 10, 210n25, 210n27, 211n32, 229n11
Shapiro, Chaim Elazar, 131
Shapiro, Raisa, 220n45
Shmeruk, Chone, 3, 12, 28, 94
Schnaper, Ber, 103
Shneiderman, Shmuel Leyb, 220n47, 242n26
Sholem Aleichem, 23; *A konsilium fun doktoyrim*, 129–132, 201, 235n13, 235n16
Shore, Marci, 17, 214n48, 214n58, 215n60, 245n55
Sienkiewicz, Henryk, 160
Sitkiewicz, Piotr, ix, 4, 209n14, 209n16, 222n72, 224n5, 243n28
Słonimski, Antoni, 10, 17, 37, 160, 162, 165, 208n6, 214n58, 215n60, 242n25
Słonimski, Hayyim Selig, 162
Słowacki, Juliusz, 160
Snyder, Timothy, 211n28, 236n21
Spinoza, Baruch, 38, 139, 146, 237nn32–33, 239n56
Spivak, Gayatri, 25, 216n78
Stanislawski, Michael, 55
Stauter-Halsted, Keely, 212n35
Stern, Anatol, 208n6, 214n58
Sternbach, Herman, 42, 48, 50
Stryjkowski, Julian, 216n78, 243n29
Studio, 42, 47, 125
Subcarpathian Review. See *Przegląd Podkarpacia*
Suchoff, David, 25, 208n7
Suss, Nosn, 109
Sutzkever, Avrom, 94, 228n7
Świt, 198
Sygnały, 24
Syrkin, Nachman, 13
Szelińska, Józefina, 79, 111, 125, 136, 222n67, 232n56, 234n1, 237n28, 250n32
Szymaniak, Karolina, 3, 93, 102, 104, 164, 207n2, 208n9, 228n6, 230nn17–19, 231n34, 242n25, 243n32; *Być agentem wiecznej idei*, 93, 228n5, 229n10
Szymel, Maurycy, 213n42

Temporality. *See* time
Thon, August (Ozjasz), 69, 226n37
thought-figure, 117, 179; *denkbild*, 179, 233n74; *obraz-talisman* (picture-talisman) and *obraz-zagadka* (picture-riddle), 21, 144–145, 153, 185, 197, 247n4
time, 14, 23, 36, 61, 180; exegetical/mythical vs. historical/everyday, 20–21, 47, 51–52, 110, 132, 147–150, 176, 182, 193, 204–205; holiday, 51–53; homogeneous, empty, in Walter Benjamin, 52, 148; messianic (*Meshiakh-tsaytn*), 99, 178, 190; two-track, 14, 51, 135–136, 148, 154, 164, 205. *See also* Benjamin; Levinas; Manger; Schulz, Bruno: "Age of Genius," "The Book," "Fatherland," "Sanatorium," "Spring"
Timoshenko, Leonid, 214n59
Timpano, Nathan, 250n32
Tokarczuk, Olga, 189, 248n19
Torres, Anna, 93, 198, 228n5
Translationality, 2, 218n21; contexts fostering, Polish 154–176; and diasporic writing, 11, 51, 205, 218n25; and mythologizing, 44, 168, 185, 221n61; in Schulz's work, 13, 20, 26–27, 29, 31–35, 49, 150, 164; in "Wiosna," 50–51, 183–184. *See also* Korn; language; multilinguality
Truchanowski, Kazimierz, 214n53
Tsushtayer, 24, 87, 185, 189, 196; founding of, 97, 207n2, 230nn18–19; Schulz published in, 98–99, 251n40; and Yiddish culture in Galicia, 97
Tuwim, Julian, 17, 37, 38, 160, 165, 171–176, 208n6, 213n44, 214n58, 243n34, 246n69; antisemitism and, 163, 243n28, 246n67; and Polish-language fatherland ("*ojczyzna-polszczyzna*"), 45, 169, 174; "Słowo i ciało" ("The Word and the Flesh") and *Wiadomości literackie*, 162; on Yiddish language, 220n47, 246n69; "Zieleń," 171; "Żydek" ("Little Jew"), 236n25, 243n34
Twardowski, Kazimierz, 103
Tygodnik Illustrowany, 47, 82, 125–26

Uganda Plan, 130–132

Ury, Scott, 217n2
Urban, Martina, 69

Vallee, Lillian, 223n76
Van Heuckelom, Kris, 247n2, 250n30
Veidlinger, Jeffrey, 181, 241n12
Veynig, Naftali, 98, 108, 112–113, 114, 116
Vienna, 17, 41, 55, 63, 83–84, 211n31, 230n27, 235n16; Galician immigration to, 68, 86, 146; 239n55; Schulz residence in, 8, 96, 146, 180, 229n14, 239n55; Viennese art, 250n32; Viennese erotica, 180, 186, 199, 205, 250n32; and Vogel, 96, 229n14; as wartime residence, 8, 96, 229n14
Vogel, Anzelm, 95
Vogel, Debora: *Acacias Are Blooming* (*Akatsies blien, Akacje kwitną*), 91–93, 100–106, 108, 112–114, 116; aesthetic debates with Schulz, 18, 23, 84, 90–124, 97–98, 112–113; 178; *Day Figures* (*Tog figurn*), 93, 100–102, 207n2, 231n35; "A Few Observations on Today's Intelligentsia" ("*Kilka uwag o współczesnej inteligencji*"), 91; "Human Exotics" ("*Ludzkie egzotyki*"), 107–108; influence on Schulz, 6, 19, 95, 153, 196–198, 199–205; Jewish themes, treatment of, 107–110; life, 90, 95–98, 103; "Lwów's Jewish Ghetto" ("*Lwowska juderia*"), 109–110; *Mannequins* (*Manekinen*), 93, 101–102, 104–106, 108, 198, 207n2; *Montages* (*Montazhn*), 207n2, 228n6; multilinguality and language choice, 8, 25, 31, 39–41, 102–104; Polish intellectual life, 97, 176; "White Words in Poetry" ("*Vayse verter in poezye*"), 114; yiddishism and, x, 1, 6, 18, 23, 25, 40, 91–111, 122–123, 230n20, 231n34. *See also* under Szymaniak: *To Be the Agent of an Eternal Idea* (*Być agentem wiecznej idei*)
Volovici, Marc, 219n34

Wandel, Oscar, 248n21
Waśniewski, Zenon, 51, 215n63
Wat, Aleksander, 17, 160, 176, 208n6, 214n58, 215n60, 243n31
Wat, Ola, 214n58
Weingarten, Stanisław, 195, *195*

Werberger, Annette, 93, 113
Werfel, Franz, 168–169, 214n56, 245n47
Werner, Sylwia, 93
Weron, Marceli, 19, 95, 198, 201–202, 250n38, 251n39. *See also* Schulz, Bruno
Wex, Michael, 219n26
Wiadomości literackie, 8, 37, 40, 107, 208n6, 208n9, 215n60; Jewishness of, 11–12, 37, 165, 242n25; 208n6; literary award, 40, 220n36; and modern Polish culture, 162, 165, 169, 213n41, 236n25; Polish nationalist critique of, 162, 243n28; Schulz published in, 125–126, 136; Yiddishist critique of, 164–165, 208n9
Wiener, Meir, 16–17
Wierzyński, Kazimierz, 126
Wilde, Oscar, 79, 250n32
Witkiewicz, S. I. (Witkacy), 10, 57, 177, 217n9, 218n21; life, 227n2; relationship with Schulz, 97, 222n74; review of *Cinnamon Shops*, 49, 218n21, 222n75; Schulz, essay for, 177, 226n57; and Vogel, 91, 96–97, 230n21
Wojda, Dorota, 212n37
Wyka, Kazimierz, 223n76
Wyspiański, Stanisław, 78

Yohai, Simeon ben, 183

Zahra, Tara, 20, 170, 215n71, 216n72
Zangen, Benzion, 220n45
Zeitlin, Aaron (Aharon Tsaytlin), 23, 67, 216, 249n27; kabbalistic poetics, 76, 232n72, 233n74; translated by Vogel, 123, *Weizmann the Second* (*Vaytsman der tsveyter*), 239n63; *Yaakov Frank*, 189, 249n22
Zeitlin, Hillel, 76, 81, 88; and neo-Hasidism, 17, 44, 58, 75; on Orthodoxy, 75
Zemel, Carol, 195
Zionism, 39, 57, 64, 121, 124, 221n53, 237n30; cultural or spiritual, 4–5, 9, 16–17, 19, 28, 45, 55–56, 68–74, 80–82, 129–130, 138, 147, 231; and *nachtasyl* (night asylum), 236n23; political, 11–12, 29, 55–57, 70, 73, 80–89, 121, 127–134, 138, 189, 226n37, 235n12, 236n21, 240; and Vogel's family, 229n10, 231n38. *See also* Ahad Ha'am; Buber; Chwila; Ehrenpreis; Fifth Zionist Congress; Herzl; Lilien; Miesięcznik Żydowski; Nordau; Schulz, Bruno: "E. M. Lilien," "Fatherland," "Sanatorium under the Sign of the Hourglass"; Sholem Aleichem: "A Consultation of Doctors" ("A konsilium fun doktoyrim")
Zweig, Stefan, 83–86, 168

KAREN UNDERHILL is Associate Professor of Polish Jewish Studies in the Department of Polish, Russian, and Lithuanian Studies at the University of Illinois Chicago.

For Indiana University Press

Tony Brewer, Artist and Book Designer

Brian Carroll, Rights Manager

Gary Dunham, Acquisitions Editor and Director

Anna Francis, Assistant Acquisitions Editor

Brenna Hosman, Production Coordinator

Katie Huggins, Production Manager

Darja Malcolm-Clarke, Project Manager/Editor

Dan Pyle, Online Publishing Manager

Pamela Rude, Senior Artist and Book Designer

Stephen Williams, Marketing and Publicity Manager